W9-BNI-850

# Oahu

## Glenda Bendure
## Ned Friary

**LONELY PLANET PUBLICATIONS**
Melbourne • Oakland • London • Paris

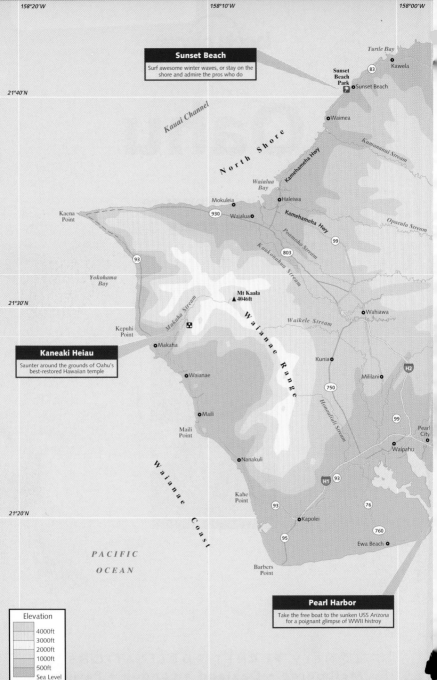

158°20'W   158°10'W   158°00'W

21°40'N

## Sunset Beach
Surf awesome winter waves, or stay on the shore and admire the pros who do

Turtle Bay
83   Kawela

Sunset
Beach
Park
Sunset Beach

Kauai Channel

Waimea

North Shore

Kamananui Stream

Waialua
Bay

Kamehameha Hwy

Mokuleia
Haleiwa
930   Waialua
Kamehameha Hwy

Kaena
Point

Opaeula Stream

Poamoho Stream

99

Kaukonahua Stream

803

93

Mt Kaala
▲ 4046ft

Yokohama
Bay

21°30'N

Waikele Stream

Wahiawa

Waianae Range

Makaha Stream

Kepuhi
Point
Makaha

## Kaneaki Heiau
Saunter around the grounds of Oahu's best-restored Hawaiian temple

Kunia
750

H2

Mililani

Waianae

Maili

Helemahili Stream

99
Pearl
City

Maili
Point

Waipahu

Nanakuli

H1   93

21°20'N

Kahe
Point

93

76

Kapolei

95

760

Ewa Beach

PACIFIC

OCEAN

Barbers
Point

## Pearl Harbor
Take the free boat to the sunken USS *Arizona* for a poignant glimpse of WWII histroy

Waianae Coast

Elevation
4000ft
3000ft
2000ft
1000ft
500ft
Sea Level

158°10'W   158°00'W

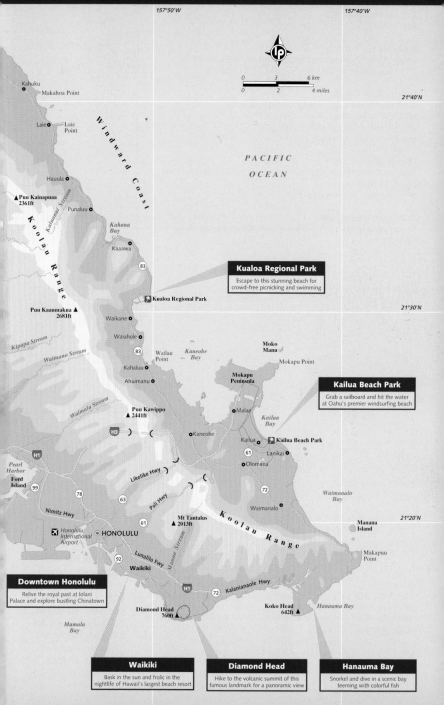

157°50'W

157°40'W

21°40'N

Kahuku

Makahoa Point

Laie
Laie
Point

**Windward Coast**

*PACIFIC*

*OCEAN*

Hauula

▲ Puu Kainapuaa
2361ft

Punaluu

*Kahana
Bay*

**Koolau Range**

Kaaawa

83

Puu Kaaumakua ▲
2681ft

*Kipapa Stream*

*Waimano Stream*

**Kualoa Regional Park**

Escape to this stunning beach for
crowd-free picnicking and swimming

Kualoa Regional Park

21°30'N

Waikane

Waiahole

Wailau
Point

*Kaneohe
Bay*

83

**Moko
Manu**

Mokapu Point

Kahaluu

**Mokapu
Peninsula**

Ahuimanu

*Waimalu Stream*

Puu Kawippo ▲
2441ft

H3

Kaneohe

Malae

*Kailua
Bay*

**Kailua Beach Park**

Grab a sailboard and hit the water
at Oahu's premier windsurfing beach

Kailua
Kailua Beach Park

61

Lanikai

Likelike Hwy

*Pearl
Harbor*

H1

Ford
Island

99

78

63

Pali Hwy

Olomana

72

*Waimanalo
Bay*

21°20'N

Nimitz Hwy

61

Mt Tantalus
▲ 2013ft

Waimanalo

*Koolau Range*

**Manana
Island**

Honolulu
International
Airport

HONOLULU

*Manoa Stream*

Makapuu
Point

92

Lunalilo Fwy

Waikiki

**Downtown Honolulu**

Relive the royal past at Iolani
Palace and explore bustling Chinatown

H1

72

Kalanianaole Hwy

Koko Head
642ft ▲

*Hanauma Bay*

Diamond Head
760ft ▲

*Mamala
Bay*

**Waikiki**

Bask in the sun and frolic in the
nightlife of Hawaii's largest beach resort

**Diamond Head**

Hike to the volcanic summit of this
famous landmark for a panoramic view

**Hanauma Bay**

Snorkel and dive in a scenic bay
teeming with colorful fish

Oahu
**2nd edition** – May 2003
**First published** – March 2000

**Published by**
**Lonely Planet Publications Pty Ltd** ABN 36 005 607 983
90 Maribyrnong St, Footscray, Victoria 3011, Australia

**Lonely Planet Offices**
**Australia** Locked Bag 1, Footscray, Victoria 3011
**USA** 150 Linden St, Oakland, CA 94607
**UK** 10a Spring Place, London NW5 3BH
**France** 1 rue du Dahomey, 75011 Paris

**Photographs**
Many of the images in this guide are available for licensing from
Lonely Planet Images.
**w** www.lonelyplanetimages.com

**Front cover photograph**
Surfboard near palm tree, Waikiki Beach, Oahu, Hawaii
(Jan Halaska)

ISBN 1 74059 201 8

text & maps © Lonely Planet Publications Pty Ltd 2003
photos © photographers as indicated 2003

Printed by SNP Security Printing Pte Ltd, Singapore

# Contents – Text

# Contents – Maps

3

# REGIONAL MAP INDEX

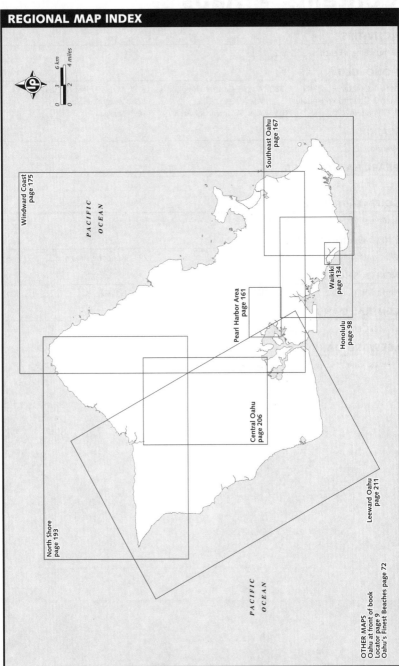

0 3 6 km
0 2 4 miles

Windward Coast
page 175

Southeast Oahu
page 167

Waikiki
page 134

Pearl Harbor Area
page 161

Honolulu
page 98

Central Oahu
page 206

North Shore
page 193

Leeward Oahu
page 211

PACIFIC
OCEAN

PACIFIC
OCEAN

OTHER MAPS
Oahu at front of book
Locator page 9
Oahu's Finest Beaches page 72

# The Authors

### Ned Friary & Glenda Bendure

Ned grew up near Boston and studied Social Thought & Political Economy at the University of Massachusetts in Amherst.

Glenda grew up in California's Mojave Desert and first traveled overseas as a high school AFS exchange student to India.

After meeting in Santa Cruz, California, where Glenda was completing her university studies, they took to the road and spent several years traveling throughout Asia and the Pacific, with a home base in Japan where Ned taught English and Glenda edited a monthly magazine. On their first trip to Hawaii, they were so taken by the islands that a two-week vacation stretched into a four-month sojourn.

Ned and Glenda now live at Cape Cod in Massachusetts. They have a particular fondness for islands and tropical climates. In addition to this Oahu guide, they are also the authors of Lonely Planet's Hawaii, Bermuda and Denmark guidebooks.

## FROM THE AUTHORS

Many thanks to the people who helped us on this project: Curt A Cottrell, Na Ala Hele Trails & Access Program Manager; Allen Tom, Sanctuary Program Manager at Hawaiian Islands Humpback Whale National Marine Sanctuary; preservation engineer Glenn Thering; Linda Delaney from the Office of Hawaiian Affairs; Jon Giffin of the Division of Forestry & Wildlife; travel consultant Teruo Koike; Honolulu science teacher Ted Brattstrom; and marine biologist Lisa King. Thanks also to those friends and travelers who shared insights and experiences with us along the way.

# This Book

This 2nd edition of *Oahu* was researched and written by Ned Friary and Glenda Bendure. It is based on the 1st edition written by the same authors. Ryan Ver Berkmoes also assisted in the research and writing of several sections and contributed some new boxed texts to this edition.

## FROM THE PUBLISHER

The 2nd edition of *Oahu* was commissioned and developed by Erin Corrigan with assistance from the series publishing manager, Susan Rimerman.

This edition was produced in Lonely Planet's Melbourne office by coordinating editor Tasmin Waby, with assistance from Elizabeth Swan and Kyla Gillzan.

Mapping was begun in the US office by Kat Smith, Laurie Mikkelsen and Bart Wright before the manuscript arrived in Australia, where Andrew Smith coordinated the cartography with the assistance of Anneka Imkamp, Alison Lyall and Csanád Csutoros.

Pablo Gastar designed the color pages. Indra Kilfolye was responsible for the layout design. The front cover design was designed by Susan Rimerman and produced by Ruth Askevold.

The project was managed by Chris Love.

Thanks to Nick Stebbing for his expertise and support during layout and Lonely Planet Images for their assistance with photos throughout the book.

# Thanks

Many thanks to the travelers who used the last edition and wrote to us with helpful hints, useful advice and interesting anecdotes:

Katrina Corcoran, Mike Earnest, Phillip East, Elizabeth Long Goldman, C Harris, Eva Himmelberg, Simon Huang, Shella Keilholz, Jim Killebrew, Vanina Killebrew, Penny Lee, Robson Lin, Jerry Muller, Kelly Nevins, Tim Nevins, James Parry, Robert Reinke, Michael Riess, Beth Thomas, Tara White, Krissy Williams, Sandra Wolf and Erin Zoski

# Foreword

## ABOUT LONELY PLANET GUIDEBOOKS

The story begins with a classic travel adventure: Tony and Maureen Wheeler's 1972 journey across Europe and Asia to Australia. There was no useful information about the overland trail then, so Tony and Maureen published the first Lonely Planet guidebook to meet a growing need.

From a kitchen table, Lonely Planet has grown to become the largest independent travel publisher in the world, with offices in Melbourne (Australia), Oakland (USA), London (UK) and Paris (France).

Today Lonely Planet guidebooks cover the globe. There is an ever-growing list of books and information in a variety of media. Some things haven't changed. The main aim is still to make it possible for adventurous travelers to get out there – to explore and better understand the world.

At Lonely Planet we believe travelers can make a positive contribution to the countries they visit – if they respect their host communities and spend their money wisely. Since 1986 a percentage of the income from each book has been donated to aid projects and human rights campaigns, and, more recently, to wildlife conservation.

Although inclusion in a guidebook usually implies a recommendation we cannot list every good place. Exclusion does not necessarily imply criticism. In fact there are a number of reasons why we might exclude a place – sometimes it is simply inappropriate to encourage an influx of travelers.

## UPDATES & READER FEEDBACK

Things change – prices go up, schedules change, good places go bad and bad places go bankrupt. Nothing stays the same. So, if you find things better or worse, recently opened or long-since closed, please tell us and help make the next edition even more accurate and useful.

Lonely Planet thoroughly updates each guidebook as often as possible – usually every two years, although for some destinations the gap can be longer. Between editions, up-to-date information is available in our free, monthly email bulletin *Comet* (**w** www.lonelyplanet.com/newsletters). You can also check out the *Thorn Tree* bulletin board and *Postcards* section of our website, which carry unverified, but fascinating, reports from travelers.

**Tell us about it!** We genuinely value your feedback. A well-traveled team at Lonely Planet reads and acknowledges every email and letter we receive and ensures that every morsel of information finds its way to the relevant authors, editors and cartographers.

Everyone who writes to us will find their name listed in the next edition of the appropriate guidebook. The very best contributions will be rewarded with a free guidebook.

We may edit, reproduce and incorporate your comments in Lonely Planet products such as guidebooks, websites and digital products, so let us know if you don't want your comments reproduced or your name acknowledged.

**How to contact Lonely Planet:**
Online: **e** talk2us@lonelyplanet.com.au, **w** www.lonelyplanet.com
**Australia:** Locked Bag 1, Footscray, Victoria 3011
**UK:** 10a Spring Place, London NW5 3BH
**USA:** 150 Linden St, Oakland, CA 94607

# Introduction

The images most people conjure up when they think of Hawaii are sights on Oahu – the beaches and high-rise hotels of Waikiki, the WWII memorials at Pearl Harbor and the towering surf at Sunset Beach.

The most developed of the Hawaiian Islands, Oahu is fittingly nicknamed 'The Gathering Place.' The island is home to 876,000 people – nearly 75% of the state's population.

Although much of Oahu is an urban scene, it's nonetheless a scenic island with rugged volcanic peaks, tropical forests, fluted mountains, aquamarine bays and valleys carpeted with pineapple fields. Oahu also has some of Hawaii's best beaches – Hanauma Bay is the most visited snorkeling spot in the Hawaiian Islands; the North Shore has Hawaii's top surfing action; and windward Kailua is Hawaii's most popular windsurfing beach.

The heart of Oahu is vibrant Honolulu. As the capital of Hawaii, Honolulu is the political, cultural and economic center of the state. The only US state capital that is located in the tropics, Honolulu boasts swaying palm trees and year-round balmy weather.

Honolulu is an attractive city with an intriguing blend of Eastern and Western influences. Cultural offerings range from Chinese lantern parades and traditional hula performances to ballet and good museums. Honolulu has fine city beaches and parks, some great hilltop views and the only royal palace in the USA. The city is also a diner's delight, with a wonderful assortment of good ethnic restaurants.

Bustling Waikiki, covering 1½ miles of sparkling beachfront at the eastern side of Honolulu, is one of the biggest resort destinations in the Pacific. Almost all of Oahu's tourist facilities are centered in Waikiki – in fact, Waikiki's hotels play host to nearly half of all visitors to the Hawaiian Islands. A monument to mass tourism, Waikiki packs an amazing array of visitor amenities: seaside restaurants, waterfront hotels, lively

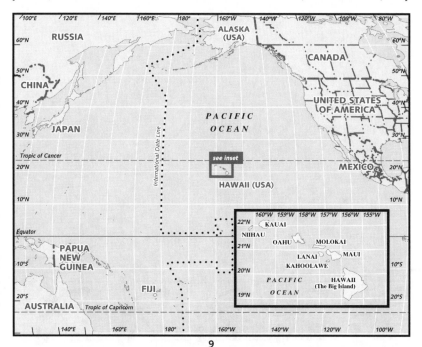

entertainment and a variety of beach activities are all close at hand.

Once the sole domain of Hawaiian royalty and the very rich, Waikiki is one of those places that has the power to lure people from far and wide. It's teeming with sunseekers strutting about in bikinis, surfers hitting the waves, retirees playing checkers at picnic tables, tourists gathering along the beach to catch the sunset, and there's music wafting from beachside bars.

Still there's much more to Oahu than its urban quarters. Lush forest reserves and lightly trodden hiking trails are just 15 minutes from downtown Honolulu, and all the rest of Oahu's sights are within an easy one- or two-hour drive from Honolulu.

Places not to be missed include the Nuuanu Pali Lookout, with its sweeping views; Kailua, with its lovely beach; and the North Shore, with its surf mania. Oahu has plenty of enjoyable off-the-beaten-path spots to explore as well, such as the community-run Hawaii's Plantation Village, the marketplaces in Chinatown and the county's botanical gardens.

# Facts about Oahu

## HISTORY

Hawaii is the northern point of the huge triangle of Pacific Ocean islands known as Polynesia, which means 'many islands.' The other two points of the triangle are Easter Island to the southeast and New Zealand to the southwest.

Whether the original Polynesian settlers had their roots in Southeast Asia, as has traditionally been thought, or whether they originated in Melanesia, as some archaeologists now believe, is a matter of debate. Either way, their migratory path apparently took them in an eastwardly direction from Melanesia to settle the southern Polynesian islands of Tonga and Samoa in around 1000 BC. Over the next 1500 years, they migrated to the more far-flung areas of Polynesia, with Hawaii being the last area settled.

Archaeological evidence indicates that the first settlers to Hawaii arrived from the Marquesas Islands around AD 500. They were followed by Tahitians, who arrived in Hawaii around AD 1000. Unlike the Marquesans, who had sparse settlements at the northwestern end of the Hawaiian chain, the Tahitians settled all of the main Hawaiian Islands.

The Tahitians were thorough colonizers, arriving in double-hulled canoes that were loaded with pigs, chickens, dogs and staple food plants such as taro and bananas.

Adept seafarers who used ocean currents and star patterns to navigate, the Tahitians were not only capable of making the 2700-mile journey north but were also able to memorize the route and retrace it. Vast waves of Tahitian migration occurred throughout the 13th and 14th centuries and archaeologists now believe that Hawaii's population probably reached a plateau of approximately 250,000 by the year 1450. The voyages back and forth continued until around 1500, when all contact between Tahiti and Hawaii appears to have stopped.

### Ancient Hawaii

The earliest Hawaiians had simple, animistic beliefs. Good fishing, a safe journey and a healthy child were all considered the result of being in tune with the spirits of nature. Their offerings to the gods consisted of prayers and a share of the harvest.

### Little People, Big Tasks

Numerous Hawaiian legends tell of a tribe of happy, elflike people called *menehunes* who came down out of the mountains to produce great engineering works in stone.

It seems likely that when the first wave of Tahitians arrived in Hawaii in about AD 1000, they conquered and subjugated the Marquesans who had settled in Hawaii centuries earlier, forcing them to build their temples, irrigation ditches and fishponds.

The Tahitian term for 'outcast' is *manahune*, and the diminutive social status the Marquesans had in the eyes of their conquerors may have given rise to tales of a dwarf-sized race.

The *menehunes* may have created the temples, but the Tahitian settlers created the legends. While the stonework still remains, the true identity of Hawaii's 'little people' has slipped into obscurity.

Around the 12th century, a powerful Tahitian kahuna (priest), Paao, arrived in Hawaii. Convinced that the Hawaiians were too lax in their worship, Paao introduced the concept of offering human sacrifice to the gods and he built the first *luakini* heiau, a type of temple where these sacrifices took place. He also established the *kapu* system, a practice of taboos that strictly regulated all social interaction.

The *kapu*s forbade commoners from eating the same food or even walking the same ground as the *alii*, or royalty, who were thought to be representatives of the gods. A commoner who crossed the shadow of a king could be put to death. *Kapu*s prohibited all women from eating coconuts, bananas, pork and certain varieties of fish.

This strict system of *kapu*s and social delineation remained intact until after the arrival of the first Westerners in the late 18th century.

**Religion** In the old Hawaiian religion there were four main gods: Ku, Lono, Kane and Kanaloa.

Ku was the ancestor god for all generations of humankind, past, present and future. He presided over all male gods while his wife, Hina, reigned over the female gods. When the sun rose in the morning, it was said to be Ku; when it set in the evening it was Hina. Like Yin and Yang, they were responsible for heaven and earth.

Ku had many manifestations, one as the benevolent god of fishing, Ku-ula (Ku of the abundant seas), and others as the gods of forests and farming. People prayed to Ku when the harvest was scarce. At a time of drought or other such disasters, a temple would be built to appease Ku.

One of the most fearful of Ku's manifestations was Kukailimoku (Ku, the snatcher of land), the war god that Kamehameha the Great worshipped. The temples built for the worship of Kukailimoku were offered sacrifices not only of food, pigs and chickens but also of human beings.

Lono was the god in charge of the elements that brought rain and an abundant harvest. He was also the god of fertility and peace.

Kane created the first man out of the dust of the earth and breathed life into him (the Hawaiian word for man is *kane*), and it was from Kane that the Hawaiian chiefs were said to have descended.

Ku, Lono and Kane together created the earth, the moon, the stars and the ocean.

Kanaloa, the fourth major god, was often pitted in struggles against the other three gods. When heaven and earth separated, it was Kanaloa who was placed in charge of the spirits on earth. Forbidden from drinking the intoxicating beverage *kava*, these spirits revolted and, along with Kanaloa, were driven to the underworld, where Kanaloa became the ruler of the dead.

Below the four main gods, there were 40 lesser gods. The best known of them was Pele, goddess of volcanoes. Her sister Laka was goddess of the hula, and another sister, Poliahu, was the goddess of snow.

The Hawaiians had gods for all occupations and natural phenomena. There was a god for the *tapa* (cloth) maker and a god for the canoe builder, as well as shark gods and mountain gods.

**Heiaus** The temples erected in ancient Hawaii, called heiaus, were built in two basic styles, both of which were constructed of lava rock. One was a simple rectangular enclosure of stone walls built directly on the ground. The other was a more substantial structure built of rocks piled high to form raised terraced platforms.

Inside the heiaus were prayer towers, taboo houses and drum houses. These structures were made of ohia wood, thatched with *pili* grass and tied with cord from the native *olona* shrub. Tikis, or god images, called *kii*, were carved of wood and placed around the prayer towers.

Heiaus were most commonly dedicated to Lono, the god of harvest, or Ku, the god of war. The heiaus built in honor of Ku were the only ones where human sacrifices took place.

Heiaus were built in auspicious sites, often perched on cliffs above the coast or in other places thought to have *mana*, or 'spiritual power.' A heiau's significance focused on the *mana* of the site rather than the structure itself. When a heiau's *mana* was gone, it was abandoned.

## Captain Cook

Hawaii was the last of the Polynesian islands to be 'discovered' by the West. This was in large part due to the fact that early European explorers who entered the Pacific around the tips of either Africa or South America centered their explorations in the Southern Hemisphere. Indeed, the great British explorer Captain James Cook spent the better part of a decade charting most of the South Pacific before chancing upon Hawaii as he sailed north from Tahiti in search of a northwest passage to the Atlantic.

On January 18, 1778, Captain Cook sighted the islands of Oahu, Kauai and Niihau. The winds favored approaching Kauai, and on January 19, Cook's ships, the *Discovery* and the *Resolution*, sailed into Kauai's Waimea Bay. Cook named the Hawaiian archipelago the Sandwich Islands in honor of the Earl of Sandwich.

The captain was surprised to find that the islanders had a strong Tahitian influence in their appearance, language and culture. The natives were eager to trade fish and sweet potatoes for iron nails and anything else made of metal, which was totally absent from their islands.

Cook, whose arrival in Hawaii happened to coincide with the *makahiki*, an annual harvest festival in honor of the god Lono, was given a warm reception. After two weeks of stocking provisions, Cook's expedition continued its journey north. Failing to find the fabled passage through the Arctic, Cook set sail back to Hawaii, where his arrival date virtually coincided with that of his initial visit to the islands one year earlier.

On January 17, 1779, Cook sailed into Kealakekua Bay on the Big Island, where a thousand canoes came out to greet him. When Cook went ashore, he was met by the high priest and guided to a temple lined with skulls. Everywhere the English captain went, people fell face down on the ground in front of him to the chant of 'Lono.'

Not only had Cook once again landed during the *makahiki* festival, but the tall masts and white sails of Cook's ships, and even the way he had sailed clockwise around the island, all fitted the legendary descriptions of how the god Lono would reappear on the scene.

Whether the priests actually believed Cook was the reincarnated Lono or whether they just used his appearance to enhance their power and add a little flair to the festivities is unknown. What is clear is that Cook never realized that both of his arrivals to Hawaii had coincided with the *makahiki* festivals – he assumed this was just the way things were in everyday Hawaii.

There's little wonder that Cook had a favorable impression of Hawaii. The islanders treated his crew with open hospitality. Hawaiian men invited the sailors to boxing matches, and the women performed dances and readily bedded down with Cook's men. For a crew that had just spent months roaming inhospitable frozen tundra, this was paradise indeed.

On February 4 the English vessels sailed north out of Kealakekua Bay but soon ran into a storm and the *Resolution* broke a foremast. Cook decided to go back to Kealakekua Bay to repair the mast – a decision that would prove to be a fatal mistake.

The ruling *alii* seemed upset with Cook's reappearance. Apparently the *makahiki* was over and not only was Cook's timing inauspicious, but so were the conditions of his return: This time he had arrived in a counterclockwise direction and with a broken sail.

Thievery became a problem for the British. After a cutter was stolen, Cook set off with a small party to capture the high chief Kalaniopuu with the intention of holding him until the cutter was returned. When Cook took the chief into custody, an angry mob cornered them. Hoping to prevent bloodshed, Cook let the chief go, but fate wasn't with the captain. As Cook was walking towards his boat, he shot at one of the armed Hawaiians who tried to block his way. The pistol misfired and the bullet bounced off the man's chest. The crowd of Hawaiians moved in on Cook with daggers and clubs.

In this freak melee on a shore of the 'Sandwich Islands,' Cook's last discovery, the life of the greatest explorer and navigator of the 18th century came to a bloody end. A week after Cook's death, the expedition's ships set sail, landing briefly on Oahu before finally leaving Hawaiian waters on March 15, 1779.

Cook and his crew left the Hawaiians a costly legacy in the iron that was turned into weapons, the diseases they introduced that decimated the natives, and the first children of mixed blood.

Some of Cook's crew returned to the Pacific, leading their own expeditions. Among them was Captain George Vancouver, who brought the first cattle and horses to Hawaii, and the ill-fated William Bligh, who captained the *Bounty*.

## Kamehameha the Great

At the time of the first European contact with Hawaii, the Hawaiian Islands were under the control of a handful of chiefs who

### Snatcher of Land

In order to amass strength, the warrior chief Kamehameha the Great became the guardian of the war god Kukailimoku, also known as the 'snatcher of land.'

This war god was embodied in a carved wooden image with a bloody red mouth and a helmet of yellow feathers. Kamehameha carried it into battle with him, and it was said that during the fiercest fighting the image would screech out terrifying battle cries.

The effects of Kukailimoku aside, Kamehameha the Great became the most successful warrior in Hawaiian history and the first king to bring all Hawaii's territory under the control of a single ruler.

were engaged in a struggle for dominance of the island chain. The main rivals were Kamehameha the Great, chief of the island of Hawaii, and Kahekili, the aging king of Maui, who in the 1780s had killed his own stepson in order to take control of Oahu.

After Kahekili died at Waikiki in 1794, a power struggle ensued and his lands were divided between two quarreling relatives. His son Kalanikupule got Oahu, while his half-brother King Kaeokulani of Kauai gained control of Maui, Lanai and Molokai. The two ambitious heirs immediately went to battle with each other, creating a rift that Kamehameha set out to exploit.

In 1795 Kamehameha swept through Maui and Molokai, conquering those islands before crossing the channel to Oahu. He landed his fleet of war canoes on the quiet beaches of Waikiki and marched up towards Nuuanu Valley to meet Kalanikupule, the king of Oahu.

The Oahu warriors were no match for Kamehameha's troops. The first heavy fighting took place around Puowaina (present-day Punchbowl), where Kamehameha's men quickly circled the fortresslike crater and drove out the Oahuan defenders. Scattered fighting continued up Nuuanu Valley, with the last big battle taking place near the current site of Queen Emma's summer palace.

The Oahuans were well prepared for the usual spear-and-stone warfare, panicked when they realized Kamehameha had brought in a handful of Western sharp-shooters with modern firearms. Under Kamehameha's command, the foreigners picked off the Oahuan generals and blasted into their ridge-top defenses.

What should have been the high-ground advantage turned into a death trap for the Oahuans when they found themselves wedged up into the valley, unable to redeploy. Fleeing up the cliffsides in retreat, they were forced to make their last stand at the narrow, precipitous ledge along the current-day Nuuanu Pali Lookout. Hundreds of Oahuans were driven over the top of the *pali* (cliff) to their deaths.

Some Oahuan warriors, including King Kalanikupule, escaped into the upland forests. When Kalanikupule surfaced a few months later, Kamehameha, as an offering to his war god, made a human sacrifice of the fallen king. Kamehameha's taking of Oahu marked the last battle ever fought between Hawaiian troops, as well as Hawaii's emergence as a united kingdom.

## The Founding of Honolulu

In 1793 the English frigate *Butterworth* became the first foreign ship to sail into what is now called Honolulu Harbor. Its captain, William Brown, named the protected harbor Fair Haven. Ships that followed called it Brown's Harbor. Over time, the name Honolulu, which means 'Sheltered Bay,' came to be used for both the harbor and the seaside district that the Hawaiians had called Kou.

As more and more foreign ships found their way to Honolulu, a harborside village of thatched houses sprang up. The port soon became a focal point for merchant ships plying the seas between the USA and Asia.

In 1809 Kamehameha the Great, who had been living in his royal court in Waikiki, decided to move to the Honolulu Harbor area, which by then had grown into a village of almost 1800 people. Intent on keeping an eye on all the trade that flowed in and out of the harbor, Kamehameha set up a residence near the waterfront. With Kamehameha's presence, Honolulu was firmly established as the center of Hawaii's commerce.

Kamehameha traded sandalwood, which was shipped to China, in exchange for weapons and luxury goods. As the trade grew, Kamehameha built harborside warehouses to store his goods and he introduced wharfage fees to build up his treasury. New England Yankees, who dominated the sandalwood trade, quickly became the main foreign presence in Honolulu.

By the time of Kamehameha's death in 1819, nearly 3500 people lived in Honolulu and it continued to boom as more foreigners arrived.

## End of the Old Religion

When Kamehameha the Great died, the crown was passed to his reluctant son Liho-liho, who was proclaimed Kamehameha II (1819–24). In reality, however, the power passed to Kaahumanu, who was Kamehameha's favorite of his 21 wives.

Kaahumanu was an ambitious woman, determined to break down the ancient *kapu* system of taboos that restricted her powers. Less than six months after Kamehameha's death, Kaahumanu threw a feast for women of royalty. Although one of the most sacred taboos strictly forbade men from eating with women, Kaahumanu forcefully persuaded Liholiho to sit beside her and join in the meal.

It was an otherwise uneventful meal, and not a single angry god manifested itself. In that one act, the old religion was cast aside, along with 600 years of taboos and restrictions. Hawaiians no longer feared being put to death for violating the *kapu*s, and a flurry of temple smashing and idol burning quickly followed.

The chiefs and kahunas who resisted were easily quelled by Liholiho, using the powerful army that Kamehameha left behind. It was the end of an era.

## Liholiho (Kamehameha II)

With Kaahumanu holding the real power, in November 1823 a floundering Liholiho set sail for England with his favorite wife to pay a royal visit to King George – although he failed to inform anyone in England of his plans.

When Liholiho arrived unannounced in London, misfitted in Western clothing and lacking in royal etiquette, the British press roasted him with racist caricatures. While being prepped in the social graces for their audience with the king, Liholiho and his wife came down with measles. They died in England within a few weeks of each other in July 1824, having never met King George.

## Missionaries & Sinners

By 1820 whaling ships sailing the Pacific began to pull into Honolulu for supplies, liquor and women. To meet their needs, shops, taverns and brothels sprang up around the harbor.

Much to the ire of the whalers, their arrival was soon followed by that of Christian

## Lost Forests

In the early 1790s American sea captains discovered that Hawaii had great stocks of sandalwood that were at a premium in China.

A lucrative three-way trade developed. From Honolulu the ships sailed to Canton and traded loads of the fragrant sandalwood in exchange for Chinese silk and porcelain, which were then carried back to New England ports and sold at a high profit. In New England the ships were reloaded with goods to be traded to the Hawaiians.

Hawaii's forests of sandalwood were so vast at this time that the Chinese name for Hawaii was Tahn Heong Sahn – the 'Sandalwood Mountains.'

In an effort to maintain the resource, Kamehameha the Great took total control over the sandalwood forests, but even under his shrewd management, the bulk of the profits ended up in the sea captains' pockets. Payment for the sandalwood was in overpriced goods; originally cannons and rifles, and later exotic items such as European furniture.

Kamehameha was careful not to deplete all his forests or overburden his subjects, but his successor Liholiho allowed local chiefs to get in on the action. These chiefs began purchasing foreign luxuries by signing promissory notes to be paid in future shipments of sandalwood.

To pay off the chiefs' rising 'debts,' commoners were forced into virtual servitude. They were used as packhorses to haul the wood, which was strapped to their backs with bands of ti leaves. The men who carted the wood were called *kua leho*, literally 'callous backs,' after the thick permanent layer of calluses that they developed. It was not uncommon for them to carry heavy loads 20 miles from the interior of the forests to ships waiting on the coast. During the height of the trade, missionaries recorded seeing caravans of as many as 3000 men carting wood.

Within a few short years after Kamehameha's death, Hawaii's sandalwood forests were exhausted. In a futile attempt to continue the trade, Oahu's governor Boki, who had heard of vast sandalwood reserves in New Hebrides, set sail in November 1829 with 500 men on an ill-conceived expedition to harvest the trees. Boki's ship was lost at sea and the expedition's other ship, not too surprisingly, received a hostile welcome in New Hebrides.

In August 1830, 20 emaciated survivors sailed back into Honolulu Harbor. Boki had been a popular, if troubled, leader in a rapidly changing Hawaii. Hawaiians grieved in the streets of Honolulu when they heard of Boki's tragedy, and his death marked the end of the sandalwood trade.

missionaries. The first missionary ship to land in Hawaii, the *Thaddeus*, sailed into Honolulu on April 14, 1820. The minister in charge of the Honolulu mission was Hiram Bingham, a staunch Calvinist who was set on putting an end to the heathen ways of the Hawaiians.

The missionaries befriended Hawaiian royalty and made inroads quickly. When Queen Kaahumanu, the widow of Kamehameha the Great, became seriously ill, Hiram's wife, Sybil Bingham, nursed the queen back to health. Shortly after, Kaahumanu showed her gratitude by passing a law forbidding work and travel on the Sabbath.

Although both the missionaries and the whalers hailed from New England, they had little else in common and were soon at odds, with the missionaries intent on saving souls and the whalers intent, after months at sea, on satisfying more earthly desires.

In January 1826 the captain of the American warship USS *Dolphin*, having arrived in Honolulu to investigate trade issues, raised a stir with the missionaries by advocating prostitution. In response, Bingham convinced the island chiefs to put a *kapu* on women, forbidding them to board ships in the harbor. After the sailors stoned Bingham's house, the women were once again allowed free contact with the crews, but the struggles between whalers and missionaries continued.

In time the missionaries gained enough influence with Hawaiian royalty to have more effective laws enacted against drunkenness and prostitution. By the peak whaling years of the mid-1800s, most whaling boats had abandoned Honolulu, preferring to land in Lahaina on Maui, where the whalers had gained an upper hand over the missionaries.

Interestingly, both groups left their marks on Honolulu. To this day the headquarters of the Protestant mission sits placidly in downtown Honolulu, while located only minutes away Honolulu's red-light district continues to attract sea-weary sailors and wayward souls.

Downtown Honolulu also became the headquarters for the emerging corporations that eventually gained control of Hawaii's commerce. It's no coincidence that their lists of corporate board members – Alexander, Baldwin, Cooke and Dole – read like a roster from the first mission ships, for indeed it

## Whaling in the Pacific

From the 1820s to 1870, Hawaii was the whaling center of the Pacific. It was a convenient way station for whalers hunting in both the Arctic and Japanese whaling grounds. At its peak, between 500 and 600 whaling ships were pulling into Hawaiian ports each year.

Hawaiians themselves made good whalers, and sea captains gladly paid a $200 bond to the Hawaiian government for each *kanaka* (native Hawaiian) allowed to join their crew. Kamehameha IV even set up his own fleet of whaling ships, which flew under the Hawaiian flag.

Whaling in the Pacific peaked in the mid-19th century and quickly began to burn itself out. In a few short years all but the most distant whaling grounds were being depleted and whalers were forced to go farther afield to make their kills. By 1860 whale oil prices were dropping as an emerging petroleum industry began to produce a less expensive fuel for lighting.

The last straw for the Pacific whaling industry came in 1871, when an early storm in the Arctic caught more than 30 ships by surprise, trapping them in ice floes above the Bering Strait. Although more than 1000 seamen were rescued, half of them Hawaiian, the fleet itself was lost.

was the sons of missionaries who became the power brokers in the new Hawaii.

## Sugar Plantations

*Ko*, or sugarcane, arrived in Hawaii with the early Polynesian settlers. Although the Hawaiians enjoyed chewing the cane for its juices, they never refined it into sugar.

The first known attempt at producing sugar in Hawaii was in 1802, when a Chinese immigrant boiled crushed sugarcane in iron pots. Other Chinese soon set up small sugar mills on the scale of neighborhood bakeries.

In 1835 a young Bostonian, William Hooper, saw a bigger opportunity in sugar and set out to establish Hawaii's first sugar plantation. Hooper convinced Honolulu investors Ladd & Company to put up the money for his venture and then worked out a deal with Kamehameha III to lease 980 acres of land for $300. His next step was to restore Hawaiian independence. Admiral Thomas raised the Hawaiian flag in Honolulu again at the site of what is today Thomas Square.

As the flag was raised, Kamehameha III uttered the words *Ua mau ke ea o ka aina i ka pono*, meaning 'The life of the land is perpetuated in righteousness,' which remains Hawaii's official motto.

In an 1853 census, Honolulu registered 11,450 residents, a full 15% of the Hawaiian kingdom's population. Though still a frontier town with dusty streets and simple wooden buildings, Honolulu was both the commercial and political center of the kingdom.

In the decades that followed, Honolulu took on a modern appearance as the monarchy erected a number of stately buildings in the city center, including St Andrew's Cathedral, Iolani Palace and the supreme court building Aliiolani Hale.

By the mid-19th century, Honolulu had a prominent foreign community composed largely of American and British expats. These foreigners were not only active in missionary endeavors but were also opening schools and starting newspapers and, more importantly, landing powerful government positions as ministry officials and consuls to the king. As the city continued to grow and Westerners wrested increasing control over island affairs from the Hawaiians, the powers of Kamehameha the Great's successors eroded.

## Kamehameha IV

Kamehameha IV had a short and rather confusing reign that lasted from 1855 to 1863. He tried to give his rule an element of European regality, à la Queen Victoria, and he and his consort, Queen Emma, established a Hawaiian branch of the Anglican Church of England. He also passed a law mandating that all children be given a Christian name along with their Hawaiian name, a statute that stayed on the books until 1967.

Kamehameha IV's reign was marked by struggles between those wanting to strengthen the monarchy and those wishing to weaken it.

## Kamehameha V

The most significant accomplishment of Kamehameha V, who reigned from 1863 to 1872, was the establishment of a controversial constitution that gave greater power to

## The Great Mahele

The Great Mahele of 1848, introduced under the urging of influential missionaries, permanently altered the Hawaiian concept of land rights: For the first time, land became a commodity that could be bought and sold.

Through the provisions of the Great Mahele, the king, who previously owned all land, gave up title to the majority of it. Island chiefs were allowed to buy some of the lands that they had controlled as fiefdoms for the king. Other lands, divided into 3-acre farm plots called *kuleana*, were made available to all Hawaiians. In order to retain title, chiefs and commoners alike had to pay a tax and register the land.

The chiefs had the option of paying the tax in property and many did so. Commoners had no choice but to pay the taxes in cash. Although the act was intended to turn Hawaii into a country of small farms, in the end only a few thousand Hawaiians carried through with the paperwork and received *kuleanas*.

In 1850 land purchases were opened to foreigners. Unlike the Hawaiians, the Westerners jumped at the opportunity, and before the native islanders could clearly grasp the concept of private land ownership, there was little land left to own. Within a few decades the Westerners, who were more adept at wheeling and dealing in real estate, owned 80% of all privately held lands. Even many of the Hawaiians who went through the process of getting their own *kuleana* eventually ended up selling it off for a fraction of its real value.

Contrary to the bright picture the missionaries had painted for Kamehameha III, the Hawaiians suddenly became a landless people, drifting into ghettos in the larger towns. In a bitter twist, many of the missionaries ended up with sizable tracts of land and more than a few of them left the church to devote themselves to their new estates.

Although Hawaiian commoners had no rights to the land prior to the Great Mahele, they were free to move around and work the property of any chief. In return for their personal use of the land they paid the chief in labor or with a percentage of their crops. In this way they lived off the land. After the Great Mahele, they were simply *off* the land.

negotiate with the *alii* for the right to use Hawaiian laborers.

In the mid-1830s Hawaii was still largely feudal. Commoners fished, farmed and lived on land that was under the domain of the local *alii*; in exchange, the commoners worked for the *alii* when needed. Therefore, before Hooper could hire any work hands, he had to first pay the *alii* a stipend to free the Hawaiians from their traditional work obligations.

The new plantation system, which introduced the concept of growing crops for profit rather than subsistence, marked the advent of capitalism and the introduction of wage labor in Hawaii. The sugar industry emerged at the same time that whalers began arriving in force, and together they became the foundation of Hawaii's economy.

## Hawaii's Immigrants

As the sugar industry boomed, Hawaii's native population declined, largely as the result of diseases introduced by foreigners.

To expand their operations, the plantation owners began to look overseas for a labor supply. They needed immigrants accustomed to working long days in hot weather, and for whom the low wages would seem like a golden opportunity.

In 1852 the plantation owners began recruiting laborers from China. In 1868 they went to Japan and in the 1870s they brought in Portuguese from Madeira and the Azores. After Hawaii's 1898 annexation to the USA resulted in restrictions on Chinese immigration, plantation owners turned to Puerto Ricans and Koreans. Filipinos were the last group of immigrants brought to Hawaii to work the fields; the first wave came in 1906, the last in 1946.

Although these six ethnic groups made up the bulk of the field hands, South Sea islanders, Scots, Scandinavians, Germans, Galicians, Spaniards and Russians all came in turn as well.

Each group brought its own culture, food and religion. Chinese clothing styles mixed with Japanese kimonos and European bonnets. A dozen languages filled the air and a unique pidgin English developed as a means for the various groups to communicate with one another.

Conditions varied with the ethnic group and the period. At the end of the 19th century,

Japanese contract laborers were paid $15 a month. After annexation, the contracts were considered to be indentured servitude and were declared illegal under US law. Still, wages as low as a dollar a day were common until the 1930s.

In all, approximately 350,000 immigrants came to Hawaii to work on the sugar plantations. A continuous flow of immigrant workers was required to replace those who invariably found better options elsewhere. Although some workers came for a set period to save money and return home, others fulfilled their contracts and then moved off the plantations to farm their own plots or start their own businesses.

Plantation towns such as Waipahu and Waialua grew up around the mills, with barber shops, beer halls and bathhouses catering to the workers. Even today a drive through these sleepy Oahuan towns, with their now defunct mills (both closed in the 1990s), offers a glimpse of plantation history.

Each of the major immigrant populations – Japanese, Chinese, Filipino and Western European – came to outnumber the native Hawaiians. Together they created the unique blend of cultures that would continue to characterize Hawaii for generations to come.

## Honolulu as Capital

In 1845, Kamehameha III, the last son of Kamehameha the Great, moved the capital of the Hawaiian kingdom from Maui to Honolulu. Kamehameha III, who ruled from 1825 to 1854, established Hawaii's first national legislature, provided for a supreme court and passed the Great Mahele Land Act, which established religious freedom and gave all male citizens the right to vote.

Hawaii's only 'invasion' by a foreign power occurred during Kamehameha III's reign. In 1843, George Paulet, an upstart British commander upset about a petty land deal involving a British national, sailed into Honolulu commanding the British ship *Carysfort* and seized Oahu for six months. In that short period, he anglicized street names, seized property and began to collect taxes.

To avoid bloodshed, Kamehameha III stood aside as the British flag was raised and the ship's band played 'God Save the Queen.' Queen Victoria herself wasn't flattered. After catching wind of the incident, she dispatched Admiral Richard Thomas to the king at the expense of elected officials. It also restricted the right to vote.

Kamehameha V, who suffered a severe bout of unrequited love, was the last king from a royal lineage that dated back to the 12th century. From childhood, he had been enraptured by Princess Bernice Pauahi, who turned down his proposals, opting instead to marry American Charles Reed Bishop. Jolted by the rejection, Kamehameha V never married, yet he also never gave up on the princess. Even on his deathbed he offered Princess Bernice his kingdom, which she declined.

As the bachelor king left no heirs, his death in December 1872 brought an end to the Kamehameha dynasty. Subsequent kings would be elected.

## Lunalilo

King Lunalilo's brief reign lasted from 1873 to 1874. His cabinet, made up largely of Americans, was instrumental in paving the way for a treaty of reciprocity with the USA.

Although the USA was the biggest market for Hawaiian sugar, US sugar tariffs ate heavily into profit margins. As a means of eliminating the tariffs, most of the plantation owners favored the annexation of Hawaii to the USA.

The US government was cool to the idea of annexation, but it warmed to the possibility of establishing a naval base on Oahu. In 1872 General John Schofield was sent to assess Pearl Harbor's strategic value. He was impressed with what he saw – the largest anchorage in the Pacific – and enthusiastically reported his findings to Washington.

Although native Hawaiians protested in the streets and the Royal Troops even staged a little mutiny, there would eventually be a reciprocity agreement that would cede Pearl Harbor to the USA in exchange for duty-free access for Hawaiian sugar.

## King Kalakaua

King David Kalakaua, who reigned from 1874 to 1891, was Hawaii's last king. Although known as the 'Merrie Monarch,' he ruled in troubled times.

The first challenge to his reign came on election day. His contender was the dowager Queen Emma, and when the results were announced her followers rioted in the streets, requiring Kalakaua to request aid from US and British warships that happened to be in Honolulu Harbor at the time.

Despite the initial turmoil, Kalakaua went on to reign as a great Hawaiian revivalist. He brought back the hula, reversing decades of missionary repression against the 'heathen dance,' and he composed the national anthem *Hawaii Ponoi*, which is now the state song. Kalakaua also tried to ensure some self-rule for native Hawaiians, who had become a minority in their own land.

Although he was unwaveringly loyal to the interest of native Hawaiians, Kalakaua was realistic about the current-day realities he faced. The king proved himself a successful diplomat by traveling to Washington, DC, and persuading President Ulysses Grant to accept a treaty giving Hawaiian sugar growers tariff-free access to US markets, which the US Congress had been resisting. In so doing, Kalakaua gained, at least temporarily, the support of the sugar plantation owners, who controlled most of Hawaii's agricultural land.

During his trip Kalakaua also managed to postpone the ceding of Pearl Harbor for eight years. He returned to Hawaii a hero – to the business community for negotiating the treaty, and to the Hawaiians for simply making it back alive. The last king to leave the islands, Kamehameha II, had come back in a coffin.

### Hawaii's *Alii*

Hawaii is the only state in the USA to have been ruled by its own monarchy. Beginning with Kamehameha the Great's 1795 unification of the islands, the reign of Hawaii's *alii* continued until the overthrow of Queen Liliuokalani by American businessmen in 1893.

Following are the dates that each of Hawaii's monarchs lived:

| | |
|---|---|
| Kamehameha the Great | c.1758–1819 |
| Kamehameha II (Liholiho) | 1797–1824 |
| Kamehameha III (Kauikeauoli) | 1813–54 |
| Kamehameha IV (Alexander Liholiho) | 1834–63 |
| Kamehameha V (Lot Kamehameha) | 1830–72 |
| Lunalilo (William C Lunalilo) | 1832–74 |
| Kalakaua (David Kalakaua) | 1836–91 |
| Liliuokalani (Lydia Liliuokalani) | 1838–1917 |

The king became a world traveler, visiting India, Egypt, Europe and Southeast Asia. Kalakaua was well aware that Hawaii's days as an independent Polynesian kingdom were numbered. To counter the Western powers that were gaining hold of Hawaii, he made a futile attempt to establish a Polynesian-Pacific empire. On a visit with the emperor of Japan, he even proposed a royal marriage between his niece Princess Kaiulani and a Japanese prince, but the Japanese declined.

Visits with other foreign monarchs gave Kalakaua a taste for royal pageantry. He returned to build Iolani Palace for what the business community thought was an extravagant $360,000. To many influential whites, the king was perceived as a lavish spender who was fond of partying and throwing public luaus.

As Kalakaua incurred debts, he became increasingly less popular with the sugar barons whose businesses were now the backbone of the economy. In 1887 they formed the Hawaiian League and developed their own armies, which stood ready to overthrow Kalakaua. The league presented Kalakaua with a list of demands and forced him to accept a new constitution strictly limiting his powers. It also limited suffrage to property owners, which at that time excluded the vast majority of Hawaiians.

On July 30, 1889, a group of 150 Hawaiians attempted to overthrow the new constitution by occupying Iolani Palace. Called the Wilcox Rebellion after its part-Hawaiian leader, it was a confused and futile attempt and the rebels were forced to surrender. Kalakaua died in San Francisco in 1891.

## Overthrow of Queen Liliuokalani

Kalakaua was succeeded by his sister, Lydia Paki Kamekeha Liliuokalani, wife of Oahu's governor John O Dominis.

Queen Liliuokalani (r.1891–93) was even more determined than Kalakaua to strengthen the power of the monarchy. She charged that the 1887 constitution, which she referred to as the 'bayonet constitution,' was illegally forced upon King Kalakaua. In a pivotal decision, the Hawaii Supreme Court upheld her contention.

In January 1893, Queen Liliuokalani was preparing to proclaim a new constitution to restore royal powers when a group of armed US businessmen occupied the Supreme Court and declared the monarchy overthrown. They announced a provisional government, led by Sanford Dole, son of a pioneer missionary.

A contingent of US sailors came ashore, ostensibly to protect the property of US citizens, but instead of going to neighborhoods where Americans lived, they marched on the palace and positioned their guns at the queen's residence. Opting to avoid bloodshed, the queen stepped down.

The provisional government immediately appealed to Washington for annexation, while the queen appealed to the same powers to restore the monarchy. To the dismay of Dole's representatives, the timing seemed to be to the queen's advantage.

Democratic president, Grover Cleveland, had just replaced a Republican administration and his sentiments favored the queen. Cleveland sent an envoy to investigate the situation and received Queen Liliuokalani's niece Princess Kaiulani, who, at the time of the coup, was in London being prepared for the throne. The beautiful 18-year-old princess eloquently pleaded the monarchy's case. She also made a favorable impression on the American press, which largely caricatured those involved in the overthrow as dour, greedy buffoons.

Cleveland ordered that the US flag be taken down and the queen restored to her throne. However, the provisional government, now firmly in power, turned a deaf ear, declaring that Cleveland was meddling in 'Hawaiian' affairs.

On July 4, 1894, Dole stood on the steps of Iolani Palace and announced that Hawaii was now a republic and he was its president. A disapproving Cleveland initially favored reversing the situation, but he realized the US public's sense of justice was weak and that ousting a government of white Americans and replacing them with native Hawaiians could backlash on his own political future. Consequently, his actions were largely limited to rhetoric.

Weary of waiting for outside intervention, in early 1895 a group of Hawaiian royalists attempted a counter-revolution that was easily squashed. Although there was no evidence that she was aware of the royalists' attempt to restore her, Liliuokalani was accused of being a conspirator and placed under arrest.

To humiliate her, the queen was tried in her own palace and referred to only as Mrs John O Dominis. She was fined $5000 and sentenced to five years of hard labor, later reduced to nine months of house arrest at the palace.

Liliuokalani spent the rest of her life in her husband's residence, Washington Place, one block from the palace. During this time she composed several songs, including the popular *Aloha Oe*, her parting song to the people of Hawaii:

Farewell to you, farewell to you *(Aloha oe, aloha oe)*; O fragrance of one who dwells in the blue; One fond embrace; Until I return; Until we meet again.

When Liliuokalani died of a stroke in November 1917, all of Honolulu came out for the funeral procession. To most islanders, Liliuokalani was still their queen.

## Annexation

With the Spanish-American War of 1898, Americans acquired a taste for expansionism, and Hawaii was an interesting prospect.

Not only was Hawaii attractive because of Pearl Harbor, it took on a new strategic importance being midway between the USA and its newly acquired possession, the Philippines. The annexation of Hawaii was approved by the US Congress on July 7, 1898. Hawaii entered the 20th century as a territory of the USA.

In just over a century of Western contact, the native Hawaiian population had been decimated by foreign diseases to which it had no immunities. It began with the venereal disease introduced by Captain Cook's crew in 1778. The whalers followed with cholera and smallpox, and Chinese immigrants brought leprosy. By the end of the 19th century, the native Hawaiian population had been reduced from an estimated 300,000 to less than 50,000.

Descendants of the early missionaries first took over the land and then the government. Without ever fighting a single battle against a foreign power, Hawaiians lost their islands to ambitious foreigners. All in all, as far as the native Hawaiians were concerned, the annexation wasn't anything to celebrate.

The Chinese and Japanese were also uneasy. One of the reasons for the initial reluctance of the US Congress to annex Hawaii was the racial mix of the islands' population. There were already restrictions on Chinese immigration to the USA, and restrictions on Japanese immigration were expected to follow.

In a rush to avoid a labor shortage, the sugar plantation owners quickly brought 70,000 Japanese immigrants into Hawaii. By the time the immigration wave was over, the Japanese accounted for more than 40% of Hawaii's population.

In the years after the reciprocity treaty negotiated by King Kalakaua, sugar production increased tenfold. Those who ruled the land ruled the government, and closer bonding with the USA didn't change the formula. In 1900, President McKinley appointed Sanford Dole the first territorial governor.

## World War I

Soon after annexation, the US Navy set up a huge Pacific headquarters at Pearl Harbor and built Schofield Barracks, the largest US army base anywhere. The military soon became the leading sector of Oahu's economy.

The islands were relatively untouched by WWI, even though the first German prisoners of war 'captured' by the USA were in Hawaii. They were escorted off the German gunboat *Grier*, which had the misfortune to be docked at Honolulu Harbor when war broke out.

## Pineapples & Planes

In the early 20th century, pineapple emerged as Hawaii's second major export crop. James Dole, a cousin of Sanford Dole, purchased the island of Lanai in 1922 and turned it into the world's largest pineapple plantation. He also established similar operations on Oahu. Although sugar remained Hawaii's top crop in export value, the more labor-intensive pineapple eventually surpassed it in terms of employment.

In 1936, Pan American airlines flew the first passenger flights from the US mainland to Hawaii, an aviation milestone that ushered in the transpacific air age. Hawaii was now only hours away from the US West Coast.

## World War II

On December 7, 1941, a wave of Japanese bombers attacked Pearl Harbor, jolting the

USA into WWII. The devastating strike, which lasted two hours, caught the US fleet by surprise. A total of 2335 US soldiers were killed and 21 ships and nearly 350 planes were lost.

After the smoke cleared, Hawaii was placed under martial law and Oahu took on the face of a military camp. Already heavily militarized, vast tracts of Hawaii's land were turned over to the US armed forces for expanded military bases, training and weapons testing. Much of that land would never be returned. Throughout the war, Oahu served as the command post for the USA's Pacific operations.

Following the attack on Pearl Harbor, a wave of suspicion landed on the *nisei* (people of Japanese descent) in Hawaii. While sheer numbers prevented the sort of internment practices that took place on the mainland, the Japanese in Hawaii were subject to interrogation, and their religious and civic leaders were sent to mainland internment camps.

Japanese language schools were closed, and many of the teachers arrested. Posters were hung in public places warning islanders to be careful about speaking carelessly in front of anyone of Japanese ancestry. *Nisei* were dismissed from posts in the Hawaiian National Guard and prevented from joining the US armed services.

Eventually Japanese-Americans were allowed to volunteer for a segregated regiment, although they were kept on the mainland and out of the action for much of the war's duration.

During the final stages of the war, when fighting was at its heaviest, the *nisei* were given the chance to form a combat unit. Volunteers were called and more than 10,000 *nisei* signed up, forming two distinguished Japanese-American regiments. One of these, the 442nd Second Regimental Combat Team, which was sent into action on the European front, became the most decorated fighting unit in US history.

The veterans returned to Hawaii with new expectations. Many went on to college using the GI Bill, and today they account for some of Hawaii's most influential lawyers, judges and civic leaders. Among the veterans of the 442nd is Hawaii's senior US senator, Daniel Inouye, who lost an arm in the fighting.

## Unionizing Hawaii

The feisty mainland-based International Longshoremen's and Warehousemen's Union (ILWU) began organizing Hawaiian labor in the 1930s.

After WWII, the ILWU organized an intensive campaign against the 'Big Five' – C Brewer, Castle & Cooke, Alexander & Baldwin, Theo Davies and Amfac – Hawaii's biggest businesses and landholders, all of which had roots in the sugar industry.

The ILWU's six-month waterfront strike in 1949 virtually halted all shipments to and from Hawaii. The union went on to organize plantation strikes that resulted in Hawaii's sugar and pineapple workers becoming the world's highest paid.

The new union movement helped develop political opposition to the staunchly Republican landowners, who had maintained a stronghold on the political scene since annexation.

In the 1950s, McCarthyism, the fanatical wave of anti-Communism that swept the mainland, spilled over to Hawaii. In the fallout, the leader of the ILWU in Hawaii, Jack Hall, was tried and convicted of being a communist.

## Statehood

WWII brought Hawaii closer to the center stage of American culture and politics.

The prospect of statehood had long been the central topic in Hawaiian political circles. Three decades had passed since Prince Jonah Kuhio Kalanianaole, Hawaii's first delegate to the US Congress, introduced the first statehood bill in 1919. It received a cool reception in Washington at that time, and there were mixed feelings in Hawaii as well. However, by the time the war was over, opinion polls showed that two out of three Hawaiian residents favored statehood.

Still, Hawaii was too much of a melting pot for many politicians to support statehood, particularly those from the rigidly segregated southern states. To the overwhelmingly white and largely conservative Congress, Hawaii's multiethnic community was too exotic and foreign to be thought of as 'American.'

Congress was also concerned with the success of Hawaiian labor strikes and the growth of membership in the ILWU. These factors combined to keep statehood at bay until the end of the 1950s.

In March 1959 the US Congress finally passed legislation to make Hawaii a state. On June 27 a plebiscite was held in Hawaii, with more than 90% of the islanders voting for statehood.

On August 21, 1959, after 61 years of territorial status, Hawaii became the 50th state of the USA.

## Hawaiian Sovereignty

Over the past decade, a Hawaiian sovereignty movement, intent on righting some of the wrongs of the past century, has become a forefront political issue in Hawaii. Growing discontent over the mismanagement of Hawaiian Home Lands and the heightened consciousness created by the 1993 centennial anniversary of Queen Liliuokalani's overthrow have served as rallying points. Things are still in a formative stage, and a consensus on what form sovereignty should take has yet to emerge.

Ka Lahui Hawaii, the largest of the many Hawaiian sovereignty groups, has adopted a constitution for a Hawaiian nation within the USA, similar to that of 300 Native American groups on the mainland who have their own tribal governments and lands. Ka Lahui Hawaii wants all Hawaiian Home Lands, as well as the title to much of the crown land taken during annexation, turned over to native Hawaiians. These lands include nearly 1¾ million acres that were held by the Hawaiian kingdom at the time of the 1893 overthrow.

Other native Hawaiian groups are also calling for self-determination. Some favor the restoration of the monarchy, others focus on monetary reparations, but the majority is looking at some form of a nation-within-a-nation model.

One sovereignty demand was addressed in November 1993, when US president Bill Clinton signed a resolution apologizing 'to Native Hawaiians for the overthrow of the Hawaiian kingdom on January 17, 1893, with participation of agents and citizens of the USA, and the deprivation of the rights of Native Hawaiians to self-determination.' The apology went on to 'acknowledge the ramifications of the overthrow' and expressed a commitment to 'provide a proper foundation for reconciliation.'

Ka Lahui introduced state legislation to establish their group as the stewards of a new Hawaiian nation, and two other sovereignty bills were also introduced. To sort out the disparity between the three bills, the state legislature established the Hawaiian Sovereignty Advisory Commission to create a mechanism for native Hawaiians to determine what form sovereignty should take.

## Hawaiian Home Lands

In 1920, under the sponsorship of Prince Jonah Kuhio Kalanianaole, the congressional delegate for the Territory of Hawaii, the US Congress passed the Hawaiian Homes Commission Act. The act set aside almost 200,000 acres of land for homesteading by native Hawaiians, who were by this time the most landless ethnic group in Hawaii. The land was but a small fraction of the crown lands that were taken from the Hawaiian kingdom when the USA annexed the islands in 1898.

Under the legislation, people of at least 50% Hawaiian ancestry were eligible to apply for 99-year leases at $1 a year. Originally, most of the leases were for 40-acre parcels of agricultural land, although more recently residential lots as small as a quarter of an acre have been allocated.

Hawaii's prime land, already in the hands of the sugar barons, was excluded from the act, and much of what was designated for homesteading was on far more barren turf. Still, many Hawaiians were able to make a go of it. Presently, there are about 6500 native Hawaiian families living on about 30,000 acres of homestead lands.

Like many acts established to help native Hawaiians, administration of the Hawaiian Home Lands has been riddled with abuse. The majority of the land has not been allocated to native Hawaiians but has been leased out at bargain rates to big business, ostensibly as a means of creating an income for the administration of the program.

In addition, the federal, state and county governments have illegally, and with little or no compensation, taken large tracts of Hawaiian Home Lands for their own use. The Lualualei Naval Reservation alone constitute one-fifth of all homestead lands on Oahu, despite the fact that more than 5000 Oahuans of native Hawaiian descent remain on the waiting list – some for as long as 30 years.

The commission itself, however, became a source of conflict, as all 20 of the commission members were chosen by the governor, and only 12 of those were selected from nominees submitted by native Hawaiian organizations. As a consequence of this, some groups, such as Ka Lahui and the Nation of Hawaii, refused to participate in the commission.

In the summer of 1996, a commission-sponsored mail-in vote, which was open to all people of Hawaiian ancestry, was held on the ballot question, 'Shall the Hawaiian People elect delegates to propose a native Hawaiian government?' It was a first-step vote to determine if native Hawaiians wanted to establish a sovereignty process that would be based on electing delegates and holding a convention to chart out their future.

Of the 80,000 ballots mailed to native Hawaiians worldwide, some 30,000 were returned. The initiative passed, with 73% voting yes and 27% against, but in many ways it was a far more divided vote. Some native Hawaiians, including members of Ka Lahui, felt the process was co-opted by the state, which had provided funding for the ballot, and they boycotted the vote. The controversial commission itself disbanded after the vote, and the state declared it would not provide funding for the delegate elections and convention. A nonprofit group, Ha Hawaii, which includes former members of the commission, then spent two years raising funds for that purpose.

In 1999, the Ha Hawaii-organized election took place for the selection of 85 delegates to form a Hawaiian Convention aimed at charting the sovereignty course. However, many groups boycotted this election as well, claiming the Ha Hawaii vote was influenced by the state and the process itself was flawed. Consequently, the voter turnout was only 8.7% – fewer than 9000 of the 102,000 eligible voters participated. With so few people embracing the election, no consensus on a forum for debating sovereignty issues developed.

The focus has since turned to the courts. In February 2000 the US Supreme Court struck down a Hawaii law that had allowed for only persons of native Hawaiian ancestry to vote for trustees of the Office of Hawaiian Affairs, the leading organization

that provides social and economic benefits to people of Hawaiian ancestry. The ruling had far-reaching ramifications that included nullifying future sovereignty elections.

The conservative court ruled that native Hawaiians are a racial group, not a tribe that has a political relationship with the USA, and thus it was discriminatory to disallow non-native residents from voting in such elections.

Native Hawaiians fear that scores of government-funded programs, from health care to housing, that have been set up to specifically benefit them are now endangered. Hawaii's representatives to the US Congress are trying to counter this situation by creating federal recognition for native Hawaiians as a sovereign people, similar to the status given to most American Indians on the US mainland. A legislative bill attempting to do this, sponsored by Hawaii's US Senator Daniel Akaka, was introduced to the US Congress in 2000; it was not passed by Congress then, and has since gone through several revisions. If the bill is enacted it will give federal recognition to Native Hawaiians and grant them the right to move ahead with self-government.

There are several qualifications to Akaka's bill, including that the form of native government that emerges must be approved and ratified by the state of Hawaii before it will be certified by the US government.

## GEOGRAPHY

The Hawaiian Islands stretch 1523 miles in a line from Kure Atoll in the northwest to the Big Island in the southeast. Hawaii is the southernmost state in the USA.

The equator is 1470 miles south of Honolulu, and all the main Hawaiian Islands are in the Tropic of Cancer. Oahu shares the same latitude as Hong Kong, Bombay and Mexico's Yucatán Peninsula. Honolulu is located 2557 miles from Los Angeles, 3847 miles from Tokyo and 5070 miles from Sydney.

Hawaii's eight major islands are, from largest to smallest, Hawaii (the Big Island), Maui, Oahu, Kauai, Molokai, Lanai, Niihau and Kahoolawe. Together, they have a land area of 6470 sq miles, which includes 96 small nearshore islands with a combined area of less than 3 sq miles. Hawaii's boundaries also include the Northwestern

Hawaiian Islands, 33 tiny islands that lie scattered across a thousand miles of ocean west of Kauai; their combined land area is just 5 sq miles. In total, Hawaii is a bit smaller than Fiji and a bit larger than the US state of Connecticut.

Oahu, which covers 594 sq miles, is the third-largest Hawaiian island. It basically has four sides, with distinct windward and leeward coasts and north and south shores. The island's extreme length is 44 miles, and its width is 30 miles. Oahu's highest point, Mt Kaala at 4020ft, is in the Waianae Range.

## GEOLOGY

The Hawaiian Islands are the tips of massive mountains created by a crack in the earth's mantle that has been spewing out molten rock for more than 25 million years. The hot spot is stationary, but the ocean floor is part of the Pacific Plate, which is moving northwest at the rate of about 3 inches a year. (The eastern edge of this plate is California's San Andreas fault.)

As weak spots in the earth's crust pass over the hot spot, molten lava bursts through as volcanoes, creating underwater mountains. Some of these finally emerge above the water as islands.

Each new volcano eventually creeps northward past the hot spot that created it. The farther from the source the volcano is, the lower the volcanic activity, until it is eventually cut off completely and then becomes cold.

Once the lava stops, the forces of erosion – wind, rain and waves – slowly wash the mountains away. In addition, the settling of the ocean floor causes the land to gradually recede.

On Oahu, two separate volcanoes arose about two million years ago to form the island's two mountain ranges, Waianae and Koolau, which slice the island from the northwest to the southeast. Oahu's last gasp of volcanic activity occurred about 10,000 years ago, when the tuff cones of Diamond Head and Koko Head erupted.

Hawaii's volcanoes are shield volcanoes, which are formed not by explosion but by a slow buildup of layer upon layer of lava. They rise from the sea with gentle slopes and a relatively smooth surface. It's only after eons of facing the elements that their surfaces

become sharply eroded. It's for this reason that the most fluted cliffs in Hawaii – those on the Na Pali Coast on Kauai and the Koolau Range on Oahu – are on the two oldest main Hawaiian Islands.

## CLIMATE

Hawaii's climate is typically warm and sunny. It's unusually pleasant for the tropics, as near-constant trade winds prevail throughout the year. Although there can be spells of stormy weather, particularly in the winter, much of the time the rain falls as short daytime showers accompanied by rainbows.

In Honolulu the average daily maximum temperature is 84°F and the minimum is 70°F. Temperatures are a bit higher in summer and a few degrees lower in winter. The highest temperature on record is 94°F and the lowest is 53°F.

Rainfall varies greatly with elevation, even within short distances. Waikiki has an average annual rainfall of only 25 inches, whereas the Lyon Arboretum in the upper Manoa Valley, at the northern side of Honolulu, averages 158 inches. Mid-afternoon humidity averages 56%.

Average water temperatures in Waikiki are 77°F in March, 82°F in August.

The **National Weather Service** provides recorded weather forecasts for **Honolulu** (☎ 973-4380) and all **Oahu** (☎ 973-4381), as well as for **marine conditions** (☎ 973-4382).

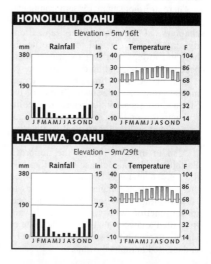

You can also find current weather information online at **w** www.hawaii.edu/news/hhp .weather.html.

## ECOLOGY & ENVIRONMENT

Hawaii has one of the world's most isolated and fragile ecosystems. Hawaiian native species are highly sensitive to habitat degradation and over the past century numerous species have become extinct, including more than a third of all native forest birds. Today, fully half of Hawaii's native flora and fauna is either threatened or endangered.

Vast tracts of native forest have long been cleared to give way to the monocrop cultures of sugarcane and pineapple. In the 1960s the advent of mass tourism posed new challenges to the environment, most notably the rampant development of land-hungry golf courses. In the past two decades the number of golf courses on Oahu has jumped from just a handful to 37, and the total acreage given over to these golf courses now rivals that used for plantation agriculture.

In terms of air quality, Oahu has no polluting heavy industry. However, Honolulu, being on the dry and less windy leeward side of the island, occasionally has moderate levels of vehicle-related pollution. As for general aesthetics, roadside billboards are not allowed and overall, the level of environmental awareness is more advanced here than on much of the US mainland.

There are more than 150 environmental groups in Hawaii, running the gamut from chapters of international organizations fighting to save the rain forests to neighborhood groups working to protect local beaches from impending development.

One of the most broad-based environmental groups is the Hawaii chapter of the Sierra Club. Its activities range from political activism on local environmental issues to weekend outings for eradicating invasive plants from the island's native forests.

Also in the forefront is the nonprofit Earthjustice Legal Defense Fund (formerly the Sierra Club Legal Defense Fund), which presses legal challenges against abuses to Hawaii's fragile environment. For instance, in conjunction with Greenpeace Hawaii, they filed a lawsuit that forced the state of Hawaii to prohibit jet skis in waters used by endangered humpback whales.

A different approach is taken by the Nature Conservancy of Hawaii, which protects Hawaii's rarest ecosystems by buying up tracts of land and working out long-term stewardships with prominent landholders. On Oahu, the Nature Conservancy manages Ihiihilauakea Preserve, a 30-acre site containing a crater with a unique vernal pool above Hanauma Bay, and the Honouliuli Preserve, a 3692-acre tract on the southeastern slope of the Waianae Range, which is home to 45 rare plant and animal species.

## FLORA & FAUNA

The Hawaiian Island chain, 2500 miles from the nearest continental land mass, is the most geographically isolated place in the world.

All living things that reached Hawaii's shores were carried across the ocean on the wind or the waves – seeds clinging to a bird's feather, a floating *hala* plant, or insect eggs in a piece of driftwood. Fern and moss spores, able to drift thousands of miles in the air, were probably the first plant life to arrive on the newly emerged volcanic islands.

It's estimated that before human contact, a new species managed to take hold in Hawaii only once every 100,000 years. New arrivals found specialized habitats ranging from desert to rain forest and elevations climbing from sea level to nearly 14,000ft. Each species evolved to fit a specific niche in its new environment.

Over 90% of Hawaii's native flora and fauna are found nowhere else on earth and some have evolved so thoroughly that it's not possible to trace them to any continental ancestor. Many of Hawaii's birds may have evolved from a single species, as is thought to have been the case with more 30 species of native honeycreeper.

Having evolved with limited competition and few predators, Hawaii's native species generally fare poorly among more aggressive introduced flora and fauna. They are also highly sensitive to habitat destruction. When Westerners first came to Hawaii, the islands had 70 native bird species. Of those, 24 are now extinct and an additional 36 are threatened with extinction.

The first Polynesian settlers to arrive weren't traveling light. They brought food and medicinal plants, chickens, dogs and pigs. The pace of introducing exotic species escalated with the arrival of Europeans, starting with Captain Cook, who dropped off goats and left melon and pumpkin seeds. The next Western visitors left cattle and horses.

Prior to human contact, Hawaii had no land mammals save for monk seals and hoary bats. The introduction of free-ranging pigs, cattle and goats, which grazed and foraged at will, devastated Hawaii's fragile ecosystems and spelled extinction for many plants.

Released songbirds and game birds spread avian diseases to the native Hawaiian birds which did not have the immunities to fight off foreign pathogens. Erosion, deforestation and the thousands of introduced plants that compete with and choke out native vegetation have all taken their toll.

The invasion of exotic species continues today. One of the latest alien species to surface is the giant day gecko, a native of Madagascar that is thought to have arrived on Oahu as part of the illegal pet trade. At least two of the footlong, neon green creatures have been found on Oahu and there are fears they may have gained a foothold on the island.

Today, more than 25% of all the endangered species in the USA are Hawaiian plants and animals. Of the approximately 2400 different native plants, half are either threatened or endangered.

## Flora

Oahu is abloom year round with colorful tropical flowers. Perhaps no flower is more closely identified with Hawaii than the hibiscus, whose lush blooms are worn by women tucked behind their ears. Thousands of varieties of hibiscus bushes grow in Hawaii; on most, the flowers bloom early in the day and drop before sunset. The variety most frequently seen is *Hibiscus rosa-sinensis*, commonly known as the red (or Chinese) hibiscus, which is used as a landscape hedge throughout Oahu.

Other flowers seen in gardens include blood-red anthurium, brilliant orange bird-of-paradise, colorful bougainvillea, red ginger, torch ginger, shell ginger, fragrant jasmine and gardenia, and various heliconias with bright orange and red bracts. Monkeypod, plumeria and poinciana are three of the more common flowering trees.

Native coastal plants include *pohuehue (Ipomoea brasiliensis)*, a beach morning glory with pink flowers which is found on the sand just above the wrack line; beach *naupaka (Scaevola sericea)*, a shrub with oval leaves and a small white five-petal flower that looks as if it's been torn in half; and Oahu's official flower, the low-growing *ilima (Sida fallax)*, which has delicate yellow-orange blossoms.

There are a number of native forest trees that are also easy to identify. The *ohia lehua (Metrosideros collina)*, with its red pom-pom flowers, grows in barren areas as a shrub and on more fertile land as a tree. *Koa (Acacia koa hawaiiensis)*, found at higher elevations, grows up to 100ft high and is unusual in that the young saplings have fernlike compound leaves, while mature trees have flat crescent-shaped phyllodes. The *kukui* tree *(Aleurites moluccana)*, brought to the island by the early Polynesian settlers, has oily nuts the Hawaiians used for candles, hence its common name, candlenut tree; it's recognizable in the forest by its light silver-tinged foliage.

Two trees found along the coast that were well utilized in old Hawaii are *hala (Pandanus odoratissimus)*, also called pandanus or screw pine, whose spiny leaves were used for thatching and weaving; and the coconut palm, or *niu (Cocos nucifera)*, which thrives in coral sands and produces about 75 coconuts a year.

Also expect to see *kiawe (Prosopis pallida)*, a non-native tree found in dry coastal areas. A member of the mesquite family, *kiawe* is useful for making charcoal but is a nuisance for beachgoers, as its sharp thorns easily pierce soft sandals.

If you want to learn more about Hawaii's flora, Oahu has some excellent botanical gardens. Foster Botanical Garden in the Chinatown area and the Lyon Arboretum on the northern side of Honolulu both have excellent collections of unique native and exotic species.

## Fauna

The most prominent urban birds are pigeons, doves, red-crested cardinals and common mynas. The myna, introduced from India, is a brown, speckled bird that congregates in noisy flocks, walks rather than hops, and is plentiful.

For those who get into the woods, Oahu has a few native forest birds worth seeking

**Frigate bird**

out. The *elepaio*, a brownish bird with a white rump, and the *amakihi*, a small yellow-green bird, are the most common endemic forest birds on Oahu. The *apapane*, a vivid red honeycreeper, and the *iiwi*, a bright vermilion bird, are less common.

Most of the islets off Oahu's windward coast are sanctuaries for seabirds, including terns, noddies, shearwaters, Laysan albatrosses, tropicbirds, boobies and frigate birds. Moku Manu ('Bird Island'), off Mokapu Peninsula in Kaneohe, has the greatest variety of species, including a large number of sooty terns that lay their eggs directly on the ground. Because the nesting birds are sensitive to human disturbance,

visitors are not allowed at all on Moku Manu and are restricted on the other islands.

However, if you have a pair of binoculars you can enjoy bird-watching right from the coast. Great frigate birds, aerial pirates that snatch food from other birds in midair, are commonly seen circling above Waimanalo Bay; graceful in flight, they are easily identifiable by their 7ft wingspan and distinctively forked tail. Another bird that can be spotted soaring along the cliffs of the windward coast is the red-tailed tropicbird, which has a white body with a trailing red tail.

Oahu has an endemic genus of tree snail, the *Achatinella*. In former days the forests were loaded with these colorful snails, which clung like gems to the leaves of trees. They were too attractive for their own good, however, and up until the early 20th century, hikers were collecting them by the handful. The deforestation of habitat and the introduction of a cannibal snail and predatory rodents have been even more devastating. Of 41 *Achatinella* species, only 19 remain and all are endangered.

Oahu has wild pigs and goats in its mountain valleys. A more interesting introduced species is the brush-tailed rock wallaby, which was accidentally released in 1916 and is now residing in the Kalihi Valley, north of Honolulu. Although rarely seen, the wallabies are of keen interest to zoologists because they may be the last members of a subspecies that's now extinct in their native Australia.

Hawaii has a rich and varied marine life. Almost 700 fish species live in Hawaiian waters, with nearly one-third of those found nowhere else in the world. Oahu's near-shore waters harbor large rainbow-colored parrotfish, some 20 different kinds of butterfly fish, numerous varieties of wrasses, bright yellow tangs, white spot damsels, picasso triggerfish, odd-shaped filefish and ballooning pufferfish, just to name a few. There are also green sea turtles, manta rays and moray eels.

Several types of whales frequent Hawaiian waters, though it is the migrating humpback, with its acrobatic breaches and tail flips, that most people want to see. Luckily for whale watchers, humpback whales are coast-huggers, preferring waters with depths of less than 600ft. They can sometimes be seen in winter from the beaches along

## From the Brink of Extinction

One of the Pacific's rarest marine creatures is the Hawaiian monk seal *(Monachus schauinslandi)*, so named for the cowl-like fold of skin at its neck and for its solitary habits. The Hawaiian name for the animal is *ilio holo kai*, meaning 'the dog that runs in the sea.'

The species has remained nearly unchanged for 15 million years, though in the past century it has been in danger of dying out completely. The annual birth rate for Hawaiian monk seal pups is between 150 and 175 a year, but due to shark attacks and other predators, the majority of pups don't reach maturity.

Fortunately, conservation efforts, including the relocation of some seals to create a better male-female ratio, appear to be bringing the seals back from the edge of extinction. The total Hawaiian monk seal population is estimated at approximately 1300 seals.

Although their prime habitat is the uninhabited Northwestern Hawaiian Islands, monk seals do occasionally haul up on Oahu's more remote northwest beaches, near Kaena Point.

ADRIANA MAMMARELLA

**Picasso triggerfish**

Oahu's west coast. See the boxed text 'Humpback Whales' for more information. Other migratory whales in Hawaiian waters include the fin whale, minke whale and right whale; all are baleen whales.

Hawaii's year-round resident whales, which are all toothed whales, include the sperm whale, false killer whale, pigmy killer whale, beaked whale, melon-head whale and, most common of all, the pilot whale. The latter is a small whale that often travels in large pods and, like most whales, prefers deep offshore waters.

Numerous dolphins – including spinner, bottlenose, slender-beaked, spotted, striped and rough-toothed varieties – are found in the waters around Hawaii.

## GOVERNMENT & POLITICS

Hawaii has three levels of government: federal, state and county. Honolulu is the seat of both the state and county government.

Hawaii has a typical state government with executive power vested in the governor, who is elected to a four-year term.

The state's lawmaking body is a bicameral legislature. The state Senate includes 25 members, elected for four-year terms from the state's 25 senatorial districts. The House of Representatives has 51 members, each elected for a two-year term.

For local administration, Hawaii is divided into four county governments. Unlike the mainland states, Hawaii has no separate municipal governments, so the counties provide services, such as police and fire protection, that elsewhere in the USA are usually assigned to cities.

## Humpback Whales

Hands-down, the most popular wintering visitor to Hawaii is the humpback whale *(Megaptera novaeangliae)*. Humpbacks, the fifth largest of the great whales, reach lengths of 45ft and weigh 40 to 45 tons.

They're great performers, known for their acrobatic displays, which include arching dives, lob-tailing, breaching and fin splashing. In breaching, humpbacks jump almost clear out of the water and then splash down with tremendous force.They save the best performances for breeding time. Sometimes several bull whales will do a series of crashing breaches to gain the favor of a cow, often bashing into one another, even drawing blood, before the most impressive emerges the winner.

Once one of the most abundant of the great whales, humpbacks were hunted almost to extinction and are now an endangered species. At the end of the 19th century an estimated 15,000 humpbacks remained. They were still being hunted as late as 1966, when the International Whaling Commission enforced a ban on their slaughter.

The entire population of North Pacific humpbacks is now thought to be about 4000. An estimated two-thirds of those winter in Hawaii, while most of the others migrate to Mexico.

Humpbacks feed all summer in the plankton-rich waters off Alaska, developing a layer of blubber that sustains them through the winter. One of the toothless whales, humpbacks gulp huge quantities of water and then strain it back out through the filterlike baleen in their mouths, trapping krill and small fish. They can eat close to a ton of food a day.

During their winter sojourn in the warm tropical waters off Hawaii, humpbacks mate and give birth. Their gestation period is 10 to 12 months. Mothers stay in shallow waters once their calves are born, apparently as protection from shark attacks. This also makes them easy to see from shore. At birth, calves are about 12ft long and weigh 3000lb. They are nursed for about six months and can put on 100 pounds a day in the first few weeks. Adults go without eating while wintering in Hawaii.

Humpbacks don't arrive in Hawaii en masse, but start filtering in around November. They can be found throughout the islands, including near Oahu, though their most frequent wintering spot is the shallow waters around Maui and Molokai.

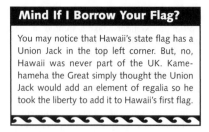

## Mind If I Borrow Your Flag?

You may notice that Hawaii's state flag has a Union Jack in the top left corner. But, no, Hawaii was never part of the UK. Kamehameha the Great simply thought the Union Jack would add an element of regalia so he took the liberty to add it to Hawaii's first flag.

The City & County of Honolulu is the unwieldy name attached to the single political entity governing all of Oahu. It is administered by a mayor and a nine-member council, elected for four-year terms.

## ECONOMY

Tourism is Hawaii's largest industry and accounts for about one-third of the state's income. Hawaii gets nearly 7 million visitors a year, and approximately half of them visit Oahu. In total, tourists spend about $11 billion in the state annually.

The second largest sector in the economy is the US military, pumping out about $3 billion annually. Hawaii is the most militarized state in the nation and nearly 25% of the land on Oahu is controlled by the armed forces. In all, there are more than a hundred military installations, from small ridge-top radar stations to huge bases.

Oahu is the hub of the Pacific Command, which directs military activities from western USA to eastern Africa. The navy, which accounts for 40% of Hawaii's military presence, is centered at Pearl Harbor, home of the Pacific Fleet.

Sugar and pineapple, which once formed the backbone of Hawaii's economy, have been scaled back dramatically in recent years. Although sugar production continues on other islands, it was phased out entirely on Oahu in 1996. Nonetheless, nearly one-fifth of Oahu is still used for agricultural purposes, mostly for growing pineapples.

The unemployment rate generally hovers around 5% statewide and on Oahu as well. In terms of employment in Oahu, tourism accounts for about 30% of jobs, followed by defense and other government employment, which together account for around 20% of all jobs.

The cost of living is 20% higher in Honolulu than in the average US mainland city, while wages are 10% lower. For those stuck in service jobs, which represent the most rapidly growing sector of the Hawaiian economy, it can be tough to get by.

## POPULATION & PEOPLE

Oahu's population is 876,000, with Honolulu accounting for nearly half of the total. Other sizable population centers are Pearl City, Kailua, Kaneohe and Kapolei.

Hawaii is the most multiracial state in the US. There is no ethnic majority – everyone in Hawaii belongs to a minority. Oahu's ethnic breakdown, which is similar to Hawaii as a whole, is 20% Japanese, 19% Caucasian, 20% part-Hawaiian (less than 1% pure Hawaiian), 19% mixed ancestry other than part-Hawaiian, 12% Filipino and 5% Chinese, with numerous other Pacific and Asian minorities.

Race is generally not a factor in marriage. On average, islanders have a 50/50 chance of marrying someone of a race different than their own, and the majority of children born in Hawaii are *hapa*, or of mixed blood.

## EDUCATION

Hawaii is the only US state to have a public education system run by the state, rather than county or town education boards. Education accounts for approximately one-third of the state budget.

Under Hawaii state law, all children between the ages of six and 18 are expected to attend school. More than 80% of all students are enrolled in the state's public school system, with the remainder in private schools.

Schools operate on a two-semester system; the first semester is from the first week of September to late December, the second from early January to the first week in June.

About a quarter of all adults living in Hawaii have completed at least four years of college. As with secondary education, the state is the main provider of higher education. Approximately 20,000 students attend the state-run University of Hawaii (UH) at Manoa, north of Waikiki. There are also four community college campuses on Oahu: Honolulu Community College, Kapiolani Community College, Leeward Community College and Windward Community College.

In addition, there are private colleges operating on Oahu: a Hawaii campus of Brigham Young University, in Laie; Chaminade University, in Honolulu; and Hawaii Pacific University, also in Honolulu.

## ARTS
### Hula

Perhaps no art form is more uniquely Hawaiian than the hula. There are many different schools of hula, all very disciplined and graceful in their movements.

Most ancient hula dances expressed historical events, legendary tales and the accomplishments of the great *alii*. Hand gestures, facial expressions hip sway and dance steps all conveyed the story. They were performed to rhythmic chants and drum beatings, serving to connect with the world of spirits. Eye movement was very important; if the story was about the sun, the dancer's eyes would gaze upward, and if about the netherworld, they would gaze downward. One school, the *hula ohelo*, was very sensual, with movements suggesting the act of procreation.

Traditional hula dancers wore tapa cloth – not the now familiar grass skirts, which were introduced from Micronesia only a hundred years ago.

The Christian missionaries found the hula too licentious and suppressed it. The dance might have been lost forever if not for King David Kalakaua, the 'Merrie Monarch,' who revived it in the latter half of the 19th century.

Hula *halaus* (schools) have had an influx of new students in recent years. Some practice in public places, such as school grounds and parks, where visitors are welcome to watch. Although many of the *halaus* rely on tuition fees, others receive sponsorship from hotels or shopping centers and give weekly public performances in return.

There are also numerous island-wide hula competitions, one of the biggest being the Prince Lot Hula Festival held each July at the Moanalua Gardens.

### Music

Contemporary Hawaiian music gives center stage to the guitar, which was first introduced to the islands by Spanish cowboys in the 1830s. The Hawaiians made it uniquely their own, however. In 1889, Joseph Kekuku, a native Hawaiian, designed the steel guitar, one of only two major musical instruments invented in what is now the USA. (The other

---

### The Beat Goes On

The *pahu hula*, a knee drum carved from a breadfruit or coconut log, with a sharkskin drum head, was traditionally used solely at hula performances. Other hula musical instruments include *ke laau* sticks, used to keep the beat for the dancers; *iliili*, stone castanets; *puili*, rattles made from split bamboo; and *uliuli*, gourd rattles decorated with colorful feathers. Even today, if you catch one of the more authentic hula performances, you'll likely see a number of these instruments still being used.

---

is the banjo.) The steel guitar is usually played with slack-key tunings and carries the melody throughout the song.

Slack-key guitar, a type of tuning in which some of the guitar strings are slackened from the conventional tuning in order to produce a harmonious, soulful sound, is also a 19th-century Hawaiian creation and one that has come back into the spotlight in recent times. Some of Hawaii's more renowned slack-key guitar players include Cyril Pahinui, Keola Beamer, Raymond Kane, Dennis Kamakahi and Atta Isaacs Jnr, and also the late Gabby Pahinui and Sonny Chillingworth.

The ukulele, which is so strongly identified with Hawaiian music, was actually derived from the *braginha*, a Portuguese instrument introduced to Hawaii in the 19th century. In Hawaiian, the word 'ukulele' means 'jumping flea.'

Both the ukulele and the steel guitar were essential to the lighthearted, romantic music popularized in Hawaii from the 1930s to the 1950s; *My Little Grass Shack*, *Lovely Hula Hands* and *Sweet Leilani* are classic examples. Due in part to the 'Hawaii Calls' radio show, which for more than 30 years was broadcast worldwide from the Moana Hotel in Waikiki, this music became instantly recognizable as Hawaiian, conjuring up images of hula dancers swaying under palm trees in a tropical paradise. Troy Fernandez and Ledward Kaapana are among the present-day masters of the ukulele.

One current sound is Jawaiian, which is a blending of Hawaiian music and Jamaican reggae. Some of the better-known musicians who emphasis Jawaiian music are Bruddah Waltah, Hoaikane, the Kaau Crater Boys and Kulana.

Other popular contemporary Hawaiian musicians include vocalist-composer Henry Kapono; Hapa, the duo of Kelii Kanealii and Barry Flanagan, who fuse folk, rock and traditional Hawaiian elements; Daniel Ho, an accomplished guitarist and ukulele player who blends Hawaiian sounds with jazz and Asian influences; and Kealii Reichel, a charismatic vocalist and hula dancer known for his Hawaiian ballads and poetic chants.

## Literature

There are plenty of books that offer vivid descriptions of life in Hawaii, from classics to contemporary novels.

*A Hawaiian Reader*, which is edited by A Grove Day and Carl Stroven, is an excellent anthology with 37 selections, both fiction and nonfiction, about writers' experiences in Hawaii. It starts with a log entry by Captain James Cook and includes writings from early missionaries as well as Mark Twain, Jack London, Somerset Maugham, David Malo, Isabella Bird, Martha Beckwith and others. If you only have time to read one book about Hawaii, this inexpensive paperback is a great choice.

OA Bushnell is one of Hawaii's best-known contemporary authors. The University of Hawaii Press has published his titles *The Return of Lono*, a historical novel of Captain Cook's final voyage; *Kaaawa*, about Hawaii in the 1850s; *The Stone of Kannon*, about the first group of Japanese contract laborers to arrive in Hawaii; and its sequel *The Water of Kane*.

*Stories of Hawaii* is a collection of 13 of Jack London's yarns about the islands.

## Ancient Crafts

**Tapa Weaving** In ancient Hawaii, women spent much of their time beating *kapa* (tapa cloth) or preparing *lauhala* for weaving.

Tapa made from the *wauke* (paper mulberry tree) was the favorite material. The bark was carefully stripped, then pounded with wooden beaters. The beaters were carved with different patterns that then became the pattern of the tapa. Dyes were made from charcoal, flowers and sea urchins.

Tapa had many uses in addition to clothing, from food containers to burial shrouds. After the missionaries introduced cotton cloth and Western clothing, the art of tapa-making slowly faded away. Today, most of the tapa for sale in Hawaii is from Samoa and has bold designs, unlike traditional Hawaiian tapa, which had more delicate patterns.

*Lauhala* **Weaving** *Lauhala* weaving uses the *lau* (leaves) of the *hala* (pandanus) tree. Preparing the leaves for weaving is hard, messy work due to the razor-sharp spines along the leaf edges and down the center.

In old Hawaii, *lauhala* was woven into mats and floor coverings, but today smaller items like hats, placemats and baskets are most common.

**Wooden Bowls** The Hawaiians had no pottery and made their containers using either gourds or wood. Wooden food bowls were most often made of kou or milo, two native woods that didn't leave unpleasant tastes.

Hawaiian bowls were free of designs and carvings. Their beauty lay in the natural qualities of the wood and in the shape of the bowl alone. Cracked bowls were often expertly patched with dovetailed pieces of wood. Rather than decrease the value of the bowl, patching suggested heirloom status and such bowls were among the mostly highly prized.

**Featherwork** The Hawaiians were known for their elaborate featherwork. The most impressive items were the capes worn by chiefs and kings. The longer the cape, the higher the rank of its wearer. Capes made from the yellow feathers of the now extinct *mamo* bird were the most highly prized.

The *mamo* was a predominantly black bird with a yellow upper tail. An estimated 80,000 mamo birds were caught to create the cape that Kamehameha the Great wore. It's said that bird catchers would capture the birds, pluck the desired feathers and release them otherwise unharmed. Feathers were also used to make helmets and leis.

*Talking to the Dead*, by Sylvia Watanabe, is an enjoyable read about growing up as a second-generation Japanese-American in postwar Honolulu.

## Painting & Sculpture

There are many artists who draw inspiration from Hawaii's rich cultural heritage and natural beauty.

Well-known Hawaiian painter Herb Kawainui Kane creates detailed oil paintings that focus on the early Polynesian settlers and Kamehameha the Great's life. His works are mainly on display in museums and at gallery collections in resorts.

Another notable native Hawaiian artist is Rocky Kaiouliokahihikoloehu Jensen, who does wood sculptures and drawings of Hawaiian gods, ancient chiefs and early Hawaiians with the aim of creating sacred art in the tradition of *makaku*, or 'creative artistic *mana*.'

Honolulu artist Pegge Hopper paints traditional Hawaiian women in relaxed poses using a distinctive graphic design style and bright washes of color. Her work has been widely reproduced on posters and postcards.

## Crafts

Some of Hawaii's most impressive crafts are ceramics, particularly *raku* work, a style of Japanese earthenware; bowls made of native woods, such as koa and milo; and baskets woven of native fibers.

Hawaiian quilting is another unique art form. The concept of patchwork quilting was introduced by the early missionaries, but the Hawaiians, who had at that time only recently taken to Western cotton clothing, didn't have a surplus of cloth scraps – and the idea of cutting up new lengths of fabric simply to sew them back together again in small squares seemed absurd. Instead, the Hawaiian women created their own designs using larger cloth pieces, typically with stylized tropical flora on a white background.

Leis, or garlands, are a more transitory art form. Although the leis most visitors wear are made of fragrant flowers such as plumeria and tuberose, traditional leis of *mokihana* berries and maile leaves were more commonly worn in old Hawaii. Both types are still made today.

## RELIGION

Oahu's population is diverse in terms of religion. In addition to the standard Christian denominations, the island has numerous Buddhist temples and Shinto shrines. There are also Hindu, Taoist, Tenrikyo, Jewish and Muslim houses of worship.

Christianity has the largest following, with Catholicism being the predominant religious denomination. Interestingly, the United Church of Christ, which includes the Congregationalists who initially converted the islands, now claims only about half as many members as the Mormons and one-tenth as many as the Catholics.

# Facts for the Visitor

## HIGHLIGHTS

Vibrant Waikiki is the venue for scores of tourist activities, with sunbathing, water sports and people-watching among the highlights. At the less-touristy end of Waikiki is Kapiolani Park, a grand public park with an aquarium, zoo and facilities for everything from concerts to tennis.

Don't miss a walk around downtown Honolulu's historic district, which sports the state capitol, early mission church sites and the only royal palace in the USA. Another delightful place is the adjacent Chinatown area, with its lively markets and ethnic restaurants. While you're there, stroll through Foster Botanical Garden, which has some of the island's loftiest trees and rarest plants.

For a city of its size, Honolulu has some surprisingly good museums. The renowned Bishop Museum will give you a great introduction to Hawaiian culture. The Honolulu Academy of Arts has a high-quality fine arts collection, while the more recently established Contemporary Museum displays modern art in a lovely estate setting.

The most visited attraction in all of Hawaii is the USS *Arizona* Memorial at Pearl Harbor, the site of the surprise Japanese attack that brought Americans into WWII.

A trip around southeast Oahu offers fine scenery and a glimpse of one of the less-developed sides of the island, including Hanauma Bay with its striking scenery and good snorkeling.

For phenomenal surf, you can't beat the North Shore, which draws the world's top surfers with its monstrous winter waves. If you'd rather try your hand at windsurfing, then Kailua's superb beach, with its steady breezes, is the place to go.

If you want to get off the beaten path, there are also less touristy beaches, such as Kaihalulu Beach on the sleepy Windward Coast, and plenty of quiet hiking trails, such as the remote Kaena Point on the Waianae Coast. For more on Oahu's beaches see the boxed text 'Oahu's Top Beaches' in the Activities chapter.

## SUGGESTED ITINERARIES

Oahu is convenient to get around; no place is more than 1½ hours drive from Honolulu,

so the island is easy to explore on day trips from a single base. There's no need to pack your bags and move around.

If you only have one week in Oahu, you can follow this suggested itinerary to see the highlights. Day one, explore Waikiki, have fun in the sun, rent a surfboard, catch a hula show, and enjoy the night scene. On day two, stroll through Chinatown, sample some delicious and inexpensive ethnic cuisine, then see some of the historic buildings of nearby downtown Honolulu.

Next day, tour southeast Oahu, stopping to snorkel at Hanauma Bay and windsurf or kayak at Kailua Beach Park. On day four, visit the USS *Arizona* Memorial at Pearl Harbor – but get there in the morning to beat the crowds. Finish the afternoon off at the untouristy Ala Moana Beach Park.

Venture up to the North Shore, catch some of the world's top surf action at Sunset Beach and cool down with a shave ice at Haleiwa on day five. On day six, make a tour of the Windward Coast, starting with the scenic Pali Hwy, dropping by Byodo-In temple and picnic at either Kualoa or Malaekahana Beach.

On your final day, hike to the summit of Diamond Head for a good workout and sweeping city views, then reward yourself with a Mai Tai on the beach at sunset.

## PLANNING
### When to Go

Oahu is a great place to visit any time of the year. Although the busiest tourist season is in winter, that has more to do with weather *elsewhere*, as many visitors are snowbirds escaping cold winters back home. Essentially, the weather in Hawaii is agreeable year-round. It's a bit rainier in the winter and a bit hotter in the summer, but there are no extremes as cooling trade winds modify the heat throughout the year.

In terms of cost, spring and fall are slower times, so you're more likely to find better deals on accommodation and airfares during this period. The busiest period is from mid-December to the first week of April.

Naturally, for certain activities there are peak seasons. For instance, if you're a board surfer, you'll find the most awesome waves in winter, whereas if you're a windsurfer, you'll find the best wind conditions in summer.

## Maps

The ubiquitous free tourist magazines contain simple island maps, but if you're going to be renting a car and doing any exploring at all it's worth picking up a good road map, especially for navigating around Honolulu.

The American Automobile Association (AAA) puts out a reliable road map of Honolulu and Oahu. Members of AAA or an affiliated automobile club can get a free map from the **AAA office** *(Map 3; ☎ 593-2221; 1270 Ala Moana Blvd, Honolulu)* or from its local affiliate before leaving home.

If you're not an AAA member, you can buy a similar road map published by Rand McNally in convenience stores throughout Oahu for a few dollars.

The 200-page *Bryan's Sectional Maps Oahu* atlas, which maps out and indexes virtually every street on the island, is the most comprehensive source, but it's more detailed than most visitors will need. It can be purchased at bookstores around Oahu.

The United States Geological Survey (USGS) publishes topographical maps of Oahu, both as full-island and detailed sectional maps. Despite the precise geographic detail, the practical use of these maps is limited for casual visitors by its unruly size and infrequent updates. Maps can be ordered from the **USGS** *(☎ 888-275-8747; W www .usgs.gov; Map & Book Sales, Denver Federal Center, Denver, CO 80225)*. In Honolulu, USGS maps, nautical charts and other specialty maps can be purchased at the **Pacific Map Center** *(☎ 545-3600; Suite 206A, 560 N Nimitz Hwy, Honolulu)*.

## What to Bring

Oahu has balmy weather and a casual attitude towards dress so, for the most part, packing is a breeze. It's essentially summer all year long. For tourist activities, shorts, sandals and a cotton shirt are the standard day dress. A light jacket or sweater will be the warmest clothing you'll need.

Pack light. You can always pick up something with a floral Hawaiian print when you get there and dress island-style. An aloha shirt and lightweight slacks for men, and a cotton dress for women, is pretty much regarded as 'dressing up' in Hawaii. Only a few of the most exclusive restaurants require anything fancier.

If you have plans for excursions to the other islands, note that the 'upcountry' areas of both Maui and the Big Island (Hawaii) can get quite nippy and warrant an extra layer of clothing.

If you plan on camping on Oahu, public camping grounds require tents (they're a good idea anyway because of mosquitoes), but you won't need anything more than the lightest sleeping bag.

Consider bringing binoculars for watching dolphins, whales and birds. You may want to bring along a snorkel, mask and fins, although you can also buy or rent them at reasonable prices once you get here. Actually, you don't need to worry too much about what to bring, because just about anything you forget to pack you can easily buy on Oahu.

## TOURIST OFFICES

The Hawaii Visitors and Convention Bureau (HVCB) provides free tourist information. On request, it will mail you a magazine containing general Hawaii-wide tourist information and a booklet listing member hotels and restaurants. HVCB information is also available at W www.gohawaii.com.

## Local Tourist Offices

The **Hawaii Visitors & Convention Bureau** *(☎ 800-464-2924; e info@hvcb.org; www.go hawaii.com)* runs a 24-hour call center where you can ask questions; the helpful staff will also mail you general tourist information on Oahu and the rest of Hawaii.

To pick up tourist brochures in person, visit the **HVCB visitor information office** *(☎ 924-0266; Suite 502, Waikiki Shopping Plaza, 2250 Kalakaua Ave, Waikiki; open 8am-4:30pm Mon-Fri, 8am-noon Sat & Sun)*.

In addition to this service, you can order a free, glossy tourist magazine containing visitor-related information on Oahu by calling ☎ 877-525-6248.

## Tourist Offices Abroad
The following are the contact details for HVCB representatives abroad:

**Australia** (☎ 02 9955 2619, fax 9955 2171) Suite 2, Level 2, 34 Burton St, Milsons Point, NSW 2061

**Canada** (☎ 604-669-6691, fax 683-9114) Comprehensive Travel Industry Services, Suite 104, 1260 Hornby St, Vancouver, BC V6Z 1W2

**Germany** (☎ 61 02 722 411, fax 02 722 409) American Venture Marketing, Herderstrasse 6-8, 63263 Neulsenburg

**Japan** (☎ 03 3201 0430, fax 3201 0433) Kokusai Bldg, 2nd floor, 3-1-1 Marunouchi, Chiyoda-ku, Tokyo 100-0005

**Korea** (☎ 02 777 0033, fax 757 6783) Travel Press, Seoul Center Bldg, 12th floor, 91-1 Sokong-dong, Chung-ku, Seoul 100-070

**New Zealand** (☎ 09 379 3708, fax 309 0725) 18 Shortland St, Auckland

**Taiwan** (☎ 02 8768 1681, fax 8768 1122) Federal Transportation Company, 7th floor, No 41, Dungshin Rd, Taipei 110

**UK** (☎ 020 8941 8116, fax 8941 4011) Box 208, Sunbury on Thames, Middlesex TW16 5RJ

## VISAS & DOCUMENTS
The conditions for entering Hawaii are the same as those for entering any other state in the USA.

### Passport & Visas
With the exception of Canadians, who need only proper proof of Canadian citizenship (such as a citizenship card with photo ID or a passport), all foreign visitors must have a valid passport, and most visitors also need a US visa.

However, there is a reciprocal visa-waiver program in which citizens of certain countries may enter the USA for stays of 90 days or less without first obtaining a US visa. Currently these countries are: Andorra, Argentina, Australia, Austria, Belgium, Brunei, Denmark, Finland, France, Germany, Iceland, Ireland, Italy, Japan, Liechtenstein, Luxembourg, Monaco, Netherlands, New Zealand, Norway, San Marino, Singapore, Slovenia, Spain, Sweden, Switzerland, the UK and Uruguay.

Under the visa-waiver program you must have a roundtrip ticket that is nonrefundable in the USA and you will not be allowed to extend your stay beyond the 90-day period.

Other travelers will need to obtain a visa from a US consulate or embassy. In most countries the process can be done by mail.

Your passport should be valid for at least six months longer than your intended stay in the USA and you'll need to submit a recent photo (37mm x 37mm) with the application. Documents of financial stability and/or guarantees from a US resident are sometimes required, particularly for those from third world countries.

Visa applicants may be required to 'demonstrate binding obligations' that will ensure their return back home. Because of this requirement, those planning to travel through other countries before arriving in the USA are generally better off applying for their US visa while they are still in their home country rather than while on the road.

The validity period for US visitor visas depends on what country you're from. The length of time you'll be allowed to stay in the USA is ultimately determined by US immigration authorities at the port of entry.

**Visa Extensions** If you want to stay in the USA longer than the date stamped on your passport, apply for an extension by contacting the Honolulu office of the **Immigration & Naturalization Service** (☎ 532-3721; 595 Ala Moana Blvd) before the expiration date stamped in your passport.

### Travel Insurance
Foreign visitors should be aware that health care in the USA is very expensive. So, it's a good idea to take out a travel insurance policy, which usually covers medical expenses, luggage theft or loss, and cancellations or delays in your travel arrangements.

There are a wide variety of policies available and the exact coverage depends on the policy you buy, so get your insurer or travel agent to explain the details. Check the small print, since some policies exclude 'dangerous activities,' which can include scuba diving, motorcycling and anything to do with parachutes.

Although you may find a policy that pays doctors or hospitals directly, you should be aware that many doctors and medical clinics in Hawaii will demand payment at the time of service. If you have to claim later, keep all documentation. Some policies ask you to call (reverse charges) a center in your home country for an immediate assessment of your problem. Check whether the policy covers ambulances or an emergency flight home.

It's best to purchase travel insurance as early as possible. If you buy it the week before you fly, you might find, for instance, that you're not covered for delays to your flight caused by a strike that may have been in force before you took out the insurance.

Purchasing your ticket with a credit card often provides travel accident insurance and may also give you the right to reclaim your payment if the operator doesn't deliver. Ask your credit card company, or the issuing bank, for details.

### Driver's License & Permits

Visitors over the age of 18 can legally drive in Hawaii as long as they have a valid driver's license issued by a country that is party to the United Nations Conference on Road & Motor Transport – which covers virtually everyone.

However, car rental companies will generally accept valid foreign driver's licenses only if they're in English. So if yours isn't, it's best to bring an international driver's license along with your home license. The national automobile association in your home country can provide one for a small fee.

### Other Documents

All visitors, including Americans, should keep in mind that all US airlines require passengers to present a photo ID as part of the airline check-in procedure.

All foreign visitors (other than Canadians) must bring their passport. US and Canadian citizens may want to bring along a passport as well, in the event they are tempted to extend their travels beyond Hawaii.

All visitors should bring their driver's license and any health insurance or travel insurance cards.

Members of Hostelling International (HI) will be able to take advantage of lower hostel rates at Oahu's HI hostels with their membership cards.

Although Hawaii doesn't offer a lot of student discounts, if you have a student card, bring it along anyway, as it may occasionally win you a discount at museums and other sights.

Members of senior citizen organizations such as the American Association of Retired Persons (AARP) and the Canadian Association of Retired Persons (CARP) can get an occasional hotel or car rental discount by showing their cards.

Members of the American Automobile Association (AAA) or other affiliated automobile clubs can get car rental, airfares and some sightseeing admission discounts with their membership cards.

Divers should bring their certification with them.

### Copies

Before you leave home, you should photocopy all important documents (passport data page, credit cards, travel insurance policy, air tickets, driver's license etc). Leave one copy with someone at home and keep another with you, separate from the originals.

It's also a good idea to store details of your vital travel documents in Lonely Planet's free online Travel Vault in case you lose the photocopies or can't be bothered with them. Your password-protected Travel Vault is accessible online anywhere in the world – create it at ⓦ www.ekno.lonelyplanet.com.

## EMBASSIES & CONSULATES
### US Embassies

US embassies abroad include the following:

**Australia** (☎ 02 6214 5600) 21 Moonah Place, Yarralumla, Canberra, ACT 2600
**Canada** (☎ 613-238-5335) 490 Sussex Drive, Ottawa, Ontario K1N 1G8
**France** (☎ 01 43 12 2222) 2 avenue Gabriel, 75008 Paris
**Germany** (☎ 030 8305-0) Neustadtische Kirchstrasse 4-5, 10117 Berlin
**Ireland** (☎ 1 668 8777) 42 Elgin Rd, Ballsbridge, Dublin 4
**Italy** (☎ 64 67 41) Via Veneto 119/A, 00187 Rome
**Japan** (☎ 03 3224 5000) 10-5, Akasaka 1-chome, Minato-ku, Tokyo
**Netherlands** (☎ 70 310 9209) Lange Voorhout 102, 2514 EJ, The Hague
**New Zealand** (☎ 04 462 6000) 29 Fitzherbert Terrace, PO Box 1190, Thorndon, Wellington
**UK** (☎ 020 7499 9000) 24/31 Grosvenor Square, London W1A 1AE

### Consulates in Oahu

There are several consulates in Honolulu, including the following:

**Australia** (☎ 524-5050) 1000 Bishop St
**Germany** (☎ 946-3819) 252 Paoa Place
**Italy** (☎ 531-2277) Suite 201, 735 Bishop St
**Japan** (☎ 543-3111) 1742 Nuuanu Ave
**Netherlands** (☎ 531-6897) Suite 7, 02745
  Fort St Mall
**New Zealand** (☎ 547-5117) Suite 414, 900
  Richards St
**Philippines** (☎ 595-6316) 2433 Pali Hwy

## CUSTOMS

US Customs allows each person age 21 or older to bring 1 quart of liquor and 200 cigarettes duty-free into the USA. Most fresh fruits and plants are restricted from entry into Hawaii and there's a strict quarantine on animals.

## MONEY

There are nearly 150 banks located throughout Oahu, so it is never a problem finding one in the major towns. The Bank of Hawaii, Hawaii's largest bank, has a branch right at the airport and another branch in central Waikiki. Elsewhere around Oahu, banks can easily be found in central areas and in shopping centers.

For information on banking hours, see Business Hours, later in this chapter.

### Currency

As is true throughout the USA, the US dollar is the only currency that is used in Hawaii.

The US dollar ($) is divided into 100 cents (¢). Coins come in denominations of 1 (penny), 5 (nickel), 10 (dime), 25 (quarter) and 50 (half dollar). Notes ('bills') come in denominations of $1, $5, $10, $20, $50 and $100. There is also a one-dollar coin that the government has tried unsuccessfully to bring into mass circulation and a two-dollar note that is out of favor but still occasionally seen.

### Exchange Rates

At the time of going to print, exchange rates were as follows:

| country | unit | | US dollars |
|---|---|---|---|
| Australia | A$1 | = | US$0.57 |
| Canada | C$1 | = | US$0.63 |
| euro zone | €1 | = | US$0.88 |
| Japan | ¥100 | = | US$0.77 |
| New Zealand | NZ$1 | = | US$0.43 |
| UK | UK£1 | = | US$1.42 |

### Exchanging Money

**Cash** If you're carrying foreign currency, it can be exchanged for US dollars at larger banks, such as the ubiquitous Bank of Hawaii, or at the exchange booths at Honolulu International Airport.

**Traveler's Checks** The main benefit of traveler's checks is that they provide protection from theft and loss. Large companies such as American Express and Thomas Cook generally offer efficient replacement policies.

Foreign visitors who carry traveler's checks will find it much easier if the checks are in US dollars. Restaurants, hotels and most stores accept US dollar traveler's checks as if they're cash, so if that's what you're carrying, odds are you'll never have to use a bank or pay an exchange fee.

Keeping a record of the check numbers and those you have used is vital when it comes to replacing lost checks, so you should keep this information separate from the checks themselves.

For refunds on lost or stolen American Express traveler's checks, call ☎ 800-221-7282; for lost MasterCard traveler's checks, call ☎ 800-223-9920.

**ATMs** Automated teller machines (ATMs) are a convenient way of obtaining cash from a bank account within the USA or abroad. Plus, using an ATM card eliminates the necessity of carrying around a bundle of traveler's checks.

Major banks such as the Bank of Hawaii and First Hawaiian Bank have extensive ATM networks throughout Oahu that will give cash advances on major credit cards (MasterCard, Visa, American Express, Discover and JCB) and allow cash withdrawals with affiliated ATM cards. Most ATM machines in Hawaii accept bank cards from both the Plus and Cirrus systems, the two largest ATM networks in the USA.

In addition to traditional bank locations, you can also find ATMs at most grocery stores, in mall-style shopping centers and in many convenience stores.

**Credit Cards** Major credit cards are widely accepted throughout Hawaii, including at car rental agencies and most hotels, restaurants, gas stations, shops and larger grocery stores. Most recreational and tourist activities can also be paid for by credit card.

The most commonly accepted cards in Hawaii are Visa, MasterCard and American Express, although JCB, Discover and Diners Club cards are also accepted by a fair number of businesses.

Note, however, that some B&B establishments and condominiums, particularly those handled through rental agencies, do not accept credit cards, so it is best to inquire in advance.

If you lose your credit cards or they are stolen, you should contact the company immediately. Toll free reporting numbers include **American Express** (☎ 800-992-3404), **MasterCard** (☎ 800-826-2181) and **Visa** (☎ 800-336-8472).

**International Transfers** It will be easier to transfer money from your home bank if you've authorized someone back home to access your account. Specify the town, the bank and the branch to which you want your money directed, or ask your home bank to tell you where there is a suitable one, and make sure that you get the details right.

You can find some of the necessary information on the websites of Hawaii's two largest banks **Bank of Hawaii** (W www.boh .com) and **First Hawaiian Bank** (W www .fhb.com).

## Costs

How much money you need for your trip to Oahu depends on your traveling style. Some people get by quite cheaply while others rack up huge balances on their credit cards.

Airfares to Hawaii is usually one of the heftier parts of the budget. Fares vary greatly, particularly from the US mainland, so shop around. (Note that Honolulu stopovers are often thrown in free, or for a nominal charge, on trips between North America and Asian or Pacific countries.)

If you want to rent a car, budget for about $50 a day for the rental fee, gas and parking. However, a car is not essential for exploring most of the island, as Oahu has a good, inexpensive bus system that charges just $1.50 per ride no matter how far you travel.

The Waikiki/Honolulu area has a wide range of accommodations. The least expensive places to stay are the two HI-affiliated youth hostels and the handful of private hostel-type places – all have dorm beds for under $20. After that, there are rooms at Ys for $30 and a few budget Waikiki hotels which start around $50. Waikiki has lots of middle-range hotels in the $75 to $125 range, as well as luxury beachfront hotels that fetch triple that rate.

Because a lot of Hawaii's food is shipped in, grocery prices average 25% higher than on the US mainland. Due to the shipping costs, bulky items such as cereal have the highest markups, while compact items such as canned tuna have the lowest. Waikiki restaurants generally reflect these higher food prices, but Oahu's plethora of less-touristy neighborhood restaurants are excellent value, with prices generally comparable to those you'll find on the mainland.

The good news for visitors is that lots of things in Oahu are free of charge. There are no parking or entrance fees at beaches (except for Hanauma Bay); free hula shows abound in Waikiki; and some of Oahu's main sightseeing attractions – such as the USS *Arizona* Memorial – do not charge admission.

## Tipping & Bargaining

Tipping practices in Hawaii are the same as in the rest of the USA. In restaurants, waiters expect a tip of about 15%, while 10% is generally sufficient for taxi drivers, hair stylists and the like. Hotel bellhops are typically tipped $1 or $2 per bag, depending on the weight.

In Hawaii, prices are generally fixed. However, some bargaining takes place in markets where you buy from individual vendors, such as the Aloha Flea Market at Aloha Stadium and at the International Market Place in Waikiki.

## Taxes

Hawaii has a 4.17% state sales tax that is tacked onto virtually everything, including all meals, groceries, car rentals and accommodations. An additional 7.24% room tax brings the total tax added to accommodation bills to 11.41%. Another tax targeted at visitors is a $3-a-day 'road use' tax imposed upon all car rentals.

## POST & COMMUNICATIONS

By world standards, the US Postal Service is both reliable and inexpensive.

There are 35 post offices on Oahu. The main Honolulu **post office** *(open 7:30am-8:30pm Mon-Fri, 8am-4:30pm Sat)* is not in central Honolulu, but is at the side of the airport at 3600 Aolele St, opposite the inter-island terminal.

You can get detailed 24-hour postal information, including the business hours for every post office in Hawaii, by dialing toll-free ☎ 800-275-8777.

Private shippers such as **United Parcel Service** *(UPS; ☎ 800-742-5877)* and **Federal Express** *(FedEx; ☎ 800-463-3339)* also ship to both domestic and foreign locations.

### Postal Rates

Postage rates for first-class mail within the USA are 34¢ for letters up to 1oz (23¢ for each additional ounce) and 21¢ for post-cards. First-class mail between Hawaii and the mainland is sent by air and usually takes three to four days.

International airmail rates for letters up to 1oz are 60¢ to Canada or Mexico, 80¢ to other countries. Postcards cost 50¢ to Canada or Mexico, 70¢ to other countries.

The cost for parcels airmailed anywhere within the USA is $3.50 for up to 1lb, $3.95 up to 2lbs. For heavier items, rates differ according to the distance mailed.

### Receiving Mail

All general delivery mail sent to you in Honolulu must be picked up at Honolulu's main post office, next to the airport. Mail sent general delivery to the Waikiki post office or other Honolulu branches will go to the main post office or be returned to sender.

To receive mail in Honolulu, have it addressed to you as follows:

Your name
c/o General Delivery, Main Post Office
3600 Aolele St, Honolulu, HI 96820-3600

It's also possible to have general delivery mail sent to you in Kailua. To do so, have it addressed to you as follows:

Your name
c/o General Delivery, Kailua Post Office
335 Hahani St, Kailua, HI 96734-9998

For general delivery service, domestic mail will usually be held for 10 days, international mail for 30 days. You'll need to present photo identification to collect your mail.

Most hotels will also hold mail for incoming guests. In addition, the **American Express office** *(☎ 926-5441; Hyatt Regency Hotel, Waikiki; open 7am-5pm daily)* will hold mail for 30 days for American Express card holders. It will not accept parcels or anything that must be signed for.

Have mail addressed to you as follows:

Your name
c/o American Express, Client Mail Service
2424 Kalakaua Ave, Honolulu, HI 96815

### Telephone

All phone numbers within the USA consist of a three-digit area code followed by a seven-digit number. All of the Hawaiian Islands share the same area code (808). The area code is not used when making calls from one Oahu number to another.

All phone numbers listed in this book beginning with 800, 877 or 888 are toll-free numbers from the US mainland, unless otherwise noted. The same numbers are sometimes toll free from Canada as well.

Pay phones can readily be found in public places such as shopping centers and beach parks. Local calls cost 50¢ at pay phones. Any call made from one point on Oahu to any other point on Oahu is a local call. Calls from Oahu to the other Hawaiian Islands are long distance.

To dial direct from one Hawaiian island to another from a pay phone, the rate is $1.40

### Telephone Area Code

The telephone area code for all of Hawaii is 808. The area code is not used when making calls on the same island, but it must be added to all Hawaiian phone numbers when calling from outside the state and when calling from one Hawaiian island to another.

Because the area code is not dialed when making a local call, the phone numbers in this book do not include the area code. Just remember, if you're dialing from home before arriving in Oahu, to add 808 to the local number.

for the first minute and 15¢ for each additional minute.

Most hotels add a service charge of $1 for each local call made from a room phone and most also have hefty surcharges for long-distance calls. Public phones, which can be found in most hotel lobbies, are cheaper. You can pump in coins, use a phonecard or make collect calls from pay phones. You can make toll-free calls from pay phones without inserting any money.

For directory assistance for Oahu phone numbers dial ☎ 1-411, and for elsewhere in Hawaii dial ☎ 1-808-555-1212.

**International Calls** To make an international call direct from Hawaii, dial ☎ 011 + country code + area code + number. (An exception is to Canada, where you instead dial ☎ 1 + area code + number.) For international operator assistance dial ☎ 0 (zero). The operator can provide specific rate information and tell you which time periods are the cheapest for calling – these vary with the country being called.

If you're calling Hawaii from abroad, the international country code for the USA is '1,' and all calls to Hawaii are then followed by the area code 808 and the seven-digit local number.

**Phonecards** There's a wide range of local and international phonecards. Lonely Planet's ekno Communication Card is aimed specifically at travelers and provides cheap international calls, a range of messaging services, free email, travel information and an online travel vault, where you can securely store all your important documents. However, for just making local calls, you're usually better off with a local card. You can join ekno online at ⓦ www.ekno.lonely planet.com, or by phone from the USA by dialing ☎ 1-800-707-0031. Once you have joined, check the ekno website for the latest access numbers and updates on new features.

**Fax**

Faxes can be sent and received through the front desks of most hotels. There are also business centers that offer reasonably priced fax services, such as Kinko's, which has several branches in Honolulu. For additional information, see the boxed text 'For Business Travelers' later in this chapter.

## Email & Internet Access

One way to stay connected is to travel with your laptop. But if you're coming from outside the USA, be sure the power supply is compatible, otherwise you may need to bring along a universal AC adapter and a plug adapter. Keep in mind that the telephone socket may be different from that at home as well, so ensure that you have at least a US RJ-11 telephone adapter that works with your modem.

Major Internet service providers such as **America Online** *(AOL;* ⓦ *www.aol.com)* have dial-in nodes in Hawaii and throughout the USA. If you access your Internet email at home through a local ISP, your best options are either to open an account with a global ISP, or to rely on public access points to collect your mail.

You can collect mail by opening a free email account such as **Hotmail** *(*ⓦ *www .hotmail.com)*. You can then access your mail on any Internet-connected machine. Most Oahu hostels have cheap online computers and there are cybercafés and business centers, such as Kinko's, that offer inexpensive online computer access as well.

If you're carrying a laptop, you may want to check with your hotel in advance to see if the room comes with a phone jack that can accommodate modem hookups; many Oahu hotels now have these data ports in at least some of their rooms.

## DIGITAL RESOURCES

The World Wide Web is a rich resource for travelers. You can research your trip, hunt down bargain airfares, book hotels, check on weather conditions and chat with locals and other travelers about the best places to visit (or avoid!).

There's no better place to start your Web explorations than the Lonely Planet website (ⓦ www.lonelyplanet.com). Here you'll find succinct summaries on traveling to best places on earth, postcards from other travelers and the Thorn Tree bulletin board, where you can ask questions before you go or dispense advice when you get back. You can also find travel news and updates for many of our most popular guidebooks, and the subwwway section links you to the most useful travel resources elsewhere on the Web.

In addition to this, ⓦ www.honoluluad vertiser.com, ⓦ www.surfhawaii.com and

**W** www.planet-hawaii.com are useful websites that have links to a wealth of Hawaii information. Other websites are suggested throughout this book under specific topics.

## BOOKS

There is a wealth of books available on everything from culture and history to Oahu's best beaches and surfing spots. The books that follow are just a few of the recommended titles.

### Lonely Planet

If you're planning to visit any of the Hawaiian Islands other than Oahu, you'll want to pick up Lonely Planet's *Hawaii*, which is packed with comprehensive information on traveling throughout Hawaii.

*Diving & Snorkeling Hawaii*, by Casey Mahaney and Astrid Witte Mahaney (Lonely Planet Pisces Books), is a perfect companion for anyone who is planning on diving or snorkeling in Hawaii. It includes lots of color photos illustrating sites and fish.

### History, People & Culture

*Hawaii's Story by Hawaii's Queen*, by Queen Liliuokalani (Mutual Publishing), written in 1897, is an autobiographical account of Liliuokalani's life and the circumstances surrounding her 1893 overthrow.

*The Betrayal of Liliuokalani: Last Queen of Hawaii, 1838-1917*, by Helena G Allen (Mutual Publishing), is an insightful account not only of the queen's life, but also of missionary activity and foreign encroachment in Hawaii.

*Hawaiian Antiquities*, by David Malo (Bishop Museum Press), written in 1838, was the first account of Hawaiian culture written by a Hawaiian. It gives an in-depth history of Hawaii before the arrival of the missionaries.

*Shoal of Time*, by Gavan Daws (University of Hawaii Press), is a comprehensive and colorful history covering the period from Captain Cook's 'discovery' of the islands to statehood.

*Fragments of Hawaiian History*, by John Papa Ii and translated by Mary Kawena Pukui (Bishop Museum Press), is a firsthand account of old Hawaii under the *kapu* system. Ii lived in Hawaii at the time of Kamehameha the Great and the arrival of the first Westerners.

*The Hawaiian Kingdom*, by Ralph S Kuykendall (University of Hawaii Press), is a three-volume set written from 1938 to 1967. It covers Hawaiian history from 1778 to 1893 and is considered the definitive work on that period.

*Merchant Prince of the Sandalwood Mountains*, by Bob Dye (University of Hawaii Press), tells the story of Chun Afong, Hawaii's first Chinese millionaire, in the context of the turbulent social and economic changes of the 18th century.

*Keneti*, by Bob Krauss (University of Hawaii Press), is a biography of Kenneth 'Keneti' Emory, the esteemed Bishop Museum archaeologist who, over the years, sailed with writer Jack London, worked with anthropologist Margaret Mead and surfed with Olympian Duke Kahanamoku. He spent much of his life uncovering the ruins of villages and temples throughout the Pacific, recording them before they disappeared forever.

*Nana I Ke Kumu (Look to the Source)*, by Mary K Pukui, EW Haertig and Catherine A Lee (Hui Hanai), is a fascinating two-volume collection of information on Hawaiian cultural practices, social customs and beliefs.

*Na Wahi Pana O Koolau Poko*, by Anne Kapulani Landgraf (University of Hawaii Press), focuses on the historical sites of Windward Oahu. The book has 82 high-quality duotone photographs accompanying Hawaiian/English text.

*Streetcar Days in Honolulu: Breezing Through Paradise*, by McKinnon Simpson and John Brizdle, is a fun nostalgia book covering the years 1889 to 1941 from the perspective of a trolley rider.

For books specific to the events surrounding Pearl Harbor, turn to the boxed text 'The Element of Surprise' in the Pearl Harbor chapter.

### Mythology

*The Kumulipo*, by Martha Beckwith (University of Hawaii Press), is a translation of the Hawaiian chant of creation. The chant of 2077 lines begins in the darkness of the spirit world and traces the genealogy of an *alii* (royal) family said to be the ancestors of humankind.

*Hawaiian Mythology*, also by Martha Beckwith (University of Hawaii Press), has comprehensive translations of Hawaii's old myths and legends.

*The Legends and Myths of Hawaii* (Mutual Publishing) is a collection of legends as told by King David Kalakaua, with a short introduction to Hawaiian culture and history as well.

## Natural History

*The Many-Splendored Fishes of Hawaii*, by Gar Goodson (Stanford University Press), is one of the better of several small, inexpensive fish-identification books on the market and has good descriptions and 170 color drawings.

*Hawaii's Fishes: A Guide for Snorkelers, Divers and Aquarists*, by John P Hoover (Mutual Publishing), a more expensive and comprehensive field guide, covers more than 230 reef and shore fishes of Hawaii. It's fully illustrated with color photographs and gives insights on island dive sites.

The Hawaii Audubon Society's *Hawaii's Birds* is the best pocket-sized guide to the birds of Hawaii. It includes color photos and descriptions of all the native birds and many of the species that have been introduced to the Hawaiian Islands.

For a more comprehensive book, there's *A Field Guide to the Birds of Hawaii & the Tropical Pacific* by H Douglas Pratt, Phillip L Bruner and Delwyn G Berrett (Princeton University Press). The book contains nearly 50 pages of color plates.

*Mammals in Hawaii*, by P Quentin Tomich (Bishop Museum Press), is an authoritative book on the mammals in Hawaii, with interesting stories on how they arrived in the islands. Coverage includes whales, dolphins and such oddities as the Australian rock-wallabies that were accidentally released in 1916 and now reside in Oahu's Kalihi Valley.

*Plants and Flowers of Hawaii*, by S Sohmer and R Gustafson (University of Hawaii Press), has good-quality color photos and descriptions of more than 130 native plants of Hawaii, including information on their habitats and evolution.

The new *Manual of the Flowering Plants of Hawaii*, by Warren L Wagner, Derral R Herbst and SH Sohmer (Bishop Museum Press), has in-depth information on Hawaiian flora, including some of the rare and endangered species that have recently been categorized.

*Practical Folk Medicine of Hawaii*, by LR McBride (Petroglyph Press), has descriptions of many native medicinal plants and their uses.

A good general book on flora and fauna is *Plants and Animals of Hawaii* by local biologist Susan Scott (Bess Press). It discusses various environments, including reefs, shorelines, forests and wetlands, and details plants and animals of the islands, both native and introduced. There are interesting tidbits on medicinal uses, origins and the like.

## Outdoor Activities

*The Beaches of Oahu*, by John RK Clark (University of Hawaii Press), is a comprehensive book detailing the island's coastline and every one of its beaches, including water conditions, shoreline geology and local history.

*Surfer's Guide to Hawaii: Hawaii Gets All the Breaks*, by Greg Ambrose (Bess Press), describes the top surfing spots throughout the islands, including Oahu's world-famous Sunset Beach and Banzai Pipeline. Entertaining and witty, it's packed with everything you need to know about surfing in Hawaii.

*The Hiker's Guide to Oahu*, by Stuart Ball (University of Hawaii Press), covers 53 hikes on Oahu. The author, a former president of the Hawaiian Trail & Mountain Club, gives information on length, difficulty and direction to the trailhead for each hike. Walks are described in detail and accompanied by topographical maps.

Also worth considering is *Oahu Trails*, by Kathy Morey (Wilderness Press), which covers 43 hikes and provides maps and detailed directions for each, including curious tidbits of information.

*Mountain Biking the Hawaiian Islands*, by Oahu resident John Alford (Ohana Publishing), is an excellent resource for mountain bikers, covering the public trails open to bikers, with maps and descriptions.

## General

*Hotel Honolulu*, by intrepid travel novelist Paul Theroux, explores the life of a washed-up writer who manages a rundown hotel in Waikiki. Lots of fun is poked at clichéd elements of Hawaii, something that Theroux, a part-time Hawaii resident himself, is intimately familiar with.

*From the Skies of Paradise, Oahu* is an aerial photography book with color plates by renowned photographer Douglas Peebles and text by Glen Grant (Mutual Publishing). All parts of Oahu – cities, beaches, mountains and fields – are beautifully photographed, with accompanying narratives that incorporate Hawaiian myths and legends.

*Architecture in Hawaii*, by Rob Sandler (Mutual Publishing), is a coffee-table book with striking color photographs of Hawaii's most notable buildings, the majority of which are in Honolulu. More than 150 buildings are detailed, from thatched cottages to the royal palace, covering some two centuries of island architecture. There are also biographies of Hawaii's top architects.

Another good large-format book is *Hawaii: The Islands of Life* (Signature Publishing), which has beautiful photos of the flora, fauna and landscapes being protected by the Nature Conservancy of Hawaii. The text is by author Gavan Daws.

### Reference

*Atlas of Hawaii* (University of Hawaii Press), by the University of Hawaii's Department of Geography, will catch the interest of trivia buffs and statisticians alike, with its 350 pages of data, maps and tabulations covering everything from land ownership to seasonal ocean wave patterns.

*Place Names of Hawaii*, by Mary Kawena Pukui, Samuel H Elbert and Esther T Mookini (University of Hawaii Press), is a glossary of 4000 Hawaiian place names. The meaning and background of each name is explained.

*Hawaiian Dictionary*, by Mary Kawena Pukui and Samuel H Elbert (University of Hawaii Press), is the authoritative work on the Hawaiian language. It's written in both Hawaiian-English and English-Hawaiian, with 30,000 entries. There's also an inexpensive pocket-sized version, with 10,000 Hawaiian words.

There are many other Hawaiian-language books on the market, including grammar texts, conversational self-study guides and books on pidgin.

### Mail-Order Sources

The following Hawaiian publishers will send catalogs of their titles that can be ordered by mail:

Bess Press (☎ 734-7159, 800-910-2377, ⓦ www.besspress.com) 3565 Harding Ave, Honolulu, HI 96816
Bishop Museum Press (☎ 848-4135, ⓦ www.bishopmuseum.org/bishop/press) 1525 Bernice St, Honolulu, HI 96817
University of Hawaii Press (☎ 956-8255, 888-847-7377, ⓦ www.uhpress.hawaii.edu) 2840 Kolowalu St, Honolulu, HI 96822

## LIBRARIES

Hawaii has a statewide system of public libraries, with 22 branches in Oahu. The main library is in downtown Honolulu, next to Iolani Palace, and there are also branches in Waikiki and Kailua.

Visitors can borrow books only after applying for a Hawaii library card; a visitor's card valid for three months costs $10 and can be issued on the spot.

Most of the libraries have good Hawaiiana sections, with lots of books on culture, history, flora and fauna. Most also subscribe to Hawaii's daily newspapers as well as to a few mainland newspapers.

Some libraries also have computers that are online. Although a few librarians may sometimes bend the rules, officially you need a library card to use the computers.

## FILMS

Dozens of feature movies have been filmed on Hawaii, and scores of others have used footage of Hawaii as the backdrop. Although the island of Kauai, with its lush landscapes and striking Na Pali Cliffs, is the darling of the movie industry, Oahu has played a role in numerous notable films as well.

*Picture Bride* (1993), which stars Yuki Kudoh, with a cameo by Toshiro Mifune, is one of the few films to insightfully delve into island life. Filmed on Oahu, it depicts the blunt realities of 19th-century Hawaiian plantation life for a Japanese mail-order bride.

Movies specific to the events surrounding WWII and Pearl Harbor (including the ever-popular *Tora! Tora! Tora!* and the mildly popular *Pearl Harbor)* are covered in the boxed text 'The Element of Surprise' in the Pearl Harbor Area chapter.

The following movies were filmed at least partially on Oahu: *From Here to Eternity* (1953), starring Burt Lancaster and Deborah Kerr, with its classic love scene on the beach at Halona Cove; *Hawaii* (1966), filmed in part on the Waianae Coast and starring Julie Andrews and Max von Sydow; *A Very Brady Sequel* (1996), in which the Brady Bunch pops up in Waikiki; and *Godzilla* (1998), starring Matthew Broderick, and Steven Spielberg's *Jurassic Park* (1993), both of which shot scenes at Kualoa Ranch on Oahu's Windward Coast.

## NEWSPAPERS & MAGAZINES

Hawaii's two main papers are the *Honolulu Advertiser* (ⓦ www.honoluluadvertiser.com) and *Honolulu Star-Bulletin* (ⓦ www.starbulletin.com), which are both published daily. Both have excellent websites that allow you to browse the papers online.

In addition, Oahu has numerous weekly or monthly newspapers, many of which can be picked up for free around the island. The most useful of these for visitors is the *Honolulu Weekly* (ⓦ www.honoluluweekly.com), a progressive paper with an extensive entertainment section.

Several mainland newspapers are also widely available, including *USA Today*, the *Wall Street Journal* and the *Los Angeles Times*. Look for them in the lobbies of larger hotels and in convenience stores. The best place to get international newspapers is at **Borders** *(Ward Centre, 1200 Ala Moana Blvd, Honolulu)*, which carries an impressive selection from around the world.

As for magazines, *Honolulu*, *Aloha* and *Hawaii Magazine* are the main general interest publications about Hawaii. *Honolulu* is geared more towards residents and is published monthly. *Aloha* and *Hawaii Magazine* have more visitor-oriented feature articles and are both published six times a year. All of these magazines can be purchased at news racks and bookstores around the island.

There are also numerous free tourist magazines, such as *This Week Oahu* and *Spotlight's Oahu Gold*, which can readily be found at the airport and in street-corner racks all around Waikiki. Although the tourist magazines are mostly composed of paid advertising, they can still be a good source of visitor information. They contain simple maps, a bit of current event information and discount coupons for everything from hamburgers to sunset cruises.

## RADIO & TV

Oahu has about 30 commercial AM and FM radio stations as well as three public radio stations. Radio station Da KINE (105.1 FM) plays classic Hawaiian music. Hawaii Public Radio is on KHPR (88.1 FM), KKUA (90.7 FM) and KIPO (89.3 FM).

Hawaii has commercial TV stations representing all the major US networks and cable network stations, including tourist information and Japanese-language channels. Almost anything you can watch on the mainland you can watch in Hawaii. Cable channels 10 and 11 feature continuous visitor information and ads geared to tourists.

For some local flavor, the evening news on Channel 2 ends with some fine slack-key guitar music by Keola and Kapono Beamer and clips of people waving the *shaka* sign.

## VIDEO SYSTEMS

If you purchase videos in Hawaii, make sure they're compatible with your home system. North America uses the NTSC system, which is incompatible with the PAL system used in Europe, Asia and Australia.

## PHOTOGRAPHY
### Film & Equipment

Both print and slide film are readily available on Oahu. If you're going to be in Hawaii for any length of time, consider having your film developed there, because the high temperature and humidity of the tropics greatly accelerate the deterioration of exposed film. The sooner it's developed, the better the results.

Kodak and Fuji have labs in Honolulu, and drugstores and camera shops usually send film to those labs. **Longs Drugs** *(Upper Level, Ala Moana Center, Honolulu • 2220 S King St, Honolulu)* is one of the cheapest places for both purchasing film and having it developed. Slides generally take two to three days, prints a day or two, and the cost is lower than at camera shops. There are also numerous places in Waikiki that do one-hour photo processing.

### Technical Tips

Oahu is a great place for photography. There's an abundance of interesting subjects, from the architecture in downtown Honolulu to landscapes, hula dancers and beach scenes.

Because of the sunny climate, a few precautions are needed. Most important, don't leave your camera in direct sun any longer than necessary. A locked car can heat up like an oven in just a few minutes, seriously damaging the film.

Sand and water are intense reflectors and in bright light they'll often leave foreground subjects shadowy. You can try compensating by adjusting your f-stop (aperture) or attaching a polarizing filter, or both, but the most effective technique is to take photos in the gentler light of early morning and late afternoon.

## TIME

When it's noon in Honolulu, the time in other parts of the world is as follows: 1pm in Anchorage, Alaska; 2pm in Los Angeles, California; 5pm in New York, New York; 10pm in London, England; 11pm in Paris, France; 7am the next day in Tokyo, Japan; 8am the next day in Sydney and Melbourne, Australia; and 10am the next day in Auckland, New Zealand.

Hawaii does not observe daylight saving time. Therefore, the time difference is one hour greater during those months when other countries observe daylight saving.

And then there's 'Hawaiian Time,' which is either a slow-down-the-clock pace or a euphemism for being late.

Hawaii has about 11 hours of daylight in midwinter and almost 13½ hours in midsummer. In midwinter, the sun rises at about 7am and sets at about 6pm. In midsummer, it rises before 6am and sets after 7pm.

## ELECTRICITY

Electricity is 110/120V, 60 cycles, and a flat two-pronged plug is used, the same as everywhere else in the USA.

## WEIGHTS & MEASURES

Hawaii, like the rest of the USA, uses the imperial system of measurement. Distances are in feet, yards and miles. Three feet equals 1 yard (.914m); 1760 yards or 5280ft are 1 mile.

Dry weights are in ounces (oz), pounds (lb) and tons (16oz are 1 pound; 2000lb are 1 ton), but liquid measures differ from dry measures. One pint equals 16 fluid oz; 2 pints equal 1 quart, a common measure for liquids such as milk, which is also sold in half gallons (2 quarts) and gallons (4 quarts). Gasoline is measured in US gallons (1 gallon equals 3.79L).

For those unaccustomed to the imperial system, there is a metric conversion table on the inside back cover of this book.

## LAUNDRY

Many hotels and hostels have coin-operated washers and dryers. In addition, there are numerous public coin laundries. The average cost is about $1 to wash a load of clothes and another dollar to dry.

## TOILETS

The sanitation standard is very high in Hawaii. Public toilets are free to use and easy to find – at least in comparison to the US mainland. Virtually every beach park has toilet facilities (also referred to as rest rooms), as do larger shopping centers and most hotel lobbies. Fast-food restaurants are another possibility, though they're generally intended for customers only.

## HEALTH

Hawaii is a very healthy place to live and to visit. Because Oahu is 2500 miles from the nearest industrial center, there's little air pollution. The main exception – and it's quite rare – occurs when unfavorable winds carry ash and haze from eruptions at Kilauea volcano on the Big Island over to Oahu.

Hawaii ranks first out of all the 50 US states in life expectancy, which is about 76 years old for men and 81 years old for women.

There are few serious health concerns. The islands are free of most tropical nasties such as malaria and cholera, and you can drink water directly out of the tap, although all stream water needs to be boiled or treated.

No immunizations are required to enter Hawaii or any other port in the USA.

Be aware that there are many poisonous plants in Hawaii, so you should never taste a plant that you cannot positively identify as edible.

If you're new to the heat and humidity, you may find yourself easily fatigued and more susceptible to minor ailments. Acclimatize yourself by slowing down your pace and setting your body clock to the more kicked-back 'Hawaiian Time.' Drink plenty of liquids.

If you're planning on a long outing or anything strenuous, be sure to take enough water along and don't push yourself.

## Emergency Medical Care

Oahu has several hospitals with 24-hour emergency services, including **Queen's Medical Center** (☎ 538-9011; 1301 Punchbowl St, Honolulu) and **Straub Clinic & Hospital** (☎ 522-4000; 888 S King St at Ward Ave, Honolulu). For 24-hour service in Kailua, there's the **Castle Medical Center** (☎ 263-5500; 640 Ulukahiki St).

Divers with the bends are brought to the **UH Hyperbaric Treatment Center** (☎ 587-3425; 347 N Kuakini St, Honolulu).

A **suicide and crisis line** (☎ 521-4555) operates 24 hours a day. Dial ☎ 911 for all ambulance emergencies.

## Medical Problems & Treatment

**Sunburn** This is always a concern in the tropics, because the closer you get to the equator the fewer of the sun's rays are blocked out by the atmosphere. Don't be fooled by what appears to be a hazy overcast day – you can get sunburned surprisingly quickly, even through clouds.

Sunscreen with a high SPF (sun protection factor) is recommended. If you're going into the water, put on one that's water-resistant. Snorkelers may want to wear a T-shirt if they plan to be out in the water for a long time. You'll not only be protecting yourself against sunburn, but also potential skin cancer and premature aging of the skin.

Fair-skinned people can get both first- and second-degree burns in the hot Hawaiian sun, and wearing a sun hat for added protection is a good idea. The most severe sun is between 10am and 2pm.

**Prickly Heat** An itchy rash, prickly heat is caused by excessive perspiration trapped under the skin. It usually strikes people who have just arrived in a hot climate and whose pores have not yet opened sufficiently to cope with increased sweating. Keeping cool by bathing often or resorting to air-con may help until you acclimatize.

**Heat Exhaustion** Dehydration or salt deficiency can cause heat exhaustion. Take time to acclimatize to high temperatures and make sure you get sufficient liquids. Salt deficiency is characterized by fatigue, lethargy, headaches, giddiness and muscle cramps, and in this case salt tablets (available at drugstores) may help. Vomiting or diarrhea can deplete your liquid and salt levels.

**Heat Stroke** This serious, sometimes fatal condition occurs when the body's heat regulating mechanism breaks down and the body temperature rises to dangerous levels. Long, continuous periods of exposure to high temperatures can leave you vulnerable to heat stroke. Avoid strenuous activity in open sun when you first arrive.

Symptoms of heat stroke include feeling unwell, sweating very little or not at all and a high body temperature (102°F to 106°F). When sweating has ceased, the skin becomes flushed and red. Severe, throbbing headaches and lack of coordination also occur, and the sufferer may be confused or aggressive. Eventually they may become delirious or convulsive. Hospitalization is essential, but meanwhile get patients out of the sun, remove their clothing, cover them with a wet sheet or towel and fan them continually.

**Fungal Infections** The same climate that produces lush tropical forests also promotes a prolific growth of skin fungi and bacteria. Hot-weather fungal infections are most likely to occur between the toes or fingers or in the groin.

To prevent fungal infections, it's essential to keep your skin dry and cool and allow air to circulate. Choose loose cotton clothing rather than artificial fibers, and sandals rather than shoes. If you do get an infection, wash the infected area daily with a disinfectant or medicated soap. Rinse and dry well and then apply an antifungal powder.

**Motion Sickness** Eating lightly before and during a trip will reduce the chances of motion sickness. If you are prone to motion sickness, try to find a place that minimizes disturbance – near the wing on aircraft or close to the midpoint on boats. Fresh air usually helps; breathing cigarette smoke or reading doesn't. Commercial motion-sickness preparations, which can cause drowsiness, have to be taken before the trip commences. Ginger is a natural preventative and is available in capsule form.

**Jet Lag** When a person travels by air across more than three time zones, they usually experience jet lag. It occurs because many of the functions of the human body (such as temperature, pulse rate and emptying of the bladder and bowels) are regulated by internal 24-hour cycles. These effects will usually be gone within three days of arrival, but to minimize the impact of jet lag:

- Rest for a couple of days prior to departure; try to avoid staying up late and last-minute dashes for traveler's checks and the like.

- Try to select flight schedules that minimize sleep deprivation; arriving late in the day means you can go to sleep soon after you arrive. For very long flights, try to organize a stopover.

- Avoid excessive eating (which bloats the stomach) and alcohol (which causes dehydration) during the flight. Instead, drink plenty of noncarbonated, nonalcoholic drinks such as fruit juice or water.

- Make yourself comfortable by wearing loose-fitting clothes and perhaps bringing an eye mask and ear plugs to help you sleep.

- Try to sleep at the appropriate time for the time zone you are traveling to.

- Avoid smoking.

**HIV & AIDS** Infection with the human immunodeficiency virus (HIV) may lead to acquired immune deficiency syndrome (AIDS), which is a fatal disease. Any exposure to blood, blood products or body fluids may put the individual at risk. The disease is often transmitted through sexual contact or dirty needles – vaccinations, acupuncture, tattooing and body-piercing can be as dangerous as intravenous drug use.

If you have any questions regarding AIDS while on Oahu, contact the **AIDS/STD Hotline** (☎ 922-1313).

**Cuts & Scratches** Cuts and skin punctures are easily infected in Hawaii's hot and humid climate, and infections can be persistent. Keep any cut or open wound clean and treat it with an antiseptic solution. Keep the area protected, but where possible avoid bandages, which can keep wounds wet.

Coral cuts are even more susceptible to infection because tiny pieces of coral can get embedded in the skin. These cuts are notoriously slow to heal, as the coral releases a weak venom into the wound.

**Pesky Creatures** Although Hawaii has no land snakes, it does have its fair share of annoying mosquitoes, as well as centipedes, which can give an unpleasant bite. There are also bees and ground-nesting wasps, which, like the centipede, generally pose danger only to those who are allergic to their stings. (For information on stinging sea creatures, see Ocean Safety, under Dangers & Annoyances, later in this chapter.)

This being the tropics, cockroaches are plentiful, and although they don't pose much of a health problem, they do little for the appetite. Lodgings with kitchens tend to have the most problems. If you find that the place where you're staying is infested, you can always call the manager or the front desk and have them spray poisons – which are no doubt more dangerous than the roaches!

While sightings are not terribly common, Hawaii does have two dangerous arachnids: the black widow spider and the scorpion.

Found in much of the USA, the black widow is glossy black and has a body that's a half-inch in diameter with a characteristic red hourglass mark on its abdomen. It weaves a strong, tangled web close to the ground and inhabits brush piles, sheds and outdoor privies. Its bite, which resembles the prick of a pin, is barely noticeable, but is followed in about 30 minutes by severe cramping, which causes the abdominal muscles become boardlike, and labored breathing. Other reactions include vomiting, headaches, sweating, shaking and a tingling sensation in the fingers. In severe cases, the bite can be fatal. If you think that you've been bitten by a black widow, seek immediate medical attention.

The scorpion, confined principally to dry regions, is capable of inflicting a painful sting by means of its caudal fang. Like the black widow, the venom contains neurotoxins. Severity of the symptoms generally depends on the age of the victim, and stings can even be fatal for very young children. Symptoms are shortness of breath, hives, swelling and vomiting. You should apply diluted household ammonia and cold compresses to the area of the sting and seek immediate medical help.

While the odds of encountering a scorpion are quite low, campers should always check inside their hiking boots before putting them on!

**Dengue Fever** This viral infection has recently surfaced in Hawaii, and is transmitted by mosquitoes. Dengue fever is rapidly becoming one of the top public health problems throughout the tropical Pacific. It spreads when a mosquito bites an infected person and then passes along the virus by biting someone else.

Signs and symptoms of dengue fever include a sudden onset of high fever, severe headaches, joint and muscle pain and nausea and vomiting. A rash of small red spots sometimes appears three or four days after the onset of fever. In the early phase of illness, dengue fever may be mistaken for other infectious diseases, including influenza. Minor bleeding such as nosebleeds may occur in the course of the illness but this does not mean that you have progressed to the potentially fatal hemorrhagic fever.

You should seek medical help as soon as possible if you think you may be infected. There is no specific treatment for dengue fever. Aspirin should be avoided as it increases the risk of hemorrhaging.

There is no vaccine for dengue fever. The best protection is to avoid mosquito bites at all times by covering up, using insect repellents containing the compound DEET and using mosquito nets.

**Leptospirosis** Visitors to Hawaii should be aware of leptospirosis, a bacterial disease found in freshwater streams and ponds. The disease is transmitted from animals such as rats, mongooses and wild pigs.

Humans most often pick up the disease, which enters the body through the nose, eyes, mouth or cuts in the skin, from swimming or wading in water contaminated by animal urine. Leptospirosis can exist in any fresh water, including idyllic-looking waterfalls, because the water may have washed down the slopes through animal habitats.

Because hikers account for many of the cases, the state posts leptospirosis warnings at trailheads. One of the most effective precautions is to avoid unnecessary freshwater crossings, especially if you have open cuts.

Symptoms can occur within two to 20 days after exposure and may include fever, chills, sweating, headaches, muscle pains, vomiting and diarrhea. More severe symptoms include blood in the urine and jaundice. Symptoms may last from a few days to several weeks. Although deaths have been attributed to the disease, they are relatively rare.

**Ciguatera Poisoning** Ciguatera is a serious illness caused by eating fish affected by ciguatoxin, which herbivorous fish can pick up from marine algae. There is no ready way of detecting ciguatoxin, and it's not diminished by cooking. Symptoms of food poisoning usually occur three to five hours after eating.

Ciguatoxin is most common among reef fish (which are not commonly served in restaurants) and it hasn't affected Hawaii's deep-sea fish, such as tuna, marlin and mahimahi. The symptoms, if you do eat the wrong fish, include nausea, stomach cramps, diarrhea, paralysis, tingling and numbness of the face, fingers and toes and a reversal of temperature feelings, so that hot things feel cold and vice versa. Extreme cases can result in unconsciousness and even death. Vomit until your stomach is empty and get immediate medical help.

## SOCIAL GRACES
In many ways, contemporary Hawaiian culture resembles contemporary culture in the rest of the USA.

Hawaiians listen to the same pop music and watch the same TV shows as Americans on the mainland. Honolulu has night clubs and ballroom dancing, bands and classical orchestras, junk food and nouvelle cuisine. The wonderful thing about Hawaii, however, is that the mainland influences largely stand beside, rather than engulf, the culture of the islands.

Not only is traditional Hawaiian culture an integral part of the social fabric of Hawaii, but so too are the customs of the ethnically diverse immigrants who have made the islands their home. Honolulu is more than just a meeting place of East and West; it's a place where the cultures merge, typically in a manner that brings out the best of both worlds.

In recent decades, there's been a Hawaiian cultural renaissance. Hawaiian language classes are thriving and there is a concerted effort to reintroduce Hawaiian words into modern speech. Hula classes are concentrating more on the nuances behind hand movements and facial expressions than on the dramatic hip-shaking that sells tickets to dance shows. Many Hawaiian artists and craftspeople are returning to traditional mediums and themes.

Certainly the tourist centers have long been overrun with packaged Hawaiiana that seems almost a parody of island culture, from plastic leis to theme-park luaus. But fortunately for the visitor, the growing interest in traditional Hawaiian culture is having a positive impact on the tourist industry, and authentic performances by hula students and Hawaiian musicians are increasingly easier to find.

## WOMEN TRAVELERS

Women travelers are no more likely to encounter problems in Hawaii than elsewhere in the USA. The usual precautions apply when it comes to potentially dangerous situations such as hitchhiking and walking alone at night. If you're camping, select your camping ground carefully; you may want to opt for camping areas with caretakers.

If you are the victim of an assault, call the **police** *(☎ 911)*. Women who have been abused or sexually assaulted can also call the **Sex Abuse Treatment Center's 24-hour hotline** *(☎ 524-7273)*.

## GAY & LESBIAN TRAVELERS

Hawaii is a popular vacation spot for gays and lesbians. The state has strong minority protections and a constitutional guarantee of privacy that extends to sexual behavior between consenting adults.

Still, most of the gay scene is low key; public hand-holding and other outward signs of affection between gays are not commonplace. In terms of nightlife, the main gay club scene is centered in Waikiki.

The following sources can help gay and lesbian visitors to become oriented to the islands.

The volunteer-run **Gay & Lesbian Community Center** *(☎ 951-7000; ⓦ www.glcc-hawaii.org; Box 22718, Honolulu, HI 96823)* is a good source of local information for gay women and men. The center has support groups, movie nights and a library.

A good website for general information on gay issues is ⓦ www.gayhawaii.com; it also has links to a variety of gay and lesbian sites that cover items from travel and entertainment to politics.

**Pacific Ocean Holidays** *(☎ 923-2400, 800-735-6600, fax 923-2499; Box 88245, Honolulu, HI 96830)* is a company that can arrange vacation packages for gay men and women.

## A Glitch in Getting Hitched

Gay marriages in Hawaii? In recent years, it looked as if travelers of all persuasions might be able to tie the knot in Hawaii, as the state took center stage in the movement to legalize same-gender marriages. The debate even took on a national scope, with conservatives in the US Congress taking up legislation to make sure any changes that might be approved in Hawaii didn't spill over into other states.

In December 1996 a Hawaii judge ruled that state prohibitions against same-sex marriages violated the equal protection clause of Hawaii's constitution, which explicitly bans gender discrimination. In July 1997, Hawaii became the first US state to extend broad rights to domestic partners. To make the law more acceptable to the vocal conservatives who oppose gay marriages, it covers any two adults who cannot legally marry, including not just same-sex couples, but also others such as a mother and adult child or two siblings living together. Those who register are covered on an umbrella of items ranging from medical insurance to survivorship rights.

In the eyes of Hawaii legislators, the domestic partnership law was a compromise, meant to quiet both the pro and con voices in the controversy over gay marriages.

However, in response to the domestic partnership law, conservative members of the state legislature put forth an amendment to Hawaii's state constitution allowing the legislature 'to reserve marriage to opposite-sex couples only.' This amendment was overwhelmingly passed by Hawaii voters in the November 1998 elections. Progressives challenged the legality of the state constitutional amendment on the grounds that it violates the US Constitution's equal protection clause, but the Hawaii Supreme Court has let it stand.

In 2000, Vermont legislators – quietly and free of the national attention that had focused on Hawaii – voted to make their state the first in the USA to legally sanction same-sex marriages.

## DISABLED TRAVELERS

Overall, Hawaii is an accommodating destination for travelers with disabilities, and Waikiki in particular is considered one of the more accessible destinations in the USA. Many of the larger hotels throughout Hawaii have wheelchair-accessible rooms and as more of them renovate their facilities, accessibility improves.

General access is getting much better, too. The Waikiki Beach area, for instance, has been extensively renovated with curb cuts and lots of low-profile ramps throughout. And the Department of Parks and Recreation now provides all-terrain wheelchairs that allow disabled visitors to access the shoreline at a growing number of Oahu beaches, including Ala Moana, Hanauma, Sans Souci and Kailua; the wheelchairs are free of charge.

The **Commission on Persons with Disabilities** *(☎ 586-8121; Room 101, 919 Ala Moana Blvd, Honolulu, HI 96814)* distributes the *Aloha Guide to Accessibility*, which contains detailed travel tips for physically disabled people. It has general information and covers things such as airport access on the major islands. The guide is free, whether you request it by mail or get it online at w www.hawaii.gov/health/dcab.

In terms of getting around on Oahu, most of island's modern fleet of public buses have wheelchair lifts. To find out which buses have lifts, call ☎ 848-5555 or consult a bus schedule, which uses a wheelchair symbol to indicate routes with lifts. In addition, disabled travelers can contact the **Honolulu Public Transit Authority** *(☎ 454-5050)* for information on Handi-Van curb-to-curb service and other provisions for the disabled.

For travel plans in general, **Accessible Vans of Hawaii** *(☎ 871-7785, 800-303-3750; 296 Ahamaha St, Kahului, HI 96732)* books accessible accommodations, rents accessible vans and arranges various activities for disabled travelers in the Honolulu area, as well as on the island of Maui. **Hawaiian Rent All** *(☎ 949-3961; 1946 S Beretania, Honolulu)* rents wheelchairs and walkers.

Those with a physical disability may want to get in touch with their national support organization (preferably the 'travel officer' if there is one) before leaving home. They often there have libraries devoted to travel

and can put you in touch with travel agents who specialize in tours for the disabled.

For instance, the UK-based **Royal Association for Disability & Rehabilitation** *(Radar; ☎ 020 7250 3222; Unit 12, City Forum, 250 City Rd, London EC1V 8AF)* publishes a useful guide called *Holidays and Travel Abroad: A Guide for Disabled People*; the book is available by post for UK£6.

In the USA, the **Society for the Advancement of Travel for the Handicapped** *(SATH; ☎ 212-447-7284; w www.sath.org; Suite 610, 347 Fifth Ave, New York, NY 10016)* publishes a quarterly magazine and has various information sheets on travel for the disabled.

## SENIOR TRAVELERS

Hawaii is a popular destination for retirees and lots of discount schemes are available. The applicable age for discounts has been creeping lower as well.

For instance, Oahu's biggest hotel chain, Outrigger, offers across-the-board discounts of 20% to anyone 50 years of age or older, and if you're a member of the American Association of Retired Persons (AARP), they'll usually increase the discount another 5%. Such discounts are available from other hotels as well, so be sure to inquire.

The nonprofit AARP is a good source for travel bargains. For information on joining this advocacy group for Americans 50 years of age and older, contact **AARP** *(☎ 800-424-3410; Membership Center, 3200 E Carson St, Lakewood, CA 90712)*.

For information on senior bus passes, which can make getting around Oahu a bargain, see the Bus section in the Getting Around chapter.

## TRAVEL WITH CHILDREN

Families with children will find lots to do on Oahu. In addition to beaches, swimming pools and a range of water sports, there are lots of other outdoor activities and cool sightseeing attractions for kids of all ages.

Successful travel with young children requires planning and effort. Try not to overdo things; even for adults, attempting to do too much can cause problems. Include children in the trip planning, because if they've helped to work out where you will be going, they will be much more interested when they get there.

## Fun for Kids

Although tourism officials tend to slant their promotions toward adults, Oahu has plenty of attractions of interest to children. These range from heavily touristed sites such as the family oriented **Polynesian Cultural Center** (☎ 293-3333, 800-367-7060; 55-370 Kamehameha Hwy Laie) on the Windward Coast, and Leeward Oahu's **Hawaiian Waters Adventure Park** (☎ 674-9283; 400 Farrington Hwy, Kapolei) to low-key local activities that visitors seldom stumble across.

The nonprofit **Hawaii Nature Center** (☎ 955-0100; 2131 Makiki Heights Drive, Honolulu), at the Makiki Forest baseyard, has a Sunday program of 'Keiki Nature Adventures' that provides a great way for visiting children to join Hawaiian children in nature projects and narrated hikes; activities typically last a few hours and are open to children as young as age five.

If you feel like staying closer to your hotel, Waikiki offers a wide range of activities right at the beach. Older children can take surfing lessons from the pros and children of all ages can hop aboard an outrigger canoe for an easier ride across the surf.

Young children may enjoy visiting the petting section of the **Honolulu Zoo** (☎ 971-7171; Kapiolani Park, Waikiki), where they can encounter some of the tamer creatures up close. Older children may want to sign up for the zoo's **elephant encounter** (☎ 971-7174), which includes a lecture by the keepers on elephant care and behavior as well as the opportunity – when the beasts are in a good mood – for children to feed the elephants.

The nearby **Waikiki Aquarium** (☎ 923-9741; 2777 Kalakaua Ave, Waikiki) can be a fascinating place – not only does it have the usual colorful array of tropical fish, as well as monk seals and sharks, but there's also a touch-tank geared specifically for children.

The free **Pleasant Hawaiian Hula Show** (☎ 945-1851; 2805 Monsarrat Ave, Waikiki), which like the zoo and aquarium is in Kapiolani Park, offers a fun little music and dance performance and is followed by a photo opportunity where parents can snap photos of their kids posing with the hula dancers.

For those vacationing with children, Lonely Planet's *Travel with Children*, by Cathy Lanigan, is packed full of valuable tips and interesting anecdotal stories. Also, see the boxed text 'Fun for Kids.'

If you're traveling with infants and come up short once you arrive on Oahu, you can contact **Hawaiian Rent All** (☎ 949-3961; 1946 S Beretania, Honolulu), which rents cribs, car seats and high chairs.

## USEFUL ORGANIZATIONS
### State Parks
The **Division of State Parks** (☎ 587-0300; w www.hawaii.gov/dlnr/dsp/dsp.html; Box 621, Honolulu, HI 96809) provides a free brochure to Hawaii's state parks, including camping information and a brief description of each park.

### Environmental Groups
The **Sierra Club** (☎ 538-6616; w www.hi.sierraclub.org; Box 2577, Honolulu, HI 96803) offers guided hikes, maintains trails and is involved in conservation projects throughout Hawaii. Contact them for recorded information on upcoming hikes. For other information on Sierra Club activities, write or visit the website.

The **Earthjustice Legal Defense Fund** (☎ 599-2436; w www.earthjustice.org; 4th floor, 223 S King St, Honolulu, HI 96813) plays a leading role in protecting Hawaii's fragile environment through court action.

The **Nature Conservancy of Hawaii** (☎ 537-4508; w www.tnc.org; 923 Nuuanu Ave, Honolulu, HI 96817) protects some of Hawaii's endangered ecosystems by acquiring land and arranging long-term stewardships with landowners. On Oahu, it manages a small crater above Hanauma Bay that has a unique vernal pool and is home to a rare species of fern, and, in the Waianae Range, it is the steward of a large tract of land that is the habitat of 45 rare plant and animal species.

### American Automobile Association
The **American Automobile Association** (AAA; ☎ 593-2221; w www.aaa-hawaii.com; 1270 Ala Moana Blvd, Honolulu) can provide AAA members with information on motoring in Hawaii, including detailed Honolulu and Hawaii road maps. Members are also

## For Business Travelers

Those traveling on business will find that some of the larger Waikiki hotels, such as Hilton Hawaiian Village, offer personal computer rentals and other specialized services geared for business travelers. Some of the hotels in the Outrigger chain have small business centers where guests can rent work desks equipped with computers, printers and modem hookups and arrange other business services.

One city hotel, the Executive Centre Hotel in downtown Honolulu, is geared specifically for business travelers. All the rooms at the Executive have private-line phones with voice mail and data ports and the hotel's business center has work stations, laptop rentals and secretarial services.

In addition, the chain business center Kinko's, which has several offices in Honolulu, offers reasonably priced on-site computer rentals, with major word processing programs, scanning capabilities and color printing. It also has inexpensive photocopying services.

If you have any last-minute business needs as you're leaving Hawaii, there's a business center in the central departure lobby of Honolulu International Airport that offers photocopy, fax and mail services and work station rentals.

entitled to discounts on car rentals, air tickets and some hotels and sightseeing attractions. It also provides members with emergency road service and towing (☎ 800-222-4357).

For information on joining AAA on the mainland before arrival in Hawaii, call ☎ 800-564-6222. Membership dues vary by state but average $60 the first year, $45 for subsequent years.

## DANGERS & ANNOYANCES
### Theft & Violence
As a traveler you're often fairly vulnerable and when you do lose things it can be a real hassle. The most important things to guard are your passport, important papers, tickets and money. It's best to always carry these next to your skin or in a sturdy pouch on your belt.

Be careful even in hotels; don't leave valuables lying around in your room. Those planning to stay in hostels should bring a padlock to secure their belongings in the hostel lockers.

For the most part, Oahu is a safe place. Honolulu has a lower violent crime rate than most other US cities, but like any city, crime does occur and reasonable precautions are advisable.

Petty theft is one crime that ranks high on Oahu. Watch your belongings and never leave anything unattended on a beach. Most accommodations have a place where you can store your valuables.

It is important to be aware that Hawaii is notorious for rip-offs from parked rental cars. The people who break into these cars are

good at what they do; they can pop a trunk or pull out a lock assembly in seconds to get to the loot inside. What's more, they do it not only when you've left your car in a secluded area to go for a long hike, but also in crowded parking lots where you'd expect safety in numbers.

It's certainly best not to leave anything of value in your car any time you walk away from it. If for some reason you feel you must, at least pack things well out of sight *before* you've pulled up to the place where you're going to leave the car.

If you're unlucky enough to have something stolen, immediately report it to the nearest police station. If your credit cards or traveler's checks have been taken, notify your bank or the relevant company immediately.

Other than rip-offs, most hassles encountered by visitors are from drunks. While Waikiki Beach is well patrolled by the police, you should be aware of the environment on other beaches at night and in places where young guys hang out to drink.

### Touts
There's been a clampdown on the hustlers who used to push time-shares and other con deals from every other street corner in Waikiki. They're not totally gone – there are just fewer of them (and some have metamorphosed into 'activity centers'). If you see a sign touting car rentals for $5 a day, you've probably found one.

Time-share salespeople will offer you all sorts of deals, from free luaus to sunset cruises, if you'll just come to hear their 'no obligation' pitch. *Caveat emptor.*

## Tsunamis

Tsunamis, or tidal waves, are not common in Hawaii but when they do hit they can be severe.

Tsunamis are generated by earthquakes or other natural disasters. The largest tsunami known to have hit Hawaii was in 1946, the result of an earthquake in the Aleutian Islands. Waves reached a height of 55.8ft, entire villages were washed away and 159 people died. Since that time, Hawaii has installed a modern tsunami warning system, which is aired through yellow speakers mounted on telephone poles. They're tested on the first working day of each month at 11:45am for about one minute.

If you're in a low-lying coastal area when a tsunami approaches, the main rule is to immediately head for higher ground. Tsunami inundation maps in the front of the Oahu white pages phone book show susceptible areas and safety zones.

## Earthquakes

There is a great deal of seismic activity in the Hawaiian Islands, although most of it takes place on the island of Hawaii (the Big Island), well to the southeast of Oahu. Should you be in an area where an earthquake occurs there are several precautions you can take to minimize the risk of injury. If you're indoors, take cover under a desk or table and stay clear of windows and anything that's in danger of falling such as mirrors, bookcases and file cabinets. If you're outdoors, get into an open area away from buildings, trees and power lines. If you're in a car driving, pull over to the side of the road away from overpasses and power lines and stay inside the car until the shaking stops.

## OCEAN SAFETY

Drowning is the leading cause of accidental death for visitors. If you're not familiar with the water conditions, ask someone before jumping in. Most major Oahu beaches have daytime lifeguards, but if there's no lifeguard on duty, local surfers are generally helpful – they'd rather give you the lowdown on water conditions than pull you out later. It's best not to swim alone in any unfamiliar place.

## Shorebreaks

Shorebreaks occur where waves break close to or directly on shore. They are formed when ocean swells pass abruptly from deep to shallow waters. If they are only a couple of feet high, they generally don't pose a threat for novice bodysurfers. Otherwise, they're for experienced bodysurfers only.

Large shorebreaks can hit with a hard, slamming downward force. Broken bones, neck injuries, dislocated shoulders and loss of wind are the most common injuries, although anyone wiped out in the water is a potential drowning victim as well.

## Rip Currents

Rip currents, often referred to as rips, are fast-flowing currents of water within the ocean, moving from shallow nearshore areas out to sea. They are most common in high surf conditions, forming when water from incoming waves builds up near the shore. Essentially, the waves are coming in faster than they can flow back out.

The water then runs along the shoreline until it finds an escape route out to sea, usually through a channel or out along a point. Swimmers caught in the current can be ripped out to deeper water.

Although rips can be powerful, they usually dissipate 50 to 100 yards offshore. Anyone caught in one should either go with the flow until it loses power or swim parallel to shore to slip out of it. Trying to swim against a rip current can exhaust even the strongest of swimmers.

## Undertows

Undertows are common along steeply sloped beaches when large waves backwash directly into incoming surf. The outflowing water picks up speed as it flows down the slopes. When it hits an incoming wave, the outflow curls under the wave, creating an undertow. Swimmers caught in an undertow can be pulled beneath the surface. The most important thing is not to panic. Go with the current until you get beyond the wave.

## Rogue Waves

You should never turn your back on the ocean. Waves don't all come in with equal height or strength. An abnormally high 'rogue wave' can sweep over shoreline ledges such as those circling Hanauma Bay. You need to be particularly cautious during high tide and in conditions of stormy weather or high surf.

| Strong Current | Man-Of-War | Sharp Coral |

| High Surf | Dangerous Shorebreak | Waves On Ledge |

Look for signs that indicate dangerous conditions

Some people think rogue waves don't exist because they have never seen one. But that is precisely the point – you don't always see them.

## Coral

Most coral cuts occur when swimmers are pushed onto the coral by rough waves and surges. Diving gloves are helpful when snorkeling over shallow reefs. Avoid walking on coral, which will not only cut your feet, but also seriously damages the coral.

## Sea Urchins

*Wana*, or spiny sea urchins, have long brittle spines that can puncture the skin and break off, causing burning and possible numbness. The spines sometimes inflict a toxin and can cause an infection. You can try to remove the spines with tweezers or by soaking the area in hot water, although more serious cases may require surgical removal.

## Sharks

More than 35 varieties of sharks are found in Hawaiian waters, including nonaggressive whale sharks and basking sharks, which can reach lengths of 50ft. Because Hawaiian waters are abundant with fish, sharks in Hawaii are well fed and most pose little danger to humans.

Sharks are curious and will sometimes investigate divers, although they generally just check things out and continue on their way. If they start to hang around, however, it's probably time for you to go.

Outside of the rarely encountered great white shark, the most dangerous shark in Hawaiian waters is the tiger shark, which averages about 20ft in length and is identified by vertical bars along its side. The tiger shark is not terribly particular about what it eats and has been known to chomp down on pieces of wood (including surfboards) floating on the ocean surface.

Should you come face to face with a shark the best thing to do is move casually and quietly away. Don't panic, as sharks are attracted by things that thrash around in water.

Some aquatic officials suggest thumping an attacking shark on the nose or sticking your fingers into its eyes, which may confuse it long enough to give you time to escape. Indeed, some divers who dive in shark waters carry a billy club or bang stick. Swimmers should avoid murky waters. After heavy rains, sharks sometimes come in and linger around river mouths.

Sharks are attracted by blood. Some attacks on humans are related to spearfishing, when a shark is going after a diver's bloody catch and the diver gets in the way. Sharks are also attracted by shiny things and by anything bright red or yellow, which might influence your choice of swimsuit color.

Unpleasant encounters with sharks are extremely unlikely, however. According to the University of Hawaii Sea Grant College, only about 30 known unprovoked shark attacks occurred in Hawaii between 1900 and 1990; about a third of them were fatal. In recent years, though, the number of reported sharks and shark attacks has increased, with attacks throughout Hawaii now occurring on average at a rate of about three a year.

## Jellyfish

Take a peek into the water before you plunge in to make sure it's not jellyfish territory. These gelatinous creatures, with sac-like bodies and stinging tentacles, are fairly common around Hawaii.

The most encountered type is the box jellyfish, which are most apt to be seen eight to 10 days after the full moon, when they come into shallow nearshore waters in places such as Waikiki. Only a couple of inches in diameter, they're hard to see as they stay just below the surface of the water and look like small pieces of cellophane. They're not keen on the sun, and as the day heats up, they retreat from shallow waters, so beachgoers mostly encounter them in the morning.

The sting of a jellyfish varies from mild to severe, depending on the variety. The box jellyfish sting is quite painful, but unless you have an allergic reaction to their venom, jellyfish stings are generally not dangerous.

## Portuguese Man-of-War

The Portuguese man-of-war is a colonial hydrozoan, or a colony of coelenterates (radially symmetrical invertebrate animals), rather than a solitary coelenterate like the jellyfish. Its body consists of a translucent, bluish, bladderlike float, which in Hawaii generally grows to 4 or 5 inches long. Known locally as 'bluebottles,' they're most often found on the Windward Coast, particularly after storms.

The sting of a Portuguese man-of-war is painful, similar to a bee sting except that you're likely to get stung more than once from clusters of long tentacles containing hundreds of stinging cells. These tentacles can reach up to 50ft in length, but in Hawaii they tend to be much shorter. Even touching a bluebottle a few hours after it's washed up on shore can result in burning stings.

If you get stung, quickly remove the tentacles and apply vinegar or a meat tenderizer containing papain (derived from papaya) to neutralize the toxins – in a pinch, you could use urine as well. For serious reactions, including chest pains or difficulty in breathing, seek medical attention immediately.

## Fish Stings

Encounters with venomous sea creatures in Hawaiian waters are rather rare. You should, however, learn to recognize scorpionfish and lionfish, two related fish that can inject venom through their dorsal spines if they are touched. Both are sometimes found in quite shallow water.

The Hawaiian lionfish, which grows up to 10 inches, is strikingly attractive with vertical orange-and-white stripes and feathery appendages that contain poisonous spines; it likes to drift along the reef, particularly at night. The scorpionfish is more drab in appearance, has shorter and less obvious spines, is about 6 inches in length, and tends to sit immobile on the bottom or on ledges.

The sting from either fish can cause a sharp burning pain, followed by numbness around the area of the sting, nausea and headaches. Immediately put the affected area in water that is as hot as you can bear (take care not to unintentionally scald the area due to numbness) and go for medical treatment.

## Cone Shells

Cone shells – which take their name from their conical shape and most commonly have brown or black patterns – should be left alone unless you're sure they're empty. There's no safe way of picking up a live cone shell, as the animal inside has a long, harpoonlike tail that can dart out and reach anywhere on its shell to deliver a painful sting. The wound should be soaked in hot water and medical attention sought.

A few species, such as the textile cone, whose shell is decorated with brown diamond or triangular shapes, have a venom so toxic that in extreme cases the sting could even be fatal.

## Eels

*Puhi*, or moray eels, are often spotted by snorkelers around reefs and coral heads.

They're constantly opening and closing their mouths to pump water across their gills, which makes them look far more menacing than they actually are.

Eels don't attack, but will protect themselves if they feel cornered by fingers jabbing into the reef holes or crevices where they live. Eels have sharp teeth and strong jaws and may clamp down if someone sticks a hand in their door.

## EMERGENCIES

For police, fire and ambulance emergencies anywhere on Oahu, dial ☎ 911. The inside front cover of the Oahu phone book lists other vital service agencies, such as poison control and coast guard rescue.

If you're unfortunate enough to have something stolen, report it immediately to the police. If your credit cards or traveler's checks have been taken, notify your bank or the relevant company as soon as possible. For the phone numbers of the major credit card and traveler's check companies, see Money earlier in this chapter.

Foreign visitors who lose their passport should contact their consulate in Honolulu. Some consulate phone numbers are listed earlier in this chapter; a complete list can be found under 'Consulates' in the yellow pages of the Oahu phone directory.

## LEGAL MATTERS

Anyone arrested in Hawaii has the right to have the representation of a lawyer, from the time of their arrest to their trial, and if a person cannot afford a lawyer, the state will provide one for free. If you want to hire a lawyer, the **Hawaii State Bar Association** (☎ 537-9140) can make referrals; foreign visitors may want to call their consulate for advice.

The minimum drinking age in Hawaii is 21. It's illegal to have open containers of alcohol in motor vehicles, and drinking in public parks or on the beaches is also illegal.

Drunk driving is a serious crime and you can incur stiff fines, jail time and other penalties if caught. In Hawaii, anyone caught driving with an alcohol blood level of 0.08% or greater is guilty of driving 'under the influence' and will have their driver's license taken away on the spot. Further punishment depends upon one's driving record, but if this is a first offense you're looking at a mandatory 90-day license suspension and alcohol

abuse counseling and possibly two to five days in prison, with a fine of up to $1,000.

As in most places, the possession of marijuana and nonprescription narcotics is illegal in Hawaii. Be aware that US Customs has a zero-tolerance policy for drugs; federal authorities have been known to seize boats after finding even minute quantities of marijuana on board.

For consumer issues, Hawaii's **Department of Commerce & Consumer Affairs** (☎ 587-1234) has a handy recorded information line that provides information on your rights regarding refunds and exchanges, time-share contracts, car rentals and similar topics.

## BUSINESS HOURS

Office hours are usually 8:30am to 4:30pm Monday to Friday, although there can be a variance of half an hour in either direction. Shops in central areas and malls, as well as large chain stores, are usually open into the evenings and on weekends, and some grocery stores are open 24 hours.

Banks are generally open from 8:30am to 4pm Monday to Thursday and 8:30am to 6pm Friday. However, bank branches inside grocery stores keep longer hours, typically 10am to 7pm Monday to Friday and 10am to 3pm Saturday and Sunday.

## PUBLIC HOLIDAYS & SPECIAL EVENTS

With its diverse cultural heritage and good year-round weather, Oahu has a seemingly endless number and variety of holidays, festivals and sporting events. The highlights are listed here.

As events and venues may change a little from year to year, it's best to check activity schedules in local papers or inquire at the **Hawaii Visitors and Convention Bureau** (☎ 923-1811, 800-464-2924; e info@hvcb .org; Suite 801, 2270 Kalakaua Ave, Waikiki, HI 96815). Water sports in particular are reliant on the weather and on the surf, so any schedule is tentative.

Note: When a public holiday falls on the weekend, it is often celebrated on the nearest Friday or Monday instead.

### January

**New Year's Eve** Firecrackers and fireworks are shot off through the night to welcome the first day of the year. January 1 is a public holiday

**Chinese New Year** Beginning at the second new moon after the winter solstice (mid-January to mid-February), Chinese New Year sees lion dances and strings of firecrackers go off. The Narcissus Festival, part of the celebrations, runs for about five weeks and includes arts, crafts, food booths, a beauty pageant and coronation ball. Events are held all around Honolulu; Chinatown is the center stage.

**Martin Luther King Jr Day** This public holiday honors the civil rights leader. It is observed on the third Monday in January.

**Sony Open in Hawaii** This PGA tour golf tournament takes place in early January at the Waialae Country Club in Kahala with a hefty $3 million purse

**Cherry Blossom Festival** This festival runs from January through February. It features a variety of Japanese cultural events at various locations around Oahu, including tea ceremonies, *mochi* pounding and *taiko* drummers.

**Ala Wai Challenge Canoe Festival** Held the third Sunday in January, this outrigger canoe festival takes place along the Ala Wai Canal in Waikiki

## February

**NFL Pro Bowl** The annual all-star game of the National Football League is held at Aloha Stadium near the beginning of the month

**Hawaiian Ladies Open** The PGA Tour golf tournament takes place in mid-February at Kapolei Golf Course

**Presidents Day** A public holiday observed on the third Monday in February

**Great Aloha Run** A popular 8.2-mile fun run from Aloha Tower to Aloha Stadium held on Presidents Day

## March

**Honolulu Festival** Held during the second weekend in March, festivities include plays, street performances, kite making, Japanese *bon odori* (dances) and a parade through Waikiki

**St Patrick's Day** March 17 is celebrated with a parade of bagpipers and marching bands from Fort DeRussy, down Kalakaua Ave in Waikiki to Kapiolani Park

**Prince Kuhio Day** This state holiday on March 26 honors Prince Jonah Kuhio Kalanianaole, Hawaii's first delegate to the US Congress

**Good Friday** The Friday before Easter is a public holiday

## April

**Jungle Jam** Honolulu Zoo in Waikiki sponsors free concerts of Hawaiian music on Sunday afternoons in April

**International Bed Race** This offbeat wheeled-bed race, from Fort DeRussy to Kapiolani Park, is held in late April

## May

**May Day** Known as Lei Day in Hawaii, on the first day of May, everybody dons a lei. There are lei-making competitions and Oahu crowns a lei queen at Kapiolani Park.

**Molokai Challenge** Held in late May, this 32-mile kayak race across the treacherous Kaiwi Channel starts at Kaluakoi Resort on Molokai and finishes at Koko Marina on Oahu

**Memorial Day** Held on the last Monday in May, this public holiday honors soldiers killed in battle. At the National Memorial Cemetery of the Pacific at Punchbowl, there's a service with taps, a 21-gun salute and a flyover by fighter planes; music is usually by the Royal Hawaiian Band. There are also events at the USS *Arizona* Memorial.

**50th State Fair** Featuring games, rides and exhibits, this event runs for four weekends from late May into June at the Aloha Stadium

## June

**Pan-Pacific Festival** Held the first weekend in June, this Japanese-American festival features marching bands, costumed performers and other street entertainment throughout Honolulu and a parade to Kapiolani Park in Waikiki

**King Kamehameha Day** A state holiday, King Kamehameha Day is celebrated on or near June 11. The statue of Kamehameha opposite the Iolani Palace is ceremoniously draped with leis and there's a parade from downtown Honolulu to Kapiolani Park, where there are hula shows, music and crafts.

**King Kamehameha Hula & Chant Competition** One of Hawaii's biggest hula contests is held at the Blaisdell Center in Honolulu near the end of June

## July

**Independence Day** The fourth of July is a public holiday, celebrated in Oahu with fireworks at Ala Moana Beach Park and a parade to Kapiolani Park

**Hawaii International Jazz Festival** Held four consecutive nights in mid-July at the atmospheric Hawaii Theatre, this festival features both local and national jazz performers

**Prince Lot Hula Festival** Held at Moanalua Gardens on the third Saturday of the month, this event features hula competitions among Hawaii's major hula schools and traditional Hawaiian games

**Transpacific Yacht Race** On the July 4 weekend of odd-numbered years, sailboats leave southern California and arrive in Honolulu 10 to 14

days later. The 'Transpac,' which has been held for nearly a century, is the country's oldest long-distance sailboat race.

## August

**Obon** Observed in July and August, this event is marked by Japanese *bon odori* (dances) to honor deceased ancestors. The final event is a floating lantern ceremony at Waikiki's Ala Wai Canal on the evening of August 15.

**Ki Hoalu Festival** Featuring some of Hawaii's top slack-key guitarists, a free concert is held at Ala Moana Beach Park

**Ko Olina International Billfish Tournament** This deep-sea fishing tournament takes place mid-month at the Ko Olina Marina in Leeward Oahu

**Admission Day** This public holiday, celebrating the anniversary of Hawaiian statehood, is observed on the third Friday in August

## September

**Labor Day** This public holiday is observed on the first Monday in September

**Aloha Week** A celebration of all things Hawaiian, held in mid-September, with cultural events, contests, canoe races and Hawaiian music. Other festivities include a street fair in downtown Honolulu and a parade in Waikiki.

**Na Wahine O Ke Kai** Hawaii's major annual women's outrigger canoe race starts at sunrise at Kaluakoi, Molokai, and ends 40 miles later at Waikiki's Fort DeRussy Beach. It's held near the end of the month.

## October

**Discoverers Day** This public holiday (known as Columbus Day on the mainland) is observed on the second Monday in October

**Princess Kaiulani Commemoration Week** Held throughout the third week in October, this event honors Hawaii's last princess with festivities, hula shows and other activities in Waikiki

**Na Molokai Hoe** Hawaii's major men's outrigger canoe race is held midmonth. It starts after sunrise on Molokai and finishes at Waikiki's Fort DeRussy Beach about five hours later. Teams from Australia, Germany and the US mainland join Hawaiian teams in this annual competition, which was first held in 1952.

## November

**General Election Day** Falling on the second Tuesday in November (during election years) this is a public holiday

**Veterans Day** Honoring the nation's veterans, this public holiday is observed on November 11

**Hawaii International Film Festival** Featuring about 175 films from Pacific Rim and Asian nations, films are shown throughout Oahu for

## Hawaiian Weddings

Many visitors come to Hawaii not only for their honeymoon, but to make their wedding vows as well.

Getting married in Hawaii is a straightforward process. The state requires that the prospective bride and groom appear in person together before a marriage license agent and pay $50 for a license, which is given out on the spot. There's no waiting period and no residence, citizenship or blood-test requirements. The legal age for marriage is 18, or 16 with parental consent.

Full information and forms are available from the **Department of Health** (☎ 586-4544; *Marriage License Office, Box 3378, 1250 Punchbowl St, Honolulu, HI 96813; open 8am-4pm Mon-Fri*).

Numerous companies provide wedding services. One of these, **Affordable Weddings of Hawaii** (☎ 923-4876, 800-942-4554, fax 396-0959; *PO Box 26475, Honolulu, HI 96825*) will mail out a brochure with helpful tips on planning your wedding, choosing a location, photography and other services. The Reverend KC Russ of Affordable Weddings can provide a nondenominational service, starting at $100 for a simple weekday ceremony and going up to $1000 for more elaborate packages.

For something more romantic, you can sail off the coast of Honolulu at sunset on *Capt Ken's Love Boat*, a private 40ft yacht. The captain's a nice guy and makes the outing lots of fun, yet is appropriately serious when it comes to the ceremony. The whole package with flowers, champagne, dinner, limousine service and a three-hour cruise costs around $1000, but you could go as low as $350 for a simpler one-hour cruise. It's arranged through **Tradewind Charters-Wedding at Sea** (☎ 973-0311, 800-829-4899, fax 396-5094; **e** *captken@hawaii.rr.com; 796 Kalanipuu St, Honolulu, HI 96825*).

a week around mid-November, with the schedule listed in the Honolulu papers

**Triple Crown of Surfing** Consisting of three professional competitions that draw the world's top surfers to Oahu's North Shore, the events begin in November and run through December, with the exact dates and locations depending on when and where the surf's up

**Thanksgiving** This national holiday is celebrated on the fourth Thursday in November

## December

**Pearl Harbor Day** In commemoration of the Japanese attack on Oahu, special ceremonies are held at the USS *Arizona* Memorial on December 7

**Bodhi Day** The Buddhist Day of Enlightenment is celebrated on December 8, with ceremonies at Buddhist temples

**Honolulu Marathon** In terms of the number of runners, this is the third-largest marathon in the USA. It's run on the second Sunday of the month along a 26-mile course from the Aloha Tower to Kapiolani Park.

**Christmas** Festivals and craft fairs are held around Oahu throughout the whole month. December 25 is a public holiday.

**Aloha Bowl** This big collegiate football game is held at Aloha Stadium on Christmas Day and televised nationally

## COURSES
### University of Hawaii

In Oahu, the main venue for courses is the University of Hawaii at Manoa, which offers both full-time university attendance and summer school. For information on undergraduate studies contact the Admissions & Records Office of the **University of Hawaii** (☎ 956-8975; Room 001, 2600 Campus Rd, Honolulu, HI 96822). For information on graduate studies, contact the **Graduate Division** (☎ 956-8544; Room 354, Spalding Hall, 2540 Maile Way, Honolulu, HI 96822).

The summer session consists primarily of two six-week terms. For a catalog, contact the **Summer Session** (☎ 956-5666; Room 1001, 2500 Dole St, Krauss Bldg, Honolulu, HI 96822).

There are also shorter, noncredit recreation and craft classes organized through **Campus Leisure Programs** (☎ 956-6468), which are open to the general public. Most classes, such as hula, massage, surfing or slack-key guitar, meet once or twice a week and cost around $50 for a month-long session. Of particular interest to short-term visitors are the one-day outdoor programs, such as hiking outings ($10).

### Other Courses

While short-term visitors can't join a traditional hula *halau* (school), where students commit themselves for years to the tutelage of their instructor, even the casual visitor can learn the basics of hula by taking the free lessons offered at the Royal Hawaiian Shopping Center in Waikiki. The instructors are patient and cater to both short-term visitors and to Waikiki residents who attend classes on a more regular basis.

For those who want to try their hand at other Hawaiian crafts, the Royal Hawaiian Shopping Center in Waikiki also offers free mini-classes in ukulele playing, lei making and Hawaiian quilting. For details, see Free Entertainment in the Waikiki chapter.

For courses in a more natural setting, the **Hawaii Nature Center** (☎ 955-0100; 2131 Makiki Heights Drive, Honolulu), at the Makiki Forest baseyard, holds weekend workshops. Topics include such things as ancient Hawaiian games, taro patch farming, ikebana (Japanese flower arranging) and jewelry making with natural fibers and shells. Though most of its participants are islanders, visitors are also welcome and it's a nice way to rub elbows with locals. Classes typically last two hours, and the cost is $10 for nonmembers.

The **Japanese Cultural Center of Hawaii** (☎ 945-7633; 2454 S Beretania St, Honolulu) offers a wide variety of courses to the general public, such as kanji calligraphy, tea ceremony, haiku and Japanese brush art. However, sessions generally last one to three months and are intended to be taken on an ongoing basis. Of more interest to visitors are the shorter workshops and one-day lectures on topics such as the significance of Japanese swords, Noh masks and Japanese cooking demonstrations. Registration for the day courses generally cost under $10, while the longer sessions cost between $75 and $125, depending on the course and duration.

## WORK

US citizens can pursue employment in Hawaii as they would in any other state. Foreign visitors who are in the USA for tourist purposes are not legally allowed to take up employment.

As Hawaii has had a relatively slow economy in the wake of the September 11 attacks on the USA, the job situation is not particularly rosy. Much of the economy is tied to the service industry, with wages hovering close to the minimum wage. For visitors, the most common work is waiting on tables, and if you're young and energetic there are job possibilities in many of the restaurants and clubs.

If you're hoping to find more serious 'professional' employment, you should note that Hawaii is considered a tight labor market, with a lack of diversified industries and a relatively immobile labor force. Professional jobs that do open up are generally filled by established Hawaii residents.

A good online resource is W www.surfha waii.com, which contains the 'help wanted' ads from Oahu's largest daily, the *Honolulu Advertiser*.

For more information on employment in Hawaii, contact the **State Department of Labor & Industrial Relations** (☎ *586-8700; 830 Punchbowl St, Honolulu, HI 96813*).

## ACCOMMODATIONS

Oahu has a wide range of accommodations, from inexpensive hostels to high-priced luxury resorts.

Unless otherwise noted, the accommodation rates given throughout this book are the same for singles and doubles and don't include the 11.41% room tax.

### Reservations

A reservation will guarantee the specific dates for which you need accommodations. Be aware, however, that most reservations require deposits. Once you have either sent a deposit or guaranteed it with a credit card, there may be restrictions on getting a refund if you change your mind.

Many B&Bs, hotels and condominiums will only refund your money if they receive your cancellation a set number of days in advance; three days for a hotel and 30 days for other accommodations is typical, but this varies widely among places. Some places may issue only a partial refund, and in some cases, you may forfeit your entire deposit altogether. Be sure to clearly establish the cancellation policies and other restrictions before making a deposit.

### Camping

Camping is allowed at numerous county beach parks, one botanical garden and four state parks. There are, however, no full-service private camping grounds of the Kampgrounds Of America (KOA) type that are popular on the US mainland. Although Oahu's camping grounds are fairly well spread around the island, none of them are in Waikiki or the central Honolulu area.

All county and state camping grounds on Oahu are closed on Wednesday and Thursday nights, ostensibly for maintenance, but also to prevent permanent encampments by the homeless.

Camping grounds are at their busiest on weekends, particularly three-day holiday weekends, and throughout the summer, as those are the times Hawaii residents are most apt to camp.

Although thousands of visitors use these camp sites each year without incident, rip-offs are not unknown, especially at roadside camping grounds, so keep an eye on your belongings. Because of turf issues and an undercurrent of resentment by some residents against outsiders, camping along the Waianae Coast is not recommended for nonresidents.

**State Parks** Oahu has four state parks: Sand Island State Recreation Area and Keaiwa Heiau State Recreation Area, on the outskirts of Honolulu, and Malaekahana State Recreation Area and Kahana Valley State Park on the Windward Coast.

State parks require a permit to camp, which costs $5 per night per site. Camping is limited to five nights per month in each park. Another camping permit for the same park will not be issued until 30 days have elapsed.

Permit applicants must be at least 18 years old and provide their address and phone number as well as an identification number (driver's license, passport or Social Security number) for each camper in the group.

Permit applications can be made no more than 30 days before the first camping date. As permits are issued on a first-come, first-served basis, it's best to apply as soon as possible; if you have a change of plans, be sure to cancel so that other campers get a chance to use the space.

Applications may be made by phone, mail or in person to the **Division of State Parks** (☎ *587-0300; Room 131, 1151 Punch-bowl St; postal address Box 621, Honolulu, HI 96809; open 8am-3:30pm Mon-Fri*).

**County Beach Parks** Camping is free with a permit at the following county beach parks: Mokuleia and Kaiaka Bay Beach Parks on the North Shore; Hauula, Swanzy and Kualoa Beach Parks on the Windward Coast; Bellows Field, Waimanalo and Waimanalo Bay Beach Parks in southeast Oahu; and Nanakuli, Lualualei (summer only) and Keaau Beach Parks on the Waianae Coast.

Camping is allowed from 8am Friday to 8am Wednesday, except at Swanzy and Bellows Field beach parks, which are open only on weekends.

County camping permits are not available by mail but can be picked up between 7:45am and 4pm Monday to Friday at the **Department of Parks & Recreation** (☎ 523-4525; 650 S King St) in downtown Honolulu in the Honolulu Municipal Building on the corner of King and Alapai Sts.

Camping permits are also available from satellite city halls, including the one at the **Ala Moana Center** (☎ 973-2600; 1450 Ala Moana Blvd, Honolulu; open 9am-4:30pm Mon-Thur, 9am-5:45pm Fri, 8am-4pm Sat). Other satellite city halls are in **Kailua** (☎ 261-8575; Keolu Shopping Center, 1090 Keolu Drive; open 7:45am-4:30pm Mon-Fri); **Kaneohe** (☎ 235-4571; 46-024 Kamehameha Hwy; open 7:45am-4:30pm Mon-Fri); and **Wahiawa** (☎ 621-0791; 330 N Cane St; open 7:45am-4:30pm Mon-Fri).

**County Botanical Gardens** At the base of the Koolau Range, **Hoomaluhia Park** (☎ 233-7323), an inland park in Kaneohe on the Windward Coast, is unique among the county camping grounds in that it's operated by the botanical gardens division. With a resident caretaker and gates that close to noncampers at 4pm, the park is one of the safest places to camp on Oahu. Like other county camping grounds, there's no fee.

Camping is allowed on Friday, Saturday and Sunday nights only. You can get a permit in advance at any satellite city hall, or simply go to the park between 9am and 4pm daily to get a permit; if you decide to go straight to the park, call first to be sure space is available.

For more details on the botanical garden, see the Hoomaluhia Park section in the Windward Oahu chapter.

**Backcountry Camping** The state forestry division allows backcountry camping along some valley and ridge trails, including in Hauula on the Windward Coast (see the Hauula section in the Windward Coast chapter for more details).

All backcountry camping requires a permit from the **Division of Forestry & Wildlife** (☎ 587-0166; Room 325, 1151 Punchbowl St, Honolulu, HI 96813; open 7:45am-4:15pm Mon-Fri). Permits are issued during opening hours. There are no fees.

**Camping Supplies** Internal-frame backpacks and lightweight, two-person tents are rented at **The Bike Shop** (Map 3; ☎ 596-0588; 1149 S King St, Honolulu). The rate for either item is $35 for up to three days, $70 for a week.

**Omar The Tent Man** (☎ 677-8785; 94-158 Leoole St, Waipahu) rents sleeping bags or external-frame backpacks for $15 for up to three days or $20 per week, and stoves or lanterns for $14 for up to three days, $18 a week. He also rents four-person cabin-tents for $52 for up to three days, $57 a week.

## Hostels

There are two Hostelling International/American Youth Hostels (HI/AYH) hostels in Oahu: Hostelling International Waikiki in the center of Waikiki and Hostelling International Honolulu near the University of Hawaii.

US citizens/residents can join **HI/AYH** (☎ 202-783-6161, fax 783-6171; W www .hiayh.org; PO Box 37613, Washington, DC, 20013) by calling and requesting a membership form or by downloading a form from the website and mailing or faxing it. Membership is free for those under 18 years of age, $25 annually for those aged 18 to 54 and $15 annually for those 55 and older.

Non-US residents can buy a HI membership in their home countries. If you do not already have a membership when you arrive, you can still stay in US hostels by purchasing 'Welcome Stamps' for each night you stay in the hostel. When you have six stamps, your stamp card becomes a one-year membership card valid at HI hostels around the world. The stamps cost $3 each but buying them allows you to stay at the hostel members' rate, which is $3 less than nonmembers are charged. You receive a stamp for each night you stay.

In addition to the two HI hostels, there are a number of private businesses providing hostel-like dorm accommodations around

Waikiki. These make finding a cheap place to crash much easier than it has been in days past. Most of these places occupy older apartment buildings; some have a cluster of units, while others have taken over a whole complex. They all cater to backpackers and draw a fairly international crowd. There are no curfews or other restrictions, except that to avoid taking on local boarders, some places occasionally require travelers to show a passport or an onward ticket.

Despite the 'hostel' in their names, these private businesses are not members of the HI association, and in most cases, visitors should expect lower standards than those found in US mainland or European hostels.

Hosteling is a very fluid scene on Oahu. There are few businesses in Hawaii that change as quickly – a change in management can see a shabby operation become newly respectable, or a good place quickly become uninviting. All factors considered, it may be wise to avoid making a long-term commitment (advance payments typically aren't refunded) until after you arrive and have had a look around.

## YMCAs/YWCAs

Although much overlooked, Ys provide another budget accommodation option. In Honolulu, there are two YMCAs and one YWCA that provide lodgings. Unlike the hostels, these Ys are not geared solely for tourists and they offer simple, inexpensive rooms (private or semiprivate) rather than dorms. Although none are in Waikiki, the largest operation, the Central Branch YMCA, is conveniently located just outside Waikiki near the Ala Moana Center. For details, see Places to Stay in the Honolulu chapter.

One YWCA outside of Honolulu, the YWCA Camp Kokokahi in Kaneohe, also offers visitor accommodations.

## B&Bs

Oahu B&Bs are rooms in private homes (or separate units at the side of the home), not full-fledged inns with paid staff or business signs out front. There aren't many B&Bs on Oahu, largely due to strict county restrictions that make it difficult to establish new businesses and limit B&Bs already in operation to renting only two guest rooms.

Many of those that do exist are in the Kailua-Kaneohe area. B&Bs are scarce in Honolulu, although there are a few places available through reservation services, mostly in the city outskirts in areas such as Diamond Head and Manoa Valley.

Out of consideration of their neighbors and guests, B&B hosts, many of whom are often out during the day, discourage unannounced drop-ins. For this reason, B&Bs are not placed on maps in this book. Even if you're hoping to book for the same day, you'll need to call first, though same-day reservations are usually hard to get, because many places are booked weeks, or even months, in advance.

Prices are typically between $60 and $100 per room. Many require a minimum stay of two or three days.

Due to state codes that place restrictions on serving home-cooked meals, many B&Bs instead offer a continental breakfast (such as coffee, fruit, juice, bread and pastries), or provide food for guests to cook their own.

This book includes a number of B&Bs that can be booked directly, but there are others that can be booked only through B&B reservation services. The following are reputable agencies:

**Affordable Paradise Bed & Breakfast** (☎ 261-1693, fax 261-7315, Ⓦ www.affordable-paradise.com) 332 Kuukama St, Kailua, HI 96734 – Books reasonably priced B&Bs and cottages throughout Oahu

**All Islands Bed & Breakfast** (☎ 263-2342, 800-542-0344, fax 263-0308, Ⓦ www.all-islands.com) 463 Iliwahi Loop, Kailua, HI 96734 – Books host homes around Oahu, including many in Kailua

**Bed & Breakfast Hawaii** (☎ 822-7771, 800-733-1632, fax 822-2723, Ⓦ www.bandb-hawaii.com) Box 449, Kapaa, HI 96746 – One of the larger statewide services and books several places on Oahu

## Hotels

Some 90% of Oahu's 40,000 hotel rooms are in Waikiki. Unlike the other Hawaiian Islands where resort hotels are in multiple destinations, all but two of Oahu's resort hotels are found in the Waikiki and Honolulu area.

In many hotels, the rooms and amenities are the same, with only the views varying. Generally, the higher the floor, the higher the price, and an ocean view will commonly bump up the bill by 50% to 100%. If you're paying extra for a view, you might want to ask to see the room first, since Waikiki certainly doesn't have any truth-in-labeling laws governing when a hotel can call a room 'ocean-view.' Although some 'ocean views' are the real thing, others are mere glimpses of the water as seen through a series of high-rise buildings.

Most Oahu hotels now have the same standard rates year-round, but some hotels still have different rates for high and low seasons. When the latter is the case, this book gives both rates. The high season is usually December 15 to April 15, but it can vary by a few weeks in either direction, depending on the hotel. The rest of the year is the low season. Even with those hotels that don't automatically switch to a lower standard rate in the low season, bargains are the norm, with special promotions and deals popping up to fill empty rooms. During the low season, not only can the rates become cheaper, but getting the room of your choice without advance reservations is far easier as well.

In Hawaii, as elsewhere, hotels commonly undercut their standard published rates in order to remain as close to capacity as possible. Some hotels simply offer discounted promotional rates to pick up the slack, but a few of the larger chains, such as Outrigger, often throw in a free rental car. Before booking any room, it's worth asking the hotel if it's running any specials – some places actually have room/car packages for less than the 'standard' room rate!

The **Hawaii Visitors and Convention Bureau** (☎ 923-1811, 800-464-2924; e info@hvcb.org; Suite 801, 2270 Kalakaua Ave, Waikiki, HI 96815) will mail you a free annual accommodations guide that lists member hotels, addresses and prices. It includes virtually all of Oahu's top-end hotels and most of those in the moderate price range but it's a bit sketchy on the budget end of accommodations.

## Rental Accommodations

Most tourist accommodations in the Waikiki area are in hotels, not condominiums, so the sort of lease-free monthly condo rentals that are readily found in tourist locales elsewhere in Hawaii are not so easily found here.

Most condos are filled with long-term residents, but you can look in the classified sections of Honolulu's two daily newspapers (see Newspapers earlier in this chapter) to

## Travel Clubs

Travel clubs provide handsome discounts on accommodations. Essentially, hotels try to fill vacant rooms at the last minute by offering cut rates to members of these clubs. In many cases, you aren't allowed to book more than 30 days in advance and room availability is limited during the busiest periods.

Many of Hawaii's largest hotel chains, including Outrigger, participate in the two travel clubs listed below. Both clubs allow members to book hotels directly, so they're easier to use than travel clubs that act more like reservation services.

The most popular club is the **Entertainment** (☎ 800-374-4464) program, which produces an annual book to Hawaii that lists scores of hotels offering members 50% off standard hotel rates. It also includes numerous Oahu restaurants with two-for-one meals. The Hawaii book, which includes a membership card, can be ordered by phone for $46, or purchased in Hawaii at bookstores.

Another club, **Encore** (☎ 800-444-9800), offers the same 50% room discounts and a similar list of hotels as Entertainment, but the dining benefits are more marginal. Annual membership costs $69.

One important difference between the two is that Entertainment membership is valid for a one-year period beginning and ending December 1 – a problem for travelers who arrive in November and stay into December. Encore, on the other hand, is valid for 12 months from the time you enrol.

Keep in mind that the number of businesses participating in these programs varies significantly with the economy. When hotel occupancy is low, participation booms, and when the economy is brisk, more businesses pull out of the clubs or add restrictions.

Certainly these clubs work best for those who visit Hawaii for longer periods of time and have flexibility with hotel preferences and dates.

Riding Oahu's big waves

CASEY & ASTRID WITTE MAHANEY

Hanauma Bay, Southeast Oahu

ANN CECIL

Sunset on Diamond Head, Waikiki

Honolulu

Aloha Tower Marketplace, Honolulu

see what's available. Just keep in mind that the vacation-rental listings can be meager, particularly in the winter season. If you're willing to sign a lease, the selection will be larger. Expect a modest one-bedroom condo to cost about $1000 a month, a studio about $800; Honolulu is one of the most expensive housing markets in the USA.

Another option is to share a house or apartment with others. Start by perusing the 'Rentals to Share' listings in the classified ads in the newspaper. Try also grocery store bulletin boards, which commonly have a notice or two posted by individuals looking for roommates. Another resource is the University of Hawaii, where there's a board listing rooms for rent in shared student households.

## FOOD

Eating in Oahu can be a real treat, since the island's ethnic diversity gives rise to hundreds of different cuisines. You can find every kind of Japanese food, an array of regional Chinese cuisines, spicy Korean specialties, native Hawaiian dishes and excellent Thai and Vietnamese food.

Generally, the best inexpensive food is found outside of Waikiki, Oahu's main tourist area. There are good, cheap neighborhood restaurants to explore throughout greater Honolulu – two particularly rewarding locales are the Chinatown and University of Hawaii areas.

Oahu also has many upscale restaurants run by renowned chefs. Although these feature gourmet foods of all types, including traditional continental fare, the most prevalent influence is the increasingly popular style dubbed 'Pacific Rim' or 'Hawaii Regional' cuisine. This type of cooking incorporates fresh island ingredients, borrows liberally from Hawaii's various ethnic groups and is marked by creative combinations such as *kiawe*-grilled freshwater shrimp with taro chips, wok-charred *ahi* with island greens, and Peking duck in ginger-*lilikoi* sauce.

And of course there is plenty of American chain restaurants to be found throughout Oahu. There is also a scattering of nonfast-food chain restaurants such as Chili's and Sizzler steak house, but with so many good island-owned eateries, Oahu is a great place to eat local.

## Hawaiian Food

The traditional Hawaiian feast marking special events is the luau. Local luaus are still commonplace in modern Hawaii for events such as baby christenings. In spirit, these local luaus are far more authentic than anything you'll see at a commercial tourist luau, but they're family affairs and the short-stay visitor would be lucky indeed to get an invitation to one.

The main dish at a luau is *kalua* pig, which is roasted in a pitlike earthen oven called an *imu*. The *imu* is readied for cooking by building a fire and heating rocks in the pit. When the rocks are glowing red, layers of moisture-laden banana trunks and green ti leaves are placed over the stones. A pig that has been slit open is filled with some of the hot rocks and laid on top of the bed.

Other foods wrapped in ti and banana leaves are placed around it. It's all covered with more ti leaves and a layer of coconut-frond mats and topped with dirt to seal in the heat, which then bakes and steams the food. The process takes about four to eight hours depending on the size of the pig and the amount of food added. Anything cooked in this style is called *kalua*.

Wetland taro is used to make *poi*, a paste pounded from cooked taro corms. Water is added to make it puddinglike and its consistency is measured in one-, two- or three-finger *poi* – which indicates how many fingers are required to bring it from bowl to mouth, one-finger *poi* being the thickest. *Poi* is highly nutritious and easily digestible, but it's a bit of an acquired taste. It is sometimes fermented to give it a zingier flavor.

*Laulau* is fish, pork and taro wrapped in a ti leaf bundle and steamed. *Lomi* salmon (also sometimes called *lomilomi* salmon) is made by marinating thin slices of raw salmon with diced tomatoes and green onions.

Other Hawaiian foods include baked *ulu* (breadfruit), *limu* (seaweed), *opihi* (the tiny limpet shells that fishers pick off the reef at low tide) and *pipikaula* (beef jerky). *Haupia*, the standard dessert for a Hawaiian meal, is a firm pudding made of coconut cream thickened with cornstarch or arrowroot.

In Hawaiian food preparation, ti leaves are indispensable, functioning as a biodegradable version of both aluminum foil and paper plates: food is wrapped in it, cooked in it and served on it.

Because it's harder to find than other ethnic cuisines, many visitors only taste traditional Hawaiian food at expensive tourist luaus or by sampling a dollop of *poi* at one of the more adventurous hotel buffets. Still, Oahu does have a few neighborhood restaurants that specialize in Hawaiian food, including **Ono Hawaiian Food** *(Kapahulu Ave, Waikiki)*. For more information, see Places to Eat in the Waikiki chapter.

## 'Local' Food

The distinct style of food called 'local' usually refers to a fixed-plate lunch with 'two scoop rice,' a scoop of macaroni salad and a serving of beef stew, mahimahi or teriyaki chicken, generally scoffed down with chopsticks. A breakfast plate might have Spam, eggs, *kimchi* (a vegetable pickle) and, always, two scoops of rice.

These plate meals are the standard fare in diners and lunch wagons. If it's full of starches, fats and gravies, you're probably eating local.

## Snacks

*Pupus* is the local term used for all kinds of munchies or hors d'oeuvres. Boiled peanuts, soy-flavored rice crackers called *kaki mochi* and sashimi are common *pupus*.

Another island favorite is *poke*, which is raw fish marinated in soy sauce, oil, chili peppers, green onions and seaweed. It comes in many varieties – sesame *ahi* is particularly delicious and goes well with beer.

Another popular snack is crack seed, a Chinese food that can be sweet, sour, salty or some combination of the three. It's often made from dried fruits such as plums and apricots, although more exotic ones include sweet and sour baby cherry seeds, pickled mangoes and *li hing mui*, one of the sour favorites. Crack seed shops commonly sell dried cuttlefish, roasted green peas, candied ginger, beef jerky and rock candy as well.

Hawaii residents love their shave ice, a treat that's as common on the islands as ice cream is elsewhere. Shave ice is similar to mainland snow cones, only better. The ice is shaved as fine as powdery snow, packed into a paper cone and drenched with sweet fruit-flavored syrups. Many islanders like the ones with ice cream and/or sweet adzuki beans at the bottom, while kids usually opt for rainbow shave ice, which has colorful stripes of different syrups.

# DRINKS
## Nonalcoholic Drinks

Tap water is safe to drink, although some people prefer the taste of bottled water, which is readily available in grocery stores and at the ubiquitous ABC discount stores.

Cans of Hawaiian-made fruit juices such as guava-orange or passionfruit can be found at most stores. If you're touring around, you might want to toss a couple of fruit drinks into your daypack. These juices make a good alternative to sodas since they don't explode when shaken and the drinks taste good even when they're not chilled.

## Alcoholic Drinks

The minimum drinking age in Hawaii is 21. It's illegal to have open containers of alcohol in motor vehicles, and drinking in public parks or on the beaches is also illegal. All grocery stores sell liquor as do most of the smaller food marts.

Tedeschi Vineyards, a winery on Maui, makes a surprisingly good pineapple wine that can be picked up at wine shops and grocery stores throughout Oahu.

---

## Fish

Fresh fish is readily available throughout Oahu. It's generally on the expensive side at places that cater to tourists, but it can be quite reasonable at neighborhood restaurants. Some of the most popular locally caught fish include the following:

| Hawaiian Name | Common Name |
| --- | --- |
| *ahi* | yellowfin tuna |
| *aku* | skipjack tuna |
| *au* | swordfish, marlin |
| *kaku* | barracuda |
| *mahimahi* | a fish called 'dolphin' (not the mammal) |
| *mano* | shark |
| *onaga* | red snapper |
| *ono* | wahoo |
| *opah* | moonfish |
| *opakapaka* | pink snapper |
| *papio* or *ulua* | jack fish |
| *uhu* | parrotfish |
| *uku* | gray snapper |

## In Search for the Perfect Mai Tai

Sun, sand and Mai Tais: all critical ingredients for the perfect Hawaii trip. But like most other features of the islands, the drink is an import, invented by Trader Vic at his restaurant in California in the late 1940s. Like so many other things 'Hawaiian,' the drink has evolved in myriad ways from its lime-juice based original.

In the worst examples, Mai Tais combine aspects of cough syrup and bug spray (if you see a bright red maraschino cherry garnish, run!). But when a Mai Tai is good it is very, very good; flavored with fresh juices underlaid by fine rum and liqueur.

Our quest to find the best Mai Tai started on Waikiki Beach. Our low expectations and natural cynicism weren't low enough for the miserable Mai Tais we were served at the Royal Hawaiian Hotel. The hotel's beach bar calls itself the Mai Tai Bar, but it should really be the Mineral Water Bar – you'll need one to get the drink's taste out of your mouth. Orange was the predominant flavor and it wasn't good. The drinks were weak and the presentation screamed: 'Sucker!' We quickly left.

We didn't fare any better at the nearby Outrigger Reef Hotel. This Mai Tai bizarrely tasted of cola and came in a simple plastic cup.

Cynicism mounting and expectations falling even lower, we moved down the beachfront to the Sheraton Moana Surfrider – which has the same corporate roots as the Royal Hawaiian Hotel. But happily the latter's recipe *hasn't* made the trip down the beach.

Sitting under the huge banyan tree, we were served beautiful drinks with spears of sugarcane for stirrers. Fresh fruit flavors mixed with the alcohol in a concoction that was tangy and complex, not overly sweet. We were compelled to order more to confirm our findings. Better yet, the enthusiastic staff shared their recipe:

### Moana Surfrider Mai Tai
**Ingredients**
1 oz light rum
1 oz dark rum
2 oz sweet and sour mix
1 oz fresh orange juice
1 oz fresh pineapple juice
½ oz orgeat syrup
½ oz orange curaçao
½ oz rock candy syrup

Mix together, pour over rocks, garnish with fresh fruit

Sadly, we had more mediocre Mai Tais elsewhere on Oahu, most seem designed to 'shut the tourists up.' A very notable exception was served at the delightful Indigo restaurant and bar in Honolulu's Chinatown: lots of fruit juices and not too sweet.

**Ryan Ver Berkmoes**

Honolulu has a couple of microbreweries, the most popular being the waterfront Gordon Biersch, located at the Aloha Tower Marketplace. Gordon Biersch brews good German-style lagers, including both light and dark varieties.

And, of course, at every beachside bar you can order one of those colorful tropical drinks topped with a fruit garnish. Three favorites are: piña colada, with rum, pineapple juice and cream of coconut; Mai Tai, a mix of rum, grenadine and lemon and pineapple juices; and Blue Hawaii, a vodka drink colored with blue curaçao.

## ENTERTAINMENT

Oahu has a lively and varied entertainment scene, ranging from beachside hula shows and traditional Hawaiian music to theater performances and rock concerts. The vast majority of entertainment takes place in Waikiki and central Honolulu.

The best place to look for up-to-date entertainment information is in the free *Honolulu Weekly* newspaper and in the Friday edition of the *Honolulu Advertiser*. For more information, see the Entertainment sections in the destination chapters. For festivals, fairs and sporting events, see Public Holidays & Special Events earlier in this chapter.

## Luaus

Oahu's two main commercial luaus, **Paradise Cove** (☎ 973-5828; *92-1089 Aliinui Drive, Kapolei*) and **Germaine's Luau** (☎ 949-6626; *440 Olai St, Kapolei*), are both huge, impersonal affairs held nightly out in the Kapolei area. Both luaus cost around $50, which includes the bus ride from Waikiki hotels (about one hour each way), a buffet dinner, drinks, a Polynesian show and related hoopla. Children pay about half price.

A pricier, but less crowded, luau is held beachside in Waikiki at the **Royal Hawaiian Hotel** (☎ 931-7194; *2259 Kalakaua Ave, Waikiki*) on Monday; the cost is $81 for adults, $48 for children ages 5 to 12.

With all luaus, it's best to book in advance because if a large tour group arrives in town they can easily sell out.

## SPECTATOR SPORTS

Some of the most popular spectator sports in Oahu are surfing, boogie boarding and windsurfing contests, many of which command high purses and bring out scores of onlookers. By far the best is the Triple Crown of Surfing, the world's top surfing event, which takes place at Sunset Beach, Banzai Pipeline and other North Shore locales beginning in late November.

Road races also attract crowds of spectators, especially the Honolulu Marathon, which is held in mid-December and is now one of the largest marathons in the USA.

The **University of Hawaii** (☎ 956-4481) basketball, volleyball and football teams have a strong local following; call for ticket information and schedules.

The state has a winter baseball league that plays from October through December and includes players from Japanese, Korean and US minor-league baseball organizations. One of the four teams, the Honolulu Sharks, has its home field at the University of Hawaii's **Rainbow Stadium** (☎ 956-4481). Call for ticket information; schedules are printed in the sports pages of the Honolulu papers.

Hawaii does not have teams in the national football, baseball or basketball leagues, but near the beginning of February, Honolulu does host the National Football League Pro Bowl, an all-star game held at the Aloha Stadium. The island also hosts the Aloha Bowl, a nationally televised collegiate football game held on Christmas Day. For ticket information on the bowl games, contact the **Aloha Stadium ticket office** (☎ 486-9300) as far in advance as possible.

Oahu is also host to PGA events that attract top golfing pros, including the Sony Open in Hawaii, at the Waialae Country Club in Kahala in early January; the Hawaiian Ladies Open at Kapolei Golf Course in mid-February; and, on the Senior PGA Tour, the Turtle Bay Championship at the Turtle Bay Links in late September.

## SHOPPING

For many people shopping is an integral part of a vacation, and Oahu offers plenty of opportunities to rid your pockets of extra cash.

Honolulu is a large, cosmopolitan city with scores of sophisticated shops selling designer clothing, jewelry and the like. Most of the more fashionable shops are either in Waikiki or have branches there.

Of course, there are also lots of kitsch souvenir shops selling imitation Polynesian souvenirs, from Filipino shell hangings and carved coconuts to cheap jewelry and wooden tiki statues. Not surprisingly, the largest collection of such shops is in Waikiki.

In addition, Waikiki has no shortage of swimsuit and T-shirt shops or quick-stop convenience marts. The prolific ABC discount stores (34 in Waikiki at last count) are often the cheapest places to buy more mundane items such as beach mats, sunblock and other vacation necessities.

### Handicrafts

There are many fine craftspeople in Oahu and choice handicrafts are easily found around the island.

Some of the most prized items are native-wood bowls, which are often made of beautifully grained Hawaiian hardwoods, such as koa and milo. Hawaiian bowls are not decorated or ornate, but are shaped to bring out the natural beauty of the wood. The thinner and lighter the bowl, the finer the artistry and greater the value. Wood bowls can run anywhere from $100 to a few thousand dollars. If you're curious to see the various grains of different woods, there's an excellent display (not for sale) of wooden bowls in the hallway lobby of the **Outrigger Reef Hotel** (2169 Kalia Rd, Waikiki).

Oahu has some very skilled potters, many influenced by Japanese styles and aesthetics. Good *raku* work in particular can be found in island shops, and prices are generally reasonable.

*Lauhala*, the leaves of the pandanus tree that were once woven into the mats that Hawaiians slept on, are now woven into placemats, hats and baskets – all of which make long-lasting souvenirs.

For general crafts, you'll usually find the best deals at one of the craft shows that periodically take place in city parks (check the newspapers for schedules). Otherwise, there are numerous shops specializing in crafts in the Honolulu area.

## Aloha Clothing

Hawaii's island-style clothing is colorful and light, often with prints of tropical flowers.

The aloha shirt is a Hawaii creation, the product of Ellery Chun, a Honolulu tailor who created the original aloha shirt in 1931. It was influenced by two things: the baggy checkered shirts worn by plantation workers and the then-popular children's shirts made from colorful kimonos. Aloha shirts have been *the* island dress for men ever since. Today, the classiest aloha shirts are those made of lightweight cotton with subdued colors (like those of reverse fabric prints).

For women there's the muumuu, a loose, comfortable, full-length Hawaiian-style dress that, like the aloha shirts, is often made of cotton or rayon.

For new aloha clothing, there are endless shops along the streets in Waikiki. Most department stores also have aloha clothing sections. Bargain-hunters can sometimes find used aloha shirts and muumuus at thrift shops and swap meets (see the boxed text 'Bargain Hunting' in the Pearl Harbor chapter). And if you want to see the very best in antique aloha shirts, visit Bailey's Antique Shop in Waikiki (see Shopping in the Waikiki chapter).

## Jewelry

For local-made jewelry, the premium product in Hawaii is the delicate Niihau shell lei. These necklaces, made from tiny seashells that wash up on the island of Niihau, are one of the most prized Hawaiiana souvenirs. Niihauans painstakingly string the tiny shells into finely handcrafted spiral strands with intricate patterns. Niihau shell leis don't come cheap – the best pieces cost thousands of dollars and are sold at top-end jewelry stores around Honolulu. Even if you're not buying, they're fun to go and admire.

One environmental plus about Niihau shells is that they're gathered after they have completed their life cycle and not harvested live from the ocean, as are many other shell products that utilize live animals taken from fragile reef ecosystems.

Black-coral jewelry, on the other hand, is always from coral that has been harvested alive from reefs. While it is now illegal to remove these precious corals from Hawaiian reefs, black coral is still found in Hawaii jewelry shops, largely because of grandfather clauses on coral collected before restrictions went into effect. Nonetheless, it's a loophole you could drive a truck through, since there's really no way to determine when the coral was collected, and buying it just encourages more coral hunters. Foreign visitors who buy black coral may get an unpleasant shock at customs, as the importation of black coral is banned by over 100 countries.

## Music

CDs and cassettes of Hawaiian music make for good souvenirs. You'll find excellent collections of both classic and contemporary music at record shops around Oahu.

Perhaps no music seems more distinctively Hawaiian than slack-key guitar music. Some of the top names to look for in slack-key guitar recordings are Cyril Pahinui, Keola Beamer, Raymond Kane, Atta Isaacs Jr and Gabby Pahinui.

Some of the hot contemporary Hawaiian musicians with several recordings to choose from are Hapa, a duo that melodically fuses folk, rock and traditional Hawaiian elements; Daniel Ho, an accomplished guitarist and ukulele player who blends Hawaiian sounds with jazz and Asian influences; and Kealii Reichel, a vocalist who specializes in Hawaiian ballads and poetic chants.

Both Borders and Tower Records (see Shopping in the Honolulu chapter) have handy headphone set-ups available that allow you to listen to Hawaiian-music CDs before you buy.

## Food

The standard edible souvenir is macadamia nuts, either plain or covered in chocolate. But there are a large number of food products made in Hawaii, such as macadamia nut butters, *lilikoi* (passionfruit) preserves and mango chutney, that all make convenient, compact gift items.

Another popular food item is Hawaiian-grown coffee. Oahu has recently begun harvesting its own crop – Waialua coffee – but more revered in gourmet circles is Kona coffee, which is grown on the cool hillsides of the Big Island. Note that 'Kona blend' is only 10% Kona coffee – if you want the real thing, make sure it says 100%.

Pineapples are not a great choice in the souvenir department. Not only are they heavy and bulky, but they're likely to be just as cheap at home.

For those who enjoy cooking Japanese food, Hawaii is a good place to pick up ingredients that might be difficult to find back home. Most grocery stores have a wide selection of things such as dried seaweed, *mochi* and *ume* plums.

## Flowers

Beautiful, fragrant flower leis – those traditional necklaces of flowers that are used to

### Lei'd in Hawaii?

Don't assume that lovely lei draped around your neck is purely Hawaiian. Island flower growers have had such a problem keeping up with the demand for the blossoms used in leis that they now import flowers from Southeast Asia. A spurt in tourism and a decline in nursery farming has forced Hawaii lei makers to go farther afield to get at least some of their flowers. Dendrobium orchids imported from Thailand, for example, are now commonly found in leis, especially during the winter months when they become particularly scarce in Hawaii.

greet visitors – are short-lived but delightful to wear. There are numerous lei shops in Oahu, including some at the airport, several in Chinatown (where most leis are made, and the prices are generally cheaper) and in some Waikiki hotel lobbies.

Tropical flowers such as orchids, anthuriums and proteas make good gifts if you're flying straight home. Proteas stay fresh for about 10 days and then can be dried. For additional details, see the boxed text 'Agricultural Inspection' in the Getting There & Away chapter.

Foreign visitors will need to check with their airline in advance, however, as there are usually restrictions against transporting agricultural products across international borders.

# Activities

Oahu has an exhaustive variety of recreational activities available. Of course, it's a great place for most anything that has to do with the water, including swimming, snorkeling, diving, surfing, windsurfing and kayaking. But it also has good opportunities for land-based activities such as hiking, jogging, tennis, golf and horseback riding. Or, if you prefer to take to the sky, you could even try your hand at skydiving.

To avoid any unpleasant surprises, before jumping in the water make sure you take a read of Ocean Safety in the Facts for the Visitor chapter.

Oahu is ringed with white sand beaches, ranging from crowded resort strands to quiet hidden coves. The island has more than 50 beach parks, most with rest rooms and showers; about half are patrolled by lifeguards.

Oahu's four distinct coastal areas have their own peculiar seasonal water conditions. When it's rough on one side, it's generally calm on another, which means you can find places to swim and surf year round.

The south shore, which extends from Barbers Point to Makapuu Point, encompasses some of the most popular beaches on the island, including legendary Waikiki Beach. The Windward Coast extends from Makapuu Point to Kahuku Point and, true to its name, is the best side of the island for windsurfing.

The North Shore, which extends from Kahuku Point to Kaena Point, has spectacular waves in winter (from December to March) but can be as calm as a lake during the summer months (from June to September). The leeward Waianae Coast extends from Kaena Point to Barbers Point and typically has conditions similar to the North Shore with big surf in the winter but suitable swimming conditions in summer.

## SURFING

Hawaii lies smack in the path of all the major swells that race unimpeded across the Pacific, so it comes as no surprise that surfing got its start in these islands hundreds of years ago with the early Hawaiians.

Oahu boasts some 594 defined surfing sites, nearly twice as many as any of the other Hawaiian Islands. There's good surfing throughout the year, with the biggest waves hitting from November to February along the North Shore. Summer swells, which break along the south shore, are usually not as frequent and not nearly as large as the northside winter swells.

Oahu's North Shore not only lays claim to Hawaii's top surf action but also plays host to some of the world's top surfing competitions. The winter swells at Waimea, Sunset Beach and the Banzai Pipeline can bring in towering 30ft waves, creating the conditions that legends are made of. The other hot winter surf spot is at Makaha Beach on the Waianae Coast.

In summer, when the south shore sees its finest surfing waves, Waikiki and Diamond Head have some of the best breaks.

If you're looking for gentle breaks, Waikiki is a good spot during the winter months.

Oahu has two telephone services that are geared to surfers. The **Surf News Network** (☎ 596-7873) has a recorded surf line, updated several times a day, reporting on winds, wave heights and tides. The **National Weather Service** (☎ 973-4383) also provides recorded tide and surf conditions.

You'll find the knockout website **Hawaii Surfing News** (W *www.holoholo.org/surf news*) is brimming with everything from surf conditions to upcoming surfing events.

## The First Surfers

Surfing is a Hawaiian creation that was as popular in pre-colonial Hawaii as it is today. When the waves were up, everyone was out. There were royal surfing grounds and spots for commoners as well. There were even coastal temples where Hawaiians paid their respects to the surfing gods before hitting the waves.

Boards used by commoners were made of breadfruit or koa wood and were about 6ft long. Only the *alii* were free to use the long *olo* boards, which were up to 16ft in length and made of *wiliwili*, the lightest of native woods. The boards were highly prized possessions and were carefully wrapped in tapa cloth and suspended from the ceilings of homes.

## Lessons & Rentals

The county's **Haleiwa Surf Center** (☎ 637-5051; Haleiwa Alii Beach Park, Haleiwa) on the North Shore, holds free surfing lessons from 9am to 11am on Saturday and Sunday mornings between September and April. Surfboards are provided – all you need to bring is a swimsuit and sunscreen!

**Surf-N-Sea** (☎ 637-9887; 62-595 Kamehameha Ave, Haleiwa) rents surfboards for $5 for the first hour, $3.50 each additional hour, or $24 a day. In addition, Surf-N-Sea gives two-hour surfing lessons for $65, including board rental. It also sells new and used surfboards.

**Planet Surf** (☎ 638-5060; cnr Pupukea Rd & Kamehameha Hwy, Waimea), opposite Pupukea Beach Park, rents surfboards for $17 to $20 per 24 hours.

In Waikiki, surfing lessons can be arranged from the beach concession stands at Kuhio Beach Park. The going rate for a private one-hour lesson is $40; the cost drops to $30 per person if there are two or more people. The Waikiki concession stands also rent surfboards for around $8 an hour or $25 a day.

**Go Nuts Hawaii** (☎ 926-3367; 159 Kaiulani Ave, Waikiki) also rents surfboards for $17 to $20 per 24 hours.

## BODYSURFING

Bodysurfing is the technique of surfing a wave without a board, using only your body for the ride. With larger, offshore breaks, the arms are typically kept at the sides of the body, while with steep shore breaks, usually at least one arm is held out in front for control.

The island's two hottest (and most dangerous) spots for expert bodysurfers are Sandy Beach Park and Makapuu Beach Park, both in southeastern Oahu. Other top shore breaks are at Makaha on the Waianae Coast; Waimea Bay on the North Shore; Kalama Beach in Kailua; and Pounders in Laie on the Windward Coast.

Waimanalo Beach Park and nearby Bellows Field Beach Park, on the Windward Coast, have gentle shore breaks good for beginner bodysurfers.

## BOOGIE BOARDING

In boogie boarding, you ride the waves with your upper body supported by a foam board

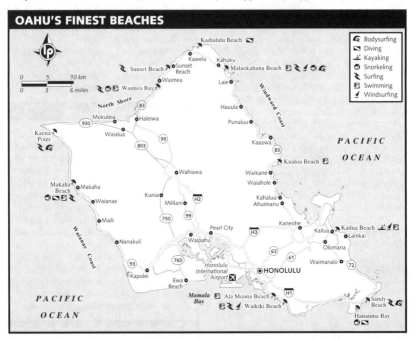

that's a couple of feet long, with your lower body trailing in the water. A very popular boogie boarding spot is the Kapahulu Groin in Waikiki.

When both bodysurfing and boogie boarding, donning a pair of fins (flippers) can provide an added measure of propulsion.

## Rentals

If you're going to be doing much boogie boarding, you may be better off buying your own board. However, there are plenty of places to rent them.

The concession stands on Waikiki Beach generally charge about $6 an hour, or $20 a day for boogie board rentals.

On the North Shore, **Planet Surf** (☎ 638-5060; cnr Pupukea Rd & Kamehameha Hwy, Waimea), opposite Pupukea Beach Park, rents boogie boards for $10 a day.

In Haleiwa, **Surf-N-Sea** (☎ 637-9887; 62-595 Kamehameha Ave, Haleiwa) rents boogie boards for $4 for the first hour, $3 for each additional hour.

**Kailua Sailboards & Kayaks** (☎ 262-2555; 130 Kailua Rd, Kailua), in the Kailua Beach

---

## Oahu's Top Beaches

The following are a dozen of the island's top beaches:

**Waikiki Beach** (p139) Oahu's most touristy beach, brimming with activity. Not only is there good swimming, but you can also take surfing lessons from former pros, rent all sorts of watersports gear, ride an outrigger canoe or join a sunset sail. And if you're into people-watching, this is the hottest spot west of Rio.

**Ala Moana Beach** (p111) This long, uncrowded beach is Oahu's favorite for swimming laps. It's also a great place to escape the tourist crowd and go local...yet it's just a mile beyond Waikiki.

**Hanauma Bay** (p169) Yes, there are too many people in the water, and yes, they stir up the sand and cut visibility, but go anyway, as it's for good reason everyone's here. The fish are plentiful, colorful and in-your-face-close, making this Oahu's top snorkeling spot. It's also a good place for diving.

**Sandy Beach** (p170) It's long, glorious and – you bet – sandy! Sandy Beach also boasts the most challenging shore break on Oahu, making it the top beach for advanced bodysurfers. In addition, there's good board surfing when the swells are big.

**Kailua Beach** (p177) Not only is this gorgeous sandy beach the island's top windsurfing destination, but it's also the best place for ocean kayaking. Even for novices it's easy, and you can rent equipment and get lessons for both sports right on the beach.

**Kualoa Beach** (p185) Arguably Oahu's most scenic beach, Kualoa is backed by precipitous green mountains and overlooks an ancient

Hawaiian fishpond. It's a good beach for kids, with shallow waters and safe swimming.

**Malaekahana Beach** (p190) Not only does this lovely beach have good year-round swimming, but it's also popular with families because of its wide range of water activities, including bodysurfing, board surfing, windsurfing and snorkeling. It's also an ideal beach for camping.

**Kaihalulu Beach** (p194) Looking for seclusion? You'll find it at this remote gem on Oahu's northern tip. It's a great place for beachcombing, long walks and basking in the sun. It can also be a fun diving spot when the seas are calm.

**Sunset Beach** (p195) Home to the Triple Crown of Surfing, this beach is synonymous with monstrous winter waves. It's also a good party beach and a great place to catch – yeah, you guessed it – the sunset.

**Waimea Bay** (p198) Here's a beach with a split personality. In winter, it has awesome surf fit for daredevils, while in summer it mellows out to swimming-pool calm good for snorkeling and swimming.

**Kaena Point** (p218) This remote beach – at the end of the road on the Waianae Coast – is a great place for winter whale-watching. The 2½-mile trail around Oahu's westernmost tip makes this the island's best hiking beach as well.

**Makaha Beach** (p215) The best winter surfing on the leeward side of the island can be found off this splendid beach. In summer, there's good snorkeling, diving and swimming.

Center, rents boogie boards for $12 for half a day.

## DIVING

Hawaiian waters offer good year-round diving. There's excellent visibility, with water temperatures ranging from 72°F to 80°F.

The marine life around the islands is superb. Almost 700 fish species live in Hawaiian waters, and nearly one-third of those are not found anywhere else in the world. In addition to colorful tropical fish, divers often see spinner dolphins, green sea turtles, manta rays and moray eels. There are also all sorts of hard and soft corals, waving anemones, sea urchins, sponges and shellfish. Because of their volcanic origins, the Hawaiian Islands harbor underwater caves, canyons and steep vertical walls.

Oahu's top summer dive spots include the caves and ledges at Three Tables and Shark's Cove in Waimea on the North Shore and the Makaha Caverns off Makaha Beach on the Waianae Coast. On the south shore, Hanauma Bay has calm diving conditions most of the year. There are a number of other popular dive spots between Hanauma and Honolulu that provide good winter diving. Two-tank dives for certified divers average $90.

If you want to experience diving for the first time, some of the dive operators offer a short beginner's 'try scuba' course for nondivers, which includes a brief instruction, followed by a shallow beach or boat dive. The cost generally ranges from $75 to $100, depending upon the operation and whether a boat is used.

For those who want to jump into the sport wholeheartedly, a number of shops offer full, open-water PADI certification courses, which can sometimes be completed in as

little as three days and cost around $400. If you're staying in Waikiki, many dive shops will provide transportation from your hotel.

There are numerous dive shops on Oahu. The following shops are all five-star PADI operations:

**Aaron's Dive Shop** (☎ 262-4158, e aarons@ aloha.com) 307 Hahani St, Kailua
**Breeze Hawaii Diving Adventure** (☎ 735-1857, e aloha@breezehawaii.com) 3014 Kaimuki Ave, Honolulu
**Dive Authority-Honolulu** (☎ 596-7234) 333 Ward Ave, Honolulu
**Hawaiian Island Aquatics** (☎ 622-3483) 1640 Wilikina Drive, Wahiawa
**Ocean Concepts** (☎ 696-7200, e ocw@ocean concepts.com) 85-371 Farrington Hwy, Waianae
**See In Sea Scuba** (☎ 528-2311, e info@diveha waii.com) 670 Auhai St, Honolulu
**South Sea Aquatics** (☎ 922-0852, e ssa@ aloha.net) 2155 Kalakaua Ave, Honolulu
**Waikiki Diving Center** (☎ 922-2121, e info@ waikikidiving.com) 424 Nahua St, Honolulu

## SNORKELING

Donning a mask and snorkel allows you to turn the beach into an underwater aquarium, offering a view of coral gardens and abundant reef fish.

Hawaii's nearshore waters harbor hundreds of kinds of tropical fish. Expect to see large rainbow-colored parrotfish munching coral on the sea floor, schools of silver needlefish glimmering near the surface, as well as brilliant yellow tangs, odd-shaped filefish, ballooning pufferfish and an assortment of butterfly fish.

Because of all the action in the water, Waikiki Beach is not a particularly good place for snorkeling – Sans Souci Beach, on Waikiki's eastern side, is the best bet as it still has some coral.

However, just a short bus ride from Waikiki is scenic Hanauma Bay in southeastern Oahu, the island's most frequented year-round snorkeling spot. At Hanauma Bay there are thousands of brilliant tropical fish near the beach on the inside of the reef, which is why the place gets packed with visitors. On the down side, because of the heavy use, Hanauma Bay's inner reef, which is in shallow water, has very little live coral left. The less frequented ocean side of the reef, which can be reached through a narrow

Moorish idol fish

## Considerations for Responsible Diving

The popularity of diving is placing immense pressure on many sites. Please consider the following tips when diving and help preserve the ecology and beauty of reefs:

• Avoid touching living marine organisms with your body or dragging equipment across the reef. Polyps can be damaged by even the gentlest contact. Never stand on corals, even if they look solid and robust. If you must hold onto the reef, only touch exposed rock or dead coral.

• Be conscious of your fins (flippers). Even without contact, the surge from heavy fin strokes near the reef can damage delicate organisms. When treading water in shallow reef areas, take care not to kick up clouds of sand. Settling sand can easily smother the delicate organisms of the reef.

• Practise and maintain proper buoyancy control. Major damage can be done by divers descending too fast and colliding with the reef.

• Make sure you are correctly weighted and that your weight belt is positioned so that you stay horizontal. If you have not dived for a while, have a practice dive in a pool before taking to the reef. Be aware that buoyancy can change over the period of an extended trip: initially you may breathe harder and need more weight; a few days later you may breathe more easily and need less weight.

• Take great care in underwater caves. Spend as little time within them as possible as your air bubbles may be caught within the roof and thereby leave previously submerged organisms high and dry. Taking turns to inspect the interior of a small cave will lessen the chances of damaging contact.

• Resist the temptation to collect or buy corals or shells. Aside from the ecological damage, taking home marine souvenirs depletes the beauty of a site and spoils the enjoyment of others. The same goes for marine archaeological sites (mainly shipwrecks). Respect their integrity; sites are typically protected from looting by law.

• Ensure that you take home all your rubbish and any litter you may find as well. Plastics in particular are a serious threat to marine life. Turtles can mistake plastic for jellyfish and eat it.

• Resist the temptation to feed fish. You may disturb their normal eating habits, encourage aggressive behavior or feed them food that is detrimental to their health.

• Minimize your disturbance of marine animals. In particular, do not ride on the backs of turtles as this causes them great anxiety. In Hawaii, this will also subject you to stiff penalties.

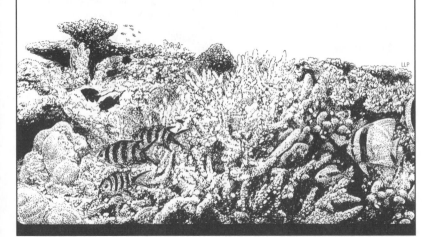

channel, has plenty of live coral and is accessible to confident swimmers.

During the calm water season on the North Shore, Pupukea Beach Park in Waimea provides excellent snorkeling in pristine conditions with far less activity than Hanauma. The catch is that Pupukea Beach Park can only be snorkeled when the waters are tranquil, which is roughly from May to October; the rest of the year the waters can be outright treacherous.

## Rentals

Some travelers cart along their own mask, snorkel and fins, but if you prefer to travel without the extra weight, these can readily be rented once you arrive on Oahu.

**Aqua Zone** (☎ 923-3483; 2335 Kalakaua Ave, Waikiki), located in the lobby of the Outrigger Waikiki hotel, rents snorkel sets for $10 a day.

**Snorkel Bob's** (☎ 735-7944; 702 Kapahulu Ave), about a mile out of Waikiki, rents snorkel sets from $4 to $9 a day, $10 to $30 a week, depending on the quality.

**Surf-N-Sea** (☎ 637-9887; 62-595 Kamehameha Hwy, Haleiwa) rents snorkel sets for $6.50 for a half day, $9.50 for 24 hours.

**Planet Surf** (☎ 638-5060; cnr Pupukea Rd & Kamehameha Hwy, Waimea), opposite Pupukea Beach Park, rents snorkel sets for $5 a day, $20 a week.

**Kailua Sailboards & Kayaks** (☎ 262-2555; 130 Kailua Rd, Kailua) rents snorkel sets for $12 a day.

If you're going to Hanauma Bay, you can rent snorkel sets at the beachside concession stand for $6 for the day.

## WINDSURFING

Oahu has lots of windsurfing activity, with some windsurfing spots ideal for beginners and other locales boasting advanced wave-riding conditions.

Kailua Bay is Oahu's top windsurfing spot. It has good year-round trade winds and both flat-water and wave conditions in different sections of the bay. The best winds are usually in summer. At that time, Kailua's predominant winds are typically east-to-northeast trades running 8 to 15 knots, though when high-pressure systems come in, they can easily double that.

Other good windsurfing spots include Diamond Head Beach, for speed and jumps;

Laie, for open-water cruising; Mokuleia Beach Park, for consistent North Shore winds; and Backyards, off Sunset Beach, with the island's highest sailable waves. In Waikiki, Fort DeRussy Beach is the main windsurfing spot.

## Lessons & Rentals

**Naish Hawaii** (☎ 262-6068, 800-767-6068; 155A Hamakua Drive, Kailua) – as in windsurfing champion Robbie Naish – has its shop in downtown Kailua, but can deliver equipment to Kailua Beach. The shop sells and rents equipment. Rental rates vary with the board and rig: beginner equipment costs $20 for two hours or $30 for a full day; intermediate and advanced equipment is $35/45 per half/full day. Naish Hawaii gives introductory group lessons for $35 for three hours. For $55 you can get a 1½-hour private lesson that includes an additional two hours of board use.

The other major player is **Kailua Sailboards & Kayaks** (☎ 262-2555; 130 Kailua Rd, Kailua), which rents beginner equipment for $29/39 per half/full day, or $160 for a week; high-performance boards cost $39/49 for a half/full day, or $199 for a week. Three-hour beginner's lessons cost $49 for a group lesson; private lessons cost $35 an hour. Kailua Sailboards & Kayaks also offers a package that includes transportation from Waikiki, lessons and gear for $69, leaving Waikiki at 8am and returning at 3pm.

The two main Kailua windsurfing shops set up vans at Kailua Beach Park from 9am to 5pm Monday to Friday and 9am to 1pm Saturday, renting boards and giving lessons.

**Waikiki Pacific Windsurfing** (☎ 949-8952), at the Prime Time Sports concession stand on Fort DeRussy Beach, rents windsurfing equipment for $25 an hour, $50 for half a day; add $15 more for an hour-long lesson.

**Surf-N-Sea** (☎ 637-9887; 62-595 Kamehameha Ave, Haleiwa), rents windsurfing equipment at $12 for the first hour and $8 for each additional hour. Two-hour windsurfing lessons are available for $65.

## KAYAKING

Ocean kayaking has become quite popular in Hawaii, spurred in part by the newer types of stable kayaks that are suitable for beginners.

On Oahu, the favorite kayaking spot is Kailua Beach, which has a couple of uninhabited nearshore islands within the reef that you can paddle to. Landings are allowed on nearby Moku Nui, which has a beautiful beach good for sunbathing and snorkeling, and on Popoia Island (Flat Island), which you can walk around. With the Kailua companies listed under Kayaking you can arrange to pick up your kayak at the beach.

Busy Waikiki is not the most ideal place for kayaking, but there are kayak rentals available right on the beach here as well. Nearby Fort DeRussy Beach has fewer swimmers and catamarans to share the water with, and makes a better bet than the central Waikiki Beach strip.

## Rentals

**Twogood Kayaks Hawaii** (☎ 262-5656; 345 Hahani St, Kailua) rents and sells kayaks. One-person kayaks rent for $25/32 per half/full day; two-person kayaks cost $32/42 per half/full day.

**Kailua Sailboard & Kayaks** (☎ 262-2555; 130 Kailua Rd, Kailua) has one- and two-person kayaks at the same rate as Twogood. In addition, it offers a $59 package that includes transportation from Waikiki plus the kayak rental and lunch, leaving Waikiki at 8am and returning at 3pm.

In Waikiki, **Prime Time Sports** (☎ 949-8952), on Fort DeRussy Beach, rents one-person kayaks for $10 an hour, two-person kayaks for $20 an hour.

## FISHING

Hawaii has excellent deep-sea fishing. Popular sport fishes include Pacific blue marlin, black marlin, yellowfin tuna, wahoo and *mahimahi*.

Charter fishing boats leave from Kewalo Basin in Honolulu and typically charge about $650 for a full-day charter that can accommodate up to six people, or $135 per person if you want to join a group. The price includes all gear, but not food or beverages. The **Hawaii Charter Skippers Association** (☎ 591-9100; e hcsa@msn.com; No 110, Kewalo Basin, 1085 Ala Moana Blvd, Honolulu) books outings on several boats.

Licenses are not required for saltwater fishing when the catch is for private consumption. There are, however, seasons, size limits and other restrictions on taking *ula*

(spiny lobster), crab, octopus (*hee* in Hawaiian, and also called *tako* or squid), *opihi* (a kind of limpet), *limu* (seaweed) and certain species of fish. Clams and oysters cannot be taken.

Also, seek local advice before eating your catch, as ciguatera poisoning (see Health in the Facts for the Visitor chapter) has become more common in recent years.

In addition to ocean fishing, the state maintains two public freshwater fishing areas on Oahu. The main one is the 300-acre Wahiawa Reservoir in central Oahu, which is stocked with largemouth and smallmouth bass, bluegill sunfish, channel catfish, *puntat* (Chinese catfish), tilapia, carp, *tucunare*, *oscar* and *pongee*. It's open year round.

Much more restricted is the Nuuanu Reservoir, which is off the Pali Hwy north of Honolulu, and is open only on selected weekends in May, August and November. Comprising about 25 acres, it's stocked mainly with channel catfish but also has *puntat* and tilapia.

Licenses, which are required for freshwater fishing, are available for nonresidents at $10 for a week or $20 for a month (free for those ages 65 and older). To obtain a fishing license, contact the **Division of Aquatic Resources** (☎ 587-0100; Room 131, 1151 Punchbowl St, Honolulu; open 7:45am-3:30pm Mon-Fri).

## HIKING

Oahu has some good hiking opportunities. Despite all the development on the island, it's surprising how much of the land is still in a natural state. There are numerous trails, including pleasant jaunts just minutes by bus from Waikiki, and backcountry hikes that are farther afield.

## Trails

The most popular hike on Oahu is the trail that starts inside Diamond Head crater and climbs three-quarters of a mile up to its summit. It's easy to reach from Waikiki and ends with a panoramic view of the city. For further details see the Diamond Head section of the Southeast Oahu chapter.

Another nice, short hike is the Manoa Falls Trail, north of Waikiki, where a peaceful walk through an abandoned arboretum of lofty trees leads to a waterfall. For further details see the Upper Manoa Valley section in the Honolulu chapter.

The Tantalus and Makiki Valley area has the most extensive trail network around Honolulu, with fine views of the city and surrounding valleys. Amazingly, though it's just 2 miles above the city hustle and bustle, this lush forest reserve is unspoiled and offers quiet solitude. For more details see Tantalus & Makiki Heights in the Honolulu chapter.

At Keaiwa Heiau State Park, northwest of Honolulu, the Aiea Loop Trail leads 4½ miles along a ridge that offers views of Pearl Harbor, Diamond Head and the Koolau Range. For additional details on this park, see the Pearl Harbor chapter.

On the westernmost point of Oahu, there's the Kaena Point Trail, a scenic coastal hike through a natural area reserve. It's the most popular hike in that area, but there are also inland forestry trails nearby. For details see Kaena Point State Park in the Waianae Coast chapter.

On Oahu's windward side, a pleasant hour-long hike leads out to Makapuu lighthouse (see the Southeast Oahu chapter for details), and there's another easy coastal trail at Kahana Valley State Park (see the Windward Coast chapter). For a hardier walk on the Windward Coast, there are two forestry trails in the Hauula area, the most popular being the 2½-mile Hauula Loop Trail, which offers nice views of both the coast and forest. For details see Hauula in the Windward Coast chapter.

In addition, there are short walks from the Nuuanu Pali Lookout and at Hoomaluhia Park in Kaneohe; see the Pali Hwy and Kaneohe sections of the Windward Coast chapter for details.

## Guided Hikes

Notices of hiking club outings are generally listed in the Friday editions of the *Honolulu Star-Bulletin* and *Honolulu Advertiser*

By joining one of these outings, you get to meet and hike with ecology-minded islanders. It may also be a good way to get to the backwoods if you don't have a car, as they often share rides. Wear sturdy shoes and, for the longer hikes, bring lunch and water.

Naturalists from the **Hawaii Nature Center** (☎ 955-0100; 2131 Makiki Heights Drive, Honolulu), at the Makiki Forest baseyard in

Honolulu's Tantalus and Makiki Valley area, lead hikes on either Saturday or Sunday, most weekends. Trails range from short walks of a mile or two, geared for families, to strenuous all-day hikes suitable for fit adults only. The cost is $8 for nonmembers. Reservations are required.

The **Sierra Club** (☎ 538-6616; Box 2577, Honolulu, HI 96803) leads hikes and other outings on Saturday and Sunday. These range from easy 2-mile hikes to strenuous 10-mile treks. Most outings meet at 8am at the Church of the Crossroads (Map 4), 2510 Bingham St, Honolulu. The hike fee is $3.

The **Hawaii Audubon Society** (☎ 528-1432; 850 Richards St, Honolulu) leads birdwatching hikes once a month, usually on a weekend. The suggested donation is $2. Binoculars, and a copy of *Hawaii's Birds*, which is readily available in bookstores, are recommended.

The **Hawaiian Trail & Mountain Club** (Box 2238, Honolulu, HI 96804) has guided hikes every weekend, although some are for members only. The hike fee is $3. Hikes generally range from 3 to 12 miles and cover the full gamut from novice to advanced in level of difficulty. For a copy of their hiking schedule, send a stamped, self-addressed envelope to the club.

## Safety Tips

Some of Oahu's hiking trails take you into steep, narrow valleys with gullies that require stream crossings. The main rule to remember is if the water begins to rise, it's not safe to cross, as a flash flood may be imminent.

Flash floods give little warning. Hikers caught in them have reported hearing a sudden loud crack and then seeing a wall of water pour down the stream bed, leaving just seconds to reach higher ground. If the water starts to rise or you hear a rumbling, get up on a bank immediately and wait it out. Don't try to cross the stream if the water reaches above your knees.

Other than flash floods, landslides and falling rocks are the biggest dangers on trails. Be wary of swimming under high waterfalls, as rocks can dislodge from the top, and be careful on the edge of steep cliffs, since cliffside rock in Hawaii tends to be crumbly.

Darkness sets in soon after sunset in Hawaii, and ridge-top trails are not the place to be caught unprepared. It's a good idea to carry a flashlight when you're hiking, just in case.

Long pants will protect your legs from the overgrown parts of the trail, and sturdy footwear with good traction is advisable. Hawaiian trails tend to be quite slippery when wet, so a walking stick always makes a good companion.

Oahu has no snakes, no poison ivy, no poison oak and few dangers from wild animals. There's a slim possibility of meeting up with a large boar in the backwoods, but they are unlikely to be a problem unless cornered.

## WALKING TOURS

Details of suggested self-guided walking tours are provided in the Waikiki, and Honolulu and Chinatown chapters of this book. In addition, there are a handful of cultural groups that offer insightful guided walking tours in these areas.

The **Waikiki Historic Trail** (☎ 841-6422) tours are free, fun and easy to join. It is not complicated – you just show up at 9am any weekday at the Duke Kahanamoku statue at Kuhio Beach Park. Led by native Hawaiian guides, the 90-minute tour is an easy stroll that emphasizes the history of Waikiki and tales of Princess Kaiulani, Prince Kuhio and other Hawaiian royalty who lived and played here a century ago.

There are a couple of organizations providing walking tours of Chinatown, which are peppered with historical insights on this intriguing part of town. With each organization, there's a $5 fee to join the tour, and there's no need for reservations.

The **Hawaii Heritage Center** (☎ 521-2749) leads walking tours of Chinatown from 9:30am to 11:30am Friday. Meet on the sidewalk in front of **Ramsay Galleries** (1128 Smith St, Honolulu).

The **Chinese Chamber of Commerce** (☎ 533-3181; 42 N King St, Honolulu) leads walking tours of Chinatown from 9:30am to noon on Tuesday for $5. Meet at the chamber office.

The **Mission Houses Museum** (☎ 531-0481; 553 S King St, Honolulu), in downtown Honolulu, offers a two-hour guided walk of the capital area, with commentary on the many period buildings and pivotal historical events that took place in this neighborhood. Walks leave from the museum at 10am

Thursday. The cost is $20, but that also includes admission to the museum.

## GOLF

A lot of turf on Oahu has been given over to the creation of golf courses. At last count, the island had a total of 37 courses – six municipal, seven military and 24 others that are either resort, public, private or semi-private courses.

These range from unpretentious municipal courses with affordable fees and relaxed settings to members-only private country clubs with resident pros and ultramanicured surroundings. For the best values head to the municipal courses.

## Municipal Courses

Of Oahu's six municipal golf courses, five have 18 holes. Greens fees at these courses are $42 per person, plus an optional $16 for a gas-powered cart. The fee for the other municipal golf course, the nine-hole course at Kahuku, is $10 per person, and it's a walking-only course.

The **reservation system** (☎ 296-2000) is the same for all municipal courses: call it and key information into the recorded system as prompted. The earliest bookings are taken just three days in advance for visitors and one week in advance for resident golfers.

The only municipal course near Waikiki is the Ala Wai Golf Course, which lays claim to being the 'busiest in the world.' Local golfers who are allowed to book earlier in the week usually take all the starting times, leaving none for visitors. However, visiting golfers who don't mind a wait may show up at the Ala Wai Golf Course window and get on the waiting list; as long as the entire golfing party waits at the course, they'll usually get you on before the day is over. If you come without clubs, you can rent them for about $25 at the 18-hole courses and $12 at Kahuku.

The following is a list of Oahu's municipal courses:

**Ala Wai Golf Course** (☎ 733-7387) Kapahulu Ave, Waikiki – Inland of the Ala Wai Canal; 18 holes, par 70

**Ewa Villages Golf Course** (☎ 681-0220) 91-1760 Park Row St, Ewa – 18 holes, par 72

**Kahuku Golf Course** (☎ 293-5842) South Golf Course Rd, Kahuku – Only 9 holes, par 35, no carts

**Pali Golf Course** (☎ 266-7612) 45-050 Kame-hameha Hwy, Kaneohe – 18 holes, par 72
**Ted Makalena Golf Course** (☎ 675-6052)
Waipio Point Access Rd, Waipahu – 18 holes, par 71
**West Loch Golf Course** (☎ 675-6076) 91-1126 Okupe St, Ewa Beach – 18 holes, par 71

## Non-Municipal Courses

All of the following courses are par 72, 18-hole courses unless noted otherwise. The regular rates are given, but there are often generous discounts if you're staying at one of the resort hotels affiliated with a course, or if you simply tee off at other than prime time. Rates at these courses include use of an electric cart.

**Makaha Valley Country Club** (☎ 695-9578; 84-627 Makaha Valley Rd, Makaha) is a great choice if you want to go local. The course can be tough in spots, but it offers great views of the Waianae Range and the coast. Greens fees are $100, but if you have a US driver's license it drops to $65.

**Koolau Golf Course** (☎ 236-4653; 45-550 Kionaole Rd, Kaneohe), named the number one course on Oahu by *Golf Digest*, is the most challenging course on the island. It may well be the most scenic too, nestled at the foot of the lush Koolau Range. Greens fee are $150.

**Waikele Golf Club** (☎ 676-9000; 94-200 Paioa Place, Waipahu) was designed by renowned golf course architect Ted Robinson, who did a masterful job incorporating the ridge and ocean views with the rolling fairways. Greens fee are $130.

**Turtle Bay Resort Golf Club** (☎ 293-8574; Turtle Bay Hilton, Kahuku) is an unbeatable choice for being right on the water. There are two adjacent courses here with a total of 27 holes. The more challenging side is the 18-hole Palmer Course, which was designed by golf pro Arnold Palmer and hosted the Senior PGA Tour in 2001. Greens fee are $140.

**Ko Olina Golf Club** (☎ 676-5300; 92-1220 Aliinui Drive, Ewa Beach), one of Oahu's newest resort courses, opened in 1990 and has already hosted both an LPGA Tour and a senior PGA Tour. It's well suited to golfers of all levels. Greens fees are $165.

## TENNIS

Oahu has 182 county tennis courts throughout the island. If you're staying in Waikiki, the most convenient locations are the 10 lighted courts at **Ala Moana Beach Park**; the 10 unlighted courts at the **Diamond Head Tennis Center**, at the Diamond Head end of Kapiolani Park; and the four lighted **Kapiolani Park** courts, opposite the Waikiki Aquarium. Court time at these county facilities is free and on a first-come, first-served basis.

If you're up in Kahuku, the **Turtle Bay Resort** (☎ 293-8811; 57-091 Kamehameha Hwy, North Shore) has 10 courts and charges $12 per person per day, with one-hour playing time guaranteed. The resort also has a pro shop and gives lessons.

## CYCLING

Cycling is gradually becoming more mainstream on Oahu. The county publishes a nifty free 'Bike Oahu' map that shows which roads are suitable for novice and experienced cyclists. All public buses now have bike racks, making it easy to head out one way by bike, and return by bus.

Although cycling along roads isn't a problem – other than traffic and the shortage of bike lanes – getting off the beaten path is a bit more complicated, since access to public forests and trails is limited.

On densely populated Oahu, mountain bikers are often pitted against hikers, and access issues are still in the formative stage. For instance, bikes have been banned from the off-road Tantalus trails, Honolulu's main forest trail network, because tire tracks were causing trail erosion. Although the Tantalus trails are closed to cyclists, the paved Tantalus Drive, which is also open to vehicle travel, remains a popular biking route.

One excellent forest trail that is open to mountain bikers is the Maunawili Trail, a scenic 10-mile trek that connects the mountain crest at the Nuuanu Pali Lookout with Waimanalo on the Windward Coast. For details on the Maunawili Trail, see The Pali Hwy in the Windward Coast chapter.

The nonprofit **Hawaii Bicycling League** (☎ 735-5756; w www.hbl.org) holds bike rides around Oahu nearly every Saturday and Sunday, ranging from 10-mile jaunts to 60-mile treks. Some outings are geared strictly to road travel and others include off-road sites. Rides are free and open to the public; the main requisite is that helmets are worn.

For information on getting around Oahu by bike, including bicycle rentals and where to pick up cycle maps, see Bicycle in the Getting Around chapter.

## JOGGING

Islanders are big on jogging. In fact, it's estimated that Honolulu has more joggers per capita than any other city in the world. Kapiolani Park and Ala Moana Park are two favorite jogging spots. There's also a 4.8-mile run around Diamond Head crater which is a well-beaten track.

Oahu has about 75 road races each year, from 1-mile fun runs and 5-mile jogs to competitive marathons, biathlons and triathlons. For an annual schedule of running events with times, dates and contact addresses, contact the **Department of Parks & Recreation** (W *www.co.honolulu.hi.us; City & County of Honolulu; 650 S King St, Honolulu, HI 96813)* or view the schedule on its website.

Oahu's best-known race is the Honolulu Marathon, which in recent years has mushroomed into the third-largest marathon in the USA. Held in mid-December, it's an open-entry event, with an estimated half of the 25,000 entrants being first-time marathon runners. For information, send a stamped, self-addressed envelope to **Honolulu Marathon Association** (W *www.hono lulumarathon.org; No 208, 3435 Waialae Ave, Honolulu, HI 96816)* or download an entry form from their website. Those writing from overseas are asked to include two international response postage coupons.

The Department of Parks & Recreation holds a Honolulu Marathon Clinic at 7:30am most Sundays at the Kapiolani Park Bandstand. It's free and open to everyone from beginners to seasoned marathon runners. Participants join groups of their own speed.

The comprehensive, bimonthly magazine *Hawaii Race* (☎ 538-0330; W *www.hawaii race.com)* includes upcoming race schedules for all of Hawaii, as well as qualification details and actual entry forms for the major races. It can be picked up free in Hawaii or by annual subscription for $15/24 to addresses within/outside the USA.

## HORSEBACK RIDING

While there's no horseback riding offered in the Honolulu area, there are a couple of options on the windward side of the island.

**Correa Trails** (☎ 259-9005; 41-050 Kala nianaole Hwy, Waimanalo) offers one-hour guided trail rides along the Koolau Range, with scenic views of the ocean. The $50 fee includes free transportation to and from Waikiki. There are rides four times a day Wednesday to Sunday.

**Kualoa Ranch** (☎ 237-8515; 57-091 Kame hameha Hwy; Kualoa), opposite Kualoa Regional Park, has one-hour trail rides for $35 and 1½-hour rides for $49, along the foot of the Koolau Range. There are rides an average of four times a day.

**Turtle Bay Resort** (☎ 293-8811; 57-091 Kamehameha Hwy, Kahuku), on the North Shore, offers daily 45-minute trail rides for $35 and 1½-hour sunset rides for $65.

## SKYDIVING & GLIDER RIDES

Skydiving and glider rides are offered at the **Dillingham Airfield** (68-760 Farrington Hwy, Mokuleia) on the North Shore. Sometimes there are discounted deals, so always ask about specials and promotions.

For around $200, **Skydive Hawaii** (☎ 637-9700) will attach you to the hips and shoulders of a skydiver so you can jump together from a plane at 13,000ft, freefall for a minute and finish off with 10 to 15 minutes of canopy ride. The whole process, including some basic instruction, takes about 1½ hours. Participants must be at least 18 years of age and weigh less than 200 pounds. Arrangements can also be made to take up experienced skydivers for solo jumps. Planes take off daily, weather permitting.

**Glider Rides** (☎ 677-3404) offers 20-minute flights on an engineless piloted glider craft, which is towed by an airplane and then released to slowly glide back to earth. Flights leave daily between 10:30am and 5:30pm, weather permitting. The cost is $100 for one person or $120 for two.

**Soar Hawaii** (☎ 637-3147) generally offers the best prices for glider rides, with deals that can be as low as $35 per person for a 20-minute ride. For thrill seekers, it also offers acrobatic rides ($110) that feature barrel rolls, spirals and wingovers – a ride you won't soon forget.

## CRUISES

Numerous sunset sails, dinner cruises and party boats leave daily from Kewalo Basin, just west of Ala Moana Park. Rates range from $25 to $100, with dinner cruises averaging about $65. Many provide transport to and from Waikiki and advertise various come-ons and specials; check the free tourist magazines for the latest offers.

**Navatek Cruises** (☎ 973-1311; 500 Ala Moana Blvd, Honolulu) offers various cruise options aboard a sleek, high-tech catamaran designed to minimize rolling. Of most interest are the two-hour whale-watching cruises ($45), which operate from January to April, leaving at 8:30am and again at noon daily. The boat leaves from Pier 6, near the Aloha Tower.

A handful of small catamarans depart from Waikiki Beach, including the **Manu Kai** (☎ 946-7490), which docks behind the Duke Kahanamoku statue and charges $10 for one-hour sails. The **Mai Ta'i** catamaran (☎ 922-5665), which departs from the beach in front of the Sheraton Waikiki, offers 1½-hour sails for $20, and longer sunset sails for $30.

**Atlantis Submarines** (☎ 973-9811) has a 65ft, 48-passenger sightseeing submarine that descends to a depth of 100ft. The tour lasts 1¾ hours, including boat transport to and from the sub. About 45 minutes are spent cruising beneath the surface around a ship and two planes that were deliberately sunk to create a dive site here. Tours leave from Hilton Hawaiian Village on the hour from 11am to 3pm daily. The cost for adults is $90 for the 11am or 3pm outing, $60 for the others. The cost for children 12 and younger is $40 on all trips.

# Getting There & Away

## AIR

Honolulu is a major Pacific hub and an intermediate stop on many flights between the US mainland and Asia, Australia, New Zealand and the South Pacific. Passengers on any of these routes are usually allowed to make a stopover in Honolulu.

### Honolulu International Airport

Honolulu International is a modern airport that has been extensively upgraded and expanded. Although it can be a pretty busy place, it's not particularly difficult to get around.

The airport offers all the expected services, including fast-food restaurants, newsstands, lounges, sundry shops, lei stands, gift shops, duty-free shops and a medical clinic, which has a nurse on duty 24 hours a day.

There's a visitor information booth, car rental counters and hotel/condo courtesy phones in the baggage claim area. You can also pick up *This Week Oahu*, *Spotlight's Oahu Gold* and other free tourist magazines from nearby racks.

If you do arrive early for a flight and are looking for something to do, the free Pacific Aerospace Museum which is located in the main departure lobby, has multimedia displays on aviation.

**Money** There are **Thomas Cook** foreign exchange booths spread around the airport, including in the international arrival area *(open 5:30am-until last foreign flight arrives)* and in the central departure lobby *(open 8:30am-4:30pm)*, next to the barber shop. On the opposite side of the same barber shop is an American Express ATM that gives cash advances on major credit cards and cash withdrawals for ATM cards using the Cirrus and Plus systems. Because Thomas Cook adds on some hefty transaction fees, using the ATM may be a more economical option.

If you're in no hurry, you can avoid needling transaction fees by going to the **Bank of Hawaii** *(open 8:30am-4pm Mon-Thur, 8:30am-6pm Fri)* on the ground level of the terminal, across the street from baggage claim D.

**Baggage Storage** The airport's coin-operated lockers and its baggage storage service were shut down following the September 11 attacks on the USA because of security concerns. At the time of writing, it was not known if any storage services will ever resume, but you can contact the airport by phoning ☎ 836-6547 to get the latest information.

**Intra-Airport Shuttle** The free **Wiki Wiki Shuttle** *(6am-10:30pm daily)* connects the more distant parts of the airport by linking the main terminals with the inter-island terminals. The shuttle can be picked up streetside in front of the main lobby (on the upper level) and also in front of the inter-island gates.

### Airlines

The following airlines have scheduled flights to Honolulu International Airport: Air Canada, Air New Zealand, All Nippon Airlines, Aloha Airlines, America West Airlines, American Airlines, China Airlines, Continental Airlines, Delta Air Lines, Garuda Indonesia, Hawaiian Airlines, Japan Airlines, Korean Air, Northwest Airlines, Philippine Airlines, Qantas Airways, Singapore Airlines, TWA and United Airlines.

## Buying Tickets

There are numerous airlines that fly to Hawaii and a variety of fares are available. Rather than just walking into the nearest travel agency or airline office, it pays to do a bit of research and shop around first.

You might want to start by perusing the travel sections of magazines and large newspapers, like the *New York Times*, the *San Francisco Chronicle* and the *Los Angeles Times* in the USA; the *Sydney Morning Herald* or Melbourne's *The Age* in Australia; and *Time Out* or *TNT* in the UK.

Airfares are constantly in flux. Fares vary with the season you travel, the day of the week you fly, your length of stay and the flexibility the ticket provides for flight changes and refunds. Still, nothing determines fares more than business, and when things are slow, regardless of the season, airlines typically drop fares to fill the empty seats.

The airlines each have their own requirements and restrictions, which also seem to be constantly changing. For the latest deals, browse travel services on the Internet, visit a knowledgeable travel agent or simply start calling the different airlines and compare ticket prices.

When you call, it's important to ask for the lowest fare, since that's not always the first one the agent will quote you. Each flight has only a limited number of seats available at the cheapest fares. When you make reservations, the agents will generally tell you the best fare that's still available on the date you give them, which may or may not be the cheapest fare that the airline is currently offering. If you make reservations far enough in advance and are a little flexible with dates, you'll usually do better.

In addition to a straightforward roundtrip ticket, a stop in Hawaii can also be part of a Round-the-World or Circle Pacific ticket.

### Round-the-World (RTW) Tickets

These tickets, which allow you to fly on the combined routes of two or more airlines, can be a good deal if you're coming from a great distance and want to visit other parts of the world in addition to Hawaii.

In most cases a 14-day advance purchase is required. After the ticket is purchased, dates can usually be changed without penalty and tickets can be rewritten to add or delete stops for an extra fee. There's an almost endless variety of possible airline and destination combinations. Because of Honolulu's central Pacific location, Hawaii can be included on most RTW tickets.

British Airways (BA) and Qantas offer a couple of interesting RTW tickets that allow you to combine routes covering the South and Central Pacific regions, Asia and Europe. One version, the One World Explorer, is based on the number of continents you visit, requires traveling to a minimum of four continents and allows four stops in each continent visited; extra stops can be added for an additional US$150 each. The One World Explorer costs US$3700 in the USA, A$2999 in Australia and UK£950 in the UK.

A second, similarly priced BA-Qantas ticket is the Global Explorer, which is based instead on the total miles flown, allowing 26,000 miles of travel. The main advantage of the Global Explorer is that it allows travel on a couple of additional partner airlines, so you could, for instance, travel from Australia to Johannesburg on South African Airways, something that isn't allowed with the One World Explorer.

Although the BA-Qantas RTW tickets are among the most popular and reliable, there are many other airlines teaming up to offer similar deals. A good travel agent can advise you on what's currently available.

### Circle Pacific Tickets

These tickets allow wide-ranging travel within the Pacific Rim area, including a stop in Hawaii. They're essentially a take-off of the RTW ticket but instead of requiring you to continue in one general direction, these tickets allow you to circle back around the Pacific Rim.

Circle Pacific tickets can be with a single carrier or with two airlines linking up to allow stopovers along their combined Pacific Rim routes. Rather than simply flying from Point A to Point B, you are able to swing through much of the Pacific and eastern Asia, taking in a variety of destinations – as long as you keep traveling in the same circular direction.

Circle Pacific routes generally cost around US$2600 when purchased in the USA and A$3000 when purchased in Australia. Some Circle Pacific fares tack on an additional charge for more than four stopovers, while others, including those offered by Air New

Zealand, allow unlimited stops. The Air New Zealand Circle Pacific ticket can make for a good island-hopping itinerary, allowing travel, for instance, from Los Angeles to New Zealand, Australia and a number of South Pacific islands, with a return to the USA via Honolulu.

Another interesting variation is the Circle Micronesia pass with Continental Airlines, which departs from Los Angeles or San Francisco and combines Honolulu with the islands of Micronesia. The price depends on how much of Micronesia you opt to see. If you only go as far as Guam, it's US$1280; if you go to Palau, at the westernmost end of Micronesia, it's US$1700. The pass allows for four stops; additional stops can be added for US$50 each.

These Circle Pacific tickets have a seven-day advance purchase requirement and allow a maximum stay of six months.

**Discount Fares from Honolulu**  Honolulu is a good place to get discounted fares to virtually any place around the Pacific. Fares vary according to the month, airline and demand, but often you can find a roundtrip fare to Los Angeles or San Francisco for around US$300; to Tokyo for US$450; to Hong Kong for US$500; to Beijing, Saigon or Sydney for US$700; and to Bali for US$750.

If you don't have a set destination in mind, you can sometimes find some great on-the-spot deals. The travel pages of the Sunday *Honolulu Advertiser* have scores of advertisements by travel agencies with discounted overseas fares.

Some of the more significant travel agencies that specialize in discount tickets are:

**King's Travel** (☎ 593-4481, **W** www.reallycheap
fares.com) 725 Kapiolani Blvd, Honolulu
**Panda Travel** (☎ 734-1961) 1017 Kapahulu Ave,
Honolulu
**Royal Adventure Travel** (☎ 732-4646) 126
Queen St, Honolulu

## Travelers with Special Needs

If you have special needs of any sort – you require a vegetarian diet, are taking a baby with you or have a medical condition that warrants special consideration – you should let your airline know as soon as possible so they can make arrangements accordingly.

Remind them when you reconfirm your reservation and again when you check in at the airport. It may also be worth calling several airlines before you book your ticket to find out how each of them handles your particular needs.

Most international airports, including Honolulu International Airport, will provide an escorted cart or wheelchair from check-in desk to plane when needed, and have ramps, lifts, accessible toilets and reachable phones. Aircraft toilets, on the other hand, are likely to present a problem for some disabled passengers; travelers should discuss this with the airline at an early stage and, if necessary, with their doctor.

As a general rule, children under two travel for 10% of the standard fare (or free on some airlines) as long as they don't occupy a seat. They don't get a baggage allowance either. 'Skycots,' baby food and diapers should be provided by the airline if requested in advance. Children between two and 12 can usually occupy a seat for half to two-thirds of the full fare, and do get a baggage allowance.

## Departure Tax

Taxes and fees for US airports are normally included in the price of tickets when you buy them, whether they're purchased in the USA or abroad.

When you book flights you may notice that those with the fewest connections are often cheaper; that's due to airport fees that are charged each time you land. Typically, for each US airport you fly into, including connections and stopovers, there's an airport user fee of US$2 to US$3 tacked on to your ticket price.

There's also a new airport security tax, which was enacted after the September 11 terrorist attacks, of US$2.50 for each departure you make from a US airport, ostensibly to cover the more thorough screening given to departing passengers.

Other fees that may be added to the ticket price are a US$6 airport departure tax on all passengers leaving the USA for a foreign destination and a US$6.50 North American Free Trade Agreement (NAFTA) tax on all passengers entering the USA from a foreign country.

There are no additional departure taxes to pay when leaving Hawaii.

## US Mainland

There's a lot of competition among airlines flying to Honolulu from the major mainland cities, and at any given time, any one of the airlines could have the cheapest fare.

Typically, the lowest roundtrip fares from the US mainland to Honolulu are about US$700 to US$1000 from the East Coast and US$350 to US$575 from the West Coast. For those flying from the East Coast, there are times when it may be significantly cheaper to buy two separate tickets – one to the West Coast with a low-fare carrier such as Southwest Airlines, and then a separate ticket to Honolulu.

Although conditions vary, the cheapest fares are generally for midweek flights and have advance purchase requirements and other restrictions. They are usually nonrefundable and have hefty penalties for changes after ticketing, although most airlines make allowances for medical emergencies.

The following airlines fly to Honolulu from both the East and the West Coasts: American Airlines, Continental Airlines, Delta Air Lines, Northwest Airlines, TWA and United Airlines.

In addition, Hawaiian Airlines flies to Honoulu from Las Vegas, Los Angeles, Portland, San Diego, San Francisco and Seattle. Aloha Airlines offers flights to Honolulu from Las Vegas, Oakland and Orange County, California.

Flight time to Honolulu is about 5½ hours from the West Coast, 11 hours from the East Coast.

## Canada

Air Canada offers flights to Honolulu from Vancouver and from other Canadian cities via Vancouver. The cheapest roundtrip fares to Honolulu are around C$600 from Vancouver, C$750 from Calgary or Edmonton and C$1200 from Toronto. These fares are for midweek travel, generally allow a maximum stay of either 30 or 60 days and have advance purchase requirements.

## Australia

Qantas flies to Honolulu from Sydney or Melbourne (via Sydney, but with no change of plane), with roundtrip fares ranging from A$1199 up to A$1679, depending on the season. These tickets allow a maximum stay of 60 days.

## New Zealand

Air New Zealand has Auckland-Honolulu roundtrip fares for NZ$1599. These tickets, which have to be purchased at least seven days in advance, allow stays of up to six months; one free stopover is allowed and others are permitted for an additional NZ$100 per stop.

## South Pacific Islands

Hawaiian Airlines flies to Honolulu from Tahiti and American Samoa. From American Samoa a roundtrip fare starts at US$600. From Tahiti to Honolulu roundtrip fares begin at US$725.

For travel from Fiji, Air New Zealand offers a roundtrip ticket for US$750. Air New Zealand also flies to Honolulu from Tonga, the Cook Islands and Western Samoa, with roundtrip tickets beginning at around US$600 from Western Samoa and US$750 from Tonga and the Cook Islands.

## Micronesia

Continental Airlines has nonstop flights from Guam to Honolulu with roundtrip fares from US$900.

A more exciting way to get from Guam, however, would be Continental's Island Hopper, which stops en route at the Micronesian islands of Chuuk, Pohnpei, Kosrae and Majuro before reaching Honolulu. A one-way ticket with free unlimited stopovers is US$730 and there is no advance purchase requirement. If you're coming from Asia, this is a good alternative to a nonstop transPacific flight and a great way to see some of

### Agricultural Inspection

All luggage and carry-on bags leaving Hawaii for the US mainland are checked by an agricultural inspector using an X-ray machine. You cannot take out gardenia, jade vine or roses, even in leis, although most other fresh flowers and foliage are permitted. You can bring home pineapples and coconuts, but most other fresh fruits and vegetables are banned. Other things not allowed to enter mainland states include plants in soil, fresh coffee berries, cactus and sugarcane.

Seeds, fruits and plants that have been certified and labeled for export aren't a problem.

the Pacific's most remote islands without having to spend a lot of money.

## Europe
The most common route to Hawaii from Europe is west via New York, Chicago or Los Angeles. If you're interested in heading east with stops in Asia, it may be cheaper to get a RTW ticket (see Round-the-World Tickets earlier in this chapter) instead of returning the same way.

The lowest American Airlines roundtrip fares from London, Paris and Frankfurt to Honolulu are usually around US$1200. The best deals are for travel between Monday and Thursday. United Airlines, Delta Air Lines and Continental Airlines have a similarly priced service to Honolulu from a number of European cities.

You can usually beat the published airline fares at bucket shops and other travel agencies specializing in discount tickets. London is arguably the world's headquarters for bucket shops, and they are well advertised. Two good, reliable agencies for cheap tickets in the UK are **Trailfinders** (☎ 020-7628-7628; 1 Threadneedle St, London) and **STA Travel** (☎ 020-7361-6262; 86 Old Brompton Rd, London).

## Asia
Japan Airlines flies to Honolulu from Tokyo, Osaka, Nagoya, Fukuoka and Sapporo. Roundtrip fares vary a bit with the departing city and the season but, except at busier holiday periods, they're generally around ¥150,000 for a ticket valid for three months.

The American carriers Continental Airlines and Northwest Airlines also have several flights to Honolulu from Japan, with ticket prices that are competitive with those of Japan Airlines.

An interesting alternative, if you're only going one way, is to fly from Japan to Guam (¥74,000) and then pick up a Continental Airlines ticket that allows you to island-hop through much of Micronesia on your way to Honolulu – for around the same cost of a direct one-way Japan-Honolulu ticket.

There are numerous airlines that fly directly to Hawaii from Southeast Asia. The fares given here are standard published fares, though bucket shops in places such as Bangkok and Singapore should be able to come up with much better deals.

Also, if you're coming from Southeast Asia, tickets to the US West Coast are not that much more than tickets to Hawaii, and many allow a free stopover in Honolulu, so you might want to consider adding the US West Coast on to your Hawaii trip.

Northwest Airlines flies to Honolulu from Bangkok, Hong Kong, Manila, Seoul and Singapore. Thai Airways, Korean Air and Philippine Airlines have numerous flights between Southeast Asian cities and Honolulu. Although there are some seasonal variations, the standard roundtrip fares are about US$1000 from Manila, US$1200 from Seoul and Bangkok, US$1400 from Hong Kong and US$1600 from Singapore.

## Central & South America
Most of the flights to Hawaii from Central and South America go via Houston or Los Angeles, though a few of those from the eastern cities go via New York.

United Airlines has flights from numerous cities in Mexico and Central America, including San José, Guatemala City, Mexico City and Guadalajara. Its lowest roundtrip fare from Mexico City to Honolulu is US$900.

## Within Hawaii
There are frequent flights between Honolulu and the other Hawaiian Islands.

The two main carriers, **Hawaiian Airlines** (☎ 838-1555, 800-367-5320) and **Aloha Airlines** (☎ 484-1111, 800-367-5250), have one-way fares of US$76 to US$103 for flights between Honolulu and the major airports of Lihue (on Kauai), Kahului (on Maui) and Kona and Hilo (both on the Big Island). Roundtrip fares are double the one-way fares.

However, you can save by using discount coupons rather than full-fare tickets. Both Hawaiian Airlines and Aloha Airlines sell coupon booklets containing six tickets, each good for a one-way inter-island flight between any two destinations they serve. The booklets cost around US$400 when purchased from the airlines at the airport ticket counter. These tickets can be used by different people and on any flight without restrictions, they don't have advance purchase requirements, and you can make reservations ahead of time before buying them. You can also buy individual coupons from discount travel agencies in Hawaii for around US$60.

In addition, if you have a MasterCard or Visa credit card, you can purchase Hawaiian Airlines coupons for US$67 per ticket from Bank of Hawaii ATMs, one of which is located in the inter-island terminal at the Honolulu International Airport (across from Burger King); others are located around Hawaii at the ubiquitous 7-Eleven stores. Unlike coupon books, you can buy just a single ticket when you use an ATM. You will need to use your PIN number along with your credit card.

There are also other schemes that come up from time to time. The latest is a US$55 'flex fare' that requires a seven-day advance booking and some flexibility on the time of day you fly; unlike standard tickets, flex fares are nonrefundable and there are penalties for making changes. Always ask the airline agent what promotional fares are being offered when you call to make reservations.

## SEA

In recent years, a handful of cruise ships have begun offering tours that include Hawaii. Many of these trips are referred to as 'repositioning tours,' since they typically visit Hawaii during April, May, September and October on ships that are otherwise used in Alaska during the summer months and in the Caribbean during the winter months.

Because US federal law bans foreign-flagged ships from offering cruises that carry passengers solely between US ports, a foreign port is included on all cruise trips to Hawaii. Most of these cruises last 10 to 12 days and have fares that start at around US$150 a day per person, based on double occupancy, though discounts and promotions can bring that price down. The airfare to and from the departure point is extra.

The typical cruise ship holiday is the ultimate package tour. Other than the effort involved in selecting a cruise, it requires minimal planning – just pay and show up – and for many people this is a large part of

the appeal. Keep in mind that much of your time will be spent at sea, so you'll have notably less time on the islands than someone with a comparable-length vacation who comes to Hawaii on a flight.

Because cruises cover rooms, meals, entertainment and transportation in one all-inclusive price, they can be relatively good value. While cruises will invariably cost more than lower-end independent travel, they will not necessarily cost more than a conventional package tour that covers airfare and expenses at an upscale resort hotel.

Most travel agencies have cruise ship brochures, complete with pictures of the ships and cabins, available for the taking. Brochures can also be obtained by contacting the cruise lines directly.

**Princess Cruises** (☎ 800-568-3262) generally offers cruises that go between Honolulu and Tahiti, or between Honolulu and Vancouver, Canada. Both **Royal Caribbean Cruise Line** (☎ 800-327-6700) and **Holland America Cruise Line** (☎ 800-426-0327) typically depart for Honolulu from Ensenada, Mexico or from Vancouver. **Norwegian Cruise Line** (☎ 800-327-7030) most commonly goes between Honolulu and Kiribati. Most of the cruises include stopovers in Maui, Kauai and the Big Island.

## ORGANIZED TOURS

There are a slew of package tours available to Hawaii. The basic ones just include airfares and accommodations, and others include car rentals, sightseeing tours and all sorts of recreational activities. If you're interested, travel agents can help you sort through the various packages.

For those with limited time, package tours can be the cheapest way to go. Costs vary, but one-week tours with airfare and no-frills hotel accommodations usually start around US$550 from the US West Coast, US$900 from the US East Coast, based on double occupancy. If you want to stay somewhere fancy, the price can easily climb to double that.

# Getting Around

Oahu is an easy island to get around, whether you're traveling by public bus or private car.

Compared with mainland urban centers, Oahu's traffic is generally manageable, although in Honolulu it can get quite jammed during rush hour – weekdays from 7am to 9am and 3pm to 6pm. Expect heavy traffic in both directions on the H1 Fwy during this time, as well as on the Pali and Likelike Hwys headed toward Honolulu in the morning and away from Honolulu in the late afternoon. If you're going to the airport during rush hour, give yourself plenty of extra time.

## TO/FROM THE AIRPORT

From the airport you can get to Waikiki by local bus, by airport shuttle services, by taxi or by rental car. A taxi to Waikiki from the airport will cost about $25. The main car rental agencies have booths or courtesy phones in the airport baggage claim area.

The easiest way to drive to Waikiki from the airport is to take Hwy 92, which starts out as Nimitz Hwy and turns into Ala Moana Blvd, leading directly into Waikiki. Although this route joins more local traffic, it's hard to get lost on it.

If you're into life in the fast lane, connect instead with the H1 Fwy heading east.

On the return to the airport from Waikiki, beware of the poorly marked interchange where H1 and Hwy 78 split; if you're not in the right-hand lane at that point, you could easily end up on Hwy 78. It takes about 20 minutes to get from Waikiki to the airport via H1 *if* you don't catch traffic.

## Public Bus

Travel time between the airport and Waikiki on city bus No 19 or 20 is about an hour. The fare is $1.50. The buses run about once every 20 minutes from 5am to 11:15pm Monday to Friday, and until 11:45pm Saturday and Sunday. The bus stops at the roadside median on the airport terminal's second level, in front of the airline counters. There are two stops; it's best to wait for the bus at the first one, which is in front of Lobby 4. Luggage is limited to what you can hold on your lap or store under your seat, the latter comparable to the space under an airline seat. For more information on public buses, see the Bus section that follows.

## Shuttle Bus

A few private companies, including **Super Shuttle** (☎ 841-2928, 877-247-8737), **Reliable Express** (☎ 924-9292) and **Airport Waikiki Express** (☎ 737-7407), offer shuttle service between the airport and Waikiki hotels. The ride averages 45 minutes, but can be longer or shorter depending on how many passengers are dropped off before reaching your hotel.

Board these buses at the roadside median on the ground level, in front of the baggage claim areas. The biggest company, Airport Waikiki Express, operated by Roberts Hawaii, makes frequent rounds of the airport and picks up riders without any need for advance reservations. The other companies require advance reservations (which can be made at the courtesy phones in the baggage

## Getting Oriented

Almost all visitors to Oahu land at Honolulu International Airport, the only commercial airport on the island. The airport is on the western outskirts of the Honolulu district, 9 miles west of Waikiki.

The H1 Fwy, the main south-shore freeway, is the key to getting around the island. H1 connects with Hwy 72, which runs around the southeast coast; with the Pali (61) and Likelike (63) Hwys, which go to the Windward Coast; with Hwy 93, which leads up the leeward Waianae Coast; and with H2, Hwys 99 and 750, which run through the center of the island on the way to the North Shore.

Incidentally, H1 is a US *interstate* freeway – an amusing designation for a road on an island state in the middle of the Pacific.

Directions on Oahu are often given by using landmarks. If someone tells you to go 'Ewa' (an area west of Honolulu) or 'Diamond Head' (east of Waikiki), it simply means to head in that direction. Two other commonly used directional terms that you can expect to hear are *mauka*, meaning inland side, and *makai*, meaning ocean side.

claim area), and because of this there can be longer waits for a shuttle to arrive.

Airport Waikiki Express charges $8 one way and $13 roundtrip; the other companies charge $7 one way and $10 roundtrip. All offer discounts for children.

## BUS

Oahu's public bus system, called TheBus, is extensive and easy to use. TheBus has about 80 routes, which collectively cover most of Oahu. You can take TheBus to watch windsurfers at Kailua or surfers at Sunset Beach, visit Chinatown or the Bishop Museum, snorkel at Hanauma Bay or hike Diamond Head. TheBus is also useful for short hops, such as to get from any one neighborhood in Honolulu to another.

Some of the island's prime viewpoints are beyond reach, however. For instance, TheBus doesn't stop at the Nuuanu Pali Lookout, go up to the Tantalus green belt, or run as far as Kaena Point on the Waianae Coast.

Buses stop only at marked bus stops. Each bus route can have a few different destinations. The destination is written on the front of the bus next to the number. Buses generally keep the same number when inbound and outbound. For instance, bus No 8 can take you either into the heart of Waikiki or away from it toward Ala Moana – so take note of both the number and the written destination before you jump on.

If you're in doubt, ask the bus driver. They're used to disoriented visitors, and most drivers are patient and helpful.

Overall, the buses are in excellent condition – if anything, they're a bit too modern. Newer buses are air-conditioned, with sealed windows and climate-control that sometimes seems so out of 'control' that drivers wear jackets to ward off the cold! Currently, about half of the buses are equipped with wheelchair lifts and all have bike racks that cyclists can use for free.

Although TheBus is convenient enough, this isn't Tokyo – if you set your watch by the bus here, you'll come up with Hawaiian Time. In addition to not getting hung up on schedules, buses can sometimes bottleneck, with one packed bus after another passing right by crowded bus stops. Waiting for the bus anywhere between Ala Moana and Waikiki on a Saturday night can be a particularly memorable experience.

Still, TheBus usually gets you where you want to go, and as long as you don't try to cut your travel time too close or schedule too much in one day, it's a great deal.

### Schedules & Information

Bus schedules vary with the route; many operate from about 5:30am to 8pm, though some main routes, such as those that serve Waikiki, continue until around midnight.

TheBus has a great **telephone service** (☎ 848-5555). As long as you know where you are and where you want to go, anytime between 5:30am and 10pm you can call it, and it will tell you not only which bus to catch, but also when the next one will be there. This same number also has a TDD service for the hearing impaired and can provide information on which buses are wheelchair accessible.

You can get printed timetables for individual routes free from any satellite city hall, including the one at the Ala Moana Center (though the Ala Moana one is closed on Sunday). Timetables can also be found in the downtown Honolulu library and in Waikiki at some of the McDonald's fast-food restaurants, including the one that is on the corner of Liliuokalani Ave and Kalakaua Ave.

When you pick up the timetables, be sure to grab one of the free schematic route maps, a handy brochure that maps out routes for the entire island and shows the corresponding bus numbers. These are indespensible if you're using the bus system a lot.

In addition, local convenience shops and bookstores sell commercial bus maps and schedules for around $5. These maps focus a bit more attention on reaching the main tourist destinations from Waikiki.

### Costs

The one-way fare for all rides is $1.50 for adults, 75¢ for children ages six to 18 and for seniors 65 years and older. Children under the age of six ride free. You can use either coins or $1 bills; bus drivers don't give change.

Transfers, which have a two-hour time limit stamped on them, are given free when more than one bus is required to get to a destination. If needed, ask for one when you board.

Visitor passes, valid for unlimited rides over four consecutive days, cost $15 and can be purchased at any of the ubiquitous ABC stores.

Monthly bus passes, valid for unlimited rides in a calendar month, cost $27 and can be purchased at satellite city halls, 7-Eleven convenience stores and Foodland and Star supermarkets.

Seniors (65 years and older) and disabled people of any age can buy a $25 bus pass that is valid for unlimited rides during a two-year period. Senior passes are issued at satellite city halls upon presentation of an identification card with a birth date.

For most visitors, the most convenient satellite city hall will be the one at the **Ala Moana Center** (☎ 973-2600; 1450 Ala Moana Blvd, Honolulu; open 9am-5:30pm Mon-Fri, 8am-4pm Sat). For information on other satellite city hall locations and hours, call ☎ 527-6695.

## Common Routes

Bus Nos 8, 19, 20 and 58 run between Waikiki and the Ala Moana Center, Honolulu's central transfer point. It's hardly worth checking timetables, as one of these buses comes by every few minutes throughout the day. From Ala Moana you can connect with a broad network of buses to points around the island.

Bus Nos 2, 19 and 20 will take you between Waikiki and downtown Honolulu. There's usually a bus every 10 minutes or so.

Bus No 4 runs between Waikiki and the University of Hawaii every 10 minutes.

## CAR

The minimum age for visitors to drive in Hawaii is 18, though car rental companies usually have higher age restrictions. If you're younger than age 25, you should call the car rental agencies in advance to check their policies regarding restrictions and surcharges.

You can legally drive in the state as long as you have a valid driver's license issued by a country that is party to the United Nations Conference on Road & Motor Transport – which covers virtually everyone.

However, car rental companies will generally accept valid foreign driver's licenses only if they are in English. Otherwise, most will require renters to present an international driver's license along with their home license.

## Circle-Island Route

It's possible to make a nice day excursion circling the island by bus, beginning at the Ala Moana Center. The No 52 Wahiawa–Circle Island bus goes clockwise up Hwy 99 to Haleiwa and along the North Shore. At the Turtle Bay Resort, on the northern tip of Oahu, it switches signs to No 55 and comes down the Windward Coast to Kaneohe and down the Pali Hwy then west back to Ala Moana. The No 55 Kaneohe–Circle Island bus does the same route in reverse.

The buses operate every 30 minutes from 5am to around 11pm. If you take the Circle Island route nonstop, it takes about four hours and costs just $1.50.

For a shorter excursion from Waikiki, you can make a loop around southeast Oahu by taking bus No 58 to Sea Life Park, in the Makapuu area, and then bus No 57 up to Kailua and back into Honolulu.

As you'll need to change buses on this route, ask the driver for a transfer when you first board. Transfers have time limits and aren't meant to be used for stopovers, but you can usually grab a quick break at Ala Moana. If your transfer expires while you're exploring, you'll need to pay a new $1.50 fare when you reboard the bus.

## Driving Times

Although actual driving time varies depending on traffic conditions, the average driving times and distances from Waikiki to points of interest around Oahu are as follows:

| destination | mileage (miles) | time (minutes) |
|---|---|---|
| USS *Arizona* Memorial | 12 | 30 |
| Haleiwa | 29 | 50 |
| Hanauma Bay | 11 | 25 |
| Honolulu Airport | 9 | 20 |
| Kaena Point State Park | 43 | 75 |
| Kailua | 14 | 25 |
| Laie | 34 | 60 |
| Makaha Beach | 36 | 60 |
| Nuuanu Pali Lookout | 11 | 20 |
| Sea Life Park | 16 | 35 |
| Sunset Beach | 37 | 65 |
| Waimea | 34 | 60 |
| Waipahu | 16 | 30 |

## Road Rules

Hawaii drives on the right-hand side of the road, as does the rest of the USA.

Drivers at a red light can make a right turn after coming to a full stop and yielding to oncoming traffic, unless there's a sign at the intersection prohibiting the turn.

In Hawaii, drivers and front-seat passengers are required to wear seat belts. State law also strictly requires the use of child safety seats for children ages three and younger, while four-year-olds must either be in a safety seat or secured by a seat belt. Most of the car rental companies rent child safety seats for around $5 a day, but they don't always have them on hand so it's advisable to reserve one in advance.

Speed limits are posted and enforced. If you are stopped for speeding, expect to get a ticket, as the police rarely just give warnings.

Hawaii has the most expensive gasoline in the USA. Prices on average are about 25% higher in Hawaii than on the US mainland, and typically hover around $2 a gallon.

One item of road etiquette – horn honking is considered very rude in Hawaii unless required for safety.

## Rental

Car rentals are readily available at the airport and in Waikiki. With most companies the weekly rate works out significantly cheaper per day than the straight daily rate. The daily rate for a small car such as a Geo Metro or Ford Escort, with unlimited mileage, ranges from around $30 to $45, while typical weekly rates are $150 to $200. You're usually required to keep the car for a minimum of five or six days to get the weekly rate.

Rates vary a bit from company to company, and also within each company, depending on season, time of booking and current promotional fares. If you belong to an automobile club, a frequent-flyer program or a travel club, you'll often be eligible for some sort of discount with at least one of the rental agencies, so always ask.

One thing to note when renting a car is that rates for mid-sized cars are often only a few dollars more per week than small cars. Because some promotional discounts exclude the economy-sized cars, at times the lowest rate available may actually be for a larger car.

At any given time, any one of the rental companies could be offering the best deal, so you can save money by taking a little time to shop around. Be sure to ask the agent for the cheapest rate, as the first quote given is not always the lowest.

It's always best to make reservations in advance; with most companies there's no cancellation penalty if you change your mind. Walking up to the counter without a reservation will not only subject you to higher rates, but during busy periods it's not uncommon for all the cars to be rented out already.

On daily rentals, most cars are rented on a 24-hour basis, so you could get two days' use by renting at midday and driving around all afternoon, then heading out to explore somewhere else the next morning before the car is due back. Most companies even allow an hour's grace period.

Rental rates generally include unlimited mileage, though if you drop off the car at a location that is different from where you picked it up, there's usually a drop-off fee.

Having a major credit card greatly simplifies the rental process. Without one, some agencies simply will not rent vehicles, and others will require prepayment by cash or traveler's checks, as well as a deposit (often around $300). Some do an employment verification and credit check; others don't do background checks, but they reserve the right for the station manager to decide whether to rent to you or not. If you intend to rent a car without a credit card, it's wise to make your plans well in advance.

Most car rental agencies typically request the name and phone number of the place where you're staying. Be aware that many car rental companies are loath to rent to people who list a camping ground as their address on the island, and a few specifically add 'No Camping Permitted' to their rental contracts.

The following are all international companies that operate in Honolulu; their cars can be booked from offices around the world. The telephone numbers listed are the Oahu numbers, followed by toll-free numbers in the USA:

| Alamo | ☎ 833-4585, 800-327-9633 |
| Avis | ☎ 834-5536, 800-831-8000 |
| Budget | ☎ 537-3600, 800-527-7000 |
| Dollar | ☎ 831-2330, 800-800-4000 |
| Hertz | ☎ 831-3500, 800-654-3131 |
| National | ☎ 831-3800, 800-227-7368 |

Budget, National, Hertz, Avis and Dollar all have rental cars available at Honolulu International Airport. Alamo has its operations about a mile outside the airport, on the corner of Nimitz Hwy and Ohohia St.

All things being equal, try to rent from a company with its lot inside the airport – not only is it more convenient but, more importantly, on the way back to the airport all the highway signs lead to the in-airport car returns. Having to drive around looking for a car rental agency lot outside the airport can cost you valuable time when you're trying to catch a flight.

In addition to their airport facilities, most of the international companies have multiple branch locations in Waikiki – many in the lobbies of larger hotels. When you make your reservation, keep in mind that the best rates sometimes aren't offered at the smaller branch offices, so even if you're already in Waikiki, it might be worth your while to catch a bus to the airport and pick your car up there – especially for longer rentals or if you're planning on keeping the car until you fly out of Oahu.

## Insurance

As for car insurance, rental companies in Hawaii have liability insurance that covers people and property you might hit while driving a rental vehicle. Damage to the rental vehicle itself is not covered, unless you accept the collision damage waiver (CDW) option offered by the rental agency. This added coverage is typically an additional $15 to $20 a day.

The CDW is not really insurance per se, but rather a guarantee that the rental company won't hold you liable for any damages to their car (though even then there are exceptions). If you decline the CDW, you will usually be held liable for any damages up to the full value of the car. If damages do occur and you find yourself in a dispute with the rental company, you can call the state **Department of Commerce & Consumer Affairs** (☎ 587-1234) for recorded information on your legal rights.

If you have collision coverage on your vehicle at home, it might cover damages to car rentals in Hawaii. Check with your insurance company before your trip.

Some credit cards, including many 'gold cards' issued by Visa and MasterCard, offer you reimbursement coverage for collision damages if you rent the car with their credit card and decline the CDW. If your credit card doesn't offer this service, it may be worth changing to one that does. Be aware, however, that most collision coverage provided by a credit card isn't valid for rentals of more than 15 days or for exotic models, jeeps, vans and 4WD vehicles.

## Parking

Parking can be a challenge in Honolulu's busiest areas. In Waikiki, most hotels charge $10 to $15 a day for guest parking in their garages. However, if you're willing to go a little out of your way, you can save money. At the west end of Waikiki, there's a public parking lot at the Ala Wai Yacht Harbor that has free parking for up to a maximum of 24 hours. At the east end of Waikiki, there's a large parking lot along Monsarrat Ave at Kapiolani Park that has free parking with no time limit.

In downtown Honolulu there's metered parking along some of the major roads such as Punchbowl St, and both downtown Honolulu and the adjacent Chinatown area have several reasonably priced parking garages.

Outside of Waikiki and Honolulu, parking is generally free and, with the exception of a few popular beaches, finding a space is seldom a problem.

## MOPED

Mopeds are another transportation option, though perhaps a bit daunting for the uninitiated: You have to contend with Honolulu's heavy traffic, which presents a challenge to those unaccustomed to such conditions or to those who don't have sufficient moped experience.

State law requires mopeds to be ridden by one person only and prohibits their use on sidewalks and on freeways. Mopeds must always be driven in single file and may not be driven at speeds in excess of 30mph. In Hawaii, all mopeds are limited to a maximum 2 horsepower, 50cc. To drive a moped, you must have a valid driver's license. Hawaii residents can drive mopeds at age 15, but those with an out-of-state driver's license must be at least 18 years old.

**Blue Sky Rentals** (☎ 947-0101; 1920 Ala Moana Blvd, Waikiki), on the ground floor of Inn on the Park Hotel, is the most reliable place in Waikiki to rent a moped. The rate is $23 for eight hours, $30 for 24 hours.

## HITCHHIKING

Hitchhiking is never entirely safe in any country in the world, and Lonely Planet does not recommend it. Travellers who decide to hitch should understand that they are taking a small but potentially life-threatening risk. People who nevertheless choose to hitch will be safer if they travel in pairs, let someone know where they are planning to go, keep their luggage light and with them at all times, and sit by a door.

## TAXI

Taxis have meters and charge a flag-down fee of $2.25 to start, and from there fares increase in 30¢ increments at a rate of $2.40 per mile. There's an extra charge of 40¢ for each suitcase or backpack.

Taxis are readily available at the airport and larger hotels but are otherwise generally hard to find. To phone for one, try **TheCab** (☎ 422-2222), **Charley's** (☎ 955-2211) or **City Taxi** (☎ 524-2121).

## BICYCLE

It's possible to cycle your way around Oahu, but there's a lot of traffic to contend with, especially in the greater Honolulu area. Hawaii has been slow to adopt cycle-friendly policies – a few new road projects now include cycle lanes, but such lanes are still relatively rare.

In Waikiki, the best main roads for cyclists are the one-way streets of canalside Ala Wai Blvd and beachside Kalakaua Ave, both of which have minimal cross-traffic.

The State Department of Transportation publishes a free 'Bike Oahu' map with possible routes, divided into those for novice cyclists, those for experienced cyclists and routes that are not bicycle-friendly. You can pick up the map at the HVCB visitor information center in Waikiki and at cycle rental shops around Oahu; you can also request a map from the Bicycle Coordinator at the **City & County of Honolulu** (☎ 527-5044) or peruse the map online at W www.state.hi.us/dot/highways/bike.

If you want to take your bike out of town and want the option of taking the bus for part of the journey, all public buses now are equipped with racks that can carry two bicycles. To use the bike rack, first tell the bus driver you will be loading your bike, then secure your bicycle onto the fold-down rack, board the bus and pay the regular passenger fare. There's no additional fee for bringing your bike along.

There are a couple of rules of the road to keep in mind. Any bicycle used from 30 minutes after sunset until 30 minutes before sunrise must have a headlight facing forward, and at least one red reflector mounted on the rear. Cyclists are not allowed to ride on sidewalks within a business district, such as Waikiki or downtown Honolulu. Cyclists using a roadway have all the rights and duties applicable to motor vehicle drivers, and must travel on the right side of the road, stop at red lights, etc. The state of Hawaii does not require cyclists over the age of 15 to wear helmets, but they are recommended.

For information on bike riding with a group, see the Cycling section in the Activities chapter.

### Rental

**The Bike Shop**, which has locations in Honolulu (☎ 596-0588; 1149 S King St) and Kailua (☎ 261-1553; 270 Kuulei Rd), has good-quality bikes for $16 a day, use of a helmet is included.

**Planet Surf** at the Aston Waikiki Beach Hotel (☎ 638-5648; 2570 Kalakaua Ave, Waikiki), and opposite **Pupukea Beach Park** (☎ 638-1110) in Waimea, rents bikes for $10 a day. **Go Nuts Hawaii** (☎ 926-3367; 159 Kaiulani Ave, Waikiki) rents bikes for $15 a day. Also in Waikiki are **Blue Sky Rentals** (☎ 947-0101; 1920 Ala Moana Blvd) and **Coconut Cruisers** (☎ 924-1646; 2301 Kalakaua Ave), at the side of the Royal Hawaiian Shopping Center; both rent bicycles for $20 a day.

## ORGANIZED TOURS

In addition to the following tours, information on guided cycling and hiking tours can be found in the Activities chapter.

### Bus Tours

Because Honolulu has such a good public bus system, extensive self-touring, even without a rental car, is a viable option. However, waiting for buses and walking between the bus stops and the sights does take time, and you can undoubtedly pack much more into a day by joining an organized tour.

Conventional sightseeing tours by van or bus are offered by **E Noa Tours** (☎ *591-2561)*, **Polynesian Adventure Tours** (☎ *833-3000)* and **Roberts Hawaii** (☎ *539-9400, 800-831-5541)*.

These companies offer several different tours. Polynesian Adventure Tours, for example, has a half-day tour that includes the main downtown Honolulu sights, Punchbowl Crater and the USS *Arizona* Memorial, Pearl Harbor. It also has another half-day tour of southeast Oahu that takes in Diamond Head, Hanauma Bay, Sandy Beach, Nuuanu Pali Lookout, Queen Emma Summer Palace and Tantalus. Each of these tours costs $23 for adults, $18 for children.

The mainstay for the tour companies, however, are full-day (roughly 8:30am to 5:30pm) Circle Island tours that average $55 for adults, $30 for children. A typical tour starts out with a visit to Diamond Head Crater and a drive past the southeast Oahu sights; goes up the Windward Coast, taking in the Byodo-In temple in Kaneohe; circles back along the North Shore, stopping at Sunset Beach and Waimea Falls Park; and then drives past the pineapple fields of central Oahu on the return to Waikiki. Some tours include a visit to the Polynesian Cultural Center in Laie instead of the stop at Waimea Falls Park.

## Private Trolleybuses

There are a couple of open-air, trolley-style buses that offer service between Waikiki and Honolulu's main tourist sights. Both services run along set routes, with passholders free to jump on and off the trolley as often as they like.

The **Rainbow Trolley** (☎ *539-9495)* is both the best value and the simplest service to use. It has 25 stops in all, running from Waikiki in a loop around Kalakaua Ave, past the Honolulu Zoo and along Kuhio Ave and then continuing to the Ala Moana Center, Ward Centre, Iolani Palace, Honolulu Academy of Arts, Chinatown and the Aloha Tower Marketplace. A trolley picks up at each stop about once every 20 minutes from around 8:30am to 10pm. It costs $10/18/30 for a one/two/four-day pass for adults, $5/8/10 for children under 12 years of age.

The **Waikiki Trolley** (☎ *593-2822)* is pricier and more complicated to use as it has different routes. Its 'red line' is geared for

tourists following a beaten path around Honolulu's main shopping and sightseeing attractions. There are about two dozen stops, including the Honolulu Zoo, Waikiki Aquarium, Ala Moana Center, Honolulu Academy of Arts, Iolani Palace, Aloha Tower Marketplace, Bishop Museum, Chinatown and the Ward Centre.

There's also a 'blue line,' which goes east from Waikiki and has a more limited route than the red line, stopping at the Honolulu Zoo, Waikiki Aquarium, Halona Blowhole and Sea Life Park.

Both lines depart daily from the Royal Hawaiian Shopping Center in Waikiki; the red line leaves every 20 minutes and the blue line leaves every 40 minutes, between 8:30am and 4:30pm. One-day passes cost $18/8 per adult/child for a single line; $30/10 for both lines. Multiday passes are also available.

Always verify the frequency and schedule before handing over your money, and be sure the pass you're buying has the stops you want.

The trolleybuses can be convenient if you're sticking solely to their predetermined routes, but it's a pricey alternative to the public bus, which is fairly frequent along these routes and offers a four-day pass for only $15 (see Bus earlier in this chapter).

## Tours to the Neighbor Islands

**Overnighters** If you want to visit another island but only have a day or two to spare, it might be worth looking into 'overnighters,' which are handy mini-packaged tours to the Neighbor Islands that include roundtrip airfare, car rental and hotel accommodations. Rates depend on the accommodations you select, with a one-night package typically starting at $140 per person, based on double occupancy. You can add additional days for a fee, usually about $65 per person.

The largest tour companies specializing in overnighters are: **Roberts Hawaii** (☎ *523-9323, 800-899-9323)* and **Pleasant Island Holidays** (☎ *922-1515)*.

**Cruises** The cruise ship *Norwegian Star* is operated by **Norwegian Cruise Line** (☎ *800-327-7030)*. The *Norwegian Star* makes a seven-day tour around the Hawaiian Islands. It departs from Honolulu and visits the Big Island, Maui and Kauai before returning to Honolulu.

Cruise rates start at $779 for the least-expensive inside cabin. The fares are per person, based on double occupancy, and there's an additional fee of about $100 for port charges.

The 971ft-long *Norwegian Star* is a full-fledged cruise ship, with lavish buffet meals, swimming pools and cabin space for 2240 passengers.

For information on short cruises off Oahu's shores that are available, see the Activities chapter.

Ilima *(Sida fallax)* blossom

Female flower of the papaya plant

Banana plant, blossom and fruit

Flowers, Foster Botanical Garden, Honolulu

Sea turtles, Sea Life Park, Southeast Oahu

Hawaiian monk seal, Waikiki Aquarium

Picasso triggerfish, Oahu's state fish

Indigenous red-footed booby

# Honolulu

**pop 371,650**

Honolulu, the only major city in Hawaii, is the state's center of business, culture and politics. It's been the capital of Hawaii since 1845.

Home to people from throughout the Pacific, Honolulu is a city of minorities, with no ethnic majority. Its diversity can be seen on almost every corner – the sushi shop next door to the Vietnamese bakery, the Catholic church around the block from the Chinese Buddhist temple and the rainbow of schoolchildren waiting for the bus.

Honolulu offers a wide range of things to see and do. It boasts a lovely city beach, some good museums, elegant public gardens and an abundance of good restaurants. By and large, it's an easy city to explore. The largest concentration of historical and cultural sights are clustered in downtown Honolulu and adjacent Chinatown, which are well suited for getting around on foot.

Unlike other large American cities, Honolulu doesn't have a separate municipal government – the entire island of Oahu is governed as the City and County of Honolulu. Consequently, Honolulu's boundaries are not cut and dried. Still, the city proper is generally considered to extend west to the airport and east to Kaimuki and that's the area covered in this chapter.

Waikiki, which is at the southeastern edge of Honolulu, is covered in a separate chapter.

## INFORMATION
### Money

Banks around Honolulu include a downtown branch of the **Bank of Hawaii** *(Map 2; ☎ 538-4171; 111 S King St)*, a Chinatown branch *(Map 2; ☎ 532-2480; 101 N King St)* and a university-area branch *(Map 4; ☎ 973-4460; 1010 University Ave)*.

### Post

There's a downtown **post office** *(Map 2; ☎ 800-275-8777; 335 Merchant St; open 8am-4:30pm Mon-Fri)* in the Old Federal Building. In Chinatown, there's a small **post office** *(Map 2; ☎ 800-275-8777; open 9am-4pm Mon-Fri, 9am-noon Sat)* in the Chinatown Cultural Plaza.

## Highlights

- Joining a tour of gracious Iolani Palace, home of Hawaii's last monarchs
- Strolling among the lofty trees and rare tropical plants in Foster Botanical Garden
- Slurping a steaming bowl of noodle soup in one of Chinatown's eateries
- Visiting the excellent Hawaii State Art Museum
- Swimming and sunbathing away an afternoon at glorious Ala Moana Beach Park

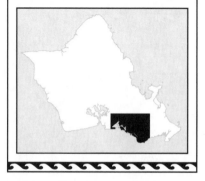

### Email & Internet Access

**Coffee Cove** *(Map 4; ☎ 955-2683; 2600 S King St; open 7am-11pm Mon-Fri, 10am-11pm Sat & Sun)*, a casual cybercafé near the University of Hawaii, has Internet access for just $1.25 per 15 minutes.

### Bookstores

A central well-stocked bookstore in the downtown area is **Bestsellers** *(Map 2; ☎ 528-2378; 1001 Bishop St)*.

There are several bookstores in the university area, including **UH Manoa Campus Bookstore** *(Map 4; ☎ 956-4338; 2465 Campus Rd)* in the Campus Center and **Rainbow Books & Records** *(Map 4; ☎ 955-7994; 1010 University Ave)*, the latter carrying both new and used books.

**Cheapo Books** *(Map 4; ☎ 943-0501; 2600 S King St)* is a great source for used titles, including hard-to-find Hawaiiana and comics. In an adjoining store, it also has CDs and a large selection of rare Hawaiian music.

# MAP 1 GREATER HONOLULU

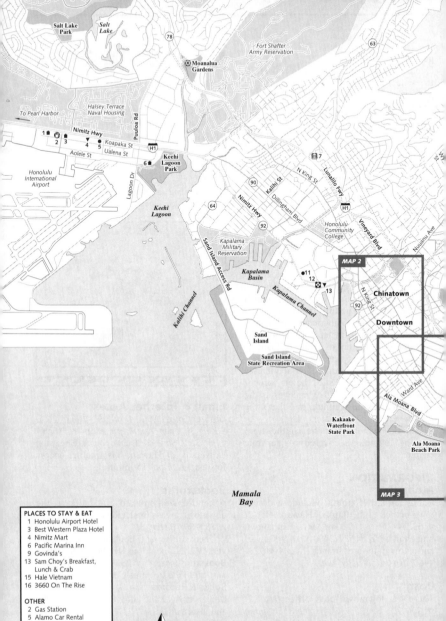

**PLACES TO STAY & EAT**
1 Honolulu Airport Hotel
3 Best Western Plaza Hotel
4 Nimitz Mart
6 Pacific Marina Inn
9 Govinda's
13 Sam Choy's Breakfast,
   Lunch & Crab
15 Hale Vietnam
16 3660 On The Rise

**OTHER**
2 Gas Station
5 Alamo Car Rental
7 Bishop Museum
8 Queen Emma Summer
   Palace
10 Royal Mausoleum State
   Monument
11 World Cafe
12 Hilo Hattie
14 Movie Museum

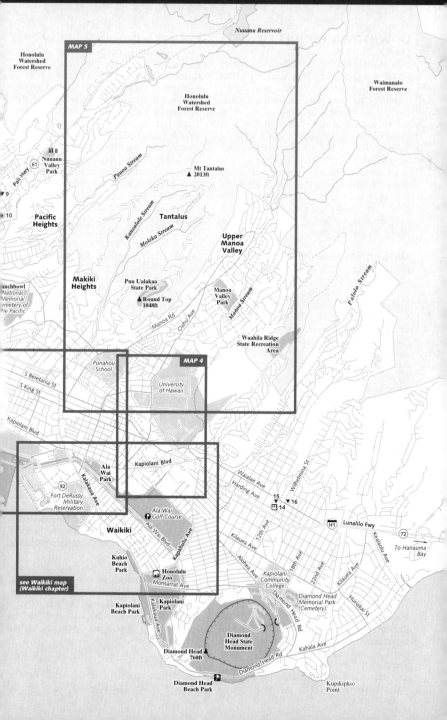

## DOWNTOWN HONOLULU (MAP 2)

Downtown Honolulu is a hodgepodge of past and present, with both sleek high-rises and stately Victorian-era buildings. Architecturally, the area has some striking juxtapositions – there's a 19th-century royal palace, a modernistic state capitol, a New England missionary church and a Spanish-style city hall all within sight of one another.

In addition to the usual sightseeing, you can soak up some local color by attending one of the free concerts given by the Royal Hawaiian Band at noon each Friday on the palace lawn or by lounging over the morning paper in the sunny courtyard of Hawaii's central library.

### Getting There & Away

If you're heading to the Iolani Palace area from Waikiki, the most frequent and convenient bus is No 2. To go directly to Aloha Tower Marketplace or the Hawaii Maritime Center from Waikiki, take bus No 19 or 20. Private trolleybuses also serve this area; see the Getting Around chapter for details.

Convenient parking lots in front of the Aloha Tower and on Pier 6 adjacent to the Hawaii Maritime Center charge $4 for up to three hours; if you have your ticket validated at a shop or restaurant, the fee is reduced to $2. There's a flat rate of $2 all day on weekends and after 4:30pm Monday to Friday.

### Walking Tour

Downtown Honolulu is ideal for strolling, with its most handsome buildings within easy walking distance of each other. You could make a quick tour in a couple of hours, but if you're up for more leisurely exploration, it's possible to spend the better part of a day poking around.

A good starting place is **Iolani Palace**, the area's most pivotal spot, both historically and geographically. If time permits, joining a guided palace tour offers a glimpse into the royal past. In any case you're free to stroll around the palace grounds. At the back side of the palace, en route to the **state capitol**, you'll find a **statue of Queen Liliuokalani**. You can enter the capitol through the rear, and exit on the Beretania St side, opposite the **war memorial**.

After turning left on Beretania St, you'll pass **Washington Place** and **St Andrew's**

**Cathedral**. In the lobby of the **State Office Tower**, directly opposite the cathedral, you'll find a colorful tile mural depicting Hawaiian royalty. From there, walk down Richards St to **No 1 Capitol District**, an elegant five-story building erected in 1928 that now houses the **Hawaii State Art Museum**. Then continue along Richards past the **YWCA**, built in 1927 by Julia Morgan, the renowned architect who designed the William Randolph Hearst San Simeon estate in California, and the Hawaiian Electric Company's four-story administration building that sports Spanish colonial architecture.

Turn right on Merchant St to see some of the historic buildings and modern skyscrapers that house Hawaii's largest corporations. Be sure to catch the free art gallery in the **First Hawaiian Center**, Hawaii's tallest high-rise.

Turn left on Bishop St and you will pass the four-story **Alexander & Baldwin Building** (c.1929); its curious facade incorporates tropical fruit, Hawaiian fish and the Chinese characters for prosperity and longevity. The building is named after Samuel Alexander and Henry Baldwin, sons of missionaries who vaulted to prominence in the sugar industry and created one of Hawaii's biggest corporations.

Turn left on Queen St and you'll immediately see the four-story **Dillingham Building**, built in 1929 in Italian Renaissance style, and now mirrored in the sleek reflective glass of the adjacent 30-story **Grosvenor Center** – a true study in contrasts.

Make your way back to Merchant St and then proceed south, where you'll find the **Old Federal Building**, the Spanish colonial structure that holds a post office, as well as **Aliiolani Hale** and a **statue of Kamehameha the Great**. Just beyond that is the historic **Kawaiahao Church** and the **Mission Houses Museum**.

As you make your way back to Iolani Palace, take a look at two classic period buildings on Punchbowl St: **Honolulu Hale** (City Hall) and the **Hawaii State Library**.

For more information on these leading sights along this walk, see individual headings.

### Iolani Palace

The beautifully restored Iolani Palace (☎ 522-0832; palace grounds free; tours *adult/child 5-12 yrs $20/5; every 15 mins; 9am-2:30pm Tues-Sat)* is the only royal palace in the USA. It was the official residence of King Kalakaua and Queen Kapiolani from 1882 to 1891 and then of Queen Liliuokalani, Kalakaua's sister and successor, for two years after that.

For history buffs, Iolani Palace is a must-see sight. There's simply no other place in Hawaii where you can get a more poignant sense of Hawaiian history during that pivotal 19th century, when Hawaiian royalty feasted, the white tax-paying business community steamed, and plots and counterplots simmered. So much happened within the walls of Iolani Palace, by monarchs and by those who overthrew them, that you can almost sense the spirits of those who were once here.

Following the overthrow of the Hawaiian kingdom in 1893, the palace became the capitol – first for the republic, then for the territory and later for the state of Hawaii.

It wasn't until 1969 that the current state capitol was built and the legislators moved out of their cramped palace quarters. The Senate had been meeting in the palace dining room and the House of Representatives in the throne room. By the time they left, Iolani Palace was in shambles, the grand koa staircase termite-ridden and the Douglas fir floors pitted and gouged.

After a multimillion-dollar renovation, the palace was restored to its former glory, and in 1978, it opened as a museum. These days, visitors must wear booties over their shoes to protect the highly polished wooden floors.

Iolani Palace was modern for its day. Every bedroom had its own full bath with hot and cold running water, copper-lined tubs, a flushing toilet and a bidet. As the tour guides like to point out, electric lights replaced the palace gas lamps a full four years before the White House in Washington got electricity.

The **throne room**, decorated in red and gold, features the original thrones of the king and queen and a *kapu* (taboo) stick made of the long, spiral, ivory tusk of a narwhal. In addition to celebrations full of pomp and pageantry, it was in the throne room that King Kalakaua danced his favorite Western dances – the polka, the waltz and the Virginia reel – into the wee hours of the morning.

Not all the events that took place here were joyous. Two years after she was dethroned, Queen Liliuokalani was brought back to the palace and tried for treason in the throne room. In a move calculated to humiliate the Hawaiian people, she spent nine months as a prisoner in Iolani Palace, her former home.

The interior of the palace can only be seen on a guided tour, which lasts about an hour; children younger than five are not admitted. Because of the palace's high upkeep expenses, the tours aren't cheap, but it's well worth the price to stroll through this unique, history-laden site. Sometimes you can join a tour on the spot, but it's advisable to call ahead for reservations.

The **palace grounds**, which are open free to the public, have a lengthy history. Before Iolani Palace was built, there was a simpler house on these grounds that was used by King Kamehameha III, who ruled for 30 years (1825–54). In ancient times it was the site of a heiau (temple).

The palace ticket window and a gift shop are in the former **barracks** of the Royal Household Guards, a building that looks oddly like the uppermost layer of a medieval fort that's been sliced off and plopped on the ground.

The **domed pavilion** on the grounds was originally built for the coronation of King Kalakaua in 1883 and is still used for the inauguration of governors and for Friday afternoon concerts by the Royal Hawaiian Band.

The **grassy mound** surrounded by a wrought iron fence was the site of a royal tomb until 1865, when the remains of King Kamehameha II and Queen Kamamalu (who both died of measles in England in 1824) were moved to the Royal Mausoleum in Nuuanu. The huge **banyan tree** between the palace and the state capitol is thought to have been planted by Queen Kapiolani.

Note that the palace was also the fictional home of Steve McGarrett's *Hawaii Five-O* crime-fighting unit.

## State Capitol

Hawaii's state capitol (☎ 587-0666; *415 S Beretania St)* is not your standard gold dome. Built in the 1960s, it was a grandiose attempt at a 'theme' design.

Its two central legislative chambers are cone-shaped to represent volcanoes; the rotunda is open to let gentle trade winds blow through; the supporting columns represent

# MAP 2 DOWNTOWN HONOLULU & CHINATOWN

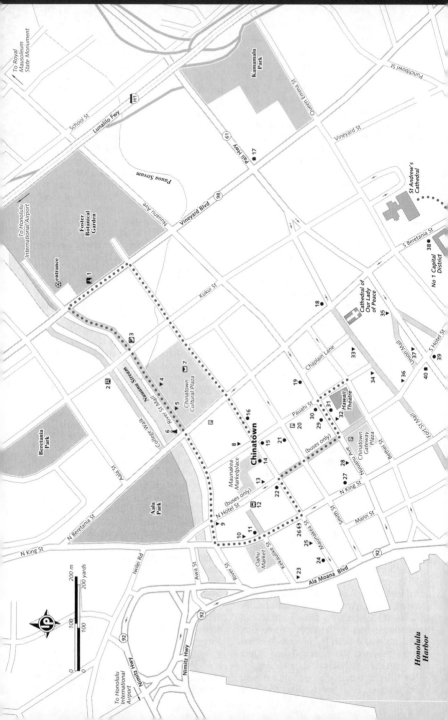

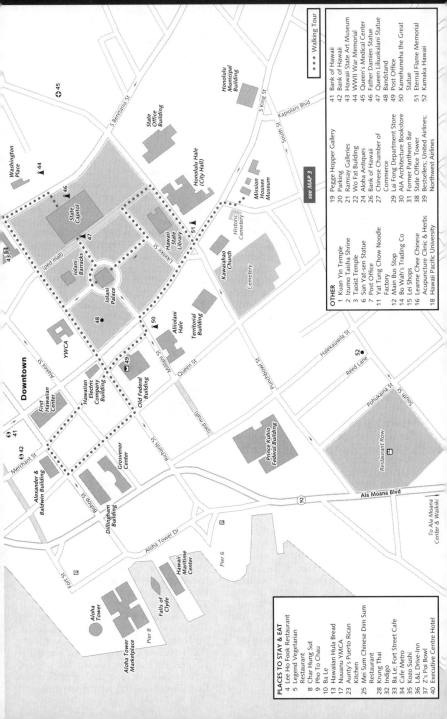

# DOWNTOWN HONOLULU & CHINATOWN  MAP 2

••• Walking Tour

see MAP 3

palm trees; and the whole structure is encircled by a large pool symbolizing the ocean surrounding Hawaii. Visitors are free to walk through the rotunda and peer through viewing windows into the two legislative chambers. Take an elevator to the top (5th) floor for its great open-air views of Honolulu.

In front of the capitol is a **statue of Father Damien**, the Belgian priest who in 1873 volunteered to work among the lepers of Molokai. He died of the disease 16 years later at age 49. The stylized sculpture was created by Venezuelan artist Marisol Escubar.

At the rear of the capitol is a life-sized bronze **statue of Queen Liliuokalani**, Hawaii's last queen. It faces Washington Place, Liliuokalani's home and place of exile for more than 20 years. The statue holds a copy of *Aloha Oe*, a patriotic hymn the queen composed; 'Kumulipo,' the Hawaiian chant of creation; and the Hawaiian constitution, a document the queen wrote in 1893 in an attempt to strengthen Hawaiian rule, but which US businessmen used as an excuse to overthrow her. The statue is often draped with leis of hibiscus or maile.

Directly opposite the state capitol on Beretania St is a sculptured **eternal torch** – a memorial dedicated to soldiers who died in WWII.

### Hawaii State Art Museum

Hawaii's first state art museum (☎ 808-586-0900; ⓦ www.state.hi.us/sfca; 250 S Hotel St; admission free; open 10am-4pm Tues-Sat) is finally open, and it was well worth the wait for both residents and visitors alike. For full details, see the boxed text 'Hawaii's New Treasure.'

### Washington Place

Washington Place, the governor's official residence, is a large colonial-style building surrounded by stately trees, built in 1846 by US sea captain John Dominis. The captain's son, also named John, became the governor of Oahu and married the Hawaiian princess who later became Queen Liliuokalani. After the queen was dethroned, she lived at Washington Place in exile until her death in 1917.

A plaque near the sidewalk on the left side of Washington Place is inscribed with the words to *Aloha Oe*, the anthem composed by Queen Liliuokalani.

### St Andrew's Cathedral

King Kamehameha IV, who reigned from 1855 to 1863, was attracted by the royal trappings of the Church of England and decided to build his own cathedral in Hawaii. He and his consort, Queen Emma, founded the Anglican Church of Hawaii in 1858.

The cathedral's cornerstone was finally laid in 1867 by King Kamehameha V. Kamehameha IV had died four years previously on St Andrew's Day – hence the church's name.

The architecture of St Andrew's Cathedral (☎ 524-2822; cnr Alakea & Beretania Sts; open 9am-5pm daily) is French Gothic, and the stone and glass used in the cathedral were shipped from England. Its most striking feature is the impressive window of handblown stained glass that forms the western facade and reaches from the floor to the eaves. In the right section of the glass you can see the Reverend Thomas Staley, the first bishop sent to Hawaii by Queen Victoria, alongside Kamehameha IV and Queen Emma.

### Aliiolani Hale

The Aliiolani Hale (House of Heavenly Kings) was the first major government building that was constructed by the Hawaiian monarchy. The building has housed the Hawaii Supreme Court since its construction in 1874 and was once also home to the state legislature. It was originally designed by Australian architect Thomas Rowe to be a royal palace, although it was never used as such.

It was on the steps of Aliiolani Hale, in January 1893, that Sanford Dole proclaimed the establishment of a provisional government and the overthrow of the Hawaiian monarchy.

A **statue of Kamehameha the Great** stands in front of Aliiolani Hale, opposite Iolani Palace. On June 11, a state holiday honoring Kamehameha, the statue is ceremoniously draped with layer upon layer of 12ft leis.

The Kamehameha statue was cast in 1880 in Florence, Italy, by American sculptor Thomas Gould. The current statue is actually a recast, as the first statue was lost at sea near the Falkland Islands. The original statue, which was recovered from the ocean floor after the second version was dedicated

## Hawaii's New Treasure

Visitors to Oahu have a new not-to-be-missed highlight: the **Hawaii State Art Museum**. Opened in November 2002, the museum culminates years of work by artists, cultural organizations and the state government, and showcases the work of artists who have lived in the islands since Hawaii became a state in 1959. Visitors immediately realize that the remarkable scenery and traditions of the state have proved incredibly inspirational for artists.

The collection makes the museum one of the best medium-sized art museums in the USA. And it's not just the works, which range from paintings to photographs to sculpture and more, but the overall design of the museum and the composition of the collection itself which are impressive. Works are displayed around inter-related themes that include island traditions, social issues, Hawaiian heritage as well as the pure beauty of the land and sea. Explanatory notes provide in-depth information on why works were chosen for display and Hawaii's confluence of Asian, Pacific and American cultures is evident throughout. The curators have done an excellent job of capturing the soul of the islands and the heart of the people. One visitor on opening day said, 'You see a beautiful sculpture and realize you know the artist and then you look at a painting and see your neighbor.'

The building itself is a work of art – the gallery is housed in the old YMCA, which was built in 1928 on prime real estate near Iolani Palace, across from the site of the future state capitol. The museum presently occupies the building's 2nd floor; with time it will be expanded to cover all five floors so that a good portion of the state's 5000-work collection can be shown. Sadly, visitors can't take a dip in the inviting courtyard swimming pool, once a refuge for scores of frolicking soldiers and seamen during WWII.

After climbing a grand staircase, visitors see a model of the canoe thought to have brought the first Polynesians to Hawaii. Behind the model is *The Discovery of Hawaii*, a painting by Herb Kawainui Kane, which is rapidly gaining iconic status in the state. It shows the awed voyagers on that first canoe as they crest a wave and catch site of an erupting volcano.

A visit to the museum can easily occupy an hour or more, but the sensible admissions policy (it's free!) means that you can pop in after visiting the palace, enjoy a few of the 360 works on exhibit and then save others for another visit.

Among the many highlights are the following:

- A series of ink drawings by Huc-Mazelet Luquiens captures the rhythm of life in Hawaii in the 1920s before tourism, the military, changing economics and population growth altered everything.
- A sculpture of shoes left on steps depicts *E Komo Mai*, the Hawaiian spirit of welcome where anybody can remove their footwear and make themselves at home. The artist, George Kahumokio, is best known for his slack-key guitar playing.
- *Ronin Samurai* is part of a 1982 series by Masami Teraoka, which uses traditional Japanese painting techniques to take a wry look at tourism. In this work a samurai and geisha are shown snorkeling in Hanauma Bay.
- *Kahoolawe Room* is a jarring painting that is Anne Miura's depiction of what her house on Maui felt like every time a Navy test bomb exploded on nearby Kahoolawe.
- A series of photographs by Mark Hamasaki continue the theme of social comment that doesn't always favor the government. The brutal assault on the land that marked the construction of the H3 highway in the 1980s is presented in stark black and white. The builders of the highway, who hired Hamasaki to record the project, definitely got more than they bargained for.
- Kids of all ages love *Introducing Ruddy Spuddy*, which comically depicts the chaos that hit painter Sally French's household when she unexpectedly inherited a potato farm in California.
- *The Drummer* by Jean Charlot is a masterpiece by the painter who spent many years in the islands before his death in 1979. It shows a local drummer intent on his music in way that will have you hearing it.

Part of the space is used for rotating special exhibits so you can always expect a surprise or two.

**Ryan Ver Berkmoes**

here in 1883, now stands in Kohala on the Big Island, where Kamehameha was born.

## Kawaiahao Church

This church (☎ 522-1333; cnr Punchbowl & King Sts; admission free; open 8am-4pm daily) is the oldest on Oahu. It was here that American missionaries originally constructed a large thatched church – which extended 54ft and seated 300 people – after their arrival in 1820.

Still, thatch wasn't quite what the missionaries had in mind. Sticking to their Western-style thinking, they designed this typical New England Congregational church with simple Gothic influences. Completed in 1842, the church is made of 14,000 coral slabs that weigh about 1000lb each. Hawaiian divers chiseled these huge blocks of coral out of Honolulu's underwater reef using elementary tools – a task that took four years.

The clock tower was donated by Kamehameha III, and the old clock, installed in 1850, still keeps accurate time. The rear seats of the church, marked by *kahili* (feather) staffs and velvet padding, were for royalty and are still reserved for descendants of royalty today.

The **tomb of King Lunalilo**, the successor to Kamehameha V, is on the church grounds at the main entrance. Lunalilo ruled for only one year before his death in 1874 at the age of 39.

The **cemetery** at the rear of the church is a fun place to poke around and is a bit like a who's who of colonial history. You'll find the gravestones of early missionaries buried alongside other important Westerners of the day, including the infamous Sanford Dole, who overthrew Queen Liliuokalani and went on to become the first territorial governor of Hawaii.

## Mission Houses Museum

This museum (☎ 531-0481; 553 S King St; tours adult/child $10/6 at 10am, 11am, 1pm & 2pm Tues-Sat) contains three of the original buildings of the Sandwich Islands Mission headquarters. The houses are authentically furnished with handmade quilts on the beds, settees in the parlor and iron cooking pots in the stone fireplaces.

The first missionaries packed more than their bags when they left Boston – they actually brought a prefabricated wooden house, now called the **Frame House**, around the Horn with them. Designed to withstand cold New England winter winds, the house's small windows instead block out Honolulu's cooling trade winds, keeping the two-story house hot and stuffy. Erected in 1821, it's the oldest wooden structure in Hawaii.

The coral-block **Chamberlain House** was the early mission storeroom, a necessity as Honolulu had few shops in those days. Upstairs are hoop barrels, wooden crates packed with dishes and the desk and quill pen Levi Chamberlain used to work on accounts. Levi was appointed by the mission to buy, store and dole out supplies to the missionary families, who survived on a meager allowance – as the account books on the desk testify.

The **Printing Office** housed a lead-type press that was used to print the Bible in the Hawaiian language.

The guided tours take in the whole shebang and last about an hour.

## Honolulu Hale

City Hall, also known as Honolulu Hale (☎ 523-2489; 530 S King St), is largely of Spanish mission design, with a tiled roof, decorative balconies, arches and pillars. Built in 1927, it bears the initials of CW Dickey, Honolulu's most famous architect of the day. The building, which is on the National Register of Historic Places, has frescoes by Einar Peterson and an open-air courtyard that's sometimes used for concerts and art exhibits. On the lawn out front is an **eternal flame memorial** erected to honor the victims of the September 11 terrorist attacks on the US East Coast.

## Hawaii State Library

The central branch of the statewide library system (☎ 586-3500; 478 S King St; open 9am-5pm Mon, Fri & Sat, 9am-8pm Tues & Thur, 10am-5pm Wed) is in a beautifully restored early-20th-century building with a grand column facade. Its collection of over half a million titles is the state's best and includes comprehensive Hawaii and Pacific sections.

The adjacent **Hawaii State Archives** (☎ 586-3617; open 8am-4:30pm Mon-Fri) is the repository for official government documents and an extensive photo collection. It's open to the public for research.

## First Hawaiian Center

The 30-story First Hawaiian Center, Hawaii's tallest building and the headquarters of the First Hawaiian Bank, occupies the block surrounded by King, Bishop, Merchant and Alakea Sts.

The building contains a worthwhile **gallery** (☎ 526-0232; 999 Bishop St; admission free; open 8:30am-4pm Mon-Thur, 8:30am-6pm Fri), which is operated in conjunction with the Contemporary Museum and features changing exhibits of modern Hawaiian art. For more information on the Contemporary Museum see Tantalus & Makiki Heights, later in this chapter.

The building itself has some notable features, including a four-story-high glass wall containing 185 prisms that was designed by New York glass artist Jamie Carpenter. *Enchanting Garden*, a flowing-water sculpture by Satoru Abe, welcomes visitors at the King St entrance.

## Fort St Mall

Fort St is a pedestrian shopping mall lined with an ever-growing number of high-rises. Although the mall is not interesting in itself, if you are downtown, it is a reasonable place to eat.

Hawaii Pacific University, an expanding private school, has much of its campus at the northern end of the mall.

The **Cathedral of Our Lady of Peace** (☎ 536-7036; 1184 Bishop St; admission free; open 8am-5pm daily), the center of the Roman Catholic Church in Hawaii, is at the northern end of the Fort St Mall. Built of coral blocks in 1843, it's older and a bit more ornate than St Andrew's Cathedral. Father Damien, who later served Molokai's leprosy colony, was ordained at the cathedral in 1864.

## Aloha Tower

Built in 1926 at the edge of the downtown district, the 10-story Aloha Tower is a Honolulu landmark that for years was the city's tallest building. In the days when all tourists arrived by ship, this icon of pre-war Hawaii – with its four-sided clock tower inscribed with the word 'Aloha' – greeted every visitor. These days, cruise ships still disembark at the terminal beneath the tower.

Take a look at the interior of the cruise ship terminal, which has wall-to-wall murals depicting early-20th-century Honolulu life. The scenes include hula dancers, Hawaiian kids diving off the pier and mainland passengers disembarking from one of the San Francisco-to-Honolulu ships that docked here during that era.

The Aloha Tower's top-floor **observation deck** (☎ 537-9260; Pier 9; admission free; open 9am-sunset daily) offers a sweeping 360-degree view of Honolulu's large commercial harbor. One caveat – the only access to the top is via an elevator that's occasionally out of commission, but you can always take in the view from one of the nearby waterfront restaurants.

In addition to the cruise ship terminal and the tower itself, the complex holds the Aloha Tower Marketplace, a shopping center with nearly 100 kiosks, stores and eateries. Fittingly, many of the shops specialize in Hawaiiana items, and most of the places to eat have harbor views.

## Hawaii Maritime Center

The Hawaii Maritime Center (☎ 536-6373; Pier 7; adult/child 6-17 yrs $7.50/4.50, child under 6 yrs free; open 8:30am-5pm daily), near the Aloha Tower, is a fantastic place to get a sense of Hawaii's history. The museum covers everything from the arrival of Captain Cook to modern-day windsurfing, with lots of offbeat tidbits that you won't find anywhere else.

Interesting displays on early tourism include a reproduction of a Matson liner stateroom and photos of Waikiki in the days when just the Royal Hawaiian and the Moana hotels shared the shore with Diamond Head. Both hotels were built by Matson in the early 1900s to accommodate the passengers they carried on their cruises. Ironically, Matson sold the hotels off to the Sheraton chain in 1959, just before the jet age and statehood launched sleepy tourism into a booming industry.

The maritime center is also home to the 266ft *Falls of Clyde*, the world's last four-masted, four-rigged ship. Built in 1878, in Glasgow, Scotland, the *Falls* was once used to carry sugar and passengers between Hilo and San Francisco. It was later converted into an oil tanker and eventually stripped down to a barge. A Hawaiian group raised funds to rescue the ship in 1963, just before it was scheduled to be sunk to create a breakwater off Vancouver. With the aid of the Bishop Museum, the *Falls* was eventually brought to Honolulu and restored. It is now registered as a National Historic Landmark. Visitors can stroll the deck and walk down into the cargo holds.

The center is also home port to the 60ft *Hokulea*, a double-hulled sailing canoe constructed to resemble the type of boat used by Polynesians in their migrations. It has made a number of voyages from Hawaii to the South Pacific, retracing the routes of the early Polynesian seafarers and using only traditional methods of navigation, such as wave patterns and the position of the stars.

## CHINATOWN (MAP 2)

A visit to Chinatown is a bit like a journey to Asia – although it's predominantly Chinese, it has Vietnamese, Thai and Filipino influences as well.

Chinatown is busy and colorful. It has a lively market that could be right off a back street in Hong Kong; fire-breathing dragons coil around the red pillars outside the Bank of Hawaii; and good, cheap ethnic restaurants abound. You can get a tattoo, consult with a herbalist, munch on moon cakes or slurp a steaming bowl of Vietnamese soup. There are temples, shrines, noodle factories, antique shops and art galleries to explore.

On Chinatown's northern boundary is a former royal estate that now encompasses the Foster Botanical Garden, the city's finest botanical garden. It offers a calm contrast to the buzz of activity found in the markets and along the busy streets.

### Getting There & Away

From Waikiki, take bus No 2 to N Hotel St in the center of Chinatown, or bus No 20 to River St on the western edge of Chinatown.

Traffic is thick and parking can be tight, so you may want to take a bus even if you have a car. However there are parking garages at the Chinatown Gateway Plaza on Nuuanu Ave and in the Hale Pauahi complex on N Beretania St north of Maunakea St. Note that N Hotel St is open to bus traffic only.

### Walking Tour

Chinatown is one of the most intriguing quarters of the city for sauntering about.

This is best done in the daytime however, not only because that's when the markets and shops are open, but also because the streets can get a little seedy after dark.

Although you could start a walking tour at virtually any street corner, a good spot to begin a loop route is in front of the **Hawaii Theatre** *(cnr Bethel & Pauahi Sts)*. Proceed up Pauahi St and make a left on Nuuanu Ave, and you'll see the now-abandoned **Pantheon Bar**, Honolulu's oldest watering hole and a favorite of sailors in days past. The **granite-block sidewalks** along Nuuanu Ave are a relic of an earlier day, built with the discarded ballasts of ships that brought tea from China in the 19th century.

Next turn right onto N Hotel St, toward the center of Chinatown. In contrast to the creeping gentrification that marks the downtown edge of Chinatown, N Hotel St still bears witness to Honolulu's seamier side. Here you'll find darkened doorways advertising 'video peeps' for 25¢ and bawdy nightspots with names like Risqué Theatre and Club Hubba Hubba.

At Maunakea St, turn left and you'll enter the heart of Chinatown, with its herbalists and noodle shops. Right on the corner of N Hotel St is one of Chinatown's oldest structures, the century-old **Wo Fat Building**, which has an ornate facade that resembles a Chinese temple. At N King St turn right and after one block you'll find the bustling **Oahu Market** with its studiously clean food stands.

At the intersection of N King and River Sts, there are some excellent neighborhood restaurants where you could stop for a bite to eat. Continue walking northeast along River St, which borders Nuuanu Stream. At N Beretania St, River St turns into a pedestrian mall, the start of which is adorned with a **statue** of Chinese revolutionary leader Sun Yat-sen. Along the mall are restaurants, a couple of religious sites and a handful of outdoor tables where old men pass the day playing mahjong and checkers. River St terminates opposite the entrance of **Foster Botanical Garden**.

After touring the gardens and the nearby **Kuan Yin Temple**, you could re-enter the main Chinatown district by heading back on Maunakea St. At the intersection of Maunakea and N Beretania, you'll find rows of small lei shops where lei makers deftly string flowers and heady fragrances fill the air.

For information on organized tours of Chinatown, see Walking Tours in the Getting Around chapter earlier in this book.

## Hawaii Theatre

The neoclassical Hawaii Theatre (☎ 528-0506; 1130 Bethel St) first opened in 1922 with silent films playing to the tunes of a pipe organ. Dubbed the 'Pride of the Pacific,' it ran continuous shows during WWII, but the development of mall cinemas in the 1970s was its undoing.

After closing in 1984, the theater's future looked dim, even though it was on the National Register of Historic Places. Theater buffs came to the rescue, formed a nonprofit group, purchased the property and spearheaded an extensive multimillion-dollar restoration.

The 1400-seat theater has a lovely interior, with trompe-l'oeil mosaics and bas-relief scenes of Shakespearean plays. It reopened in 1996 for dance, drama and music performances and is now one of the leading entertainment venues in Honolulu.

## Oahu Market

The focal point of Chinatown is the Oahu Market (cnr Kekaulike & N King Sts), a Honolulu institution since 1904.

Everything a Chinese cook needs is on display: pig heads, ginger root, fresh octopus, quail eggs, slabs of tuna, jasmine rice, long beans and salted jellyfish.

In 1984, the tenants organized and purchased the market themselves to save it from falling into the hands of developers. Today, it gets a lot of competition from a bustling newcomer, Maunakea Marketplace.

## Noodle Makers

If you look inside one of the half dozen noodle factories in Chinatown, you'll see clouds of white flour hanging in the air and thin sheets of dough running around rollers and coming out as noodles. One easy-to-find but very small shop, Yat Tung Chow Noodle Factory (150 N King St), makes nine sizes of noodles, from skinny golden thread to fat udon.

## Chinatown Cultural Plaza

This plaza, covering the better part of a block, is bordered by N Beretania St, Maunakea and River Sts. The modern complex doesn't have the character of Chinatown's older shops, but inside it's still quintessential Chinatown, with tailors, acupuncturists and calligraphers alongside travel agencies, restaurants and a Chinese news press. In a small courtyard, elderly Chinese light incense and leave mangoes at a statue of Kuan Yin.

## Taoist Temple

Organized in 1889, the Lum Sai Ho Tong Society was one of more than 100 societies started by Chinese immigrants in Hawaii to help preserve their cultural identity. This one was for the Lum clan, which hails from an area west of the Yellow River. At one time the society had more than 4000 members, and even now there are nearly a thousand Lums in the Honolulu phone book.

The society's Taoist Temple (cnr River & Kukui Sts) honors the goddess Tin Hau, a Lum child who rescued her father from drowning and was later deified. Many Chinese claim to see her apparition when they travel by boat. The temple is not usually open to the general public, but you can admire the building from the outside.

## Izumo Taisha Shrine

The Izumo Taisha Shrine (☎ 538-7778; 215 N Kukui St; open 9am-5pm daily), across the river from the Taoist temple, is a small wooden Shinto shrine built by Japanese immigrants in 1923. It was confiscated during

## Flower Power: Traditional Chinese Medicine

Chinatown herbalists are both physicians and pharmacists, with walls full of small wooden drawers each filled with a different herb. They'll size you up, feel your pulse and listen to you describe your ailments before deciding which drawers to open, mixing herbs and flowers and wrapping them for you to take home and boil together. The object is to balance yin and yang forces. You can find herbalists at the Chinatown Cultural Plaza and along N King and Maunakea Sts, including Leanne Chee Chinese Acupuncture Clinic & Herbs (☎ 533-2498; 1159 Maunakea St; open 9am-4pm Mon-Sat), where you might want to pick up a tonic like the African Sea-Coconut Cough Mixture.

WWII by the city of Honolulu and wasn't returned to its congregation until 1962.

Incidentally, the 100lb sacks of rice that sit near the altar symbolize good health, and ringing the bell placed at the shrine entrance is considered an act of purification for those who come to pray.

### Foster Botanical Garden

This botanical garden (☎ 522-7066; 180 N Vineyard Blvd; adult/child 5-13 yrs $5/1; open 9am-4pm daily), at the northern side of Chinatown, has an impressive 14-acre collection of tropical plants.

The garden took root in 1850, when German botanist William Hillebrand purchased 5 acres of land from Queen Kalama and planted the trees that now tower in the center of the property. Captain Thomas Foster bought the property in 1867 and continued planting the grounds. In the 1930s, the tropical garden was bequeathed to the city of Honolulu, and it is now a city park.

The garden is laid out according to plant groups, including sections of palms, orchids, plumeria and poisonous plants. If you've ever wondered how nutmeg, allspice and cinnamon grow, stroll through the Economic Garden. In this section, there's also a black pepper vine that climbs 40ft up a gold tree, a vanilla vine and other herbs and spices.

The herb garden was the site of the first Japanese language school in Oahu. Many Japanese immigrants sent their children here to learn how to read Japanese, hoping to maintain their cultural identity and the option of someday returning to Japan. During the bombing of Pearl Harbor a stray artillery shell exploded in a room full of students. A memorial marks the site.

At the other end of the park, the wild orchid garden makes a good place for close-up photography. Foster Botanical Garden holds many extraordinary plants. For instance, the garden's East African *Gigasiphon macrosiphon*, a tree with white flowers that open in the evening, is thought to be extinct in the wild. The tree is so rare that it doesn't have a common name.

The native Hawaiian *loulu* palm, taken long ago from Oahu's upper Nuuanu Valley, may also be extinct in the wild. The garden's chicle tree, New Zealand kauri tree and Egyptian doum palm are all reputed to be the largest of their kind in the USA.

Oddities include the cannonball tree, the sausage tree and the double coconut palm that's capable of producing a 50lb nut.

Trees are labeled, and a free self-guided tour booklet is available at the entrance. The Friends of Foster Garden provides volunteer guides who lead hour-long walking tours at 1pm Monday to Friday, included in the admission price.

### Kuan Yin Temple

The Kuan Yin Temple (☎ 533-6361; 170 N Vineyard Blvd; open daylight hrs), near the entrance of Foster Botanical Garden, is a bright red Buddhist temple with a green ceramic-tile roof. The ornate interior is richly carved and filled with the sweet, pervasive smell of burning incense.

The temple is dedicated to Kuan Yin Bodhisattva, goddess of mercy, whose statue is the largest in the prayer hall. Devotees burn paper 'money' for prosperity and good luck. Offerings of fresh flowers and fruit are placed at the altar. The large citrus fruit that is stacked pyramid-style is the pomelo, considered a symbol of fertility because of its many seeds.

Honolulu's multiethnic Buddhist community worships at the temple, and respectful visitors are welcome.

### Shopping

Chinatown can be a fun place to do some off-beat shopping. A good spot to start is the **Maunakea Marketplace** (☎ 524-3409; 1120 Maunakea St), which has a hodgepodge of shops and stalls in and around it. One of the more interesting ones is **Bo Wah's Trading Co** (☎ 537-2017; 1037 Maunakea St), where you can find everything from inexpensive rice bowls to jasmine soap and Oriental cookie molds. Nearby shops sell snuff bottles, cloisonné jewelry and freshwater rice pearls.

Chinatown is also a good place to look for art and antiques. You may want to begin your browsing at **Aloha Antiques** (☎ 536-6187; 942 Maunakea St), where about 20 vendors sell eclectic collections, including jewelry, Art Deco items, Asian ceramics and 1950s collectibles.

A few blocks away you'll find one of the best souvenirs of Hawaii: fresh leis. Along Maunakea St near Pauahi St you'll find open-air **lei shops** where you can watch the flowers being strung. Pick one up for as little as $3. The shops will pack them, too, for you to carry home on the plane.

**Lai Fong Department Store** *(☎ 537-3497; 1118 Nuuanu Ave)* also sells a curious variety of antiques and knickknacks, including Chinese silk clothing, Oriental porcelain and old postcards of Hawaii dating back to the first half of the 20th century.

For artwork, the **Pegge Hopper Gallery** *(☎ 524-1160; 1164 Nuuanu Ave)* features the works of Pegge Hopper, one of the most recognized contemporary painters in Hawaii; her prints of voluptuous Hawaiian women adorn many a wall on Oahu.

A block to the northwest is **Ramsay Galleries** *(☎ 537-2787; 1128 Smith St; closed Sun)*, a top choice which exhibits finely detailed pen-and-ink drawings of Honolulu by the internationally known Ramsay as well as changing collections of works by other local artists.

### CENTRAL HONOLULU & ALA MOANA (MAP 3)

Ala Moana means 'Path to the Sea.' Ala Moana Blvd (Hwy 92) connects the Nimitz Hwy and the airport with downtown Honolulu and continues into Waikiki. Ala Moana is also the name of the area west of Waikiki, which includes Honolulu's largest beach park and a huge shopping center.

### Ala Moana Center

The Ala Moana Center is Hawaii's biggest shopping center, with some 200 shops. When outer islanders fly to Honolulu to shop, they go to Ala Moana. Tourists wanting to spend the day at a mall usually head there too. Ala Moana Center is Honolulu's major bus transfer point and tens of thousands of passengers transit through daily, so even if you weren't planning to go to the center, you're likely to end up there.

Ala Moana has typical mall anchor stores such as Sears, Macy's, Neiman Marcus and JC Penney as well as lots of specialty shops. A favorite for local color is the Crack Seed Center, where you can scoop from jars full of pickled mangoes, candied ginger, dried cuttlefish and banzai mix.

There are also airline offices, a couple of banks, a supermarket and a food court with scores of ethnic fast-food stalls.

On the inland side of the center, near Sears, is a **post office** *(open 8:30am-5pm*

*Mon-Fri, 8:30am-4:15pm Sat)*. Also on the ground level, but at the opposite end of the row, is a satellite city hall where you can get bus schedules.

To get to the Ala Moana Center from Waikiki by car, simply head west on Ala Moana Blvd. Bus Nos 8, 19, 20 and 58 connect Waikiki with the Ala Moana Center.

### Ala Moana Beach Park

Ala Moana Beach Park, opposite the Ala Moana Center, is a fine city park with much less hustle and bustle than Waikiki. The park is fronted by a broad, golden-sand beach, nearly a mile long, which is buffered from the traffic noise of Ala Moana Blvd by a spacious, grassy area with shade trees.

This is where Honolulu residents go to jog after work, play volleyball and enjoy weekend picnics. The park has full beach facilities, several softball fields, tennis courts, and free parking. It's a very popular park, yet big enough that it never feels crowded.

Ala Moana is a safe place to swim and is a good spot for distance swimmers. However, at low tide the deep channel that runs the length of the beach can be a hazard to poor swimmers who don't realize it's there. A former boat channel, it drops off suddenly to overhead depths. If you want to measure laps, it's 500m between the lifeguard tower at the Waikiki end and the white post in the water seen midway between the third and fourth lifeguard towers.

The 43-acre peninsula jutting from the eastern side of the park is the **Aina Moana State Recreation Area**, more commonly known as **Magic Island**. During the school year, you can often find high school outrigger canoe teams practising here in the late afternoon. There's a nice walk around the perimeter of Magic Island, and sunsets can be very picturesque, with sailboats pulling in and out of the adjoining Ala Wai Yacht Harbor. This is also a hot summer surf spot.

If you're taking the bus from Waikiki, Nos 8 and 20 stop on Ala Moana Blvd opposite the beach park.

### Hawaii Children's Discovery Center

The Hawaii Children's Discovery Center *(☎ 524-5437; 111 Ohe St; adult/child 2-17 yrs $8/6.75, child under 2 yrs free; open 9am-1pm*

# MAP 3 CENTRAL HONOLULU & ALA MOANA

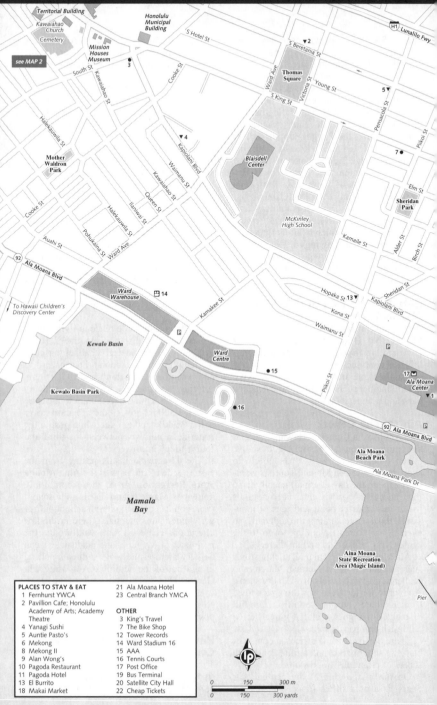

Territorial Building
Kawaiahao Church Cemetery
Honolulu Municipal Building
Mission Houses Museum
see MAP 2
South St
Kawaiahao St
Halekauwila St
Cooke St
Mother Waldron Park
Cooke St
Auahi St
Pohukaina St
Ilaniwai St
Halekauwila St
Ward Ave
92 Ala Moana Blvd
To Hawaii Children's Discovery Center
Ward Warehouse
Kewalo Basin
Kewalo Basin Park
Kamakee St
Ward Centre
S Hotel St
S Beretania St
Ward Ave
S King St
Victoria St
Young St
Thomas Square
Kapiolani Blvd
Waimanu St
Kawaiahao St
Queen St
Blaisdell Center
McKinley High School
Kamaile St
Hopaka St 13 ▼
Kona St
Waimanu St
Piikoi St
H1 Lunalilo Fwy
Pensacola St
5 ▼
7 ●
Piikoi St
Elm St
Sheridan Park
Alder St
Birch St
Sheridan St
Kapiolani Blvd
▼ 2
▼ 4
🎦 14
P
● 15
● 16
92 Ala Moana Blvd
P
17 ✉
Ala Moana Center
▼ 1
P
Ala Moana Beach Park
Ala Moana Park Dr

Mamala Bay

Aina Moana State Recreation Area (Magic Island)
Pier

**PLACES TO STAY & EAT**
1 Fernhurst YWCA
2 Pavillion Cafe; Honolulu Academy of Arts; Academy Theatre
4 Yanagi Sushi
5 Auntie Pasto's
6 Mekong
8 Mekong II
9 Alan Wong's
10 Pagoda Restaurant
11 Pagoda Hotel
13 El Burrito
18 Makai Market

21 Ala Moana Hotel
23 Central Branch YMCA

**OTHER**
3 King's Travel
7 The Bike Shop
12 Tower Records
14 Ward Stadium 16
15 AAA
16 Tennis Courts
17 Post Office
19 Bus Terminal
20 Satellite City Hall
22 Cheap Tickets

0    150    300 m
0    150    300 yards

see MAP 5

Makiki
District Park

Punahou School

Lunalilo St

Makiki St

Moleka Stream

1

Punahou St

Wilder Ave

Kinau St

Matlock Ave

Dole St

Cartwright
Park

Artesian Way

6 ▼

H1  Lunalilo Fwy

S King St

Coyne St

Liona St

S Beretania St

Punahou St

Young St

▼ 8

Artesian St

Kalakaua Ave

Rycroft St

Ahana St

11 ■

10 ●

McCully St

9 ▼

S King St

Kanunu St

Algaroba St

Keeaumoku St

12

Makaloa St

Waiola St

Kaheka St

Citron St

see MAP 4

Date St

Honolulu
Stadium State
Recreation
Area

19

Fern St

20 ●

P

Kona St

Hauoli St

Pumehana St

McCully St

Lime St

Isenberg St

Coolidge St

Mahukona St

22 ●

21

Kapiolani Blvd

Willwill St

Paani St

Hoawa St

Hausten St

Hawaii
Convention
Center

23

Atkinson Dr

Ala Wai Canal

Ala Wai
Park

Ala Wai
Yacht
Harbor

Holomoana St

Hobron Lane

Hobron Lane

Kalakaua Ave

Ena Rd

Ala Wai Blvd

Niu St

Pau St

Keoniana St

Ala Moana Blvd

92

Kuamoo St

Namahana St

Olohana St

Kalaimoku St

Kalia Rd

see Waikiki map
(Waikiki chapter)

Kuhio Ave

Laumiu

Kaiolu St

Waikiki

Dewey Court

Maluhia Rd

Lewers St

Aloha Dr

Hilton
Lagoon

Fort DeRussy
Military Reservation

Kahanamoku Beach

*Tues-Fri, 10am-3pm Sat & Sun)* is a great place to take the kids on a rainy day.

This hands-on children's museum occupies the waterfront site of the old city incinerator, though the only hint of its less than glorious past is the towering smokestack that reaches skyward from the center of the building. The centerpiece of an ambitious redevelopment plan that's returning the neighborhood to recreational use, the 37,000-sq-ft museum is adjacent to a new 30-acre waterfront park. Although older kids may find some of the displays interesting, the exhibits are principally geared to capture the interest of pre-teen children.

The museum has five main exhibit sections extending over three stories. The **Toy Box**, just off the entry, introduces children to the center via a video puppet show. **Fantastic You** explores the human body, allowing kids to walk through a mock stomach and the like. More traditional displays can be found in the **Your Town** section, where kids can drive an interactive fire engine or try their hand at being a bank teller or TV interviewer. The other two sections, **Hawaiian Rainbows** and the **Rainbow World**, relate specifically to life in Hawaii and allow children to navigate a ship, swim with dolphins and dress up in the traditional costumes of the various ethnic groups that comprise Hawaii society.

You can get to there from Waikiki via bus No 8 or 20; it's a five-minute walk from the nearest bus stop on Ala Moana Blvd to the museum.

## Honolulu Academy of Arts

The Honolulu Academy of Arts (☎ 532-8700; W *www.honoluluacademy.org; 900 S Beretania St; adult/senior or student $7/4, child under 13 yrs free; open 10am-4:30pm Tues-Sat, 1pm-5pm Sun)* is an exceptional museum, with solid Asian, European and Pacific art collections. Hawaii's only comprehensive fine arts museum, it houses nearly 40,000 pieces of artwork, which include an amazingly varied range of high quality paintings, sculptures and cultural artefacts.

The museum dates to 1927 and has a predominantly classical facade that is invitingly open and airy, with some 30 galleries branching off a series of garden courtyards. Major donors to the Honolulu Academy of Arts have included the late publishing magnate Mrs Charles Montague Cooke, whose private collection of 4500 works became the museum's founding collection, and novelist James A Michener, who left his entire holding of more than 5400 Japanese ukiyoe prints to the museum.

Don't miss the splendid Asian Courtyard, where you'll cross a lily pond to enter halls displaying an extensive collection of Asian art, ranging from serene buddhas to fierce samurai armor. Considered one of the finest Asian art collections in the USA, it gives almost equal weight to both Chinese and Japanese works of art. Among the highlights is the collection of 'Scenes of Kyoto,' painted by the renowned Japanese artist Kano Motohide. The extensive Ming Dynasty collection includes several pivotal works such as Shen Zhou's brilliant painting *Boating on an Autumn River*, which is credited with establishing a new compositional technique that had a significant effect on Ming painting styles.

In 2001, the museum added the Henry R Luce Pavilion, a lovely new contemporary wing that added 10,000 sq ft of additional exhibit space. It contains Hawaiiana artefacts and paintings reflecting Hawaiian culture on its upper level and modern art on the ground floor, including works by such modernist luminaries as Henry Moore and Georgia O'Keeffe.

European art of the 19th and 20th centuries is represented in a roomful of paintings by Henri Matisse, Paul Cézanne, Claude Monet, Paul Gauguin, Vincent van Gogh and Camille Pissarro. There's also a worthwhile collection of 16th to 18th century European artists such as Pieter de Hotch, Sir Thomas Lawrence and Carlo Bonavia and a number of Madonna-and-child oil paintings from 14th-century Italy.

The Pacific art exhibits include ceremonial carvings, ancestral figurines, war clubs and masks from Papua New Guinea, body ornaments and navigational stick charts from Micronesia and head-dresses and containers from French Polynesia. And the museum also exhibits some fine eclectic pieces, ranging from sculptures and miniature figurines from India to fertility figures and ceremonial carvings from African tribespeople.

There is a gift shop with some arty souvenirs and a recommendable lunch café overlooking a beautiful fountain courtyard. In addition, the museum's Academy Theatre is one of Oahu's top venues for showing experimental and revival film series; call the museum to see what's playing.

The Honolulu Academy of Arts can be reached by bus No 2 from Waikiki. If you are arriving by car there's street-side metered parking nearby, near the front of the museum on S Beretania St, as well as at the rear of the museum.

## UNIVERSITY AREA (MAP 4)

The University of Hawaii (UH) at Manoa, the central campus of the statewide university system, is 2 miles north of Waikiki.

The university has strong programs in astronomy, geophysics, marine sciences and Hawaiian and Pacific studies, and the campus attracts students from islands throughout the Pacific. It has approximately 17,000 students and offers degrees in 90 fields of study.

Staff at the **information center** (☎ 956-7235) in the Campus Center provide campus maps, give tours and can answer any questions you have about the university. Free one-hour **walking tours** of the campus, emphasizing history and architecture, leave from the Campus Center at 2pm Monday, Wednesday and Friday; to join a tour, simply arrive 10 minutes before the tour begins.

At the eastern side of the University of Hawaii campus is the **East-West Center** (1777 East-West Rd), a federally funded educational institution established in 1960 by the US Congress to promote mutual understanding among the people of Asia, the Pacific and the USA. Some 2000 researchers and graduate students work and study at the center, examining development policy, the environment and other Pacific issues.

Changing exhibits on Asian art and culture are displayed in the East-West Center's **Burns Hall** (☎ 944-7111; cnr Dole St & East-West Rd; admission free; open 8am-5pm Mon-Fri, noon-4pm Sun). The center occasionally has other multicultural programs open to the public, such as music concerts and scholastic seminars.

Bus No 4 runs between the university and Waikiki, bus No 6 between the university and Ala Moana.

## UPPER MANOA VALLEY (MAP 5)

The Upper Manoa Valley, on the mountain side of the university, ends at forest reserve land in the hills above Honolulu. The road up the valley runs through a well-to-do residential neighborhood before reaching the trailhead to Manoa Falls and the Lyon Arboretum.

## Manoa Falls Trail

The trail to Manoa Falls, which starts near the Lyon Aboretum, is a beautiful hike, especially for one so close to the city. The trail runs for three-quarters of a mile above a rocky streambed before ending at the falls. It takes about 30 minutes each way.

Surrounded by lush, damp vegetation and moss-covered stones and tree trunks, you get the feeling you are walking through a thick rain forest a long way from civilization. The sounds are purely natural: the chirping of birds and the rush of the stream and waterfall.

There are all sorts of trees along the path, including tall *Eucalyptus robusta*, with its soft, spongy, reddish bark; flowering orange African tulip trees; and other lofty varieties that creak like wooden doors in old houses. Many of them were planted by the nearby Lyon Arboretum, which at one time held a lease on the property.

Wild purple orchids and red ginger grow near the falls, adding a colorful element to the tranquil scene. The falls are steep and drop about 100ft into a small shallow pool. The pool is not deep enough for swimming, and occasional falling rocks make swimming inadvisable anyway. Note that the local health department warns against swimming in the water for fear of leptospirosis!

It's an easy hike, with just a 400ft gain in elevation. The trail is usually a bit muddy, but it's not too bad if it hasn't been raining recently. It does call for shoes that are more secure than mere flip-flops.

## Aihualama Trail

Just before reaching Manoa Falls, an inconspicuous trail starts to the left of the chain-link fence. This is the Aihualama Trail, well worth a little 15-minute side trip. Just a short way up, you'll get a broad view of Manoa Valley.

After walking for about five minutes, you'll enter a bamboo forest with some massive old banyan trees. When the wind blows, the forest crackles eerily. It's an engaging forest, enchanted or spooky depending on your mood.

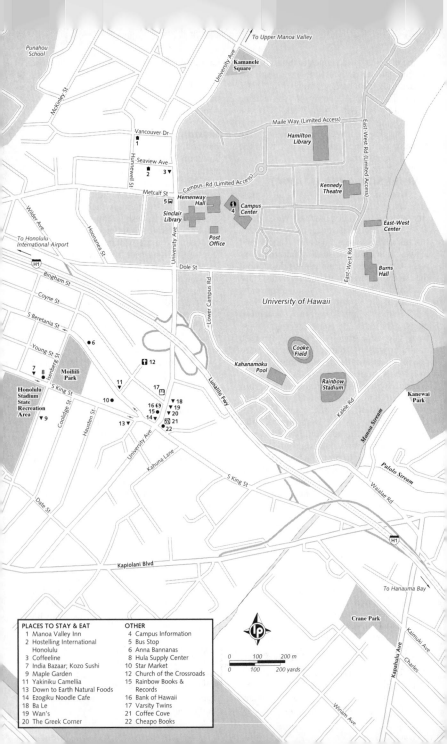

## PLACES TO STAY & EAT
1 Manoa Valley Inn
2 Hostelling International Honolulu
3 Coffeeline
7 India Bazaar; Kozo Sushi
9 Maple Garden
11 Yakiniku Camellia
13 Down to Earth Natural Foods
14 Ezogiku Noodle Cafe
18 Ba Le
19 Wan's
20 The Greek Corner

## OTHER
4 Campus Information
5 Bus Stop
6 Anna Bannanas
8 Hula Supply Center
10 Star Market
12 Church of the Crossroads
15 Rainbow Books & Records
16 Bank of Hawaii
17 Varsity Twins
21 Coffee Cove
22 Cheapo Books

0    100    200 m
0    100    200 yards

You can return to the Manoa Falls Trail or go on for another mile to Pauoa Flats, where the trail connects with the Puu Ohia-Pauoa Trail in the Tantalus area. For more trail information, see Tantalus & Makiki Heights later in this chapter.

### Lyon Arboretum

If you want to identify trees and plants you've seen along the trail to Manoa Falls, the Lyon Arboretum (☎ 988-0465; 3860 Manoa Rd; admission $2.50; open 9am-3pm Mon-Sat) is a great place to visit after your hike.

Dr Harold Lyon, after whom the arboretum is named, is credited with introducing 10,000 exotic trees and plants to Hawaii. Approximately half of these are represented in this 193-acre arboretum, which is under the auspices of the University of Hawaii. This is not a landscaped tropical flower garden, but a mature and largely wooded arboretum where related species are clustered in a seminatural state.

Among the plants in the Hawaiian ethnobotanical garden are mountain apple, breadfruit and taro; *ko*, the sugarcane brought by early Polynesian settlers; *kukui*, which was used to produce lantern oil; and ti, which was used for medicinal purposes during ancient times and for making moonshine after Westerners arrived.

A good choice among the arboretum's many short trails is the 20-minute walk up to **Inspiration Point**, which offers a view of the hills that enclose the valley. En route you'll encounter wonderful scents, inviting stone benches and lots of birdsong. The path loops through ferns, bromeliads and magnolias and passes by tall trees, including a bo tree that's a descendant of the tree Gautama Buddha sat under when he received enlightenment.

Free guided tours (call for reservations) are given at 1pm Saturday and 10am Tuesday. Helpful staff members at the reception center can provide a map of the garden and information on the arboretum's workshops and children's programs.

### Getting There & Away

From Ala Moana Center take the No 5 Manoa Valley bus to the end of the line, which is at the junction of Manoa Rd and Kumuone St. From there, it's a 10-minute walk to the end of Manoa Rd, where the Manoa Falls Trail

begins. Lyon Arboretum is at the end of the short drive just to the left of the trailhead.

To reach this area by car, simply drive to the end of Manoa Rd. Don't be fooled by the signs touting 'Falls Parking' – that parking lot has a fee, and some huckster is trying to make money out of unsuspecting tourists. There's room to park for free at the trailhead, but it's not a very secure place, so don't leave anything valuable in the car. Lyon Arboretum has a parking area adjacent to its gardens which is reserved for the arboretum visitors only.

## TANTALUS & MAKIKI HEIGHTS (MAP 5)

Just 2 miles from downtown Honolulu, a narrow switchback road cuts its way up the lush green forest reserve land of Tantalus and the Makiki Valley. The road climbs almost to the top of 2013ft Mt Tantalus, with swank, mountainside homes tucked in along the way.

Although the road is one continuous loop, the western side is called Tantalus Dr and the eastern side Round Top Dr. The 8½-mile circuit is Honolulu's finest scenic drive, offering splendid views of the city below.

The route is winding, narrow and steep, but it's a good paved road. Among the profusion of dense tropical growth, bamboo, ginger, elephant-ear taro and fragrant eucalyptus trees are easily identified. Vines climb to the top of telephone poles and twist their way across the wires.

A network of hiking trails runs between Tantalus Dr and Round Top Dr and throughout the forest reserve, with numerous trailheads off both roads. The trails are seldom crowded, which is somewhat amazing considering how accessible they are. Perhaps because the drive itself is so nice, the only walking most people do is between their car and the scenic lookouts.

The Makiki Heights area below the forest reserve is one of the most exclusive residential areas in Honolulu and the site of a the Contemporary Museum. There's a bus service as far as Makiki Heights, but none around the Tantalus–Round Top loop road.

### Puu Ualakaa State Park

From Puu Ualakaa State Park (open 7am-7:45pm daily Apr 1–early Sept, 7am-6:45pm daily Sept-Mar) you can see an incredible panorama of all Honolulu. The park entrance is 2½ miles up Round Top Dr from Makiki St. From the entrance, it's half a mile in to the lookout; bear to the left when the road forks.

The sweeping view from the lookout extends from Kahala and Diamond Head on the far left, across Waikiki and downtown Honolulu, to the Waianae Range on the far right. To the southeast is the University of Hawaii at Manoa, easily recognizable by its sports stadium; to the southwest you can see clearly into the green mound of Punchbowl Crater; the airport is visible on the edge of the coast and Pearl Harbor beyond that.

Although the best time for taking photos is generally during the day, this is also a fine place to watch evening settle over the city. Arrive at least 30 minutes before sunset to see the hills before they're in shadow.

## Contemporary Museum

The Contemporary Museum (☎ 526-0232; w www.tcmhi.org; 2411 Makiki Heights Dr; adult/senior or student $5/3; child under 13 yrs free; open 10am-4pm Tues-Sat, noon-4pm Sun) is an engaging modern art museum occupying an estate with 3½ acres of gardens.

The estate house was constructed in 1925 for Mrs Charles Montague Cooke, whose other former home is the present site of the Honolulu Academy of Arts. A fervent patron of the arts and an influential newspaper heiress, she played a founding role in both museums.

The main galleries feature changing exhibits of paintings, sculpture and other contemporary artwork by both national and international artists. A newer building on the lawn holds the museum's most prized piece, a vivid environmental installation by David Hockney based on his sets for *L'Enfant et les Sortilèges*, Ravel's 1925 opera.

Docent-led tours, conducted at 1:30pm, are included in the price of admission. There's a café serving lunch and drinks. The museum, near the intersection of Mott-Smith and Makiki Heights Drs, can be reached by the No 15 bus from downtown Honolulu.

## Makiki Valley Loop Trail

Three of the Tantalus area hiking trails – Maunalaha Trail, Makiki Valley Trail and Kanealole Trail – can be combined to make the Makiki Valley Loop Trail, a popular 2½-mile hike.

The loop goes through a lush and varied tropical forest that begins and ends in Hawaii's first state nursery and arboretum. In this nursery, hundreds of thousands of trees were grown to replace the sandalwood forests that were leveled in Makiki Valley and elsewhere in Hawaii in the 19th century.

The **Maunalaha Trail** begins at the rest rooms below the parking lot of the Makiki Forest baseyard. It crosses a bridge, passes taro patches and climbs up the eastern ridge of Makiki Valley, passing Norfolk pine, bamboo and fragrant allspice and eucalyptus trees. There are some good views along the way.

After three-quarters of a mile, you will come to a four-way junction, where you'll take the left fork and continue on the **Makiki Valley Trail**. The trail goes through small gulches and across gentle streams bordered with patches of ginger. Near the Moleka Stream crossing, there are mountain apple trees (related to allspice and guava) that flower in the spring and bear fruit in the summer. Edible yellow guava and strawberry guava also grow along the trail. There are some fine views of the city below.

The **Kanealole Trail** begins as you cross Kanealole Stream and then follows the stream back to the baseyard, three-quarters of a mile away. The trail leads down through a field of Job's tears; the beadlike bracts of the female flowers of this tall grass are often used for leis. Kanealole Trail is usually muddy, so wear shoes with good traction and pick up a walking stick.

**Getting There & Away** To get to the Makiki Forest baseyard, turn left off Makiki St and go half a mile up Makiki Heights Dr. Where the road makes a sharp bend, proceed straight ahead through a gate into the Makiki Forest Recreation Area and continue until you reach the baseyard. There's a parking lot on the right, just before the office.

You can also take the No 15 bus, which runs between downtown and Pacific Heights. Get off near the intersection of Mott-Smith and Makiki Heights Drs and walk down Makiki Heights Dr to the baseyard. It's a mile-long walk between the bus stop and the trailhead.

An alternative is to hike just the Makiki Valley Trail, which you can reach by going up Tantalus Dr 2 miles from its intersection with Makiki Heights Dr. As you come around a sharp curve, look for the wooden post marking the trailhead on the right. You can take this route in as far as you want and backtrack out or link up with other trails along the way.

## Puu Ohia Trail

The Puu Ohia Trail, in conjunction with the Pauoa Flats Trail, leads up to a lookout with a view of the Nuuanu reservoir and valley. It's nearly 2 miles one way and makes a hardy hike.

The trailhead is at the very top of Tantalus Dr, 3.6 miles up from its intersection with Makiki Heights Dr. There's a large turnoff opposite the trailhead where you can park.

The Puu Ohia Trail begins with reinforced log steps and leads past ginger, lush bamboo groves and lots of eucalyptus, a fast-growing tree that was planted to protect the watershed. About a half mile up, the trail reaches the top of 2013ft Mt Tantalus (Puu Ohia).

### The Last Records

The Bishop Museum is well respected, not only for its collections, but for the ethnological research it spearheaded throughout the Pacific. Beginning in the 1920s, supported by mainland philanthropy and Ivy League scholars, the museum organized teams of archaeologists and anthropologists and sent them to record the native cultures of the Pacific Islands before they were forever lost.

The most renowned of the researchers was Kenneth Emory, who was born in Boston but spent his early years in Hawaii, where he became fluent in the Hawaiian language. His knowledge of Hawaiian gave him the linguistic underpinnings to understand all Polynesian dialects. For five decades, he sailed on schooners and mail boats to the far corners of the Pacific, collecting film footage of native dancers, recording their songs, measuring their temples (both buildings and skulls!) and transcribing their folklore.

Emory's treatises are the most important (and sometimes the only) anthropological documentation of many Pacific Island cultures, from Lanai to Tuamotu. He was affiliated with Bishop Museum until his death at age 94 in 1992.

From Mt Tantalus, the trail leads to a service road. Continue on the road to its end, where there's a telephone company. The trail picks up again behind the left side of the building.

Continue down the trail until it reaches the Manoa Cliff Trail and go left. Walk on for a short distance until you come to another intersection, where you'll turn right onto the **Pauoa Flats Trail**. This trail leads down into Pauoa Flats and on to the lookout. The flats area can be muddy; be careful not to trip on exposed tree roots.

You'll pass two trailheads before reaching the lookout. The first is **Nuuanu Trail**, on the left, which runs three-quarters of a mile along the western side of Upper Pauoa Valley and offers broad views of Honolulu and the Waianae Range.

The second is **Aihualama Trail**, a bit farther along on the right, which takes you 1¼ miles through tranquil bamboo groves and past huge old banyan trees to Manoa Falls. If you follow this route, you can hike down the Manoa Falls Trail, a distance of about a mile, to the end of Manoa Rd and from there catch a bus back to town (see the Upper Manoa Valley section for bus details).

## ELSEWHERE IN HONOLULU
### Bishop Museum

The Bishop Museum *(Map 1; ☎ 847-3511; ⓦ www.bishopmuseum.org; 1525 Bernice St; adult/child 4-12 yrs $14.95/11.95, child under 4 yrs free; open 9am-5pm daily)* is hands down the finest Polynesian anthropological museum in the world, although the presentation can be a bit dry.

The main gallery, the **Hawaiian Hall**, has three floors of exhibits that cover the cultural history of Hawaii. The 1st floor, which is dedicated primarily to Hawaii before Westerners arrived, contains a full-sized *pili*-grass thatched house, carved temple images, shark-toothed war clubs and a number of other displays.

One of the museum's most impressive holdings is a feather cloak once worn by Kamehameha the Great. It was created entirely from the yellow feathers of the now-extinct *mamo*, a predominantly black bird with a yellow upper tail. Eighty thousand *mamo*s were caught, plucked and released to create this single cloak. To get a sense of just how few feathers each bird had available for sacrifice, look at the nearby taxidermic *mamo*, to the left of the Queen Liliuokalani exhibit.

The 2nd floor is dedicated to the varied influences of 19th-century Hawaii. Here you'll find traditional tapa cloth robes, missionary-inspired quilt work and barter items that Yankee traders brought to the islands; there is also a small whaling exhibit.

The top floor has displays on the various ethnic groups that comprise present-day Hawaii. Like Hawaii itself, it has a bit of everything, including samurai armor, Portuguese festival costumes, Taoist fortune-telling sticks and a Hawaiian ukulele made of coconut shells. To top it off, a 55ft sperm whale skeleton hangs from the ceiling.

The **Kahili Room**, a small gallery off the main hall, feature portraits of Hawaiian royalty and a display of *kahili*, the feathered staffs used at coronations and royal funerals. Other exhibits cover the cultures of Polynesia, Micronesia and Melanesia.

The museum's modern wing, the **Castle Building**, has changing natural history exhibits, some interactive, designed for children. The museum is also home to Oahu's only **planetarium** *(shows at 11:30am, 1:30pm, 2:30pm & 3:30pm daily)*; shows are included in the museum admission price.

The gift shop off the lobby sells books on the Pacific which are not easily found elsewhere, as well as some quality Hawaiiana crafts and souvenirs. There's also a snack shop open until 4pm.

To get to the Bishop Museum by bus from Waikiki or downtown Honolulu, take the No 2 School St bus to Kapalama St, and turn right on Bernice St. By car, take exit 20B off H1, go inland on Houghtailing St and turn left on Bernice St.

## Punchbowl

Punchbowl (Map 1) is the bowl-shaped remnant of a long-extinct volcanic crater. At an elevation of 500ft, it sits a mile north of the downtown district and offers a fine view of the city, out to Diamond Head and the Pacific beyond.

The early Hawaiians called the crater Puowaina, the 'hill of human sacrifices.' It's believed there was a heiau at the crater and that the slain bodies of *kapu* breakers, those who deviated from the taboos that strictly regulated all social interaction, were

brought to Punchbowl to be cremated upon the heiau altar.

Today, it's the site of the 115-acre **National Memorial Cemetery of the Pacific** *(☎ 532-3720; 2177 Puowaina Dr; admission free; open 8am-5:30pm daily Oct-Feb, 8am-6:30pm daily Mar-Sept)*. The remains of Hawaiians sacrificed to appease the gods now share the crater floor with the bodies of over 25,000 soldiers, more than half of whom were killed in the Pacific during WWII.

The remains of Ernie Pyle, the distinguished war correspondent who covered both world wars and was hit by machine gunfire on Ie Shima during the final days of WWII, lie in section D, grave 109. Five stones to the left, at grave D-1, is the marker for astronaut Ellison Onizuka, the Big Island native who perished in the 1986 Challenger space shuttle disaster. Their resting places are marked with the same style of flat granite stone that marks each of the cemetery's graves.

A huge memorial at the rear of the cemetery has eight marble courts representing different Pacific regions. The memorial is inscribed with the names of the 26,289 Americans missing in action from WWII and the Korean War. Two additional half courts have the names of 2489 soldiers missing from the Vietnam War.

For a good view of the city, walk to the lookout, 10 minutes south of the memorial.

If you're driving to Punchbowl, take the H1 to the Pali Hwy. There's a marked exit as you start up the Pali Hwy; watch closely, because it comes up quickly! From there, drive slowly and follow the signs as you wind through a series of narrow streets on the short route up to the cemetery.

By bus, take No 2 from Waikiki to downtown Honolulu and get off at Beretania and Alapai Sts, where you then transfer to bus No 15. Ask the driver where to get off. It's about a 15-minute walk to Punchbowl from the bus stop.

### Queen Emma Summer Palace

This summer palace *(Map 1; ☎ 595-3167; 2913 Pali Hwy; adult/child under 12 yrs $5/1; open 9am-4pm daily except holidays)*, on the northern side of Honolulu, is a former residence of Queen Emma, the consort of Kamehameha IV.

Emma was three-quarters royal Hawaiian and a quarter English, a granddaughter of the shipwrecked sailor John Young, who became a friend and adviser of Kamehameha the Great. The house is also known as Hanaiakamalama, the name of John Young's home in Kawaihae on the Big Island, where he served as governor.

Young left the home to Queen Emma, who often slipped away from her formal downtown home to this cooler retreat. It's a bit like an old Southern plantation mansion, with a column porch, high ceilings and louvered windows to catch the breeze.

The home was forgotten after Queen Emma's death in 1885 and was scheduled to be razed in 1915. At the last minute, the Daughters of Hawaii, a women's group founded by the descendants of missionaries, rescued the house from the wrecker's ball, and they have run it as a museum ever since.

The house is furnished in a way similar to Queen Emma's day, decorated with period furniture collected from five of Emma's homes. Items of particular note include a cathedral-shaped koa cabinet displaying a set of china from Queen Victoria; Emma's necklace of tiger claws, a gift from a maharaja of India; and feather cloaks and capes once worn by Hawaiian royalty.

There's a gift shop here selling Hawaiiana books and crafts such as koa bracelets and jewelry boxes made from native woods; it's open the same hours as the museum.

Queen Emma Summer Palace is on the Pali Hwy (Hwy 61) at the two-mile marker. By bus, take No 4 Nuuanu Dowsett, which runs about every 15 minutes from Waikiki. Be sure to let the bus driver know in advance where you're going, so you don't miss the stop.

### Royal Mausoleum State Monument

The Royal Mausoleum (Map 1; 2261 Nuuanu Ave; admission free; open 8am-4:30pm Mon-Fri) contains the remains of Kings Kamehameha II, III, IV and V, as well as King David Kalakaua and Queen Liliuokalani, Hawaii's last reigning monarchs. Conspicuously absent are the remains of Kamehameha the Great, the last king to be buried in secret in accordance with Hawaii's old religion.

The original mausoleum building, which is usually locked, is now a chapel; the caskets are in nearby crypts. Other gravestones honor Kamehameha the Great's British confidante John Young and American Charles Reed Bishop, husband of Princess Bernice Pauahi Bishop.

The Royal Mausoleum is on Nuuanu Ave, just before it meets the Pali Hwy. You can take the same No 4 Nuuanu Dowsett bus from Waikiki that serves the Queen Emma Summer Palace.

### Sand Island State Recreation Area

Sand Island (Map 1) is a 500-acre island on the western side of Honolulu Harbor. About a third of the island has been set aside as a state recreation area.

The park is heavily used by locals who camp, fish and picnic there on weekends, but because of the location at the end of an industrial area, and the noise from passing airplanes, it's not of great appeal to the casual visitor.

Sand Island is not reached from the downtown area, but via the Sand Island Access Rd, off the Nimitz Hwy (Hwy 92). The access road to the park travels 2½ miles through Honolulu's main industrial zone with warehouses, a wastewater treatment plant, oil tanks, scrap metal yards and the like. The airport runway is directly across the lagoon and the main flight path is just off the tip of the park.

The park has showers, rest rooms and a sandy beach, which, while cleaner than it's been in years past, is still far from pristine. Camping is allowed here with a permit; for more information, see Camping under Accommodations in the Facts for the Visitor chapter at the front of the book.

### Moanalua Gardens

In olden times Moanalua (Map 1) was a stopover for people who were traveling between Honolulu and Ewa, as well as a vacation spot for Hawaiian royalty. In 1884, Princess Pauahi Bishop willed the area to Samuel M Damon, and it's now privately owned by his estate.

Moanalua Gardens, maintained by the Damon Estate, is a large, grassy park with grand shade trees. The park is the site of King Kamehameha V's gingerbread-trimmed summer cottage, which overlooks a taro pond. Beyond it, a Chinese-style hall is fronted by carp ponds and stands of golden-stemmed bamboo. The center of the park has a grassy stage where the Prince Lot Hula Festival is held each July.

This is not a must-see spot, except during the festival, but it is a pleasant place to stroll if you happen to be passing by. To get there, take the Puuloa Rd/Tripler Hospital exit off Hwy 78 and then make an immediate right turn into the gardens. Unfortunately it's not practical to get here by public transport.

## PLACES TO STAY
### Near the Airport

If you have some dire need for a hotel near Honolulu International Airport, there are three hotels outside the airport, though they're along a busy highway and beneath flight paths. All three hotels provide free 24-hour transport to and from the airport, which is about 10 minutes away.

**Best Western Plaza Hotel** *(Map 1; ☎ 836-3636, 800-528-1234, fax 834-7406; e plaza hotel@aloha.net; 3253 N Nimitz Hwy; rooms $109)*, the most comfortable option, is a modern hotel with 274 pleasant rooms, each with a TV and refrigerator. The only drawback is the noise from the heavy traffic on the nearby highway that has an overpass adjacent to the front of the hotel – ask for a room at the rear. The hotel has a pool, lounge and restaurant, and nonsmoking rooms are available. Within walking distance is the Nimitz Mart center, which has a handful of fast-food eateries.

**Honolulu Airport Hotel** *(Map 1; ☎ 836-0661, 800-800-3477, fax 833-1738; e info@ honoluluairporthotel.com; 3401 N Nimitz Hwy; rooms $115)* has 308 utilitarian rooms that are a bit on the small side, but this four-story former Holiday Inn has all the usual amenities, including a lounge, pool and restaurant. Nonsmoking rooms are available. Discounts are common, including a room-and-car deal at the same price as the regular rate. The best reason to stay here is because you've arrived late at night or are flying out early.

**Pacific Marina Inn** *(Map 1; ☎ 836-1131, 800-548-8040, fax 833-0851; e pacific_ma rina_inn_2000@yahoo.com; 2628 Waiwai Loop; rooms $90)* is a mile farther east in an industrial area, but on the plus side it has the least traffic noise. This three-decker motel has small, straightforward rooms with air-con and TV, and a pool. There's often an 'airport special' of $65; call from its courtesy phone in the airport's baggage claim

area. For those with a daytime layover, there's a $40 day rate for use of the room between 6am and 2pm.

### Elsewhere in Honolulu

**Budget** A well-run hostel, in a quiet residential neighborhood near the University of Hawaii, **Hostelling International Honolulu** *(Map 4; ☎ 946-0591, fax 946-5904; e ayhalo ha@lava.net; 2323A Seaview Ave; dorm beds nonmembers/HI members $17/14, private rooms $44/38; office open 8am-noon & 4pm-midnight daily)* has seven dorm rooms with bunk beds that can accommodate up to 43 travelers. Men and women are in separate dorms, and there are also two double rooms. If you're not a Hostelling International (HI) member, there's a three-night maximum stay. HI membership is sold on site; the cost is $25 for Americans, $18 for foreign visitors. The hostel has a TV lounge, common-use kitchen, laundry room, lockers and bulletin boards with handy information for new arrivals.

**Fernhurst YWCA** *(Map 3; ☎ 941-2231, fax 949-0266; e fernywca@gte.net; 1566 Wilder Ave; beds in shared room $15, private rooms $30)* has rooms for women only in a three-story building about a mile from the university. Although the Y accepts tourists, most guests are local, because Fernhurst provides transitional housing for women in need – and the place can sometimes be full for weeks at a time. There are 60 rooms, each with two single beds and two lockable closets; two rooms share one bathroom. Rates include breakfast and dinner, except on weekends; there are limited kitchen facilities. Advance payment is required and guests must be YWCA members (membership is $30 a year). It costs $20 to rent linen, or you can bring your own. There's a laundry room, TV room and small pool.

**Central Branch YMCA** *(Map 3; ☎ 941-3344, fax 941-8821; 401 Atkinson Dr; e cen tralymca@yahoo.com; singles/doubles with shared bathroom $30/41; singles or doubles with private bathroom $53)*, on the eastern side of the Ala Moana Center, is conveniently located just outside Waikiki, and has 114 rooms in all. The rooms with shared bathroom, which are available to men only, are small and simple, resembling those in a student dorm; most have one single bed, but a few have a second bed, which allows two guys to share a room. Rooms with private bathroom, which are a bit nicer but still small and basic, are open to both men and women. Guests receive YMCA privileges, including free use of the sauna, pool and gym. The Y has a coin laundry and a TV lounge, and there are lots of cheap eats in the neighborhood.

**Nuuanu YMCA** *(Map 2; ☎ 536-3556; 1441 Pali Hwy; rooms per day/week $30/160)*, at the intersection of Pali Hwy and Vineyard Blvd, has mostly long-term tenants but rents some rooms by the day and week. Accommodations are for men only. Rooms are small and spartan, essentially just a single bed, a desk and a chair; bathrooms are shared. Guests have access to a TV lounge, the weight room and pool.

**Mid-Range** North of the Ala Moana Center, **Pagoda Hotel** *(Map 3; ☎ 941-6611, 800-367-6060, fax 955-5067; e hthcorp@world net.att.net; 1525 Rycroft St; rooms $110, studios $115)* has two sections. The rooms in the hotel itself, where you'll find the front desk and central lobby, are quiet and have the expected amenities, including air-con, TV and refrigerator. There are also studios with kitchenettes in a nearby apartment complex, but they can feel a bit removed from the main hotel – especially if you're checking in at night. There's nothing distinguished about this hotel, other than a restaurant with a carp pond, but it is one alternative to jumping into the bustling Waikiki scene.

**Top End** A restored Victorian inn on the National Register of Historic Places, you'll find the **Manoa Valley Inn** *(Map 4; ☎ 947-6019, fax 946-6168; e manoavalleyinn@aloha.net; 2001 Vancouver Dr; rooms with shared bathroom $99, with bathroom $140-190)* on a quiet side street near the University of Hawaii. The inn's common areas and the eight guest rooms are furnished with antiques, and the whole place drips with colonial character. The inn is away from the beach and sightseeing attractions, so it's best suited for people who prefer to be outside the main tourist scene – if you want to be in the thick of things, you may be bored here. Rates include continental breakfast.

**Ala Moana Hotel** *(Map 3; ☎ 955-4811, 800-367-6025, fax 944-6839; e amh.resv@gte.net; 410 Atkinson Dr; rooms $155-225)* looms above the Ala Moana Center, just west of Waikiki. The 1169 rooms, which resemble those of a chain hotel, have TV, air-con, small refrigerators and room safes. The lower rates are for lower-floor city-view rooms, with prices rising as you climb, topping out at ocean-view rooms on the 35th floor. The hotel is popular with business travelers, particularly overnighting airline crews.

**Executive Centre Hotel** *(Map 2; ☎ 539-3000, 800-922-7866, fax 523-1088; e res .exc@aston-hotels.com; 1088 Bishop St; rooms $170-250, corporate rates $124)* is Honolulu's only downtown hotel. Geared for businesspeople, it has 116 suites, each large and comfortable with modern amenities that include three phones, voice mail, two TVs, a refrigerator and a room safe. As the hotel is on the upper floors of a high-rise, most of the rooms have fine city views. The pricier rooms have ocean views and kitchen facilities. There's a fitness center, heated lap pool and a business center with secretarial services and laptop rentals. Rates include continental breakfast and the morning newspaper.

## PLACES TO EAT

Honolulu has an incredible variety of restaurants that mirror the city's multiethnic composition, and if you know where to look, it can also be quite cheap. The key is to get out of the tourist areas and eat where the locals do.

### Downtown Honolulu (Map 2)

**Restaurant Row** This rather sterile complex on the corner of Ala Moana Blvd and Punchbowl St, caters primarily to the downtown business crowd at lunchtime, with fast-food eateries and several restaurants.

**Payao** *(☎ 521-3511; dishes $7-12; open 11am-2pm Mon-Sat, 5pm-9:30pm daily)* offers an extensive menu of tasty Thai dishes, including salads, curries and noodle dishes. Most items can be ordered vegetarian or prepared with beef, chicken or shrimp.

**Sunset Grill** *(☎ 521-4409; lunch/dinner mains about $10/20; open 11am-11pm Mon-Fri, 5pm-11pm Sat & Sun)* has a varied menu with fresh fish, pastas and grilled meats at dinner, and creative salads and sandwiches at lunch. In addition to good food, the restaurant boasts an extensive wine list, including numerous selections by the glass.

**Ruth's Chris Steak House** (☎ 599-3860; mains $25-35; open 5pm-10pm daily), a high-end chain restaurant, has a reputation for consistent, top-quality steaks cooked to your liking. Top dollar, but always a good bet for steak lovers.

**Aloha Tower Marketplace** The Aloha Tower Marketplace, the waterfront shopping complex immediately west of the downtown district, is easily recognized by its landmark clock tower.

**Kapono's** (☎ 536-2161; small meals $6-10; open 11am-midnight daily), in the marketplace's waterfront courtyard, is not only a happening place for Hawaiian music, but a good spot for a drink and light eats. The menu includes snacks, sandwiches, fried calamari and the like. Happy 'hour' is a day-long event here, running from 11am to 8pm, and featuring $2 draft beers. There's live Hawaiian music from 6pm to 9pm nightly.

**Gordon Biersch Brewery Restaurant** (☎ 599-1405; mains $10-23; open 10:30am-10pm Mon-Fri, 10:30am-11pm Sat & Sun), seaside on the 1st floor, is another great spot for a drink. Hawaii's first and most successful microbrewery restaurant, it features fresh lagers made according to Germany's centuries-old purity laws. The food is also good: Hawaiian pupus, creative salads, sandwiches and pizzas are available for under $10, while the mains include specialty pastas and grilled seafood. There's live entertainment Wednesday through Saturday nights.

**Big Island Steak House** (☎ 537-4446; lunch specials $7-12, dinner mains $15-25; open 11am-10pm daily) is a decent steak restaurant with a fine water view. It specializes in thick, juicy steaks but also offers grilled fish, baby-back ribs and barbecued chicken.

**Chai's Island Bistro** (☎ 585-0011; appetizers $8-12, lunch mains $12-20, dinner mains $28-45; open 11am-4pm Mon-Fri, 4pm-10pm daily) is a spin-off of the popular Singha Thai restaurant that is located in Waikiki. It features upmarket Pacific Rim cuisine, with such specialties as crispy duck spring rolls, macadamia-crusted prawns and brandy-glazed Mongolian lamb. It is pricey and doesn't have a water view, but both the food and presentation are winners, and some of Hawaii's best musicians perform at dinner.

## Vegetarian Dining

Honolulu doesn't have many entirely vegetarian restaurants, but there are a few.

One recommendable spot is **Legend Vegetarian Restaurant** (Map 2; ☎ 532-8218; River St Mall) in Chinatown, which offers creative vegetarian Chinese food, including mock meat and seafood dishes.

In the University of Hawaii area, you'll find a vegetarian deli inside **Down to Earth Natural Foods** (Map 4; 2525 S King St), with inexpensive hot and cold takeout fare. For vegetarian Indian food there's **India Bazaar** (Map 4; ☎ 949-4840; 2320 S King St) in a little shopping center near Moiliili Park. **Coffeeline** (Map 4; ☎ 947-1615; cnr University & Seaview Aves), a cozy café opposite the university, serves up vegan soups, salads and simple vegetarian dishes.

In addition, there are many restaurants throughout Honolulu that have extensive vegetarian selections on their menus. Most Thai restaurants, including those listed in this book, have at least a page of vegetarian offerings, as do a number of Chinese and Vietnamese restaurants.

For a quick snack, Honolulu's ubiquitous Ba Le chain makes a tasty vegetarian sandwich of diced Asian vegetables on a crispy baguette.

A unique eating-out choice is **Govinda's** (Map 1; ☎ 595-3947; 51 Coelho Way; lunch buffet $7), the dining room at the Hare Krishna residence, which welcomes visitors from 11:30am to 3pm Monday to Friday to join the group over a buffet lunch of Indian dishes and salad.

The **Vegetarian Society of Hawaii** (☎ 944-8344), a nonprofit organization that aims to educate people about the benefits of vegetarianism, sponsors social activities such as lectures, picnics and dining outings. Call for a recorded message listing upcoming events.

**Fort St Mall** The Fort St Mall, a pedestrian street on the edge of the downtown district, has inexpensive restaurants within walking distance of Iolani Palace. It's convenient for sightseers and downtown workers, but is certainly not a draw if you're elsewhere around town. In addition to the places that follow, the area has lots of fast-food chains, including local favorites such as **Ba Le**, with good sandwiches, and **Kozo Sushi**, with inexpensive takeout sushi.

**Fort Street Cafe** (☎ 536-0455; 1152 Fort St Mall; dishes $4-6; open 7am-7pm Mon-Fri, 7am-4pm Sat) is usually crowded with students who come here for the cheap Asian plate lunches, *pho* (Vietnamese noodle soup) and various noodle dishes.

**L&L Drive-Inn** (☎ 521-8891; 116 S Hotel St; plate lunches $5; open 8am-6:30pm Mon-Sat), offering local-style Chinese fast food, does a bustling business at lunchtime, with items such as sweet-and-sour pork, broccoli chicken and fried noodles served from steamer trays.

**Z's Poi Bowl** (☎ 545-4225; 1108 Bishop St; plate lunches $4-6; open 6:30am-2pm Mon-Fri), a little hole-in-the-wall a block south of the Fort St Mall, features takeout plate lunches of traditional Hawaiian food. A typical plate includes selections such as *kalua* pig, *lomi* salmon, *poi* and rice.

**Cafe Metro** (☎ 533-0129; 1130 Fort St Mall; meals $6-12; open 9am-6pm Mon-Sat) is a pleasant place specializing in Tex-Mex fare. You can get standards such as tacos, enchiladas, chile relleno, served with rice and beans, and it also has salads, shrimp scampi and other items.

## Chinatown (Map 2)

For a quintessentially local dining option, head to the food court in the **Maunakea Marketplace** (N Hotel St; open 7am-3:30pm daily). Here you'll find about 20 stalls with mom-and-pop vendors dishing out homestyle Chinese, Thai, Vietnamese, Korean and Japanese food. You can get a solid meal for $5 and chow down at tiny wooden tables crowded into the central walkway.

Another takeout option is **Hawaiian Hula Bread** (☎ 536-2880; 1120 Maunakea St; open 5am-6pm Mon-Fri, 7am-2pm Sat & Sun), where you can snack on baked treats ranging from cookies to pizza. Hilo's Passion bread, with walnuts and cranberries, is its most popular.

**Ba Le** (☎ 521-3973; 150 N King St; snacks $1-5; open 6am-5pm Mon-Sat, 6am-3pm Sun) is another good place for a quick, inexpensive bite. Vegetarian sandwiches – a tangy combo of crunchy carrots, daikon and cilantro – cost just $2.25, while meat selections such as a lemongrass chicken sandwich are $3.75. For

a caffeine jolt, there's sweet, strong French coffee with milk, either hot or cold.

**Lee Ho Fook Restaurant** (☎ 536-6077; Chinatown Cultural Plaza; dishes $4-6.50; open 10am-8pm daily), on the River St mall, is a hole-in-the-wall family-run place with half a dozen tables and some of the cheapest Chinese food around. Amazingly, there are nearly a hundred items on the menu, from delicious cake noodles to beef in oyster sauce and black-bean shrimp. Unbeatable value.

**Krung Thai** (☎ 599-4803; 1028 Nuuanu Ave; plates 1/2 mains $4/5; open 10:30am-2pm Mon-Fri) is a Thai eatery on the edge of Chinatown. Lunch, the only meal served, is geared to the business community's 30-minute lunch breaks, with food ready in steamer trays. You can choose from a dozen hot mains, such as broccoli beef, cashew chicken or garlic eggplant, served with rice. There are tables in a rear courtyard where you can sit and enjoy your meal.

**Pho To Chau** (☎ 533-4549; 1007 River St; pho regular/large $4/5.20; open 8am-2:30pm daily) specializes in Vietnamese *pho* soups. It comes with a second plate of fresh basil and hot chili peppers that you add to your liking. A bowl of soup is a meal in itself. The shrimp rolls ($3) here are also excellent, and the restaurant serves some rice dishes, but just about everybody comes to this family-run place for the soup. It's so popular that even at 10am you may have to line up outside the door for one of the 16 tables. It's well worth the wait.

One of Chinatown's most-loved spots doesn't serve Chinese food at all: **Aunty's Puerto Rican Kitchen** (☎ 524-7921; 907 Kekaulike St; plates $4.50-6.25; open 7am-2pm Tues-Fri, 9am-4pm Sat) has mastered the art of making *pasteles*, a tamale-like bundle of mashed green banana filled with vegetables and pork, wrapped in a ti leaf and boiled. The Spanish rice is also excellent at this tiny hole-in-the-wall.

**Char Hung Sut** ( ☎ 538-3335; 64 N Pauahi St; open 5:30am-2pm Mon & Wed-Sat, 5:30am-1pm Sun) looks like hell outside, but the *manapua*, an Island version of the familiar Chinese *sui bao*, or steamed pork buns, are legendary.

**Mei Sum Chinese Dim Sum Restaurant** (☎ 531-3268; 65 N Pauhai St; dim sum $1.25-2.95; open 7am-8:45pm daily, dim sum until

*3pm daily)* is a small, cheery place that was chosen as one of Hawaii's 150 best restaurants by the *Honolulu Advertiser* staff. A full menu is offered, but the main draw is the multitude of small plates that make for a memorable dim sum meal.

**Legend Vegetarian Restaurant** *(☎ 532-8218; Chinatown Cultural Plaza; dishes $7-12; open 10:30am-2pm, 5:30pm-9pm Thur-Tues)* is a curious place on the River St side. This health-oriented Chinese dining spot offers some incongruously named dishes (vegetarian butter fish! sweet-and-sour vegetarian pork!) that creatively use tofu and wheat gluten to duplicate the flavors and textures of meat and seafood. Nonetheless, the restaurant is 100% vegetarian. The menu is not only imaginative but extensive as well, and the restaurant packs in a good crowd.

**Indigo** *(☎ 521-2900; 1121 Nuuanu Ave; appetizers $6-10, dinner mains $16-26; open 11:30am-2pm Tues-Fri, 6pm-9:30pm Tues-Sat)* has a relaxed, open-air courtyard and good contemporary Eurasian cuisine. Located on the Chinatown-downtown border, behind the Hawaii Theatre, it's a favorite dinner spot for theatergoers, and the crowd is a happy, eclectic mix. The creative dim sum appetizers such as tempura ahi rolls and goat cheese wontons are a special treat. Dinner features such dishes as tangerine-glazed ribs, ginger-miso salmon and mahogany duck. An award-winning wine list matches the inspired menu. The courtyard bar has an impressive, free spread at happy hour (food at 5pm, drink specials 4pm to 7pm Tuesday to Friday).

## Central Honolulu & Ala Moana (Map 3)

**Mekong** *(☎ 591-8841; 1295 S Beretania St; appetizers $4-7, mains $7-10; open 11am-2pm Mon-Fri, 5pm-9:30pm daily)* is one of the oldest Thai restaurants in Honolulu. It's a small unpretentious place with a solid reputation for good food and fair prices. The menu includes noodle dishes and a variety of curries with both vegetarian and meat versions. If it's full there's a branch operation nearby, **Mekong II** *(☎ 941-6184; 1726 S King St)*, with the same menu and hours.

**El Burrito** *(☎ 596-8225; 550 Piikoi St; combination plates $8-10; open 11am-8pm Mon-Thur, 11am-9pm Fri & Sat)*, near the Ala Moana Center, could be a neighborhood

restaurant on a back street in Mexico City. This hole-in-the-wall squeezes in about a dozen tables and serves authentic Mexican food, with fellow diners as likely to be chatting in Spanish as English.

**Auntie Pasto's** *(☎ 523-8855; 1099 S Beretania St; antipasti $5-10, mains $8-12; open 11am-10:30pm Mon-Fri, 4pm-11pm Sat & Sun)* has good Italian food at honest prices. Pasta is the specialty, with a number of vegetarian varieties such as eggplant parmesan, as well as a full range of seafood and meat choices. Although it's off the tourist track, this popular spot attracts a crowd and you may have to wait for a table – particularly on the weekend.

**Pavilion Cafe** *(☎ 532-8734; 900 S Beretania St; dishes $8-12.50; open 11:30am-2pm Tues-Sat)*, in the Honolulu Academy of Arts, has a lovely courtyard setting overlooking the museum's water fountains. It specializes in gourmet salads and sandwiches, but also has a pasta of the day ($12.50). It's a good place to relax and a wonderfully indulgent way to support the arts. Reservations are suggested, particularly if there's a special exhibit taking place at the museum.

**Pagoda Restaurant** *(☎ 941-6611; 1525 Rycroft St; breakfast dishes $4-9, lunch buffet $11, dinner buffet $19-21; breakfast 6:30am-11am Mon-Sat, lunch 11am-2pm Mon-Fri, dinner 4:30pm-9:30pm daily)*, at the Pagoda Hotel, offers a pleasant gardenlike setting bordering a carp pond. The breakfast menu is extensive, there's a rather standard lunch buffet of Japanese and American dishes and a fancier dinner buffet with a spread that includes prime rib, crab legs, sashimi, a salad bar and a dessert bar.

**Yanagi Sushi** *(☎ 537-1525; 762 Kapiolani Blvd; a la carte sushi $2-5, set meals $10-20; open 11am-2pm daily, 5:30pm-2am Mon-Sat, 5:30pm-10pm Sun)* is one of Honolulu's most popular late-night places. Not only is the sushi here top-rated, but Yanagi also offers a full line of other Japanese dinners prepared to perfection. Ask about the 'late birds' – $8 meal specials available after 10:30pm.

**Alan Wong's** *(☎ 949-2526; 1857 S King St; appetizers $8-12, mains $26-38; open 5pm-10pm daily)*, one of Hawaii's top restaurants, is a high-energy place that specializes in upmarket Hawaii Regional cuisine. Chef Wong, who won accolades at the Big Island's exclusive Mauna Lani Resort before striking out on his own, offers a creative menu that has an emphasis on fresh local ingredients. Appetizers include the likes of tempura ahi and mains feature fresh seafood such as Wong's signature dish, ginger-crusted *onaga*. Each night there's also a five-course 'tasting menu' ($65). Reservations are recommended.

**Ala Moana Center** The **Makai Market** *(open 8am-9pm Mon-Sat, 9am-6pm Sun)*, the Ala Moana Center's food court, is a circus with neon signs, hundreds of tiny tables crowded together and some 50 fast-food stalls. There's something for everyone, from salads to ice cream and warm cookies, and Chinese, Japanese, Korean, Hawaiian, Thai and Mexican specialties.

If you have the munchies, this is a good place to stop when you're between buses. It's like window-shopping – you can walk through, preview the food and select what you want. The food court is on the ocean side of the Ala Moana Center's ground floor. Some of your choices here include the following:

**Yummy Korean BBQ** *(combination plates $6)* is a similar concept to the Panda Express chain, with Korean meat mains, rice and a number of tasty pickled vegies and kimchis.

**Patti's Chinese Kitchen** *(combination plates $5.50)* is a big-volume place with a few dozen dishes to choose from. If you really want to indulge, you can get a whole roast duck for $11.75.

**Naniwa Ya Ramen** dishes up steaming bowls of authentic Japanese ramen noodles for around $6 and has *gyoza*, a tasty grilled dumpling that goes great with beer, for $3. **Panini Too** is unbeatable for its high-rise turkey sandwich ($7) on a choice of sourdough or foccacia. **Little Cafe Siam** serves tasty skewers of chicken satay in peanut sauce ($2.50), and at **Sbarro** meal-sized slices of pizza cost $3.

**Ward Centre** The shopping complex, Ward Centre *(1200 Ala Moana Blvd)*, has a couple of coffee shops and delis and about a dozen other dining spots.

**Mocha Java/Crepe Fever** *(☎ 591-9023; items $2-8; open 7am-9pm Mon-Sat, 8am-6pm Sun)*, on the center's ground level, is a popular hangout serving good fresh fruit smoothies, coffees, pastries, crepes, omelettes and other light dishes.

**Kaka'ako Kitchen** *(☎ 596-7488; meals $6-9; open 7am-10pm Mon-Sat, 7am-5pm Sun)*, at the northwestern corner of the center, offers fantastic food at bargain prices. A spin-off of the upscale restaurant 3660 On the Rise (see later), Kaka'ako uses the same fresh ingredients and creative flair as its pricier parent operation. Here, however, the food is served plate lunch style on styrofoam with brown rice and a salad of locally grown greens. You can choose from standard favorites such as *shoyu* chicken ($6) or for a bit more order a gourmet plate such as the sauteed *mahimahi* (a top choice) or the ginger-sake ahi steak. Eat here at patio tables or take it across the street to Ala Moana Beach for a picnic.

**Scoozee's** *(☎ 597-1777; dishes $8-14; open 11am-10pm Sun-Thur, 11am-11pm Fri & Sat)*, on the center's ground level, is a nouveau-Italian café with good pastas, pizzas, calzones and Italian sandwiches.

**Compadres** *(☎ 591-8307; appetizers $5-8, combination plates $10-20; open 11am-11pm Mon-Thur, 11am-midnight Fri & Sat, 11am-10pm Sun)*, on the center's upper level, is a bustling Mexican restaurant that draws a crowd and wins plenty of local awards. It not only offers the expected enchilada, fajita and taco dishes, but also has some interesting cross-cultural fare such as spicy peanut Thai quesadillas.

**Brew Moon** *(☎ 593-0088; snacks $6-9; lunch/dinner mains $12/18; open 11am-1am daily)*, a stylish, high-energy place, brews its own ales, ranging from a low-calorie 'moonlight' brew to the copper-colored 'Hawaii 5' malt. A fun way to tantalize the taste buds is with the 24oz sampler ($6) of six different ales. Brew Moon serves a wide variety of snacks, including fried calamari, grilled pizzas, burgers and sandwiches. Meals such as jambalaya chicken or sauteed fish are available at lunch and dinner.

**Ward Warehouse** The Ward Warehouse *(cnr Ala Moana Blvd & Ward Ave)*, is a shopping complex adjacent to the Ward Centre.

**Kincaid's Fish, Chop & Steak House** *(☎ 591-2005; lunch specials $10-15, dinner mains $18-30; open 11am-10pm daily)* is a pleasant place with good food and a harbor view. A favorite lunch spot for downtown businesspeople, the restaurant specializes in creative seafood dishes and steaks. The best deal is the soup-to-dessert 'early bird,' which is available from 5pm to 6pm and offers a choice of several mains for $19.

There are also a few food stalls on the ground floor that sell $6 plate lunches, including **Korean BBQ Express**, with Korean fare, and **L&L Drive-Inn**, a chain with local dishes. Also at ground level is **Coffee Works**, a little café selling coffee and pastries.

## University Area (Map 4)

Not surprisingly, the area around the University of Hawaii at Manoa supports an interesting collection of reasonably priced ethnic restaurants, coffee shops and health food stores. The following places are all within walking distance of the three-way intersection of King St, Beretania St and University Ave.

**Coffeeline** (☎ 947-1615; cnr University & Seaview Aves; dishes $3-6; open 7am-3:45pm Mon-Fri, 8am-noon Sat) is a casual student hangout serving coffees and mostly vegetarian meals. Proudly serving 'slow food,' Coffeeline offers up vegan soup, 'big hippie' sandwiches, hearty salads and a few hot dishes such as spinach lasagna. Blues and jazz music plays all day and there's a large stack of alternative magazines to browse through.

**Ezogiku Noodle Cafe** (☎ 942-3608; 1010 University Ave; dishes $5-7; open 11am-11pm daily) serves up steaming bowls of Japanese ramen, curries and fried rice. Nothing memorable, but it is on a par with similar fast-food noodle shops in Japan, and it's cheap.

**Ba Le** (☎ 943-0507; 1019 University Ave; snacks $1-5; open 7am-7:30pm Mon-Sat), a simple local chain eatery, sells good inexpensive French rolls, croissants and sandwiches, as well as Vietnamese noodle dishes and salads.

**Down to Earth Natural Foods** (☎ 947-7678; 2525 S King St; open 7:30am-9pm daily) is Honolulu's largest natural foods supermarket. It's a great place to shop, carrying everything from Indian chapatis to local organic produce, and prices are reasonable. The store also has a vegetarian deli with a salad bar and hot dishes such as tahini tofu balls or vegetable curry for $6 a pound. There's a conventional grocery store, **Star Market**, across the street.

**India Bazaar** (☎ 949-4840; 2320 S King St; meals $7; open 11am-7:30pm daily), in a little shopping plaza, is a small café selling inexpensive Indian food. Plates are dished up with your choice of three curried items, either vegetarian or chicken, plus spiced rice. Side orders of papadams, chapatis and raita cost less than $1.

**Kozo Sushi** (☎ 973-5666; 2334 S King St; a la carte sushi $1-5; open 9am-7pm Mon-Sat, 9am-6pm Sun), in the same complex as India Bazaar, is a branch of a local chain that specializes in good, inexpensive sushi. Two top choices are the fresh tuna roll and the California maki, a crab and avocado roll. Although it's mostly takeout, the shop has a couple of tables where you can sit and eat.

**Wan's** (☎ 949-3706; 1023 University Ave; dishes $6-10; open 10:30am-3:30pm, 5pm-10pm daily) is a wonderful little family-run Thai restaurant, neat as a pin. It has an extensive menu, including many vegetarian dishes. The curries are scrumptious and come in numerous versions, including Penang and yellow, but if you like things fiery go instead with the red curry, a hot and spicy version that's dubbed 'Wan's Evil Thai.'

**Maple Garden** (☎ 941-6641; 909 Isenberg St; lunch specials $6, dinner mains $6.50-10; open 11am-2pm & 5:30pm-10pm daily), around the corner from S King St, is a popular local Szechuan restaurant with delicious food at reasonable prices. There are scores of vegetarian, beef, pork, chicken, duck and seafood options. House specialties include eggplant in hot garlic sauce, black-bean prawns and smoky Szechuan duck.

**The Greek Corner** (☎ 942-5503; 1025 University Ave; sandwiches $7, mains $10-12; open 11am-1:30pm Mon-Fri, 5pm-9:30pm daily) is an inviting eatery with good Greek food, and being near the university, prices are cheaper than they'd be in a trendier part of town. Main dishes, which come with Greek salad, rice and pitta bread, include such standards as lamb kebab, moussaka and dolmades. It offers plenty of choices for vegetarians and meat eaters alike.

**Yakiniku Camellia** (☎ 946-7595; 2494 S Beretania St; lunch/dinner buffet $10/15.75; open lunch 11am-3pm, dinner 3pm-10pm daily) features tasty all-you-can-cook Korean buffets. It's quality food, and if you've worked up an appetite, it's a fine deal. The mainstay is pieces of chicken, pork and beef that you select and grill at your table. Accompanying this are 18 marinated side dishes, miso and seaweed soups, salads and fresh fruit. When selecting kimchis, keep in mind that the redder they are, the hotter they are. Everything here is authentic, right down to the vending machine selling Korean-language newspapers.

## Elsewhere in Honolulu

**Hale Vietnam** *(Map 1; ☎ 735-7581; 1140 12th Ave; mains $6-10; open 11am-10pm daily)*, in the Kaimuki area, well off the beaten path, is a top-notch local favorite with delicious Vietnamese food at moderate prices. A delightful starter is the temple rolls ($4.25), a combination of fresh basil, mint, tofu and yam rolled in rice paper. The yellow curries are also excellent and come in vegetarian, beef and chicken variations.

**Sam Choy's Breakfast, Lunch & Crab** *(Map 1; ☎ 545-7979, fax 545-7997; 580 N Nimitz Hwy; lunch mains $9-16, dinner mains $11-34; open 6:30am-10pm daily)* offers huge portions of local specialties such as fried noodles or loco moco for breakfast (along with mainland staples such as bacon and eggs), and fresh crab, crabcakes or other sandwiches for lunch, and more crab for dinner. There's also a steak and lobster combo ($34). The food is great, a high-quality change from overpriced hotel fare. The Sunday brunch buffet is a bargain at $12.50, and the restaurant's on-site Big Aloha Brewery pours some of the best micro brews in town. Reservations recommended.

**3660 On the Rise** *(Map 1; ☎ 737-1177; 3660 Waialae Ave; appetizers $10, mains $19-26; open 5:30pm-9pm Tues-Sun)* is a trendy restaurant with a loyal Honolulu following. It features 'Euro-Island' cuisine, blending continental and Island flavors. Appetizers include escargot, spicy crab cakes and specialty salads. Popular mains include red snapper steamed in a Hawaiian ti leaf, macadamia nut-crusted lamb and Black Angus garlic steak. The restaurant is 3 miles northeast of Waikiki, on Waialae Ave between 12th and 13th Aves; reservations recommended.

**Contemporary Cafe** *(Map 5; ☎ 523-3362; 2411 Makiki Heights Dr; lunch mains $8-10; open 11am-2:30pm Tues-Sat, noon-2:30pm Sun)* is a genteel treat, with a pleasant lawn setting at the Contemporary Museum in Makiki Valley. There are healthy salads, such as chicken Caesar or soba noodle with watercress, and creative sandwiches, including grilled eggplant with feta or tapenade and boursin cheese on a baguette. It's not necessary to pay museum admission if you're just having lunch – simply let the staff person at the door know that you're there for the café.

**Waioli Tea Room** *(Map 5; ☎ 988-5800; 2950 Manoa Rd; a la carte dishes $8-12, high tea $18.25; open 8am-4pm daily)* in Manoa Valley, between the University of Hawaii and the Lyon Arboretum, near Oahu Ave, is a different sort of place, a bit like stepping back a hundred years. It has a series of open-air dining rooms looking out onto gardens. In one of the gardens is the restored grass hut that author Robert Louis Stevenson stayed in during his retreat at Waikiki Beach; the cottage was dismantled and moved to this site in 1926. Another area has a chapel that's a popular wedding spot.

The main event here is the afternoon high tea, which is served on the veranda at 2:30pm daily except Monday. It's not cheap, but it's an elegant affair with fine china, a dozen-plus teas and a good selection of homemade scones and pastries. You can also get breakfast here, with waffles and omelettes, as well as lunchtime sandwiches, such as chicken curry with mango chutney, and specialty salads such as fresh ahi on Island greens. For the high tea, reservations are required and usually need to be made at least a day in advance.

## ENTERTAINMENT

Honolulu has a lively entertainment scene. The best updated listings are in the free *Honolulu Weekly*, which is easily found throughout the city, and the TGIF insert in the Friday edition of the *Honolulu Advertiser*.

## Theater & Concerts

Honolulu has a symphony, an opera company, ballet troupes, chamber orchestras and numerous community theater groups.

**Hawaii Theatre** *(Map 2; ☎ 528-0506; 1130 Bethel St)* is a popular venue for dance, music and theater. Performances range from top contemporary Hawaiian musicians such as Hapa and the Brothers Cazimero to modern dance pieces and film festivals.

**Blaisdell Center** *(Map 3; ☎ 591-2211; 777 Ward Ave)* presents concerts, Broadway shows and family events, such as the Honolulu Symphony, the Ice Capades, the American Ballet Theatre and occasional big-name rock musicians such as Sting.

**Academy Theatre** *(Map 3; ☎ 532-8768; 900 S Beretania St)*, at the Honolulu Academy of Arts, and to a lesser degree, the **East-West Center** *(Map 4; ☎ 944-7111)*, adjacent to the University of Hawaii, both present multicultural theater and concerts along the lines of Chinese opera and Japanese koto music.

There are more than a dozen theater companies on Oahu, performing everything from Broadway musicals to David Mamet satires and pidgin fairy tales. For a schedule of current theater productions, see the entertainment section of the Honolulu newspapers.

**Aloha Stadium** *(☎ 486-9300)*, on the western outskirts of Honolulu (see Pearl Harbor Area map), has the island's largest audience capacity and is the location for some of the biggest big name concerts.

## Bars & Clubs

**Anna Bannanas** *(Map 4; ☎ 946-5190; 2440 S Beretania St)* is a hot dance place not far from the university, which features blues, ska and reggae bands from 9pm to 2am Thursday to Sunday.

**Kapono's** *(Map 2; ☎ 536-2161)*, at the Aloha Tower Marketplace, has live music from 9pm to 2am Tuesday to Saturday, featuring jazz, rock and top Hawaiian musicians, including the club's namesake, Henry Kapono.

**Gordon Biersch Brewery Restaurant** *(Map 2; ☎ 599-4877)*, also at the Aloha Tower Marketplace, is a popular waterfront microbrewery with live rhythm and blues, contemporary Hawaiian and soft rock from 9pm to midnight Thursday to Saturday.

At **Indigo** *(Map 2; ☎ 521-2900; ⓦ www .indigo-hawaii.com; 1121 Nuuanu Ave; admission free)*, the Opium Den & Champagne Bar offers drink specials ($2.75 for a huge variety of flavored, vodka-based drinks related to a dry martini only by the shape of the glass) and live music every Thursday night. The multilevel restaurant's Green Room has late-night ambient DJ music and dancing on Friday and Saturday, and a bar menu is served until midnight.

**Rumours** *(Map 3; ☎ 955-4811; 410 Atkinson Dr)*, at Ala Moana Hotel, has dancing to

recorded music from 9pm to 4am Thursday to Saturday, with Latin music on Thursday, Top 40 music on Friday and hip-hop and rhythm and blues on Saturday.

**World Cafe** *(Map 1; ☎ 599-4450; 1130 Nimitz Hwy)* is one of Honolulu's most happening clubs, with everything from theme nights to concerts by the likes of Alicia Keys and modpunk band The Strokes.

## Cinemas

Honolulu has several large movie theaters showing first-run feature films, including **Ward Stadium 16** *(Map 3; ☎ 594-7000; Auahi & Kamakee Sts)*, Oahu's biggest theater with 16 screens; and **Restaurant Row 9 Cinemas** *(Map 2; ☎ 526-4171; 500 Ala Moana Blvd)*, a nine-screen multiplex at Restaurant Row.

For a cozier scene, there's the **Movie Museum** *(Map 1; ☎ 735-8771; 3566 Harding Ave)*, a fun place to watch classic oldies such as *Citizen Kane* and *Casablanca* in a theater with just 20 comfy chairs. Movies are shown on Thursday to Monday evenings and Saturday and Sunday afternoons. Reservations are recommended.

**Varsity Twins** *(Map 4; ☎ 973-5833; 1006 University Ave)*, a two-screen theater near the University of Hawaii, usually shows foreign films, art film and other alternative movies.

**Academy Theatre** *(Map 3; ☎ 532-8768; 900 S Beretania St)*, at the Honolulu Academy of Arts, showcases progressive movies, art films and avant-garde shorts.

## Free Entertainment

The Royal Hawaiian Band performs from noon to 1pm on Friday (except during August) on the lawn of the Iolani Palace (Map 2).

In the Ala Moana Center (Map 3), a courtyard area called Centerstage is the venue for free performances by hula dancers, gospel groups, ballet troupes, local bands and the like. There's something happening almost daily – look for the schedule in the Ala Moana Center's free shopping magazine.

**Mayor's Office of Culture & Arts** *(☎ 527-5666)* sponsors numerous free performances, art exhibits and musical events, ranging from street musicians in city parks to band concerts in various locales around Honolulu. Call for information on current events.

## SHOPPING

Hawaii's biggest shopping center, the **Ala Moana Center** *(Map 3; ☎ 955-9517; 1450 Ala Moana Blvd)*, has 200 stores, from chain department stores to fashionable boutiques and specialty shops. Interesting shops in the center include **The Islands' Best** *(☎ 949-5345)* and **Products of Hawaii** *(☎ 949-6866)* for locally made gifts; the **Hawaiian Quilt Collection** *(☎ 946-2233)* for beautiful quilts, pillows and kits; and **High Performance Kites** *(☎ 947-7097)* for Hawaii-made kites with Island designs.

The two other large shopping centers in central Honolulu are the **Ward Centre** *(Map 3; ☎ 591-8411; 1200 Ala Moana Blvd)* and the adjacent **Ward Warehouse** *(Map 3; ☎ 593-2376; 1050 Ala Moana Blvd)*. The larger of the two, Ward Warehouse, has about 60 stores, including two that sell some of the finest in Hawaiian-made crafts, art and silk-screened clothing: **Native Books & Beautiful Things** *(☎ 596-8885)* and **Nohea Gallery** *(☎ 596-0074)*.

The **Aloha Tower Marketplace** *(Map 2; ☎ 528-5700; Pier 9)* has about 50 shops as well as dozens of kiosks selling Hawaiian-made foods, jewelry and knickknacks. One of the more interesting stores to browse is **Martin & MacArthur** *(☎ 524-6066)*, which specializes in upmarket Hawaiiana products such as calabashes, quilts, handmade dolls and koa woodwork.

The **Hula Supply Center** *(Map 4; 941-5379; 2346 S King St)* sells feather leis, calabash gourds, hula skirts and the like.

Although they're intended for Hawaiian musicians and dancers, some of the items would make interesting souvenirs and prices are reasonable.

If you've been hankering to make your own music, **Kamaka Hawaii** *(Map 2; ☎ 531-3165; 550 South St)* specializes in handcrafted ukuleles made on Oahu, but expect to pay nearly $500. You can also find ukuleles – imported, but cheaper – at **Hawaiian Ukulele Co** *(☎ 536-3228)* at the Aloha Tower Marketplace; prices begin at $80.

You'll find good collections of classic and contemporary Hawaiian CDs at **Borders** *(Map 3; ☎ 591-8996)* at the Ward Centre and at **Tower Records** *(Map 3; ☎ 941-7774; 611 Keeaumoku St)*, just north of the Ala Moana Center. Both have handy headphone set-ups that allow you to listen to various Hawaiian-music CDs before you buy.

**Hilo Hattie** *(Map 1; ☎ 535-6500; 700 Nimitz Hwy; ⓦ www.hilohattie.com; open 8am-6pm daily)* is the place to go for all those Hawaiian gifts: sarongs, flip-flops, hundreds of Hawaiian shirts, matching muumuus, macadamia nuts, pukka shell necklaces and on and on. The selection is enormous, and touristy or not, the shop has good deals. There's also a branch on the 1st floor of the Ala Moana Center.

Finally, if you're in the Pearl Harbor area, pop in to the **Aloha Stadium Swap Meet** held on Wednesdays, Saturdays and Sundays. For more information on this market, see the boxed text 'Bargain Hunting' in the Pearl Harbor Area chapter.

# Waikiki

Waikiki is one of those places that people dream of when they think of a tropical vacation. There's good reason why it's become such a holiday mecca: Waikiki has a phenomenal seaside location, sunny year-round weather and a plethora of things to do.

The largest tourist destination in Hawaii, Waikiki fronts a glimmering white-sand beach that's lined with high-rise hotels and set against the backdrop of scenic Diamond Head.

Crowded with tourists from both Japan and North America, Waikiki has 25,000 permanent residents and some 65,000 visitors on any given day, all in an area roughly 1½ miles long and half a mile wide. It boasts 34,000 hotel rooms, 450 restaurants, 350 bars and clubs, and more shops than you'd want to count.

Waikiki has plenty of activities that can make for good fun, such as hula shows, outrigger canoe rides and sunning on the beach. Like any city scene, the deeper you dig, the more you'll find. You can also join in a Japanese tea ceremony, take a surfing lesson from an aging beachboy, or listen to a free concert by the Royal Hawaiian Band.

Although the beaches are packed during the day, at night most of the action is along the streets, where window-shoppers, time-share touts and street performers all go about their business. A variety of live music, from mellow Hawaiian to rock, wafts from clubs and hotel lounges.

Waikiki Beach has wonderful orange sunsets, with the sun picturesquely dropping down between cruising sailboats. The beach is also quite romantic to stroll at night, enhanced by the dramatic city skyline and the sounds of the surf lapping at the shore, and it's dark enough to enjoy the stars.

## ORIENTATION

Waikiki, at the southeastern side of Honolulu, is considered a neighborhood of Honolulu for most official purposes, but for practical purposes is usually referred to as an entity in itself.

Waikiki is bounded on two sides by the Ala Wai Canal, on another by the ocean and on the fourth by Kapiolani Park.

## Highlights

- Digging your toes into the sand as one of Waikiki's brilliant sunsets unfolds
- Catching one of Waikiki's many free hula performances
- Enjoying a romantic dinner at a beach-front restaurant
- Taking a surfing lesson from one of Waikiki's beachboys
- Hitting Waikiki's vibrant night scene and knocking back some Mai Tais

Waikiki
pages 134-135

Three parallel roads cross Waikiki: Kalakaua Ave, the beach road named after King David Kalakaua; Kuhio Ave, the main drag for Waikiki's buses, which is named after Prince Jonah Kuhio Kalanianaole; and Ala Wai Blvd, which borders the Ala Wai Canal.

City buses are not allowed on Kalakaua Ave, and the traffic on this multi-lane road is one way, so it's relatively smooth for driving. However, pedestrians need to be cautious, as cars tend to zoom by at a fairly fast clip.

## INFORMATION
### Tourist Offices

You can pick up brochures and general tourist literature at the Hawaii Visitors and Convention Bureau's **visitor information office** (☎ 924-0266; Suite 502, 2250 Kalakaua Ave; open 8am-4:30pm Mon-Fri, 8am-noon Sat & Sun) in the Waikiki Shopping Plaza.

Free tourist magazines, such as This Week Oahu, Spotlight's Oahu Gold and Best of Oahu, can readily be found on street corners and in hotel lobbies throughout Waikiki.

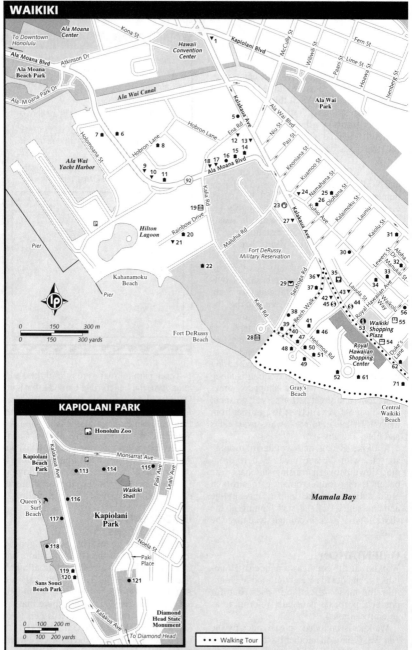

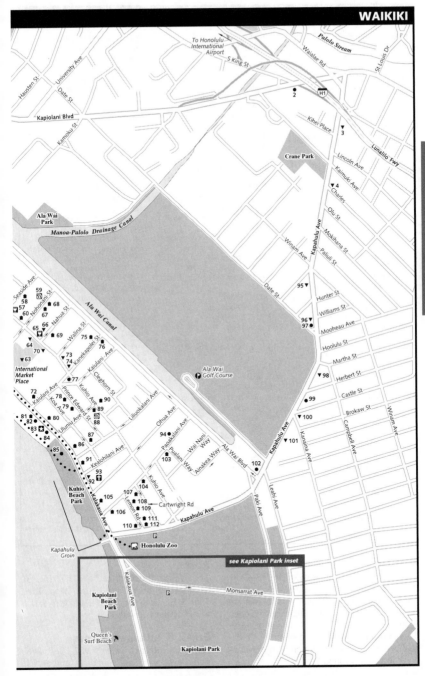

# WAIKIKI

see Kapiolani Park inset

## WAIKIKI

**PLACES TO STAY**
6   Hawaii Polo Inn
7   Hawaii Prince Hotel;
    Prince Court
8   Ohana Waikiki Hobron
11  Holiday Inn Waikiki
14  Doubletree Alana Waikiki
    Hotel
15  Island Hostel
20  Hilton Hawaiian Village;
    Bestsellers; Golden Dragon
22  Hale Koa Hotel
25  Royal Garden at Waikiki
26  Ohana Maile Sky Court
31  Coconut Plaza Hotel
32  Ohana Waikiki Surf East
33  Ohana Waikiki Surf
34  Ohana Waikiki Malia
37  The Breakers
39  Ohana Royal Islander
41  Ohana Coral Seas
46  Ohana Reef Towers
47  Ohana Waikiki Tower
48  Outrigger Reef Hotel; Shore
    Bird Beach Broiler
49  Halekulani Hotel; Orchids;
    La Mer; House Without a Key
50  Imperial of Waikiki
51  Waikiki Parc Hotel
52  Sheraton Waikiki
58  Seaside Hawaiian Hostel
60  Ohana Surf
61  Royal Hawaiian Hotel;
    Surf Room
62  Waikiki Beachcomber
    Hotel
67  Hawaiian King Hotel
68  Ilima Hotel
69  Honolulu Prince
71  Outrigger Waikiki; Duke's
    Canoe Club; Chuck's Steak
    House
72  Sheraton Princess Kaiulani
75  Aloha Surf Hotel
76  Waikiki Sand Villa Hotel
78  Hostelling International
    Waikiki
79  Waikiki Prince Hotel
80  Hyatt Regency Waikiki;
    Harry's Bar

81   Sheraton Moana Surfrider;
     The Banyan Grill; Banyan
     Veranda
86   Waikiki Circle Hotel
87   Waikiki Resort Hotel
89   Royal Grove Hotel
90   Continental Surf
91   Pacific Beach Hotel;
     Oceanarium Restaurant
103  Aston Waikiki Sunset
104  Ocean Resort Hotel Waikiki
105  Waikiki Beach Marriott
     Resort
106  Aston Waikiki Beach Hotel;
     The Poolside Bar; Planet Surf
107  Cabana at Waikiki
108  Pacific Ohana Hostel
109  Hokondo Waikiki Beachside
110  Waikiki Grand; Hula's Bar &
     Lei Stand
111  Polynesian Hostel Beachclub
112  Queen Kapiolani Hotel
119  New Otani Kaimana Beach
     Hotel; Hau Tree Lanar
120  W Honolulu Diamond Head

**PLACES TO EAT**
1   Hard Rock Cafe
3   KC Drive Inn
4   Leonard's
9   Aloha Sushi
10  Ye Olde Fox & Hound
12  Pho Tri
13  Eggs 'n Things
17  Todai
18  Singha Thai
21  Bali By The Sea; Golden
    Dragon
24  Keo's
27  Kyo-ya
36  Sapporo Ramen Nakamura
40  Patisserie
42  Planet Hollywood
43  Moose McGillycuddy's
63  Coconut Willy's
64  Saint Germain
66  La Cucaracha
70  Fatty's Chinese Kitchen
73  Food Pantry
74  Perry's Smorgy

92   Cheeseburger in Paradise
95   The Pyramids
96   Ono Hawaiian Food
98   Irifune's
100  Rainbow Drive-In
101  Sam Choy's Diamond Head
     Restaurant

**OTHER**
2   Foodland
5   Wave Waikiki
16  Blue Sky Rentals
19  Bishop Museum at Kalia
23  Gas Station
28  US Army Museum of Hawaii
29  Post Office
30  Island Treasures Antiques
35  In-Between
38  Urasenke Tea Ceremony
44  Bank of Hawaii
45  First Hawaiian Bank
53  Hawaii Visitors & Convention
    Bureau
54  Waikiki Theatres
55  IMAX Theatre Waikiki
56  Waikiki Trade Center
57  Angles Waikiki; Fusion Waikiki
59  e-c@fe
65  Scruples
77  Go Nuts Hawaii
82  Board Rentals
83  Police; Waikiki Beach Center
84  Wizard Stones of Kapaemahu;
    Duke Kahanamoku Statue
85  Hula Mound
88  Fishbowl Internet Cafe
93  St Augustine's Church;
    Damien Museum
94  Waikiki Community Center
97  Snorkel Bob's
99  Bailey's Antique Shop
102 Waikiki-Kapahulu Public
    Library
113 Kapiolani Bandstand
114 Pleasant Hawaiian Hula Show
115 Peoples Open Market
116 Tennis Courts
117 Waikiki Aquarium
118 Natatorium
121 Diamond Head Tennis Center

## Money

Waikiki has a **Bank of Hawaii** (☎ 543-6900; *2220 Kalakaua Ave; open 8:30am-4pm Mon-Thur, 8:30am-6pm Fri*) and a **First Hawaiian Bank** (☎ 943-4670; *2181 Kalakaua Ave; open 8:30am-4pm Mon-Thur, 8:30am-6pm Fri*). There are autmoated teller machines (ATMs) at those banks and at numerous other non-bank locations around Waikiki.

## Post

The Waikiki **post office** (☎ 973-7515; *330 Saratoga Rd; open 8am-4:30pm Mon, Tues, Thur & Fri, 8am-6pm Wed, 9am-1pm Sat*) is in the center of Waikiki.

## Email & Internet Access

**Fishbowl Internet Cafe** (☎ 922-7565; *2463 Kuhio Ave; open 8am-1am daily*) and **e-c@fe**

*(☎ 926-3299; 445 Seaside Ave; open 9am-1am daily)* both offer Internet access for $1 per 10 minutes.

## Bookstores

**Waldenbooks** *(☎ 922-4154; Waikiki Shopping Plaza, 2250 Kalakaua Ave)* and **Bestsellers** *(☎ 953-2378; Hilton Hawaiian Village, 2005 Kalia Rd)* both sell Hawaiiana books, travel guides and paperback fiction.

## Libraries

The **Waikiki-Kapahulu Public Library** *(☎ 733-8488; 400 Kapahulu Ave; open 10am-5pm Mon-Sat)* is a relatively small library, but it does carry mainland and Honolulu newspapers.

## Laundry

Many accommodations have on-site laundry facilities. Otherwise, **Waikiki Laundromats** *(☎ 926-2573; all open 6:30am-10pm daily)* operates public coin laundries at the Ohana Waikiki Hobron *(343 Hobron Lane)*, Ohana Coral Seas *(250 Lewers St)* and the Outrigger Waikiki *(2335 Kalakaua Ave)* hotels.

## Parking

Parking cheaply in Waikiki can be a challenge. Many of the hotels charge $10 to $15 a day for guest parking in their garages.

If you're willing to park on the outskirts of Waikiki, you can get by without spending any money. At the western end of Waikiki, there's a large public parking lot at Ala Wai Yacht Harbor, which has free parking with a 24-hour limit.

At the eastern end of Waikiki, there's a large parking lot along Monsarrat Ave at Kapiolani Park that has free parking with no time limit.

## Emergency

Dial ☎ 911 for all police, fire and medical emergency services.

**Doctors On Call** *(☎ 971-6000; 120 Kaiulani Ave)* has a 24-hour clinic with X-ray and lab facilities in the Sheraton Princess Kaiulani Hotel. The charge for an office visit is a minimum of $110 if you don't have health insurance.

## Dangers & Annoyances

There's been a clampdown on the touts and hustlers who used to push time-shares and other con deals in the Waikiki area, but they're not totally gone.

At night you can expect to see a few scantily clad prostitutes walking along Kalakaua Ave, showering most of their attention on well-dressed Japanese businessmen. If you pay them no attention, you're unlikely to have any unpleasant encounters.

For more on safety, see Dangers & Annoyances and Ocean Safety in the Facts for the Visitor chapter.

## WALKING TOUR

It's possible to make an interesting two- to three-hour walking tour of Waikiki by combining a stroll along the beach with a walk along Kalakaua Ave.

You can walk the full length of Waikiki along the sand and the sea wall. Although the beach gets crowded at midday, at other times it's usually less packed than the sidewalks along Kalakaua Ave.

A good place to begin the walk is the **Kapahulu Groin**, at the end of Kapahulu Ave, where you can observe Waikiki's top boogieboarding action. As you continue west along the beach, you can stop for a swim, watch surfers ride the offshore breaks and take a look at some of the seaside hotels.

After you reach the Halekulani Hotel, continue to the **US Army Museum of Hawaii** at the Fort DeRussy Military Reservation and then head up Beach Walk to Kalakaua Ave, where you'll turn right. On the corner of Lewers St and Kalakaua Ave is the **First Hawaiian Bank**, the interior of which has

---

### Borrowed Sands

Most of Waikiki's beautiful white sands are not its own. Tons of sand have been barged in over the years, much of it from Papohaku Beach on the island of Molokai.

As the beachfront developed, landowners haphazardly constructed sea walls and offshore barriers to protect their properties. In the process they blocked the natural forces of sand accretion, and erosion has long been a serious problem at Waikiki.

Sections of the beach are still being replenished with imported sand, although much of it ends up washing into the ocean, where it fills channels and depressions and alters the surf breaks.

notable Hawaiiana murals by the fresco artist Jean Charlot; get a free brochure describing the murals from the bank's information desk.

As you continue down Kalakaua Ave, you can take in the historic **Royal Hawaiian** and **Moana** hotels, visit the **Oceanarium** at the Pacific Beach Hotel and take a look at the **Damien Museum** behind St Augustine's Church. Upon returning to Kapahulu Groin, you might want to visit the **Honolulu Zoo** and, if you still have time, stroll around **Kapiolani Park** and see the **Waikiki Aquarium**. For more details on the sights along this walk see the sections that follow.

## BEACHES

The 2-mile stretch of white sand that runs from the Hilton Hawaiian Village to Kapiolani Park is commonly referred to as Waikiki Beach, although different sections along the way have their own names and characteristics.

In the early morning the beach belongs to walkers and joggers, and it's surprisingly quiet. Strolling down the beach toward Diamond Head at sunrise can actually be a meditative experience.

By midmorning it looks like a normal resort beach, with boogie-board and surfboard concessionaires setting up shop and catamarans pulling up on the beach offering $15 sails. By noon it is packed, and the challenge is to walk down the beach without stepping on anyone.

Waikiki Beach is good for swimming, boogie boarding, surfing, sailing and other beach activities most of the year. Between May and September, summer swells can make the water a little rough for swimming, but they also make it the best season for surfing. Because of all the activity, Waikiki beaches simply aren't that good for snorkeling; the best of them is Sans Souci.

There are lifeguards and showers at many places along the beach.

### Kahanamoku Beach

Fronting the Hilton Hawaiian Village, Kahanamoku Beach is the westernmost section of Waikiki. The beach is named for Duke Kahanamoku, the surfer and swimmer who won an Olympic gold medal in 1912 and went on to become a Hawaii celebrity.

Kahanamoku Beach is protected by a breakwater at one end and a pier at the other,

with a coral reef running between the two. It's a calm swimming area with a sandy bottom that slopes gradually.

### Fort DeRussy Beach

One of the least crowded Waikiki beaches, Fort DeRussy Beach borders 1800ft of the Fort DeRussy Military Reservation. Like all beaches in Hawaii, it's public; the federal government provides lifeguards and there are showers and other facilities. In addition, you'll find an inviting grassy lawn that has a bit of sparse shade from

## From Swamp to Resort

A little over a century ago, Waikiki was almost entirely wetlands, filled with fishponds, taro patches and rice paddies. Fed by mountain streams from Manoa Valley, Waikiki was one of Oahu's most fertile areas.

By the late 19th century, Waikiki was attracting Honolulu's more well-to-do citizens, who built gingerbread-trimmed cottages along the narrow beachfront.

Tourism took root in 1901, when the Moana opened its doors as Waikiki's first hotel. A tram line was built to connect Waikiki to downtown Honolulu, and city folk crowded aboard for weekend beach outings. Tiring quickly of the pesky mosquitoes that thrived in the wetlands, these early beachgoers petitioned to have Waikiki's 'swamps' brought under control.

In 1922 the Ala Wai Canal was dug to divert the streams that flowed into Waikiki and to dry out the wetlands. Water buffaloes were replaced by tourists, and within a couple of years, Waikiki's second hotel, the Royal Hawaiian, opened to serve passengers arriving on ocean liners from San Francisco.

The Depression and WWII put a damper on further development, and as late as 1950, Waikiki had only 1400 hotel rooms. Surfers could drive their cars to the beach and park right on the sand. In the 1960s, however, tourism took over in earnest. By 1968, Waikiki had some 13,000 hotel rooms, and in the following two decades that number more than doubled. The lack of available land finally halted the boom, but not before Waikiki's real estate prices vaulted to a level second only to downtown Tokyo.

palm trees, providing an alternative to frying on the sand.

The water is usually calm and good for swimming. When conditions are right, you can windsurf, boogie board and board surf as well. There are two **beach huts** *(open daily)*, where you can rent windsurfing equipment, boogie boards, kayaks and snorkel sets.

## Gray's Beach

Gray's Beach, the local name for the beach near the Halekulani Hotel, was named for a boarding house called Gray's-by-the-Sea that stood on the site in the 1920s. On the same stretch of beach was the original Halekulani, a lovely low-rise mansion that was converted into a hotel in the 1930s. In the 1980s, the mansion gave way to the present high-rise hotel.

Because the sea wall in front of the Halekulani Hotel is so close to the waterline, the beach fronting the hotel is often totally submerged by the surf.

The section of Gray's Beach that stretches between the Halekulani Hotel and the Royal Hawaiian Hotel varies in width from season to season, changing with the tides. The waters off the beach are shallow and calm, offering good conditions for swimming.

## Central Waikiki Beach

The area from the Royal Hawaiian Hotel to the Waikiki Beach Center is the busiest section of the whole beach and has a nice spread of sand for sunbathing.

Most of the beach has a shallow bottom with a gradual slope. There's pretty good swimming here, but there's also a lot of activity, with catamarans, surfers and plenty of other swimmers in the water. Keep your eyes open.

Offshore are Waikiki's best-known surf breaks – Queen's Surf and Canoe's Surf.

**Waikiki Beach Center** Just opposite the Hyatt Regency Waikiki the Waikiki Beach Center, has rest rooms, showers, a police station, surfboard lockers and rental concession stands.

The **Wizard Stones of Kapaemahu** – four boulders on the Diamond Head side of the police station – are said to contain the secrets and healing powers of four Tahitian sorcerers named Kapaemahu, Kinohi, Kapuni and Kahaloa, who visited from Tahiti in ancient

### Wave Like the Sea, Dude

OK, so why *are* all those people standing in front of the Duke Kahanamoku statue and waving wildly up at the sky? Could it be they're hip to the location of Waikiki's most popular webcam?

If you too want to prove to your mates that you've made it to America's most celebrated beach resort, have them log onto the Duke's webcam at **W** www.citycams.co.honolulu.hi .us. Prearrange a time when they can be online and you can be at the Duke's statue – then smile at the folks back home.

times. Before returning to their homeland, they transferred their powers to these stones.

Just east of the stones is a bronze **statue of Duke Kahanamoku** (1890–1968), Hawaii's most decorated athlete, standing with one of his longboards. Considered the 'father of modern surfing,' Duke, who made his home in Waikiki, gave surfing demonstrations on beaches around the world from Sydney, Australia, to Rockaway Beach, New York. Many local surfers took issue with the placement of the statue, which has Duke standing with his back to the sea – a position they say he never would have taken in real life. In response, the city moved the statue as far from the ocean and as close to the sidewalk as possible.

Beachside concession stands rent surfboards and boogie boards by the hour, give surfing lessons and offer inexpensive outrigger canoe rides. For details, see the Activities chapter.

## Kuhio Beach Park

Kuhio Beach Park is marked on its eastern end by Kapahulu Groin, a walled storm drain with a walkway on top that juts out into the ocean.

A low breakwater sea wall runs about 1300ft out from Kapahulu Groin, paralleling the beach. This breakwater was built to control sand erosion, and in the process, two nearly enclosed swimming pools were formed. Local kids walk out on the breakwater, which is called 'The Wall,' but it can be dangerous to the uninitiated due to a slippery surface and breaking surf.

The pool closest to Kapahulu Groin is best for swimming, with the water near the breakwater reaching overhead depths. However, because circulation is limited, the water gets murky with a noticeable film of sunscreen oil. The 'Watch Out Deep Holes' sign refers to holes in the pool's sandy bottom that can be created by swirling currents. Those who can't swim should be cautious in the deeper areas of the pool because the holes can take waders by surprise.

The park, incidentally, is named after the distinguished Hawaiian statesman Prince Kuhio, who maintained his residence on this beach. His house was torn down in 1936, 14 years after his death, in order to expand the beach.

Between the old-timers who gather each afternoon to play chess and cribbage at Kuhio's sidewalk pavilions and the kids boogie boarding off the Groin, this section of the beach has as much local color as tourist influence.

The city recently spent millions of dollars removing one lane of Kalakaua Ave fronting Kuhio Beach Park and in its place extended the beach and added water fountains, landscaping and a hula mound. All in all, it's a pleasant place to hang out.

**Kapahulu Groin** Kapahulu Groin is one of Waikiki's hottest boogie-boarding spots. If the surf's right, you can find a few dozen boogie boarders, mostly teenage boys, riding the waves. The kids ride straight for the Groin's cement wall and then veer away at the last moment, drawing 'oohs' and 'ahs' from the tourists who gather to watch them.

Kapahulu Groin is also a great place to catch one of Waikiki's spectacular sunsets.

## Kapiolani Beach Park

Kapiolani Beach Park starts at Kapahulu Groin and extends to the Natatorium, past the Waikiki Aquarium.

**Queen's Surf Beach** is the name given to the wide midsection of Kapiolani Beach. The stretch in front of the pavilion is a popular beach with the gay community. It's a pretty good area for swimming, with a sandy bottom. The section of beach between Queen's Surf and Kapahulu Groin is shallow and has a lot of broken coral.

Kapiolani Beach Park is a relaxed place with little of the frenzied activity found in front of the central strip of Waikiki hotels. It's a popular weekend picnicking spot for local families, who unload the kids to splash in the water as they line up the barbecue grills.

There's a big grassy field, good for spreading out a beach towel and unpacking a picnic basket. There are rest rooms and showers in the Queen's Surf pavilion. The surfing area offshore is called Public's.

**Natatorium** The Natatorium, at the Diamond Head end of Kapiolani Beach Park, is a 100m-long saltwater swimming pool built after WWI as a memorial for soldiers who died in that war. There were once hopes of hosting an Olympics on Oahu, with this pool as the focal point. In the end, Olympic competitions were never held here, but two Olympic gold medalists – Johnny Weissmuller and Duke Kahanamoku – both trained in this tide-fed pool.

The Natatorium is on the National Register of Historic Places. The city recently spent a hefty $11 million for restoration work that spiffed up the Natatorium's exterior but failed to restore the pool to a usable condition; now that the money has run out, it's doubtful that the pool will ever reopen.

## Sans Souci Beach Park

Down by the New Otani Kaimana Beach Hotel, Sans Souci is a nice little sandy beach away from the main tourist scene. It has showers, rest rooms and a lifeguard station.

Many residents come to Sans Souci for daily swims. A shallow coral reef close to shore makes for calm, protected waters and provides reasonably good snorkeling. More coral can be found by following the Kapua Channel as it cuts through the reef, but beware of currents that can pick up in the channel. Check conditions with the lifeguard before venturing out.

## HISTORIC HOTELS

Waikiki's two historic hotels, the Royal Hawaiian and the Moana (now the Sheraton Moana Surfrider), both retain their period character and are well worth a visit. These beachside hotels, both on the National Register of Historic Places, are a short walk from each other on Kalakaua Ave.

With its pink turrets and Moorish/Spanish architecture, the **Royal Hawaiian Hotel** is a throwback to the era when Rudolph Valentino was *the* romantic idol and travel to

Hawaii was by luxury liner. Inside, the hotel is lovely and airy, with high ceilings and chandeliers and everything in rose colors.

The hotel was originally on a 20-acre coconut grove, but over the years the grounds have been chipped away by a huge shopping center on one side and a high-rise mega-hotel on the other. Still, the small garden at the rear is filled with birdsong – a rare sound in most of Waikiki.

The **Sheraton Moana Surfrider**, which has undergone a splendid restoration, has the aura of an old plantation inn. On the 2nd floor, just up the stairs from the lobby, there's a display of memorabilia from the early hotel days, with scripts from the 'Hawaii Calls' radio show, period photographs and a short video. At 11am and 5pm on Monday, Wednesday and Friday, visitors can join free hour-long historical tours of the hotel; just show up in the lobby – reservations are not necessary.

## FORT DERUSSY

Fort DeRussy Military Reservation is a US Army post used mainly as a recreation center for the armed forces. This large chunk of Waikiki real estate was acquired by the US Army a few years after Hawaii was annexed to the USA. Prior to that, it was swampy marshland and a favorite duck-hunting spot for Hawaiian royalty.

A hotel on the property is open only to military personnel, but there's public access to the rest of the property, including the beach and the US Army Museum. The section of Fort DeRussy between Kalia Rd and Kalakaua Ave has public sidewalks that provide a shortcut between the two roads.

### US Army Museum of Hawaii

Battery Randolph, a reinforced concrete building erected in 1911 as a coastal artillery battery, houses the army museum (☎ 955-9552; admission free; open 10am-4:15pm Tues-Sun) at Fort DeRussy. This battery once held two 14-inch diameter disappearing guns with an 11-mile range that were designed to recoil down into the concrete walls for reloading after each firing. A 55-ton lead counterweight would then return the carriage to position. When the guns were fired, the entire neighborhood shook. To get a sense of how huge these guns were, go up to the roof, where you'll see one of the 7-inch replacements – despite being half the size of the original, it still has a formidable presence.

In addition to the guns and a collection of WWII tanks, there are detailed exhibits with dioramas, scale models and period photos on military history as it relates to Hawaii.

The battery houses a wide collection of weapons, including shark-tooth clubs and flintlock pistols that Kamehameha the Great used to take control of the island chain two centuries ago. Despite this small, but interesting, nod to native Hawaiian history, the bulk of the exhibits – not surprisingly – concentrates on the US military presence in Hawaii, beginning in 1898 with the Philippine-bound army troops that used Oahu as a way station.

The WWII exhibits are extensive and include displays you might not expect in a military museum, such as coverage of the unfounded suspicions that Japanese-Americans were subjected to during this period. Other exhibits concentrate on the Korean and Vietnam wars.

## BISHOP MUSEUM AT KALIA

This museum (☎ 947-2458; 2005 Kalia Rd; adult/child 4-12 yrs $11.95/9.95, child under 4 yrs free; open 9am-5pm daily), in the Hilton Hawaiian Village, is intended for people who can't make it over to the main Bishop Museum, on the western side of Honolulu.

Though the Waikiki collection is significantly smaller, it is nonetheless high quality, including Hawaiian artefacts such as stone adzes, hair ornaments and feather capes, a replica pili grass hut, one of Duke Kahanamoku's 10ft wooden surfboards and some insightful displays on the Hawaiian monarchy, Polynesian migration and the early days of Waikiki tourism.

You can learn about Hawaii here, but if you have time to get outside Waikiki, the Bishop Museum and the Hawaii Maritime Center are both better options.

## KAPIOLANI PARK

The nearly 200-acre Kapiolani Park, at the Diamond Head end of Waikiki, was a gift from King Kalakaua to the people of Oahu in 1877. Hawaii's first public park, it was dedicated to Kalakaua's wife, Queen Kapiolani.

In its early days, horse racing and band concerts were the park's biggest attractions. Although the racetrack is long gone, the

WAIKIKI

## Don't Squeeze the Fruit!

Oahu's island-wide public market program was formed in the 1970s to provide local farmers, fishers and aquaculturists opportunities to sell directly to customers. At the People's Open Market, you'll find food that's both significantly fresher and cheaper than at grocery stores – on average, you can expect prices to be about 35% lower.

Not only will you find bargain prices on fruits such as papayas, oranges and avocados, you'll also find items such as passionfruit and exotic ethnic vegetables that simply aren't sold in supermarkets.

As for market etiquette, an air horn is sounded to start the market and the organizers prohibit any sales prior to that point. It's considered bad manners to ask a vendor to reserve anything for you before the market starts. Remember that you're buying directly from the owner, so some of the testing that's commonplace in the supermarket – squeezing fruit, for instance – isn't going to make a good impression.

Try to get there early. As a matter of fact, it's best to be there before the starting time, as once the horn blows, there's a big rush, and people begin to scoop things up quickly. Everything wraps up within an hour.

There are 22 market sites in all, including a couple in the Waikiki Area: at **McCully District Park** (831 Pumehana St; open 8:15am-9:15am Wed); and at **Kapiolani Park** (cnr Monsarrat & Paki Aves; open 10am-11am Wed). For information on locations elsewhere on the island call ☎ 522-7088.

concerts continue, and Kapiolani Park is still the venue for a wide range of community activities.

The park contains the Waikiki Aquarium, the Honolulu Zoo, Kapiolani Beach Park, the Pleasant Hawaiian Hula Show grounds, the Kapiolani Bandstand, and the Waikiki Shell, an outdoor amphitheater that serves as a venue for symphony, jazz and rock concerts.

The Royal Hawaiian Band presents free afternoon concerts each Sunday at the Kapiolani Bandstand, and other activities also occur there throughout the year.

A newly dedicated octagonal memorial near the zoo's entrance contains the skeletal remains of some 200 native Hawaiians unearthed over the years by construction projects in Waikiki.

Kapiolani Park also has sports fields, tennis courts, tall banyan trees and expansive lawns ideal for just lazing about.

### Waikiki Aquarium

This interesting aquarium (☎ 923-9741; W www.mic.hawaii.edu/aquarium; 2777 Kalakaua Ave; adult/senior over 60 yrs or student/child 13-17 yrs $7/5/3.50, child under 13 yrs free; open 9am-5pm daily) dates to 1904 and just a few years back had a $3 million makeover. The aquarium has some fun interactive displays and an impressive shark gallery, where visitors can watch circling reef sharks through a 14ft window.

The aquarium is a great place to identify colorful coral and fish you've seen while snorkeling or diving. Tanks re-create various Hawaiian reef habitats, including those found in a surge zone, a sheltered reef, a deep reef and an ancient reef. There are rare Hawaiian fish with names such as the bearded armorhead and the sling-jawed wrasse, along with moray eels, giant groupers and flash-back cuttlefish wavering with pulses of light.

In addition to Hawaiian marine life, you'll find exhibits on other Pacific ecosystems. In 1985 the aquarium was the first to breed the Palauan chambered nautilus in captivity; you can see them, with their unique spiral chambered shells, in the South Pacific section. Also noteworthy are the giant Palauan clams that were raised from dime-sized hatchlings in 1982 and now measure over 2ft, the largest in the USA.

The aquarium also has an outdoor tank with two rare Hawaiian monk seals.

### Honolulu Zoo

The Honolulu Zoo (☎ 971-7171; adult/child 6-12 yrs $6/1, child under 6 yrs free; open 9am-4:30pm daily, closed Christmas & New Year's Day), at the northern end of Kapiolani Park, has been upgraded into a respectable city zoo, with some 300 species spread across 42 acres. A highlight is the naturalized African Savanna section, which has lions, cheetahs, white rhinos, giraffes, zebras, hippos and monkeys. There's also an interesting reptile section and a small petting zoo that allows children to see animals up close.

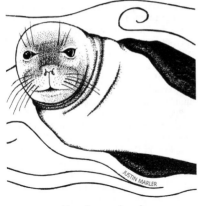

Hawaiian monk seal

The zoo's tropical bird section not only covers the usual colorful exotics, such as toucans and flamingoes, but also displays native species such as the Hawaiian stilt, the Hawaiian goose *(nene)* and the *apapane*, a bright-red forest bird.

## Pleasant Hawaiian Hula Show

The Pleasant Hawaiian Hula Show *(☎ 945-1851; 2805 Monsarrat Ave; admission free; shows 10am-11am Tues-Thur)*, near the Waikiki Shell, is a staged photo opportunity of hula dancers, ti-leaf skirts and ukuleles. The musicians are a group of older ladies who performed at the Royal Hawaiian Hotel in days gone by.

This is the scene shown on classic postcards where dancers hold up letters forming the words 'Hawaii' and 'Aloha.' The whole thing is quite touristy and heavily nostalgic, but it's entertaining and it's free.

## OTHER WAIKIKI ATTRACTIONS

The **Oceanarium** *(Pacific Beach Hotel, 2490 Kalakaua Ave)* is an impressive three-story, 280,000-gallon aquarium that forms the backdrop for two of the hotel's restaurants. Even if you're not dining in one of them, go and enjoy a view of the aquarium from the lobby. Divers enter the Oceanarium to feed the tropical fish at noon, 1pm, 6:30pm and 8pm daily.

St Augustine's Church, off Kalakaua Ave and Ohua Ave, is a quiet little sanctuary in the midst of the hotel district. In the rear of the church, a building houses the modest

**Damien Museum** *(☎ 923-2690; admission free; open 9am-3pm Mon-Fri)* honoring Father Damien, the Belgian priest famed for his work at the leprosy colony on Molokai. It has a video presentation on the colony, historical photos and a few of Damien's personal possessions.

Everyday at dawn, people walk and jog along the **Ala Wai Canal**, which forms the northern boundary of Waikiki. Late in the afternoon, outrigger canoe teams paddle up and down Ala Wai Canal and out to Ala Wai Yacht Harbor, offering photo opportunities for the passerby.

## PLACES TO STAY

Waikiki's main beachfront strip, Kalakaua Ave, is lined with high-rise hotels with $200-plus rooms. As is the norm in resort areas, most of these hotels cater to package tourists, driving the prices up for individual travelers.

Better value for money is generally found at the smaller hotels on the backstreets, with the prices dropping proportionately as you get farther from the beach. There are hotels in the Kuhio Ave area and up near the Ala Wai Canal that have rooms as nice as some of the beachfront hotels but charge half the price. If you don't mind walking 10 minutes to the beach, you can save yourself a bundle.

Some hotels raise rates in the winter, a peak time for travel to Hawaii, but the practice is becoming less common and most places now list the same rates year-round. Hotels, particularly the larger chains, operate a bit like airlines in that they'll offer discounts off their standard rates whenever business is slow. While such discounts can be found anytime there's a slump in business, they're particularly common in spring and fall, when occupancy rates are at their lowest. Always ask about discounts and promotions when making a reservation.

All rates given in the following section are standard year-round rates, unless otherwise noted. When low/high season rates are given, the low season is April to mid-December, the high season mid-December to March.

## Budget

**Hostels** In addition to the one Hostelling International (HI) hostel, several private businesses provide hostel-style accommodations around Waikiki. All are similar operations in

WAIKIKI

that they occupy small converted apartment buildings with a few dozen units. They all cater to backpackers and draw a fairly international crowd. There are no curfews or other restrictions, except that some of these places, in an effort to avoid taking on local boarders, may require travelers to show a passport or an onward ticket.

The private hostels seem to go in cycles, with the standards varying whenever there are changes in management or staffing – and that can be frequent. Consequently, if you want to play it safe, consider booking into the HI hostel or a budget hotel for at least the first few nights. Inquire about refund policies before dishing out any money at a private hostel – you can sometimes get a discount on stays of a week or more but these typically require advance payment and allow no refunds.

**Hostelling International Waikiki** (☎ 926-8313, fax 922-3798; e ayhaloha@lava.net; 2417 Prince Edward St; dorm beds $17, doubles $42; office open 7am-3am) is a 60-bed hostel on a backstreet a few short blocks from Waikiki Beach. Like other Waikiki's hostels, it's in an older low-rise apartment complex, with the units converted for hostel use mainly by adding extra beds – often in what used to be the living room. There are also five rooms for couples, with small refrigerators and private bathrooms. The maximum stay is seven nights and there's a $3 surcharge if you're not an HI member; HI membership can be purchased on-site for $25 for Americans, $18 for foreign visitors. Unlike most other HI hostels, there's no dorm lockout or curfew, and a group kitchen is accessible throughout the day. Four parking spaces are available at $5 per day. Reservations can be made by phone or fax with a credit card. You can sometimes get a bed as a walk-in, but at busy times reservations are often necessary two to three weeks in advance.

**Seaside Hawaiian Hostel** (☎ 924-3303, fax 923-2111; e info@seasidehawaiianhostel .com; 419 Seaside Ave; bed in 6-/2-bed dorm $15/17, private rooms $40) occupies an aging two-story apartment building set back in an alley off Seaside Ave. The digs aren't fancy, but the place has an inviting travelers' atmosphere and cheap rates. In addition to the dorm rooms, there are private rooms with TV and cube refrigerator, which hold

up to two people but share a bathroom with another room. Discounts of one night free are available on weekly stays. There's an open-air courtyard, a common kitchen and laundry facilities; water-sports gear can be rented at reasonable prices. The hostel has a couple of online computers ($3 per 30 minutes) available for guests. It's about a 10-minute walk from Waikiki Beach.

**Pacific Ohana Hostel** (☎/fax 921-8111; 2552 Lemon Rd; dorm beds $16.75, semiprivate rooms $36, private rooms $50) is the new kid on the block and shows promise. Dorm rooms have four beds, while the semiprivate rooms have a private bedroom but require you to pass through the dorm to enter your room or use the shared bathroom. If you want your own space, consider one of the private rooms, which is essentially a one-bedroom apartment with its own kitchen and bathroom. There's a guest lounge with a kitchen and TV.

**Polynesian Hostel Beachclub** (☎ 922-1340, fax 923-4146; e polynesian@hawaii hostels.com; 2584 Lemon Rd; dorm beds $19, singles/doubles $38/44, studios $60) is a short walk from the beach. It occupies a lackluster three-story apartment complex on a side street behind the Queen Kapiolani Hotel. It offers a variety of sleeping arrangements: You can get a bunk bed in a dorm; a bedroom in a two-bedroom apartment; or a fully private studio with a kitchen. Each apartment has its own bathroom, but only the studios have private kitchens. Guests have access to a common room with a kitchen. One drawback is the noise – particularly the garbage trucks that make their rounds on Lemon Rd around dawn.

**Hokondo Waikiki Beachside** (☎ 923-9566, fax 923-7525; e hokondo@aol.com; Suite B101, 2556 Lemon Rd; dorm beds $20-25, private rooms $55-78) is another small condo complex that's been converted into hostel-style accommodations, offering both dorm beds and private rooms. The units each have a refrigerator, a stove and a bathroom. It's straightforward, but maintains a higher standard of cleanliness than most of the other private hostels.

**Island Hostel** (☎/fax 942-8748; 1946 Ala Moana Blvd; dorm beds $16.75, private rooms $50) occupies part of an older apartment building at the western end of Waikiki. The private rooms are small but have TV, hot plates and a bathroom. The dorms in particular can feel a bit confined, but on the plus side accommodate only four people. Although it's a bit farther from the beach than other hostels, it's still within walking distance and the beach at this end of Waikiki is less crowded.

**Hotels** The **Waikiki Prince Hotel** (*☎ 922-1544, fax 924-3712; 2431 Prince Edward St; rooms $50, with kitchenettes $60)* is an excellent low-end value place, with 24 units in a six-story building next door to Hostelling International Waikiki. The rooms are simple, but they're cheery and equipped with air-con, TV and private bathroom; for just $10 extra you can opt for one with cooking facilities and a bit more space. On weekly stays, the seventh night is free. It's just a couple of minutes' walk to the beach.

**Royal Grove Hotel** (*☎ 923-7691, fax 922-7508; e rghawaiii@gte.net; 151 Uluniu Ave; rooms in old wing $43, new wing $59)* has so many retirees returning each winter to its 85 rooms that it's usually impossible to get a room in the high season without reserving. Rooms in the oldest wing are small, have no air-con, and are streetside and exposed to traffic noise. Rooms in the main wing are simple but perfectly adequate, and have air-con and lanais. Both types of rooms have TV, kitchenette and private bathroom. This is an older, no-frills hotel, but unlike other places in this price range, it has a small pool.

**Continental Surf** (*☎ 922-2232, 800-922-7866, fax 922-1718; w www.continentalsurfhotel.com; 2426 Kuhio Ave; rooms $59, with kitchenette $68)* is an uninspired place but the price is right. While the 140 rooms could benefit from some spiffing up and a fresh coat of paint, they are otherwise adequate. All of the rooms have air-con, cable TV and a refrigerator. Both the standard rooms and the kitchenette rooms are the same size. So by adding the cooking facilities, the kitchenette rooms become a bit squeezed, but if you don't mind giving up the elbow room you'll be able to save money by preparing your own meals. Expect traffic to be noisy along Kuhio Ave, but the hotel is high enough (it has 21 floors) that you can drown out most of the noise by requesting one of the upper-level rooms.

**Honolulu Prince** (*☎ 922-1616, 800-922-7866, fax 922-6223; w www.astonhotels.com;* 317 Nahua St; rooms low/high season from $75/85)*, in the Aston chain, is a reasonable choice for an economy hotel with full amenities such as cable TV, air-con and mini-refrigerators. The lowest-priced rooms are cramped, but for just $10 more you can get a roomier 'superior,' which has two double beds, a sofa bed and a lanai.

**Hawaiian King Hotel** (*☎ 922-3894, 800-545-1948; e winston@iav.com; Suite 409; 417 Nohonani St, ; rooms low season $75-105, high season $95-125)* has 18 pleasant units owned by Patrick Winston. Each has one bedroom with either a queen or two twin beds, a living room, TV, air-con, ceiling fans, lanai and a kitchen with microwave, refrigerator and hot plate. Many of the rooms also have an oven, some have a washer/dryer and all have thoughtful touches. Although it's an older complex, a lot of money has gone into these units and they have a spiffy decor that's on par with much pricier places. There are also a few unrenovated rooms – wearworn but otherwise fine, which can be as low as $49. There's a courtyard pool. Ask about discounts, as Patrick can sometimes fill last-minute vacancies at lower rates. There's a four-day minimum stay.

**Coconut Plaza Hotel** (*☎ 923-8828, 800-882-9696, fax 923-3473; e info@aston-hotels.com; 450 Lewers St; rooms from $85, studios from $100)*, in the Aston chain, is a quiet 80-room hotel near Ala Wai Blvd. Rooms have contemporary decor and full amenities, though they're on the small side. There are often promotions that can cut the rates listed above by about a third, which then makes this a good budget choice.

**Hawaii Polo Inn** (*☎ 949-0061, 800-669-7719, fax 949-4906; w www.hawaiipolo.com; 1696 Ala Moana Blvd; rooms $89)* is at the westernmost end of Waikiki. The 72 motel-style rooms are lined up in rows, with their entrances off a long outdoor corridor. While the building is simple, the rooms have been renovated and are equipped with small refrigerators, coffeemakers, air-con and TVs; some have lanais, although generally the lanai area is at the expense of room space. When things are slow, they'll commonly offer discounted rates as low as $55, which is certainly a good deal. Request a room at the back to minimize the traffic noise that comes from busy Ala Moana Blvd.

**Waikiki Grand** (☎ 923-1511, 800-321-2558, fax 923-4708; e resgra@aston-hotels .com; 134 Kapahulu Ave; rooms from $90, with kitchenette $130) is a 173-room hotel opposite the zoo. The rooms are rather small and ordinary but they have all the amenities of a tourist-class hotel, such as TV, air-con and mini-refrigerator. The hotel has a pool and is just a two-minute walk from the beach.

**The Breakers** (☎ 923-3181, 800-426-0494, fax 923-7174; e breakers@aloha.net; 250 Beach Walk; studios $94-100, suites doubles/quads $135/151) is an older low-rise hotel with 64 units surrounding a courtyard pool. In a neighborhood dominated by high-rise hotels, this Polynesian-style place is a throwback to earlier times. The staff are friendly, and the rooms are straightforward but perfectly comfortable. The studio rooms each have a double bed, a single bed and a kitchenette. Opt for the 2nd floor units, which have a lanai for just $6 more. The hotel also has large suites that have a separate bedroom with a queen bed, a living room that resembles a studio with two twin beds, a full kitchen and a table for four. All rooms have air-con, TVs, room safes and phones. Avoid the rooms closest to Saratoga Rd, which has lots of traffic.

**Waikiki Sand Villa Hotel** (☎ 922-4744, 800-247-1903, fax 923-2541; e reserve@ai hotels.com; 2375 Ala Wai Blvd; rooms low/high season from $93/106, studios $156/166 ) is on the Ala Wai Canal, a 10-minute walk from the beach. This friendly place, popular with young Japanese tourists, has an inviting pool and a row of online computers in the lobby which are free for hotel guests. The 223 rooms are compact, but most have both a double and a twin bed, and all have a TV, refrigerator and lanai. Ask for one of the corner units, which have the best views. There are also poolside studios with kitchenettes, which can sleep up to four people. Rates include a continental breakfast.

**Aloha Surf Hotel** (☎ 923-0222, 800-922-7866, fax 924-7160; w www.aston-hotels .com; 444 Kanekapolei St; rooms low/high season from $95/110) has a lively surf theme and has been recently renovated. While the lobby is fun, the rooms in this 200-unit hotel are standard fare and on the small side. Each has a small refrigerator, TV and room safe. There's a small pool and rates include a continental breakfast.

**Ocean Resort Hotel Waikiki** (☎ 922-3861, 800-367-2317, fax 924-1982; e res@ oceanresort.com; 175 Paoakalani Ave; standard rooms $98, larger rooms $140), a former Quality Inn, hosts a fair number of people on low-end package tours. Nonetheless, the 451 rooms have the same amenities as more expensive hotels, with air-con, cable TV, refrigerators and room safes. Nonsmoking rooms are available on request, and there are two pools. The larger rooms are on higher floors, which are generally quieter. When things are slow, they sometimes offer walk-in rates as low as $60, which is a real deal for this standard of hotel.

## Mid-Range

**Imperial of Waikiki** (☎ 923-1827, 800-347-2582, fax 923-7848; w www.imperialofwai kiki.com; 205 Lewers St; studios $109, suites from $139, 2-bedroom units $199) is an interesting, little-known option. This pleasant time-share rents out unfilled rooms on a space-available basis. It's a good value, especially considering it's directly opposite the exclusive Halekulani Hotel and just a two-minute walk from the beach. Studios, which can accommodate two people, have a pull-down double bed, queen sofa bed, microwave and refrigerator. The one-bedroom suites, which hold four people, have a kitchenette, a queen bed in the bedroom and a pull-down bed and queen sofa bed in the living room. There are also well-equipped two-bedroom, two-bathroom units for up to five people. There's a pool and a front desk that's open 24 hours.

**Queen Kapiolani Hotel** (☎ 922-1941, 800-367-2317, fax 922-2694; e res@queenkapio lani.com, 150 Kapahulu Ave; rooms from $125, with ocean view $175) is a 19-story older hotel at the quieter Diamond Head end of Waikiki. It has 313 rooms and a regal theme: chandeliers, high ceilings and faded paintings of Hawaiian royalty. The standard rooms vary in size, some very pleasant and others quite cramped. The best way to avoid a closet-sized space is to request a room with two twin beds instead of a single queen. Ocean-view rooms have lanais with splendid unobstructed views of Diamond Head.

**Waikiki Resort Hotel** (☎ 922-4911, 800-367-5116, fax 922-9468; e hotel@waikikire sort.com; 2460 Koa Ave; rooms from $120) is a 20-story Korean Airlines – owned hotel that, not surprisingly, books heavily with Korean guests on package tours. Rooms are small but modern with full amenities, including mini-refrigerators, room safes and lanais. A room/car deal is available for an additional $10 on listed rates.

**Holiday Inn Waikiki** (☎ 955-1111, 888-992-4545, fax 947-1799; e holinnwk@pixi .com; 1830 Ala Moana Blvd; rooms $120-130) is a recommended mid-range 200-room hotel at the western end of Waikiki. Rooms are modern and comfortable, with either two double beds or one king bed, TV, refrigerator and in many cases a lanai. There are often promotions and discounts off the regular rates, so always ask. The hotel has a pool and deck, and the beach is about a 10-minute walk away. Unlike most hotels on busy Ala Moana Blvd, the Holiday Inn is set back from the road, so it tends to be noticeably quieter.

**Ilima Hotel** (☎ 923-1877, 800-801-9366, fax 924-8371; e mail@ilima.com; 445 Nohonani St; singles $129-165, doubles $139-175) is a smaller hotel in a less hurried section of Waikiki, about a 10-minute walk from the beach. All 99 units are roomy and bright, with large lanais, two double beds, tasteful rattan furnishings and full kitchens. The rates vary according to the floor, although the rooms themselves are the same. The staff are friendly, the lobby has an interesting Hawaiiana motif, and there's a small heated pool and fitness room. Popular with business travelers and other return visitors, the Ilima offers free local phone calls and free parking, which is a rarity in Waikiki.

**Waikiki Circle Hotel** (☎ 923-1571, 800-922-7866, fax 926-8024; e info@aston-hotels .com; 2464 Kalakaua Ave; rooms $130-195) is an interesting hotel with a good central location opposite the beach. It has 104 rooms on 13 floors, all with lanai, two double beds, room safe, phone, TV and air-con. The hotel is older than others but has been renovated and the rooms are comfortable. This circular building has a back room on each floor that's called 'city view' and costs the least; although you can't see the ocean, these are farther from the road and quieter. Each floor also has two rooms with partial ocean views and five rooms with unobstructed ocean views that cost the most. Request one of the upper-floor rooms, which have the same rates but better views.

**Cabana at Waikiki** (☎ 926-5555, 877-902-2121, fax 926-5566; w www.cabanawaikiki .com; 2551 Cartwright Rd; 1-bedroom suites $135-175) caters to the gay community and is only minutes from Hula's, Waikiki's bustling gay bar. Each of the 15 units has a queen bed, queen sofa bed, full kitchen, lanai, TV and VCR. Rates include continental breakfast, use of an eight-person hot tub, and access to a men's gym.

**New Otani Kaimana Beach Hotel** (☎ 923-1555, 800-356-8264, fax 922-9404; e rooms@ kaimana.com; 2863 Kalakaua Ave; rooms from $135, studios from $160) is right on Sans Souci Beach on the quieter Diamond Head side of Waikiki. Popular with return visitors, it's a pleasantly low-key place with 125 units. All units have air-con, TV, refrigerators and lanai, and the studios add on kitchenettes.

**Aston Waikiki Beach Hotel** (☎ 922-2511, 800-922-7866, fax 923-3656; w www.aston waikiki.com; 2570 Kalakaua Ave; rooms from $140, with ocean view from $245) has just undergone a $30 million renovation after being taken over by Aston. It looks almost like a reflection of the larger Marriott across the street, and the 713 rooms here are comparable but less expensive. The best value is the Mauka Tower, an annex off to the side of the main building, where the rates are at the low end and the rooms are larger and quieter than in the main hotel.

**Royal Garden at Waikiki** (☎ 943-0202, 800-367-5666, fax 946-8777; e rghresv@ aol.com; 440 Olohana St; rooms $150-250) is a pleasant mid-sized hotel with 220 comfortable rooms. The rooms vary in decor, but all have air-con, TV, room safe and private lanai. The lowest rate is for rooms on the lower floors; as the elevator climbs so do the prices. The hotel has an elegant marble lobby, two swimming pools and an exercise room.

**Aston Waikiki Sunset** (☎ 931-1400, 800-922-7866, fax 922-8785; e info@aston-hotels .com; 229 Paoakalani Ave; units low/high season from $185/215) is a 366-unit condominium complex. The one-bedroom units each have a lanai as well as a large living room with a full kitchen. Ask about special promotions, which can substantially cut these rates, as well as AAA rates and travel-club discounts. If you're able to get a discounted rate on one of the better-furnished units, it's reasonable value.

WAIKIKI

**Doubletree Alana Waikiki Hotel** (☎ 941-7275, 800-222-8733, fax 949-0996; **w** www.alana-doubletree.com; 1956 Ala Moana Blvd; rooms from $195, suites from $240) is a stylish 313-room hotel on the western side of Waikiki. The rooms are modern with mini-bars, room safes and lanais, and the hotel has a heated outdoor pool. The published rates are on the high side, but when occupancy is low, last-minute prices are slashed, and rates as low as $79 are not uncommon – making this a good place to look for a quality room at a bargain price.

**Hale Koa Hotel** (☎ 955-0555, 800-367-6027, fax 800-425-3329; **w** www.halekoa.com; 2055 Kalia Rd; rooms from $60), on Fort DeRussy Beach, is reserved for US military personnel (both active and retired) and their families. Rates vary by the floor and by the guest's rank. This is a modern, first-class 817-room hotel with a fitness center, three swimming pools and an array of activities available for guests, and is an excellent value for those who qualify.

**Outrigger & Ohana Hotels**  Over the years, the Outrigger chain has snapped up and renovated many of Waikiki's mid-range hotels; at last count it had 19. It has now split its hotels into two categories: Ohana, which includes the more affordable properties, and Outrigger, which covers the high-end hotels. Overall, it's a well-run chain that offers high standards at reasonable prices. At any rate, with one phone call, you can check on the availability of 25% of the hotel rooms in Waikiki!

You can book any Outrigger or Ohana hotel at the following: ☎ 303-369-7777, fax 303-369-9403; **e** reservations@outrigger.com; **w** www.outrigger.com. Although you can access everything through the Outrigger website, Ohana also has its own website at **w** www.ohanahotels.com.

The chain has the following toll-free numbers: ☎ 800-688-7444 and fax 800-622-4852 from the USA and Canada; and ☎ 1-800-688-74443 and fax 1-800-622-48522 from Australia, New Zealand, Germany, the UK and Japan. Additional toll-free numbers, via AT&T USA Direct 800 service, are available from many other countries – the local AT&T representative can provide the access number.

Ask about promotional deals when making reservations. The Ohana hotels often run a 'SimpleSaver Rate,' which cuts rates as low as $69 – a great deal for this standard of hotel. The Outrigger hotels offer a similar deal called the 'Best Value Rate,' which cuts room rates to about $150. In addition, both Ohana and Outrigger commonly offer a 'Free Ride' program, which provides a free rental car when you book at the regular room rate; and a 'Fifth Night Free' program on stays of five nights.

Travelers aged 50 and older, and members of the AAA/CAA auto clubs, are entitled to discounts of about 25% off the regular room rates.

All Ohana and Outrigger hotel rooms have air-con, phone, cable TV, room safe and refrigerator.

**Ohana Coral Seas** (☎ 923-3881; 250 Lewers St; rooms $109, with kitchenette $119, 1-bedroom suites $169) is a small hotel popular with return guests, which is just a few minutes walk from the beach. Although Ohana gives the property its low-end economy rating, the 109 rooms are comfortable and adequately furnished with either one queen or two double beds, and even a lanai.

**Ohana Royal Islander** (☎ 922-1961; 2164 Kalia Rd; rooms $109-159) has 101 rooms, friendly staff and a superb location just across from Fort DeRussy Beach. The rooms in this 12-story hotel are on the small side, but are pleasant and have all the expected amenities. The best rooms for ocean views are the upper-floor corner ones, all of which end in the numbers 01. The only drawback is that the hotel is on a busy intersection, so roadside rooms on the lower floors can be noisy. Rates vary depending upon the view.

**Ohana Maile Sky Court** (☎ 947-2828; 2058 Kuhio Ave; rooms $109, with kitchenette $119) is one of Ohana's better value places if you don't mind being away from the beach. This 596-unit high-rise hotel has an inviting lobby and a central location convenient to restaurants, shops and entertainment. The rooms are so small that once you open your suitcase, you may have to dance sidewards a bit to get around the beds, but unless you're claustrophobic they're otherwise pleasant.

**Ohana Waikiki Hobron** (☎ 942-7777; 343 Hobron Lane; rooms $109, with kitchenette $119), a 612-unit hotel on the western end of Waikiki, is a reasonable choice if you're just looking for a comfortable place to sleep. There's not much space in these compact rooms, but they're modern with full amenities, and being on a back street there's less traffic noise than in many other hotels.

**Ohana Waikiki Surf** *(☎ 923-7671; 2200 Kuhio Ave; rooms $109, with kitchenette $129, suites $179)* is one of Outrigger's better deals in the Kuhio area, offering 302 rooms. Standard hotel rooms are small but otherwise quite pleasant; each has a lanai and either one queen or two twin beds. The kitchenette units are roomier, with one king or two double beds. There are also one-bedroom suites for up to four people.

**Ohana Waikiki Surf East** *(☎ 923-7671; 422 Royal Hawaiian Ave; studios $129, suites $179)*, a block north of Ohana Waikiki Surf, is recommended if preparing your own meals is a consideration, as there are kitchenettes in all of its 102 units. Both the studios and one-bedroom suites are large, and most have a sofa bed, as well as a regular king or two double beds. The accommodations are superior to many higher-priced Outriggers – the lower price simply reflects the distance from the beach and the fact that the hotel is a converted apartment building with no restaurant or other lobby facilities.

**Ohana Surf** *(☎ 922-5777; 2280 Kuhio Ave; rooms $129)* has 251 pleasant rooms, each with lanai, refrigerator and two-burner stove. Ask for a room on one of the higher floors, since these are less prone to catch the drone of traffic on busy Kuhio Ave. Although it's a couple of blocks inland, the rooms are otherwise on a par with many beachside hotels charging nearly twice the price.

**Ohana Waikiki Malia** *(☎ 923-7621; 2211 Kuhio Ave; rooms $129, suites $189)* is a 327-room high-rise hotel opposite the Ohana Waikiki Surf. Rooms are comfortable, each with a tiny one-chair lanai and, in most cases, two double beds. Some of the rooms are wheelchair accessible. Ask for an upper-floor room at the back, as they're the quietest. All rooms, regardless of the floor, have the same rate. There are also one-bedroom suites.

**Ohana Waikiki Tower** *(☎ 922-6424; 200 Lewers St; rooms $139-169, with kitchenette $149-219)* is a high-rise 439-room hotel a few minutes' walk from the beach. The rooms are inviting, with a lanai and either two doubles or a king bed. The rooms on all floors are essentially the same, with the cheapest rates applying for rooms from the 12th floor down.

**Ohana Reef Towers** *(☎ 924-8844; 227 Lewers St; rooms $129, with kitchenette $139)* is also a good deal and just a tad farther from the beach. The 479 rooms are comfortable and well equipped. The kitchenette units not only add cooking facilities, but also have a sofa bed.

**Outrigger Reef Hotel** *(☎ 923-3111; 2169 Kalia Rd; rooms $220, with ocean view $350)* is an 883-room hotel right on the beach. The rooms are nice, albeit without much character, and have the usual first-class amenities. Wheelchair-accessible rooms are available, and some floors are designated for nonsmokers only.

**Outrigger Waikiki** *(☎ 923-0711; 2335 Kalakaua Ave; rooms $230, with ocean view $335)* is the chain's other beachfront hotel. This 530-room hotel offers modern amenities and rates that rise with the view. Set on a prime stretch of sand, there's lots of activity here, from beach events to seaside dining.

## Top End

The following hotels all have standard first-class amenities, in-house restaurants and swimming pools, and all are either on the beach or across the street from it.

**Sheraton Princess Kaiulani** *(☎ 922-5811, 800-325-3535, fax 923-9912;* **W** *www.sheraton-hawaii.com; 120 Kaiulani Ave; rooms from $165)* is the Sheraton's least expensive Waikiki property. One of Waikiki's older hotels, it was built in the 1950s by Matson Navigation to help turn Waikiki into a middle-class destination, and from the outside it looks rather like an apartment complex. However, the interior is more appealing, and the 1150 rooms are modern and inviting. It's in the busy heart of Waikiki across the street from the beach.

**Waikiki Parc Hotel** *(☎ 921-7272, 800-422-0450, fax 923-1336;* **W** *www.waikikiparc.com; 2233 Helumoa Rd; standard rooms $190, with ocean view $270)* is a good-value top-end hotel with 298 rooms. Across the street from its more upmarket sister operation, the Halekulani, the Parc has a pleasantly understated elegance. Rooms are average in size, but have nice touches, such as ceramic-tile floors, shuttered lanai doors and bathtubs. The hotel offers various specials, including a 50% discount on the second room for families traveling together, and a three-night 'Parc Sunrise' package that includes free breakfast and parking and costs about 30% less than the regular room rates.

**Pacific Beach Hotel** *(☎ 922-1233, 800-367-6060, fax 922-0129; e reservation@hthcorp .com; 2490 Kalakaua Ave; rooms from $195, with ocean view from $230)* is a high-rise hotel with 831 rooms. The accommodations, although not distinguished, are pleasant, with full amenities. Nonsmoking rooms are available. There's a fitness center, and the hotel has an impressive three-story aquarium filled with tropical fish.

**Waikiki Beach Marriott Resort** *(☎ 922-6611, 800-367-5121, fax 921-5222; w www .marriotthotels.com; 2552 Kalakaua Ave; rooms from $260, with ocean view $310)* is one of Waikiki's largest hotels, with 1308 rooms in a huge block-long complex opposite the beach. The Marriott recently took over this property (formerly the Hawaiian Regent) and renovated the place, so you can expect everything to be shiny and new. Steep discounts off the standard rates are common.

**Sheraton Moana Surfrider** *(☎ 922-3111, 800-325-3535, fax 923-0308; w www.shera tonhawaii.com; 2365 Kalakaua Ave; rooms from $265, with ocean view $420)* is a delightful place to stay for those fond of colonial hotels. Built in 1901, the Moana was Hawaii's first beachfront hotel. It's undergone a $50 million historic restoration, authentic right down to the carved columns on the porte cochere. Despite the fact that modern wings have been attached to the main hotel's flanks, the Moana has survived with much of its original character intact. The lobby is open and airy with high plantation-like ceilings, reading chairs and Hawaiian artwork. The rooms in the original building were restored to their early-19th-century appearance. The furnishings on each floor are made from a different wood, for example, koa on the 5th and cherry on the 6th, and TVs and refrigerators are discreetly hidden behind armoire doors.

**Hyatt Regency Waikiki** *(☎ 921-6026, 800-233-1234, fax 923-7839; w www.hyatt waikiki.com; 2424 Kalakaua Ave; rooms from $265, with ocean view $360)* has twin 40-story towers with 1230 rooms. There's a maximum of 18 rooms per floor, so it is quieter and feels more exclusive than other hotels its size. Rooms are pleasantly decorated with rattan furnishings and vary in price depending on the view. Despite being

a high-rise, the hotel has created a nice little rainforest oasis in the form of a ground-floor atrium resplendent with cascading waterfalls and tropical plants.

**Sheraton Waikiki** *(☎ 922-4422, 800-325-3535, fax 922-9567; w www.sheratonhawaii .com; 2255 Kalakaua Ave; rooms from $280, with ocean view $450)* is the 1850-room mega-hotel that looms over the historic Royal Hawaiian Hotel. The bustling lobby resembles an exclusive Tokyo shopping center, lined with expensive jewelry stores and boutiques with French names and designer labels.

**Hawaii Prince Hotel** *(☎ 944-4411, 800-321-6248, fax 946-0811; w www.princeresorts hawaii.com; 100 Holomoana St; rooms from $300)*, managed by an exclusive Japanese chain, is a thoroughly upscale hotel. An ultra-modern high-rise that overlooks the yacht harbor, it has 521 sleek rooms, each boasting an ocean view. There's a business center with computers and secretarial services; a fitness center; and free shuttle service around Waikiki, which can be useful, as there's no beach in this neighborhood.

**Hilton Hawaiian Village** *(☎ 949-4321, 800-445-8667, fax 947-7898; w www.ha waiianvillage.hilton.com; 2005 Kalia Rd; rooms from $300, with ocean view $405)* is Hawaii's largest hotel, with some 3000 rooms in high-rise towers. The ultimate in mass tourism, it's practically a package-tour city unto itself – all self-contained for people who never want to leave the hotel grounds. It's a busy place, but it maintains a good reputation despite its size. The Hilton is on a nice beach, has some good restaurants and offers free entertainment, including Friday-night fireworks.

**Halekulani Hotel** *(☎ 923-2311, 800-367-2343, fax 926-8004; w www.halekulani.com; 2199 Kalia Rd; rooms from $325, with ocean view $440, suites from $720)* is widely regarded as Waikiki's premier hotel. The 456 rooms, which are pleasantly subdued rather than posh, have large balconies, marble vanities, deep soaking tubs and little touches such as bathrobes and fresh flowers. There are no check-in lines, instead, guests are registered in the privacy of their own room. The Halekulani has received numerous awards and is in the top-10 list of both *Conde Nast Traveler*'s best Pacific Rim Hotels and *Travel & Leisure*'s 'World's Best Service.'

**Royal Hawaiian Hotel** (☎ 923-7311, 800-325-3535, fax 924-7098; ⓦ www.sheraton hawaii.com; 2259 Kalakaua Ave; rooms in historic wing from $345, rooms in tower from $550), now a Sheraton property, was Waikiki's first luxury hotel. Despite being overshadowed by modern high-rises, the pink, Moorish-style building is still a beautiful place, cool and airy, and loaded with charm. The historic section maintains a classic appeal, with some of the rooms having quiet garden views. This section is easier to book too, as most guests prefer the modern high-rise wing with its ocean views.

**W Honolulu Diamond Head** (☎ 922-1700, 888-528-9465, fax 923-2249; ⓦ www.whotels.com; 2885 Kalakaua Ave; rooms with Diamond Head view $375, ocean view $450) is a fashionable boutique hotel located right on Sans Souci Beach, on the quieter Diamond Head side of Waikiki. Recently renovated and upgraded, it has 48 stylish, contemporary rooms with high-end amenities such as 27-inch web-TVs and down-feather bedding.

## PLACES TO EAT

Waikiki has no shortage of places to eat, although the vast majority of the cheaper ones are easy to pass up. Generally, the best inexpensive food is found outside Waikiki, where most Honolulu residents live and eat. Waikiki's top-end restaurants, on the other hand, are some of the island's best, though they can quickly burn a hole in your wallet.

### Budget

For inexpensive bakery items, try the **Patisserie** (☎ 922-4974; 2168 Kalia Rd; open 6am-9pm daily), in the lobby of the Ohana Edgewater hotel, which sells reasonably priced pastries, bread, sandwiches and coffee.

**Saint Germain** (☎ 924-4305; 2301 Kuhio Ave; snacks under $5; open 7am-9pm daily) is a new bakery with delicious croissants and pastries, as well as soups, salads and hearty sandwiches. The sandwiches are all made fresh to order with your choice of bread, including a nice crispy baguette, and a dozen vegetarian, fish and meat fillings to select from.

**International Market Place** (2330 Kalakaua Ave; plate lunches $6; open 11am-11pm daily) has a food court at its northwestern corner with about two dozen stalls

selling cinnamon buns, ice cream, pizza, sandwiches and plate lunches of Korean, Chinese, Japanese and Greek fare.

**Fatty's Chinese Kitchen** (☎ 922-9600; 2345 Kuhio Ave; open 10:30am-10:30pm daily) is a hole-in-the-wall eatery in an alley on the western side of the Miramar hotel. It serves some of the cheapest food to be found in these parts, with rice or chow mein plus one hot main for only $3.50. Add $1 for each additional main. The atmosphere is purely local, with a dozen stools lining a long bar and the cook on the other side chopping away.

**Aloha Sushi** (☎ 955-5223; 1178 Ala Moana Blvd; boxed sushi $2-6; open 9am-9pm daily), in the Discovery Bay Center, offers an interesting fast-food alternative, selling dozens of varieties of sushi at roughly the same price as a Big Mac. Mix and match them to your taste or order a pre-arranged lunch bento – either way you can get a decent takeout meal for around $5.

**Eggs 'n Things** (☎ 949-0820; 1911 Kalakaua Ave; dishes $3-8; open 11pm-2pm daily) is a bustling all-nighter. It specializes in breakfast fare, with a variety of waffles, pancakes, crepes and omelettes. The most popular deal is the 'Early Riser' special of three pancakes and two eggs that's offered from 5am to 9am for just $3.

**Pho Tri** (☎ 944-1190; 478 Ena Rd; pho $6; open 10am-10pm daily), a small eatery on the western side of Waikiki, specializes in pho, a Vietnamese noodle soup spiced with fresh green basil. The servings are generous and come with a choice of chicken or beef. If there's someone in your party who is not in the mood for soup, it also serves some simple but solid rice dishes for the same price as the *pho*.

**Ye Olde Fox & Hound** (☎ 947-3776; 1178 Ala Moana Blvd; snacks $3-5; meals $7-10; open 10am-11pm daily) is an English-style pub in the basement of the Discovery Bay Center. If you've got a craving for a Cornish pastie, shepherd's pie or other pub grub favorites, this is the place. It also offers Waikiki's cheapest mug of beer ($1) during its afternoon happy hour, which is from 2pm to 6pm daily.

**Moose McGillycuddy's** (☎ 923-0751; 310 Lewers St; snacks & mains $6-12; open for meals 7:30am-9:30pm daily) offers a varied menu. A great breakfast deal is the early-bird special (until 11am) of two eggs, bacon and toast for $1.99. The restaurant also does burgers, salads, Mexican fare and steaks.

**Sapporo Ramen Nakamura** (☎ 922-7960; 2141 Kalakaua Ave; noodle dishes $8; open 11am-midnight daily) specializes in authentic Japanese ramen. It also has tasty *gyoza*, a grilled garlic-and-pork-filled dumpling, which can be added on to the noodle dishes for a couple of dollars. The scene is like a neighborhood eatery in Tokyo, with seating at stools around a small U-shaped bar and fellow diners chatting away in Japanese.

**Perry's Smorgy** (☎ 926-0184; 2380 Kuhio Ave; breakfast $5.50, lunch $6.50, dinner $9.50; open 7am-11am, 11:30am-2:30pm & 5pm-9pm daily) features all-you-can-eat buffets in a gardenlike setting. Breakfast includes pancakes, eggs, ham, coffee and fresh tropical fruit. Lunch includes a salad bar and simple hot dishes such as fried chicken. Dinner adds a round of beef. It's a tourist crowd and the food is cafeteria quality, but if you're really hungry the price is right.

American fast-food chains can be found on virtually every other corner in Waikiki – you are seldom far from a Burger King, McDonald's or Jack in the Box (the latter open 24 hours). In addition to the usual fare, they add some island touches, such as passionfruit juice, saimin and Portuguese sausage.

**Kapahulu Ave** A nice alternative to dining in Waikiki proper can be found at a run of neighborhood restaurants on Kapahulu Ave, the road that starts in Waikiki near the zoo and runs up to the H1 Fwy.

**Leonard's** (☎ 737-5591; 933 Kapahulu Ave; pastries 65¢-$1; open 6am-9pm daily), a Portuguese bakery, is known throughout Honolulu for its *malasadas*, a type of sweet fried dough rolled in sugar and served warm – like a doughnut without the hole. Try the *haupia malasada*, filled with an addictive coconut cream, and you'll be hooked.

**KC Drive Inn** (☎ 737-5581; 1029 Kapahulu Ave; open 6am-11:30pm daily), near the H1 Fwy, has been a local favorite since the 1930s. It features Ono Ono malts (a chocolate and peanut butter blend that tastes like a liquefied Reese's Peanut Butter Cup) for $3.40 and waffle dogs (a hot dog wrapped in a waffle) for $2, as well as inexpensive breakfast fare, plate lunches, burgers and saimin for either eat-in or takeout.

**Rainbow Drive-In** (☎ 737-0177; cnr Kapahulu & Kanaina Aves; open 7:30am-9pm daily) is closer to central Waikiki than KC Drive Inn if you are on foot, and has similar fast food and just as much of a local following.

**Ono Hawaiian Food** (☎ 737-2275; 726 Kapahulu Ave; meals $8-10; open 11am-7:45pm Mon-Sat) is *the* place in the greater Waikiki area to get traditional Hawaiian food served Hawaiian-style. It's a simple little diner, crowded with aging tables and decorated with sports paraphernalia, but at dinnertime people line up on the sidewalk waiting to get in. A favorite is the *kalua* pig plate, which comes with *lomi* salmon, *pipikaula* beef jerky, *haupia* coconut pudding and either rice or poi. This is a great choice if you're looking to eat local.

**Irifune's** (☎ 737-1141; 563 Kapahulu Ave; lunch specials $7, dinner plates $10-14; open 11:30am-1:30pm & 5:30pm-9:30pm Tues-Sat), a funky little joint decorated with Japanese country kitsch, serves tasty MSG-free food. A recommended appetizer is the *gyoza* stuffed with tofu and cheese ($3.50). Top choice for dinner is the *tataki ahi*, a delicious fresh tuna which is seared lightly on the outside, sashimi-like inside, and artistically presented. Or opt for one of the combination dinners that pairs tempura with sashimi and other Japanese favorites. Alcohol is not served, but you can bring your own beer. Although few tourists come up this way, Irifune's is popular with locals and you might have to wait to be seated at dinner, but it's well worth it.

**The Pyramids** (☎ 737-2900; 758 Kapahulu Ave; lunch buffet $9, dinner mains $13-18; open 11am-2pm & 5.30pm-10pm Mon-Sat, 5pm-9pm Sun) is an atmospheric Egyptian restaurant with a scrumptious lunch buffet. The buffet features Greek salad, pitta bread, falafels, tahini, tabouleh and shawarma, a deliciously spiced meat dish that's cooked on a spit. Dinner is à la carte, with main dishes such as shish kebab, moussaka and marinated lamb. There's belly dancing nightly. If you need a break from Pacific Rim cuisine, stop here and enter another world.

## Mid-Range

**Shore Bird Beach Broiler** (☎ 922-2887; 2169 Kalia Rd; breakfast buffet $8, dinner $9-20; open 7am-11am & 4:30pm-10pm daily), at the Outrigger Reef Hotel, is a fun place to eat, with beachfront dining and reasonable prices. At one end of the dining room, there's a big common grill where you barbecue your own order – fish, steak or chicken. Meals come with a buffet bar of salad, chili, rice and fresh fruit. Get seated for dinner before 6pm and you can enjoy the sunset and take advantage of cheaper early-bird prices as well. It's a busy place, so unless you get there early, expect to wait for a table – however, this is scarcely a hardship, as you can hang out on the beach until your name's called. Shore Bird also has a breakfast buffet, but dinner is the real winner here.

**Duke's Canoe Club** (☎ 922-2268; 2335 Kalakaua Ave; breakfast buffet $10, lunch buffet $10.50, dinner mains $15-25; open 7am-10pm daily), on the beach at the Outrigger Waikiki hotel, is thoroughly recommended. This bustling restaurant takes its name from the late surfing king Duke Kahanamoku and the outrigger canoe club that was located here in earlier days. The breakfast buffet offers omelettes to order, fresh fruit and tasty pastries, while the lunch buffet centers around a salad bar and hot dishes such as chicken and *mahimahi*. Dinner, which features fresh fish and steaks, includes a grand salad bar with pasta dishes, fruit and muffins. There's live Hawaiian music nightly.

**Hard Rock Cafe** (☎ 955-7383; 1837 Kapiolani Blvd; mains $8-15; open 11:30am-11pm daily) has a Honolulu branch just over the Ala Wai Canal, on the outer edge of Waikiki. The place is enlivened by loud rock music and decorated with old surfboards and a 1959 Cadillac 'woody' wagon hanging precariously above the bar. Hard Rock serves good burgers and fries and other all-American food, including barbecued ribs and milkshakes, but it's the atmosphere as much as the food that draws the crowd.

**Planet Hollywood** (☎ 924-7877; 2155 Kalakaua Ave; mains $10-15; open 11:30am-11pm daily) competes for a similar audience and has a flashy celluloid motif, with Hollywood memorabilia lining the walls and flicks playing on big-screen TVs. Part of the attraction is the hope, however seldom realized, of catching a glimpse of one of the restaurant's Hollywood shareholders, such as Arnold Schwarzenegger or Whoopi Goldberg. The menu includes specialty salads, pizza, pasta, fancy sandwiches and the like.

**Cheeseburger in Paradise** (☎ 923-3731; 2500 Kalakaua Ave; meals $7-11; open 7am-midnight daily) is a local-theme eatery boasting an open-air tropical motif and a view (across Kalakaua Ave) of the beach. It has good sandwiches, including Black Angus burgers, Cajun chicken and vegetarian Gardenburgers, as well as Caesar and shrimp salads. There's music from 4pm to 11pm nightly.

**The Banyan Grill** (☎ 922-3111; 2365 Kalakaua Ave; snacks & plate meals $5-13; open 3pm-10pm daily) is an open-air grill in the courtyard between the beach and pool at the upscale Sheraton Moana Surfrider hotel. The chef literally cooks up your order over a barbecue pit as you sit in a lounge chair and watch. The food is simple but tasty fare which includes baby back ribs, teriyaki chicken and grilled shrimp – and the location, beneath the historic hotel's sprawling banyan tree, is particularly engaging. Here you can relax and dine with the rich and famous without breaking the bank.

**La Cucaracha** (☎ 922-2288; 2310 Kuhio Ave; dishes $8-15; open 2pm-midnight daily) may come as a surprise – who would expect an authentic family-run Mexican restaurant in the heart of Waikiki? The food is excellent. Dishes, which include rice and beans, range from soft tacos with fresh cilantro and lime to a Mexican-style steak smothered in salsa verde. Wash it all down with a potent margarita.

**Oceanarium Restaurant** (☎ 922-1233; 2490 Kalakaua Ave; breakfast buffet $13, lunch $8, dinner mains $13-26; open 7am-10pm daily), in the Pacific Beach Hotel, has standard hotel fare but a one-of-a-kind view. Its dining room wraps around a stunning three-story aquarium brimming with colorful tropical fish, including some impressive sharks and rays. At breakfast, waffles or French toast cost $7 and there's also a full buffet available. Dinner mains range from pasta to lobster, while lunch features a variety of sandwiches.

**Chuck's Steak House** (☎ 923-1228; 2335 Kalakaua Ave; dinners $17-25; open 5pm-10pm daily), on the 2nd floor of the Outrigger Waikiki hotel, has a good sunset ocean view and some excellent early-bird specials. From 5pm to 6pm you can get a teriyaki chicken or grilled *mahimahi* dinner for a reasonable $12.75 and down a few Mai Tais at just $2.50 each. The regular menu features a nice variety of steak and seafood choices. All meals come with a simple but fresh salad bar that includes slices of pineapple and melon along with the usual vegies.

**Tanaka of Tokyo** (☎ 922-4702; 2250 Kalakaua Ave; lunch $10-15, dinner $16-36; open 11:30am-2pm Mon-Fri, 5:30pm-10pm daily), in the Waikiki Shopping Plaza, is an entertaining place to dine. Its U-shaped teppanyaki tables each have a central grill that's presided over by a chef with 'flying knives,' who cooks and serves meals to the diners at his table. Meals are set courses that include salad, miso soup, rice, an appetizer and dessert. The dinner price, which is determined by the main meal selected, ranges from $16 for chicken to $36 for lobster tail. Look in the free tourist magazines for coupons that are good for half off one meal when two people dine together.

**Singha Thai** (☎ 941-2893; 1910 Ala Moana Blvd; mains $12-25; open 4pm-11pm daily) has award-winning Thai food and a troupe of Thai dancers that performs from 7pm to 9pm nightly. For starters, the shrimp salad and the hot-and-sour *tom yum* soup are tasty house specialties ($10 each). Mains include a variety of spicy curry and noodle dishes as well as some upmarket choices such as seared Hawaiian lobster tail in a ginger chili sauce. A top choice for an exotic night out.

## A Sunday Splurge

If you really want to treat yourself, Waikiki has some top-notch Sunday brunch buffets that are among the most indulgent imaginable.

Waikiki's most elegant Sunday brunch buffet is served at **Orchids** (☎ 923-2311; 2199 Kalia Rd; buffet $38; 9:30am-2:30pm) in the Halekulani Hotel. The grand spread includes sashimi, sushi, prime rib, smoked salmon, roast suckling pig, an array of salads and a thoroughly decadent dessert bar. In addition, there's a fine ocean view, orchid sprays on the tables and a soothing flute and harp duo. It's best to make advance reservations, or you may encounter a long wait.

A pleasant runner-up is the Royal Hawaiian Hotel's **Surf Room** (☎ 931-7194; 2259 Kalakaua Ave; buffet $34; 11am-2.30pm), which has an alfresco beachside setting and a fine brunch spread. It includes seafood dishes such as sashimi and Alaskan crab legs, waffle and omelette stations, prime rib, salads and tempting desserts. The main drawback is that it's nearly as pricey as Orchids, though it isn't as much of an event.

If you favor a historic colonial atmosphere over beachside dining, then there's the Sunday brunch on the **Banyan Veranda** (☎ 922-3111; 2365 Kalakaua Ave; buffet $35; 9am-1pm) at the Sheraton Moana Surfrider. It features specialty salads, sashimi, oysters on the half shell, prime rib, eggs Benedict, omelette and waffle stations and a generous dessert bar. This brunch is accompanied by live classical music.

For something less formal there's **Brunch on the Beach** – a lively event that takes place on the second Sunday of each month and draws scores of locals and tourists alike. Oceanfront Kalakaua Ave, between Kaiulani and Liliuokalani Aves, is lined with umbrella-shaded tables and transformed into a huge outdoor café. Chefs from some of Waikiki's best restaurants set up food stands, and Hawaiian musicians perform along the beach. All you pay is for the cost of the food you choose. Sample whatever you like – omelettes, fish tacos, Thai curry and dim sum are favorites among the many selections – and most items are priced under $5, so you can easily eat your fill for less than $20.

**Keo's** (☎ 922-9355; 2028 Kuhio Ave; mains $10-18; open from 5pm-11pm daily), Waikiki's other top-rated Thai restaurant, also has good food. The main drawback is that the location, roadside on busy Kuhio Ave, can be noisy. Keo's, which has long been a favorite with visiting celebs ranging from Jimmy Carter to Keanu Reeves, has a loyal following. A house specialty is the Evil Jungle Prince, a spicy curry with basil and coconut milk, which can be ordered in vegetarian, chicken, beef or shrimp versions.

**Todai** (☎ 947-1000; 1910 Ala Moana Blvd; lunch/dinner buffet $15/27; open 11:30am-2:30pm & 5:30pm-9pm daily) has amazing buffet spreads with virtually any seafood item you can think of, from Alaskan king crab legs and lobster tail to sashimi and smoked salmon. To round it out, there are salads, pastas and mouthwatering desserts. Despite being a huge operation, the place is always packed so it's wise to get there early, particularly at dinner.

## Top End

Reservations are always a good idea at any of Waikiki's top-end restaurants.

**Golden Dragon** (☎ 946-5336; 2005 Kalia Rd; appetizers $7-10, mains $15-30; open 6pm-9:30pm Tues-Sat), in the Hilton Hawaiian Village, is a top choice for fine Chinese dining, with both good food and an ocean view. Although the varied menu has some expensive specialties, many dishes, including a tasty Cantonese roast duck and a deliciously crispy lemon chicken, are priced under $20.

**Hau Tree Lanai** (☎ 921-7066; 2863 Kalakaua Ave; breakfast dishes $8-15, appetizers $7-16, mains $20-30; open 7am-10pm daily), in the New Otani Kaimana Beach Hotel, has a romantic beachfront setting right on Sans Souci Beach, at the Diamond Head end of Waikiki. Breakfast includes omelettes and some interesting dishes such as salmon Benedict, a delicious combination of seared salmon, spinach, bacon and a poached egg on a cheddar-cheese scone. Dinner features Pacific Rim specialties such as papaya chicken salad, Cajun sashimi, prawns thermidor and *hoisin* duck breast. Be sure to request one of the seaside tables in the alfresco courtyard, which is shaded by a sprawling *hau* tree.

**Sam Choy's Diamond Head Restaurant** (☎ 732-8645; 449 Kapahulu Ave; meals $20-30; open 5:30pm-9:30pm daily), about half a mile north of the zoo, offers Hawaii Regional cuisine in a contemporary setting. Unlike many other restaurateurs specializing in such fare, Choy serves guests hearty portions that include both soup and salad with main meals. Among the favorites here are the seafood *laulau* (steamed in ti leaves) and the crabmeat-stuffed fish. There are a few appetizers on the menu but because the mains are so generous, most diners forgo the first course.

**Bali By The Sea** (☎ 941-2254; 2005 Kalia Rd; appetizers $8-15, mains $26-35; open 6pm-10pm Mon-Sat), in the Hilton Hawaiian Village, is the resort's top-rated dinner restaurant. It boasts a chic decor, a splendid ocean view and a creative menu that combines both continental and Hawaiian influences. Appetizers include such varied choices as ahi poke with wasabi ginger sauce or a traditional Caesar salad with duck confit. Main dishes not only feature standards such as rack of lamb and tenderloin Wellington, but also include some excellent local fish dishes such as sake-steamed Kona lobster and macadamia-crusted *opakapaka*.

**Banyan Veranda** (☎ 922-3111; 2365 Kalakaua Ave; 4-course dinner $40; open 5:30pm-9pm daily), at the Sheraton Moana Surfrider, has a gem of a setting on the hotel's historic courtyard veranda. The menu changes nightly and features French- and Pacific Rim-influenced dishes. Dinner is accompanied by Hawaiian music and hula dancing. All in all, the Banyan Veranda makes for a very romantic night out.

**Prince Court** (☎ 956-1111; 100 Holomoana St; lunch buffet $20, dinner buffet $30/39 weekdays/weekend; open 11:30am-2pm Mon-Fri, 5pm-9pm daily) is a worthy treat. This sleek contemporary restaurant on the 3rd floor of the Hawaii Prince Hotel, offers a view of the yacht harbor and wonderful buffets of Asian and Western cuisine. All buffets have hot and cold mains, dim sum, fresh fish, salads and tempting desserts; dinner adds on a generous array of seafood dishes, including crab legs, sashimi and smoked salmon.

**Orchids** (☎ 923-2311; 2199 Kalia Rd; appetizers $12-18, mains $25-35; open 6pm-10pm daily), located in the Halekulani Hotel, has an alfresco ocean-view setting and excellent contemporary continental food. In

WAIKIKI

addition to French-inspired cuisine such as escargot and rack of lamb, the menu has some Pacific Rim dishes such as shrimp rolls and seared Hawaiian fish. Orchids also features Waikiki's top-rated Sunday brunch (for details see the boxed text 'A Sunday Splurge' earlier).

**La Mer** (☎ 923-2311; 2199 Kalia Rd; mains $30-45, fixed-price meal 4/6-course $80/105; open 6pm-9:30pm daily), in the Halekulani Hotel, is regarded by many to be Hawaii's ultimate fine-dining restaurant. It has a neoclassical French menu, with an emphasis on Provençal cuisine and a superb 2nd-floor ocean view. The dining is formal, and men are required to wear jackets (loaners are available). The menu changes daily but typically features items such as ahi with caviar, bouillabaisse and filet mignon.

**Kyo-ya** (☎ 947-3911; 2057 Kalakaua Ave; multicourse lunch $14-20, dinner $30-55; open 11am-1:30pm Mon-Sat, 5:30pm-9pm daily), a formal Japanese restaurant with kimono-clad waitresses, has Waikiki's fanciest Japanese cuisine. The menu is extensive, covering eight pages. The specialty here is the *kaiseki* dinner, a traditional Kyoto-style meal that is served with as many as a dozen small courses. Both the setting and food presentation are elegant, and it's a favorite spot among islanders for a special night out.

## ENTERTAINMENT

Waikiki has a varied entertainment scene, and you'll never have a problem finding something to do. For updated schedule information, check the free tourist magazines and local newspapers.

### Hawaiiana

Waikiki has a variety of Hawaiian-style entertainment, from Polynesian shows with beating drums and hula dancers to mellow duos playing ukulele or slack-key guitar.

You can watch some of Oahu's best hula troupes performing their music and dance for free at a couple of Waikiki venues. The most scenic is the city-sponsored **Kuhio Beach Torch Lighting & Hula Show** (Kuhio Beach Park's hula mound), which takes place at 6:30pm Monday to Thursday and 6pm Friday to Sunday. Another free hula show takes place at the **International Market Place** (2330 Kalakaua Ave) food court from 7:30pm most evenings.

The beachside courtyard at **Duke's Canoe Club** (☎ 922-2268; 2335 Kalakaua Ave), at the Outrigger Waikiki hotel, is Waikiki's most popular venue for contemporary Hawaiian music. There's entertainment from 4pm to 6pm and from 10pm to midnight daily, with the biggest names – including Kapena and Henry Kapono – appearing on weekend afternoons. Great scene – don't miss it.

At the **Banyan Veranda** (☎ 922-3111; 2365 Kalakaua Ave), in the Sheraton Moana Surfrider, you can listen to music beneath the same old banyan tree where 'Hawaii Calls' broadcast its nationwide radio show for four decades beginning in 1935. The performance schedule varies, but typically there's Hawaiian music and a hula dancer from 5:30pm to 8:30pm nightly, followed by classical musicians from 8:30pm to 10:30pm.

### Sunset on the Beach

How can you go wrong in a city where the mayor throws a beach party every weekend?

Every Saturday and Sunday evening the Mayor's Office of Culture and the Arts for the City and County of Honolulu turns Queen's Surf Beach into a festive scene that attracts an equal measure of locals and visitors. It's as much fun as going to a luau and everything is free – except for the food and that's a bargain. You can literally mingle with the mayor, who takes centerstage to kick off the event, which has been dubbed 'Sunset on the Beach.'

Hawaiian bands perform on a beachside stage from 4pm to sunset and then when darkness falls a huge screen is unscrolled above the stage and a feature movie is shown. Sometimes they opt for a movie with island connections, such as *Blue Hawaii* – the 1961 classic starring Elvis Presley – while other nights it's a popular Hollywood flick of the *Star Wars* or *Shrek* variety.

Tables and chairs are set up on the beach and out along the Kapahulu Groin. The area's eateries operate food stalls along the beach, serving up standard picnic fare such as burgers and pizza as well as tastier treats such as Panang chicken curry from Keo's and savory seafood dishes from other upmarket restaurants – and nothing is over $5.

It's all plenty of good fun and a great community experience.

**House Without a Key** (☎ 923-2311; 2199 Kalia Rd) attracts an older, genteel crowd who gather daily at the Halekulani Hotel's open-air bar for sunset cocktails, Hawaiian music and hula dancing by a former Miss Hawaii.

**Luaus** The **Royal Hawaiian Hotel** (☎ 931-7194; 2259 Kalakaua Ave; show & buffet dinner adult/child 5-12 yrs $81/48) has a beachside luau from 6pm to 8:30pm Monday, with an open bar, buffet-style dinner and Polynesian show.

The **Don Ho Show** (☎ 923-3981; Waikiki Beachcomber Hotel, 2300 Kalakaua Ave; show & dinner $52) features the saucy Honolulu musician who has been playing the Waikiki tourist scene since 1962. Seating behind an organ, he cracks jokes, plays his old pop hits such as 'Tiny Bubbles' and offers a good dose of kitsch. Performances are from 7pm Sunday to Thursday in the hotel theater. Search around and you can almost always find discount tickets.

See also the Entertainment section in the Facts for the Visitor chapter for luau shows that take place elsewhere on Oahu, but include free transportation from Waikiki.

### Bars

**The Poolside Bar** (☎ 921-6264; 2570 Kalakaua Ave), in the Aston Waikiki Beach Hotel, is a good place to linger over a cool tropical drink while soaking up the rays.

**Coconut Willy's Bar** (☎ 923-9454; 2330 Kalakaua Ave), in the bustling International Market Place, gets a bit loud but it's a great place to watch people and there's plenty of night action.

**Ye Olde Fox & Hound** (☎ 947-3776; 1178 Ala Moana Blvd), an English-style pub in the basement of the Discovery Bay Center, features live sports broadcasts on big-screen TVs and Waikiki's cheapest beer prices.

**Harry's Bar** (☎ 923-1234; 2424 Kalakaua Ave), in the Hyatt Regency Waikiki, is a fun place that not only mixes up those colorful tropical drinks with little umbrellas but also makes good alcohol-free smoothies. There is usually Hawaiian entertainment in the evening.

### Cinemas

**Waikiki Theatres** (☎ 971-5133; cnr Seaside & Kalakaua Aves; admission $7.50) is a comfortable theater with three screens showing first-run movies.

**IMAX Theatre Waikiki** (☎ 923-4629; 325 Seaside Ave; admission $10) shows a 40-minute movie of Hawaii's stunning vistas on a 70ft-wide screen, with three-dimensional visual effects. It can be a fun introduction to the landscapes of the Hawaiian islands, providing much of the same effect as zooming around in a helicopter – including the sense of motion!

### Dance Clubs

**Wave Waikiki** (☎ 941-0424; 1877 Kalakaua Ave; admission $5; open 9pm-4am daily), with an emphasis on trance, hip hop, funk and alternative music, is Waikiki's hottest dance club. The minimum age is 21.

**The Maze** (☎ 921-5800; 2255 Kuhio Ave; admission $10; open 8pm-2am Fri & Sat), in the Waikiki Trade Center, is a high energy dance club with DJs spinning music in three different rooms – the main room features progressive and trance music, the other two have anything from hip hop to Latin. The minimum age is 21.

**Scruples** (☎ 923-9530; 2310 Kuhio Ave; admission $5; open 8pm-4am daily) is a busy, disco-style, top-40 dance club in the center of Waikiki. The minimum age is 18.

**Moose McGillycuddy's** (☎ 923-0751; 310 Lewers St; admission free; open 9pm-1am Mon-Sat) is a raucous place with live bands; the music is mostly 80s and 90s rock and top 40. You have to be 21 to get in.

**Hard Rock Cafe** (☎ 955-7383; 1837 Kapiolani Blvd; admission for ages 18-20 $10, over 21 $5; open 9pm-2am Wed & most Sat & Sun) has live rock, hip hop and top 40. The minimum age is 18.

**Zanzabar Nightclub** (☎ 924-3939; 2255 Kuhio Ave; admission $5; open 9pm-4am nightly), in the Waikiki Trade Center, has something happening every night. There's always dancing but the scene varies with the night; Monday is techno and trance, Tuesday is Latin music, Wednesday is reggae, Thursday and Friday are flashbacks, Saturday is DJs and Sunday is top 40. The minimum age is 21.

### Gay & Lesbian Venues

**Hula's Bar & Lei Stand** (☎ 923-0669; 134 Kapahulu Ave; open 10am-2am daily), on the 2nd floor of the Waikiki Grand hotel, is

WAIKIKI

Waikiki's main gay venue. This open-air bar is a popular place for gay people to meet, dance and have a few drinks. It also has a nice ocean view.

Other gay spots in Waikiki are **Angles Waikiki** (☎ 926-9766; 2256 Kuhio Ave), a nightclub with dancing, a pool table and video games; **Fusion Waikiki** (☎ 924-2422; 2260 Kuhio Ave), which has karaoke and drag queen shows; and **In-Between** (☎ 926-7060; 2155 Lauula St), a gay karaoke bar open until 2am nightly.

All four of these places welcome both gay men and lesbians, though Hula's and In-Between are predominantly frequented by gay men, while Angles and Fusion tend to have a more mixed crowd.

## Concerts
**Waikiki Shell** (Kapiolani Park) hosts both classical and contemporary music concerts. For current schedule information, call the **Blaisdell Center box office** (☎ 591-2211).

## Tea Ceremonies
**Urasenke Foundation of Hawaii** (☎ 923-3059; 245 Saratoga Rd) has tea ceremony demonstrations at 10am on Wednesday and Friday, bringing a rare bit of serenity to busy Saratoga Rd. Students who are dressed in kimonos perform the ceremony on tatami mats in a formal tearoom; for those participating, the tea ceremony can be a meditative experience.

It costs $3 to be served green tea and sweets, or you can watch the ceremony for free. The ceremony lasts about 45 minutes. Although it's not always essential, you can make reservations by phone. Because guests leave their shoes at the door, they are asked to wear socks.

## Free Entertainment
A pleasant way for you to pass the evening is to stroll along Waikiki Beach at sunset and sample the outdoor Hawaiian shows that take place at the beachfront hotels. You can take a leisurely wander past the musicians playing at the Sheraton Moana Surfrider's **Banyan Veranda** (2365 Kalakaua Ave), watch bands performing beachside at **Duke's Canoe Club** (2335 Kalakaua Ave), see the poolside performers at the **Sheraton Waikiki** (2255 Kalakaua Ave) and so on down the line.

The **Royal Hawaiian Band** performs from 2pm to 3pm most Sundays, with the exception of August, at the Kapiolani Park Bandstand. It's a quintessential Hawaiian scene that caps off with the audience joining hands and singing Queen Liliuokalani's *Aloha Oe* in Hawaiian.

The Kapiolani Park Bandstand is also the site of free **Friday Bandstand Concerts** held from 5:30pm to 6:30pm each Friday. A different Hawaiian group performs each week – anything from top-notch slack-key guitar masters to blues, jazz or reggae bands.

The **Royal Hawaiian Shopping Center** (☎ 922-0588; Kalakaua Ave) offers free events at its fountain courtyard, including a nightly torchlighting ceremony at 6pm, which is followed some nights by a 30-minute Polynesian show.

The shopping center also sponsors various daytime activities. Hula lessons are given 10am to 11am Monday and Friday; lei-making lessons are from 11am to noon Monday and Wednesday; Hawaiian quilting lessons are offered 9:30am to 11:30am Tuesday and Thursday; and hour-long ukulele lessons start at 10am Tuesday and Thursday and at 11:30am Monday, Wednesday and Friday. All the classes are free, though supplies must be purchased for the quilting class.

If you want to get some exercise while you learn more about Hawaiian culture, consider joining one of the free **Waikiki Historic Trail** walking tours. These 90-minute walks, led by Native Hawaiian guides, are peppered with interesting historic tidbits on Prince Kuhio and other Hawaiian royalty who lived and played in Waikiki a century ago. The walks begin at 9am Monday to Friday in front of the Duke Kahanamoku statue at Kuhio Beach Park.

Other free things to see and do in Waikiki, which are detailed earlier in this chapter, include the Pleasant Hawaiian Hula Show in Kapiolani Park; the Damien Museum, dedicated to Father Damien; the Oceanarium, a three-story tropical fish tank at the Pacific Beach Hotel; the US Army Museum at Fort DeRussy; and tours of the historic Sheraton Moana Surfrider hotel.

And of course don't miss one of the free hula shows that are offered nightly (see the earlier Hawaiiana section for details) or the Sunset on the Beach event that takes place on weekends (see the boxed text in this section).

## SHOPPING

There are hundreds of shops in Waikiki vying for tourist dollars, including souvenir stalls, T-shirt and swimsuit shops, and fancy boutiques.

You'll never be far from one of the ubiquitous ABC discount marts, which stand on nearly every other street corner. They can be a good place to pick up vacation necessities, such as inexpensive beach mats, sunblock and sundry goods.

For cheap souvenirs, there's the **International Market Place** (☎ 923-9871), under a sprawling banyan tree in the center of Waikiki, where nearly a hundred stalls sell everything from seashell necklaces and refrigerator magnets to T-shirts and sarongs.

Numerous high-end shops along Kalakaua Ave sell designer clothing and fashionable accessories. The simplest approach is just to stroll the street and see what catches your fancy, or peruse the lobby shops of the more expensive hotels, such as the Sheraton Waikiki.

The **Royal Hawaiian Shopping Center** (☎ 922-0588; Kalakaua Ave), Waikiki's biggest shopping center, has dozens of shops selling jewelry and designer clothing, including Donna Karan, Versace and Chanel. The Royal Hawaiian also has Hawaiian-influenced gift shops, including **Little Hawaiian Craft Shop** (☎ 926-2662), which carries a range of local crafts, from *kukui*-nut key chains and quilt-pattern kits to high-quality koa bowls.

### Art in the Park

Looking for fine art at bargain prices? The best deal for buying paintings directly from island artists is the city sponsored 'Art in the Park' program, which sets up at the southern side of the Honolulu Zoo on Monsarrat Ave in Kapiolani Park. Local artists have been hanging their paintings on the zoo fence each weekend for 30 years.

The artwork is on display 10am to 4pm on Saturday and Sunday and 9am to noon on Tuesday. It's an informal open-air event that only takes place on days when it's not raining. It's possible you might find a great deal here, as many of Hawaii's better painters got their start at the fence.

For antique and used aloha shirts, **Bailey's Antique Shop** (☎ 734-7628; 517 Kapahulu Ave) has the island's widest selection, with prices from $10 to $3000. It's a great place to go and look around – almost like a museum.

The thrift shop at the **Waikiki Community Center** (☎ 523-1802; 310 Paoakalani Ave) often has used aloha clothing at bargain prices, and if you're lucky you just might find something that fits you.

For eclectic antiques, there's **Island Treasures Antiques** (☎ 922-8223; 2145 Kuhio Ave), which has lots of odds and ends, including jewelry, period glassware, old posters and Asian porcelain.

# Pearl Harbor Area

## PEARL HARBOR

On December 7, 1941, a wave of more than 350 Japanese planes attacked Pearl Harbor, home of the US Pacific Fleet.

Some 2335 US soldiers were killed during the two-hour attack. Of those, 1177 died in the battleship USS *Arizona* when it took a direct hit and sank in less than nine minutes. Twenty other US ships were sunk or seriously damaged and 347 airplanes were destroyed that fateful day.

## USS *Arizona* Memorial

Over 1.5 million people 'remember Pearl Harbor' each year by visiting the USS *Arizona* Memorial. Operated by the National Park Service, the memorial is Hawaii's most visited attraction.

The **visitor center** (☎ *422-2771; 24hr recorded information ☎ 422-0561;* **w** *www.nps.gov/usar; admission free; open 7:30am-5pm daily except Thanksgiving, Christmas & New Year's Day)* encompasses a museum and a theater as well as the offshore memorial at the sunken USS *Arizona*. The 75-minute program includes a documentary film on the attack and a boat ride out to the memorial and back.

The 184ft memorial, built in 1962, sits directly over the *Arizona* but does not touch the sunken ship. The memorial contains the ship's bell and a wall inscribed with the names of those who perished onboard. The average age of the enlisted men on the *Arizona* was just 19 years old.

From the memorial, the battleship is visible 8ft below the surface. The ship rests in about 40ft of water, and even now oozes a gallon or two of oil each day. In the rush to recover from the attack and prepare for war, the navy exercised its option to leave the men in the sunken ship. They remain entombed in its hull, buried at sea.

Pearl Harbor survivors, who act as volunteer historians, are sometimes available to give talks about the day of the attack.

There's also a small museum with interesting photos, from both Japanese and US military archives, showing Pearl Harbor before, during and after the attack. One photo is of Harvard-educated Admiral Yamamoto, the brilliant military strategist who planned

### Highlights

• Touring the USS *Arizona* Memorial for a poignant sense of the events that thrusted the USA into WWII

• Walking the deck of the USS *Missouri*, where the formal end of WWII took place

• Learning about traditional Hawaiian medicine at Keaiwa Heiau, a temple dedicated to healing

Pearl Harbor Area
page 161

the attack on Pearl Harbor – even though he personally opposed going to war with the USA. Rather than relish the victory, Yamamoto stated after the attack that he feared Japan had 'awakened a sleeping giant and filled him with a terrible resolve.'

Weather permitting, programs run every 15 minutes from 8am to 3pm (from 7:45am in summer) on a first-come, first-served basis. As soon as you arrive, pick up a ticket at the information booth (each person in the party must pick up their own ticket); the number printed on the ticket corresponds to the time the tour begins.

Generally, the shortest waits are in the morning, and if you arrive before the crowds, your wait may be less than half an hour; however, waits of a couple of hours are not unknown. The summer months are the busiest, with an average of 4500 people taking the tour daily, and the day's allotment of tickets is sometimes gone by noon.

Admission to everything, including the boat ride, which is provided by the navy, is free. The memorial and all its facilities are

*PEARL HARBOR AREA*

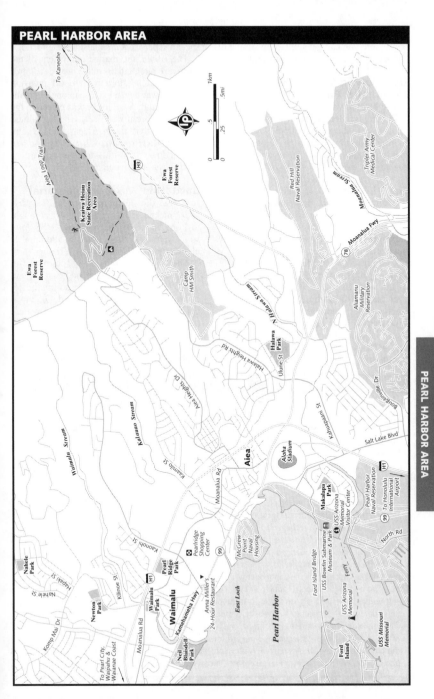

# PEARL HARBOR AREA

accessible to the disabled. There's a snack bar, where you can get something simple to eat, and a shop selling souvenirs and books.

## USS *Bowfin* Submarine Museum & Park

If you have to wait an hour or two for your USS *Arizona* Memorial tour to begin, take a stroll over to the adjacent USS *Bowfin* Submarine Museum & Park (☎ 423-1341; admission to park free, admission to submarine & museum adult/child 4-12 yrs $8/3; open 8am-5pm daily except Thanksgiving, Christmas & New Year's Day). The park contains the moored WWII submarine the USS *Bowfin*, as well as the Pacific Submarine Museum, which traces the development of submarines from their early origins to the nuclear age.

Commissioned in May 1943, the *Bowfin* sank 44 ships in the Pacific before the end of the war. Visitors can take a self-guided tour using a 30-minute recorded cassette (included in the admission). Children under four years old are not allowed on the submarine for safety reasons.

You can freely stroll around the park, view the missiles and torpedoes displayed on the grounds, look through the periscopes and inspect a Japanese *kaiten*, a suicide torpedo.

The *kaiten*, the marine equivalent of the kamikaze pilot and his plane, was developed as a last-ditch effort to ward off invasion when the war began to close in on the Japanese homeland. A volunteer was placed in the torpedo before it was fired. He then piloted the torpedo to its target. At least one US ship, the USS *Mississinewa*, was sunk by a *kaiten*. It went down off Ulithi Atoll in southwestern Micronesia in November 1944.

## Battleship *Missouri* Memorial

In 1998, the decommissioned USS *Missouri*, nicknamed 'Mighty Mo,' was brought to Ford Island by the nonprofit USS *Missouri* Memorial Association to add another element to Pearl Harbor's WWII sites.

The 887ft-long ship, one of four powerful Iowa class battleships launched near the end of WWII, served as a flagship during the decisive battles of Iwo Jima and Okinawa. On September 2, 1945, the formal Japanese surrender that ended WWII took place on the battleship's deck. The *Missouri* is now docked just a few hundred yards from the sunken remains of the USS *Arizona*; together,

## The Element of Surprise

The attack upon Pearl Harbor, which jolted the USA into WWII, caught the US fleet totally by surprise. There had, however, been warnings, some of which were far from subtle.

At 6:40am on December 7, 1941, the USS *Ward* spotted a submarine conning tower approaching the entrance of Pearl Harbor. The *Ward* immediately attacked with depth charges and sank what turned out to be one of five midget Japanese submarines launched to penetrate the harbor.

At 7:02am a radar station on the northern shore of Oahu reported planes approaching. Even though they were coming from the wrong direction, they were assumed to be American planes from the US mainland.

At 7:55am Pearl Harbor was hit. Within minutes the USS *Arizona* went down in a fiery inferno, trapping its crew beneath the surface. It wasn't until 15 minutes after the bombing started that American antiaircraft guns began to shell the Japanese warplanes.

Claims that President Roosevelt knew the attack was coming, but withheld the information because he needed an incident to propel the USA into war, are discounted by most historians. Not only is there no hard evidence to support the theory, but it makes little sense that Roosevelt would have put so much of his navy in jeopardy upon entering a war with the Japanese that clearly was going to be fought predominantly by naval forces.

If you're looking for screen versions of the battle, go with *Tora! Tora! Tora!*, which although at times dry is spot-on accurate and mostly compelling as it chronicles the American blunders that unwittingly aided the Japanese. In contrast, the huge-budget *Pearl Harbor* is a bomb in every sense of the word that displays a cynical disregard for accurately portraying the heroism and tragedy of the day. In print, the classics remain Walter Lord's *Day of Infamy* and the series of books by Gordon Prange, which includes the excellent *At Dawn We Slept*.

the ships provide a unique set of historical bookends.

Launched in 1944, the *Missouri*, with its 13-inch-thick armor plating, impressive gun turrets and 65ft-long guns, was the last battleship ever built. In 1955, after service in the Korean War, it was placed in mothballs. Then, three decades later, it was awakened from rest during the heated Reagan-era military buildup, and after costly modernization, the *Missouri* was recommissioned in 1986. The ship made a brief appearance in the Persian Gulf War and was again decommissioned in 1992.

In 1996, with the Pearl Harbor connection weighing heavily in its favor, Honolulu was chosen to become Mighty Mo's permanent home.

**Battleship *Missouri* Memorial** (☎ 973-2494; W *www.ussmissouri.com; self-guided tour adult/child 4-12 yrs $16/7; open 9am-5pm daily)* is now open to visitors. A tour of the ship takes approximately two hours. You can poke about the officers' quarters, visit the wardroom that now houses exhibits on the ship's history and walk the deck where General Douglas MacArthur accepted the Japanese surrender. The main advantage of joining a group tour is that it provides access to a 'combat engagement center' where you can watch a simulated naval battle. In addition there are tours that take in parts of the ship not open to regular visitors. The Explorer's Tour ($49) takes in large areas below decks and is a fascinating introduction into life aboard one of the largest warships ever built. Note the thickness of the armored decks and their hatches. Call for information on the special tours and their mandatory reservations (groups are usually limited to about three).

It's not possible to drive directly to Ford Island, because it's an active military facility. Instead, a trolleybus shuttles visitors to the *Missouri* from Bowfin Park, where the tickets are sold. If you're a history buff the *Missouri* is a don't-miss sight, but if your time or money is more limited visit the USS *Arizona* Memorial instead.

## Getting There & Away

The USS *Arizona* Memorial visitor center and Bowfin Park are off Kamehameha Hwy (Hwy 99) on the Pearl Harbor Naval Reservation southwest of the Aloha Stadium. If you're coming from Honolulu, take H1 west to exit 15A (Stadium/Arizona Memorial). Make sure that you follow the highway signs for the USS *Arizona* Memorial, and not the signs for Pearl Harbor. There's plenty of free parking at the visitor center.

It's easy to get there by public bus. Bus No 42 Ewa Beach is the most direct bus from Waikiki to the visitor center, taking about an hour. Bus No 20 covers the same route, but it makes a stop at the airport, adding about 15 minutes to the travel time.

The private **Arizona Memorial Shuttle Bus** (☎ 839-0911) and **Hawaii Super Transit** (☎ 841-2989) both pick up people from hotels in Waikiki several times a day, charging $3 one way or $5 roundtrip for a van ride to the visitor center. The ride usually takes about 40 minutes.

There are also private boat cruises to Pearl Harbor which leave from Kewalo

---

## Security Restrictions

Because of the symbolic significance Pearl Harbor holds, its two memorials, both of which are on military property, were considered potential terrorist targets after the September 11 attacks on America.

As a safeguard, new security measures have been enacted, and all visitors to the USS *Arizona* Memorial and the USS *Missouri* Memorial now face strict restrictions on what they can bring into these sites.

You are not allowed to bring into the USS *Arizona* Memorial visitor center, or onto either of the ship tours, *any* items that allow concealment, and this includes purses, camera bags, fanny packs (bum bags), backpacks, diaper bags, shopping bags and the like. Also, cameras or video cameras larger than 12 inches are not allowed. It's not that these items are being searched and then allowed in; they simply can't be brought into the sites at all.

If you arrive by bus, there's now a stand offering storage services located between the buildings for the two attractions. Call one or the other to confirm it is operating. If you arrive by car, of course you could put these items in your trunk, but this is something the park service has predictably and extremely cautiously advised against in the past because of potential theft from parked cars.

Basin and cost about $25 – avoid them, as they don't stop at the visitor center and their passengers are not allowed to board the USS *Arizona* Memorial.

## PEARL CITY
**pop 31,000**

Pearl City is a large urban area that is home to lots of military personnel and civilians who work on the bases, but it offers little of interest to casual visitors.

If you're just passing through and not going to Pearl City itself, stay on H1 and avoid the parallel Kamehameha Hwy (Hwy 99), which is all stop-and-go traffic through blocks of fast-food restaurants and shopping malls.

The **Pearlridge Shopping Center** (☎ 488-0981; 98-1005 Moanalua Rd), a massive shopping mall situated between the H1 and Kamehameha Hwy, has all of the usual mall stores.

A block west of the shopping center, at the drive-in theater, is the **Kam Super Swap Meet** (☎ 483-5933; 98-850 Moanalua Rd; open 5am-3pm Wed, Sat & Sun); it can be fun if you happen to be going by at the time, but by far the biggest swap meet on Oahu is at the Aloha Stadium (see the boxed text 'Bargain Hunting').

In the corner of the Pearlridge Shopping Center parking lot at Kaonohi St and Kamehameha Hwy, **Anna Miller's 24-Hour Restaurant** (☎ 487-2421; dishes $4-10) is a top-quality coffee shop that regularly wins local popularity contests. Its excellent iced tea is bottomless, the omelettes delicious and the sandwiches enormous. Should you gobble your way through your main meal and feel like some dessert, there is a range of homemade pies.

### Lost Luster

Pearl Harbor was named for the lustrous pearl oysters that thrived in its once pristine waters. Unfortunately, during the early 19th century, foreign settlers introduced cattle to the area, and the grazing livestock so denuded the nearby uplands that the hillsides above the harbor began to erode. As a result, vast quantities of mud washed into the harbor, destroying the oyster beds.

## KEAIWA HEIAU STATE RECREATION AREA

This 334-acre state park (☎ 483-2511; Aiea Heights Dr; admission free; open 7am-sunset daily) in Aiea, north of Pearl Harbor, contains an ancient medicinal temple, camping grounds, picnic facilities and a scenic hiking trail.

At the park entrance is **Keaiwa Heiau**, a stone temple built in the 1600s and used by kahuna *lapaau* (healers who used plants for medicine). The kahuna *lapaaus* used hundreds of medicinal plants and grew many on the grounds surrounding the heiau. Among those still found here are *noni*, whose pungent yellow fruits were used to treat heart disease; *kukui*, whose nuts are an effective laxative; *ulu*, whose sap was used to soothe chapped skin; and ti leaves that were wrapped around a sick person to break a fever. Not only did the herbs have medicinal value, but the heiau itself was thought to possess life-giving energy, and the kahuna *lapaau* was able to draw from the powers of both the temple and the plants.

Today, people wishing to be healed still place offerings within the heiau. The offerings reflect the multiplicity of Hawaii's cultures: rosary beads and sake cups sit beside flower leis and rocks wrapped in ti leaves.

### Aiea Loop Trail

The 4½-mile Aiea Loop Trail begins at the top of the park's paved loop road, next to the rest rooms, and ends at the camping ground, about a third of a mile below the start of the trail. This easy hike takes 2½ to three hours.

The first part of the trail goes through a eucalyptus forest and runs along the ridge. Other trees on the way include ironwood, Norfolk Island pine, guava and native ohia lehua, which has fluffy, red flowers.

Along the trail, there are sweeping vistas of Pearl Harbor, Diamond Head and the Koolau Range. About two-thirds of the way in, the wreckage of a C-47 cargo plane that crashed in 1943 can be spotted through the foliage on the eastern ridge.

### Camping

The park can accommodate 100 campers, most sites with their own picnic table and barbecue grill. Camp sites are not crowded together, but because many are open, there's

## Bargain Hunting

OK, so where's the best place to hunt for old Hawaii license plates, '50s kitsch ceramics and cheap used aloha shirts? Hands-down the honors go to the **Aloha Stadium Swap Meet** (☎ 486-6704; 99-500 Salt Lake Blvd; open 5am-3pm Wed, Sat & Sun), at Aloha Stadium in the Pearl Harbor area.

The Aloha Stadium, best known as the host to nationally televised football games and top-name music concerts, transforms itself three days a week into Hawaii's biggest and best swap meet.

For local flavor, this flea market is hard to beat, with some 1500 vendors selling an amazing variety of items, from beach towels and bananas to collectibles, antiques and crafts. It's also a fun place to mingle.

This is such a big event that there are private shuttle bus services to the swap meet from Waikiki ($6 return) which operate every hour or so on meet days; for information call **Reliable Shuttle** (☎ 924-9292) or **Affordable Shuttle** (☎ 479-3447).

not a lot of privacy either. If you are camping in winter, make sure your gear is waterproof, because it rains frequently at this 880ft elevation. The park has rest rooms, showers, a pay phone and drinking water. There's a resident caretaker by the front gate, and the gate is locked at night for security.

As with all Oahu public camping grounds, camping is not permitted on Wednesday and Thursday, and permits must be obtained in advance. For details, see Camping in the Facts for the Visitor chapter.

### Getting There & Away

From Honolulu, you should head west on Hwy 78 and then take the Stadium/Aiea turnoff onto Moanalua Rd. Turn right onto Aiea Heights Dr at the second traffic light. From here the road winds up 2½ miles to the park.

Bus No 11 (Honolulu–Aiea Heights) serves this area; however, the bus stops 1¼ miles south of the park entrance, and it is another 600 yards from the entrance to the camp sites.

**PEARL HARBOR AREA**

# Southeast Oahu

Some of Oahu's finest scenery is along the southeast coast, which curves around the tip of the Koolau Range. Diamond Head, Hanauma Bay and the island's most famous bodysurfing beaches are all just a 20-minute ride from Waikiki.

East of Diamond Head, H1 turns into the Kalanianaole Hwy (Hwy 72), following the southeast coast up to Kailua. It passes the exclusive Kahala residential area, a run of shopping centers and suburban housing developments that creep up into the mountain valleys.

The highway rises and falls as it winds its way around the Koko Head area and Makapuu Point, with beautiful coastal views along the way. The area's geological formations are fascinating, with boldly stratified rocks, volcanic craters and lava sea cliffs.

## DIAMOND HEAD

Diamond Head is a tuff cone and crater that was formed by a violent steam explosion deep beneath the surface long after most of Oahu's volcanic activity had stopped. As the backdrop to Waikiki, it's one of the best-known landmarks in the Pacific. The summit is 760ft high.

The Hawaiians called it Leahi and at its summit they built a *luakini* heiau, a type of temple used for human sacrifices. But ever since 1825, when British sailors found calcite crystals sparkling in the sun and mistakenly thought they'd struck it rich, it's been called Diamond Head.

In 1909 the US Army began building Fort Ruger at the edge of the crater. They constructed a network of tunnels and topped the rim with cannon emplacements, bunkers and observation posts. Reinforced during WWII, the fort has been a silent sentinel whose guns have never been fired. Today, there's a Hawaii National Guard base inside the crater.

Diamond Head *(admission $1; open 6am-6pm daily)* is a state monument, with picnic tables and rest rooms. The best reason to visit is to hike up to the crater rim for the panoramic view.

### Diamond Head Trail

The trail to Diamond Head summit was originally built in 1910 to service the military

**Highlights**

- Snorkeling among colorful tropical fish at Hanauma Bay
- Climbing the Diamond Head Trail to the scenic crater summit
- Marveling at the top-notch bodysurfing action at Sandy Beach
- Taking a swim in lovely Waimanalo Bay

Southeast Oahu
page 167

observation stations located along the crater rim.

Don't expect a walk in the park, as it's a fairly steep hike with a gain in elevation of 560ft. It is, however, only three-quarters of a mile to the top, and plenty of people of all ages hike to the summit. It takes about 30 minutes to reach the top. The trail is open and hot, so you might want to wear sunscreen and take along something to drink.

As you start up the trail, you can see the summit ahead, a bit to the left at roughly 11 o'clock. The crater is dry and scrubby with *kiawe*, native grasses and wildflowers. The small, yellow-orange flowers along the trail are *ilima*, Oahu's official flower.

About 20 minutes up the trail, you enter a long, dark tunnel. Because the tunnel curves, you don't see light until you get close to the end. It's a little spooky, but there is a handrail, and your eyes will adjust to make out shadows in the dark. Nevertheless, to prevent accidents, the park advises hikers to bring a flashlight.

When you step out into the light, you're immediately faced with a steep, 99-step staircase. Persevere! After this there's a shorter

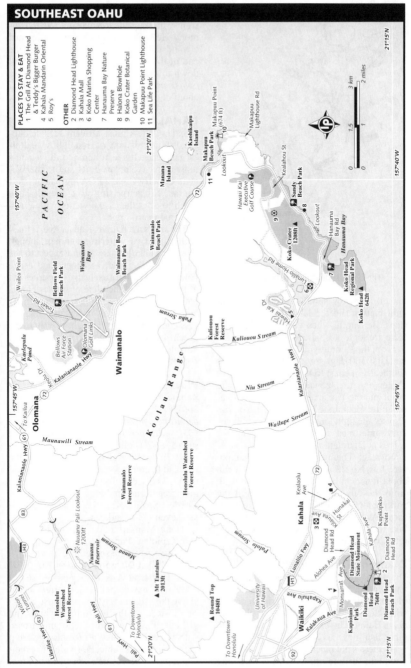

# SOUTHEAST OAHU

**PLACES TO STAY & EAT**
1 The Grill At Diamond Head
& Teddy's Bigger Burger
4 Kahala Mandarin Oriental
5 Roy's

**OTHER**
2 Diamond Head Lighthouse
3 Kahala Mall
6 Koko Marina Shopping
Center
7 Hanauma Bay Nature
Preserve
8 Halona Blowhole
9 Koko Crater Botanical
Garden
10 Makapuu Point Lighthouse
11 Sea Life Park

The *ilima* is Ohahu's official flower

tunnel, a narrow spiral staircase inside an unlit bunker and the last of the trail's 271 steps. Be careful when you reach the top – there are some steep drops.

From the summit you're rewarded with a fantastic 360-degree view that takes in the southeastern coast to Koko Head and Koko Crater and the leeward coast to Barbers Point and the Waianae Range; below is Kapiolani Park and the Waikiki Shell. You can also see the lighthouse, coral reefs, sailboats and sometimes even surfers waiting for waves at Diamond Head Beach.

To reach Diamond Head from Waikiki, take bus No 22 or 58, both of which run about twice an hour. It's a 20-minute walk from the bus stop to the trailhead at the parking lot. By car from Waikiki, take Monsarrat Ave to Diamond Head Rd and then take the right turn after Kapiolani Community College into the crater.

### Diamond Head Beach

Diamond Head Beach draws both surfers and windsurfers. Conditions are suitable for intermediate to advanced windsurfers, and when the swells are up it's a great place for wave riding. The beach has showers but no other facilities.

As there's not much to see here unless the wind and surf are up, most people coming

this way are touring by car. To get there from Waikiki, follow Kalakaua Ave to Diamond Head Rd. There's just parking lot just beyond the lighthouse. Walk east past the end of the lot and you'll find a paved trail down to the beach. If you don't have your own transport, bus No 14 runs from Waikiki about once an hour.

### KAHALA

Kahala, Oahu's most affluent seaside suburb, is home to many of Honolulu's wealthiest residents. It's also home to the island's most exclusive resort hotel and to the Waialae Country Club, a PGA tournament golf course. Not surprisingly, it doesn't have much to offer the casual visitor with a normal credit card limit.

The area's main drive, Kahala Ave, is lined with expensive waterfront homes, though most are rather low-key. Don't expect to see much from the road, as hedges and estate fences keep the more exclusive properties out of sight, and the thick line of houses blocks out virtually any view of the sea. Between the homes, there are a half-dozen shoreline access points that provide a right-of-way to the beach, but the swimming conditions aren't notable – it's mostly shallow, with sparse pockets of sand.

### Places to Stay & Eat

**Kahala Mandarin Oriental** (☎ 739-8888, 800-367-2525, fax 739-8800; **W** www.mandarin-oriental.com; 5000 Kahala Ave; rooms $310, with ocean view $500, presidential suite $3650) is on a private, quiet stretch of beach in swank Kahala. This is where the rich and famous go when they want to avoid the Waikiki scene. The guest list is Hawaii's most regal and includes Britain's Prince Charles, Spain's King Juan Carlos and the last seven US presidents.

Along Monsarrat Ave just past the zoo and Kapiolani Park, there are a couple of great places to grab something to eat.

**The Grill at Diamond Head** (☎ 732-0077; 3158 Monsarrat Ave; plate lunches $6.00-8.50) is a newcomer which offers a cut above the usual fare: you can choose brown rice instead of the ubiquitous white, and grilled salmon or portobello mushroom with vegetables make a nice change from the usual teriyaki chicken (which is excellent here). It serves delicious iced tea, too.

You'll know The Grill from the old Burgerland sign that still hangs out front.

The area also boasts an outpost of Kailua's **Teddy's Bigger Burgers** (☎ 735-9411; 3114 Monsarrat Ave; burgers $3.90-8; open 10:30am-9pm daily), with high-quality burgers, fries and milkshakes.

## KOKO HEAD REGIONAL PARK

The entire Koko Head area is a county regional park. It includes Hanauma Bay, Koko Head, Halona Blowhole, Sandy Beach Park and Koko Crater.

Koko Crater and Koko Head are both tuff cones created about 10,000 years ago during Oahu's last gasp of volcanic activity. The area is backed by Hawaii Kai, an expansive development of condos, houses, shopping centers, a marina and a golf course – all meticulously planned and rather sterile in appearance.

### Hanauma Bay Nature Preserve

Hanauma, which means 'Curved Bay,' is a gorgeous bay of sapphire and turquoise waters set in a rugged volcanic ring.

Once a popular fishing spot, the fish population was nearly depleted by the time the bay was designated a marine life conservation district in 1967. Now that they're protected, the fish swarm in by the thousands. It's a great place to go snorkeling – don't miss it!

Hanauma is both a county beach park and a state underwater park (information ☎ 396-4229; admission $3, child under 13 yrs free; open 6am-6pm Wed-Mon Nov-Mar, 6am-7pm Wed-Mon Apr-Oct, closed Tues). It has a snack bar, lifeguards, showers, rest rooms and access for the disabled.

The boldly striped lionfish

Hanauma's biggest draw is the sheer number and variety of fish. From the overlook you can peer into crystal waters and view the entire coral reef that stretches across the width of the bay. You can see schools of glittering silver fish, the bright blue flash of parrotfish and perhaps a lone sea turtle. To see an even more colorful scene, put on a mask, jump in and view it from beneath the surface.

The preserve seems to get as many people as fish. With over a million visitors a year, it's often busy and crowded. The heavy use of the bay has taken its toll, however, and the coral on the shallow reef has been damaged by all the action.

Still, efforts are being made to right the wrongs. For your part, be careful not to stand on the reef. Fish feeding by snorkelers, a practice that drew more aggressive fish into the bay, is now banned at Hanauma, resulting in a more natural balance of fish species.

Paths lead along low ledges on both sides of the bay. A 15-minute walk along the eastern path goes to the **Toilet Bowl**, a small natural pool in the lava rock. It's connected to the sea by an underwater channel, which enables water to surge into the bowl and then flush out from beneath. People going into the pool for the thrill of it can get quite a ride as it flushes down 4ft to 5ft almost instantly. However, the rock around the bowl is slippery and difficult to grip, and getting in is far easier than getting out. It definitely should not be tried alone.

A 10-minute walk along the western path will take you to a rocky point. The cove at the southern side of the point is the treacherous **Witches Brew**, so named for its swirling, turbulent waters. From here there's a nice view of Koko Crater, and green sand made of olivine can be found along the way.

When the surf is up, which is most highwind days, both paths are gated shut and entry to the ledges is prohibited. At other times you can walk out along the ledges, but be cautious; whenever the tide is high, waves can wash over the ledges – and of course a rogue wave can occur at any time.

More people drown at Hanauma than at any other beach on Oahu. Although the figure is high largely because there are so many visitors at this beach, people drowning in the Toilet Bowl or being swept off the ledges have accounted for a fair number of deaths over the years.

SOUTHEAST OAHU

**Snorkeling & Diving** Snorkeling is good at Hanauma Bay year round. Mornings are better than afternoons, as swimmers haven't yet stirred up the sand.

The large, sandy opening in the middle of the coral, known as the **Keyhole**, is an excellent place for novice snorkelers. The deepest water is 10ft, though it's very shallow over the coral, so if you have diving gloves, bring them. It's well protected and usually swimming-pool calm.

For confident snorkelers, it's better on the outside of the reef, where there are larger coral heads, bigger fish and fewer people; to get there follow the directions on the signboard or ask the lifeguard at the southwestern end of the beach. Keep in mind that because of the channel current it's generally easier getting out than it is getting back in. Don't attempt to swim outside the reef when the water is rough or choppy. Not only will the channel current be strong, but the sand will be stirred up and visibility poor, too.

Divers have the whole bay to play in, with clear water, coral gardens, sea turtles and lots of fish. Beware of currents when the surf is up; surges near the Witches Brew, on the right-hand side; and the Molokai Express, a treacherous current that runs just outside the mouth of the bay.

The beachside **concession stand** (open 8am-4:30pm daily) rents snorkel sets for $6. You'll need to either hand over $30, a credit card or your car-rental keys as a deposit.

**Getting There & Away** Hanauma Bay is about 10 miles from Waikiki via Hwy 72. The parking lot sometimes fills up by noon, so the earlier you get there the better. It costs $1 per vehicle to enter, but if you're unable to find a space, the fee will be refunded.

Bus No 22, called the Beach Bus, goes from Waikiki to Hanauma Bay (and on to Sea Life Park). On weekdays the first buses leave Waikiki from the corner of Kuhio Ave and Namahana St at 8:15am and 9:15am, with subsequent buses leaving at 55 minutes past the hour until 3:55pm, and then a final bus at 4:25pm. The Beach Bus also stops near the Honolulu Zoo at Monsarrat and Kalakaua Aves (see the Waikiki chapter for more information on the Honolulu Zoo), but it often fills to capacity before it reaches that stop.

Buses leave from Hanauma Bay to return to Waikiki at least once every hour from 11:10am to 5:40pm. On weekends the buses are more frequent (roughly twice an hour), though the schedule is more sporadic.

## Koko Head

Koko Head (not to be confused with Koko Crater) overlooks and forms the southwest side of Hanauma Bay. There are two craters atop Koko Head, as well as radar facilities on its 642ft summit. The mile-long summit road is closed to casual visitors.

The **Nature Conservancy of Hawaii** (☎ 537-4508), in Honolulu, maintains a preserve in the shallow Ihiihilauakea Crater, the larger of the two craters. The crater has a unique vernal pool and a rare fern, the *Marsilea villosa*. For information on work parties or weekend excursions to the preserve, call the Nature Conservancy.

## Halona Blowhole Area

About three-quarters of a mile past Hanauma is a **lookout** with a view of striking coastal rock formations and crashing surf. In clear weather, this part of the island also offers views of Molokai and Lanai.

A little less than a mile farther is the parking lot for the **Halona Blowhole**, where water surges through a submerged tunnel in the rock and spouts up through a hole in the ledge. It's preceded by a gushing sound, created by the air that's being forced out of the tunnel by rushing water. The action depends on water conditions – sometimes it's barely discernible, while at other times it's a real showstopper.

Down to the right of the parking lot is **Halona Cove**, the little beach where the risqué love scene with Burt Lancaster and Deborah Kerr in *From Here to Eternity* was filmed in the 1950s.

Immediately before the blowhole, a small stone monument sits atop Halona Point. It was erected by Japanese fishermen to honor those lost at sea.

Note: the public bus No 22 doesn't stop between Hanauma Bay and Sandy Beach, so visiting the Halona Blowhole area is only a practical option if you have your own transportation.

## Sandy Beach Park

Sandy Beach is the most dangerous beach on the island, when measured in terms of lifeguard rescues and broken necks. It has a punishing shore break, a powerful backwash and strong rip currents.

Huge waves break close to shore – hard to bodysurf, but if you know how, it's the best. It's equally popular with spectators, who gather to watch the bodysurfers being tossed around in the transparent waves.

Sandy Beach is wide, very long and, yes, sandy. It's frequented by sunbathers, young surfers and admirers of both. When the swells are big, board surfers hit the left side of the beach.

Red flags flown on the beach indicate hazardous water conditions. Even if you don't notice the flags, always check with the lifeguards before entering the water.

Not all the action is in the water, however. The grassy strip on the inland side of the parking lot is used by people looking skyward for their thrills – it's both a hang glider landing site and a popular locale for kite flying. If you want to try your hand at the latter, High Performance Kites sets up a van here every Sunday afternoon selling kites and offering free instruction.

The park has rest rooms and showers. Bus No 22 stops in front of the beach. **Local Chef** *(open 11am-4pm daily)*, a food wagon, sets up in the parking lot, and sells cheap burgers and plate lunches.

## Koko Crater

According to Hawaiian legend, Koko Crater is the imprint left by the magical flying vagina of Pele's sister Kapo, which was sent from the Big Island to lure the pig-god Kamapuaa away from Pele.

Inside the crater you'll find a simple county-run **botanical garden** *(admission free; open 9am-4pm daily)*, with plumeria trees, oleander, cacti and other dryland plants. To get there, take Kealahou St off Hwy 72, opposite the northern end of Sandy Beach. Just over half a mile in, turn left onto the one-lane road to Koko Crater Stables and continue a third of a mile to the garden. There is no public transportation to the crater.

## Places to Eat

The **Koko Marina Shopping Center** *(cnr Lunalilo Home Rd & Hwy 72)*, is the main place to eat in this area, with more than a dozen choices ranging from fast food to waterfront dining.

The center's **Whole In One Bagels & Juice Rush** *(☎ 394-2929; open 7am-7pm daily)* has fresh juices, makes a variety of tasty bagels and sells reasonably priced bagel sandwiches. The nearby **Kozo Sushi** *(☎ 396-8881; open 9am-7pm daily)* has good takeaway sushi that is a favorite with locals packing beach picnics – you can get a 15-piece lunch box for just $5. **Yummy Korean BBQ** *(☎ 395-4888; open 10am-7pm daily)* offers tasty barbecued plate lunches for $7, and there are waterfront tables where you can sit and eat.

**Roy's** *(☎ 396-7697, Hawaii Kai Corporate Plaza, Hwy 72; starters $8-10, mains $20-30; open 5:30pm-10pm Mon-Fri, 5pm-10pm Sat & Sun)* is the best upmarket option in Southeast Oahu, and arguably the entire island. Chef Roy Yamaguchi is a prominent force behind the popularity of Hawaii Regional cuisine, which emphasizes using fresh local ingredients and blending the lighter aspects of European cooking with Polynesian and Asian influences. A superb main dish is the blackened ahi, seared outside, rare inside and served with a fiery wasabi sauce. For dessert, the chocolate souffle is a decadent treat. Roy's is a top choice for a special night out – the food is beautifully presented and the service attentive. The restaurant also does a nice job of matching moderately priced wines with its menu. Reservations are advised and can be made weeks in advance – request a table with a sunset view.

## MAKAPUU POINT

Just over a mile north of Sandy Beach, the 647ft Makapuu Point and its coastal **lighthouse** mark the easternmost point of Oahu. The mile-long service road to the lighthouse is locked to keep out private vehicles, but you're allowed to park off the highway just beyond the gate and walk in from there. Although not difficult, it's an uphill walk and conditions can be hot and windy. There are fine coastal views along the way and at the lighthouse lookout. During the winter, whales are sometimes visible offshore.

Back on Hwy 72, about a third of a mile farther along, there's a scenic **roadside lookout** with a view down onto Makapuu Beach, with its aqua-blue waters outlined by white sand and black lava. It's an even more spectacular sight when hang gliders are taking off from the cliffs, which are Oahu's top hang-gliding spot.

From the lookout you can see two offshore islands, the larger of which is **Manana Island**, also known as Rabbit Island. This aging volcanic crater is populated by feral rabbits and burrowing wedge-tailed shearwaters. The birds and rabbits coexist so closely that they sometimes even share the same burrows. Amusingly, the island looks vaguely like the head of a rabbit, and if you try hard you may see it, ears folded back. If that doesn't work, try to imagine it as a whale.

In front of it is the smaller **Kaohikaipu Island**, which won't tax the imagination – all it looks is flat.

Divers sometimes explore the coral reef between the two islands, but to do so requires a boat.

## Makapuu Beach Park

Makapuu Beach is one of the island's top winter bodysurfing spots, with waves reaching 12ft and higher. It also has the island's best shore break. As with Sandy Beach, Makapuu is strictly the domain of experienced bodysurfers who are comfortable with rough water conditions and dangerous currents. Surfboards are prohibited. In summer, when the wave action disappears, the waters can be calm and good for swimming.

The beach, opposite Sea Life Park, is in a pretty setting, with cliffs in the background and a glimpse of the lighthouse. Two native Hawaiian plants are plentiful – *naupaka* by the beach and yellow-orange *ilima* by the parking lot. The park has public toilets.

## Sea Life Park

This park (☎ 259-7933; 41-202 Hwy 72; adult/child 4-12 yrs $24/12, child under 4 yrs free; open 9:30am-5pm daily) is Hawaii's only marine park. A highlight is its enormous 300,000-gallon aquarium filled with sea turtles, eels, eagle rays, hammerhead sharks and thousands of colorful reef fish. A spiral ramp circles the 18ft-deep aquarium, allowing you to view the fish from different depths.

There's also the usual theme park entertainment, with shows featuring imported Atlantic bottlenose dolphins giving choreographed performances. The dolphins tail walk, do the hula and give rides to a 'beautiful island maiden' – all bordering on kitsch.

The park has a large pool of California sea lions and a smaller pool with harbor seals. Another section has rare Hawaiian monk seals, comprised largely of abandoned pups that have been rescued from the wild; once they reach maturity, they're released back into their natural habitat. The park also has a penguin habitat, a turtle lagoon with green sea turtles, and a seabird sanctuary that holds red-footed boobies, albatrosses and great frigate birds.

A $3 parking fee is charged in the main lot; however, if you continue past the ticket booth to the area marked 'additional parking,' there's no fee.

You can visit the park's cafeteria without paying admission, and from there you can also get a free glimpse of the seal and sea lion pools.

Public buses No 22 (Beach Bus), No 57 (Kailua/Sea Life Park) and No 58 (Hawaii Kai/Sea Life Park) stop at the park.

## WAIMANALO BAY

Waimanalo Bay has the longest continuous stretch of beach on Oahu: 5½ miles of white sand that stretches from Makapuu Point to Wailea Point. A long coral reef about a mile offshore breaks up the biggest waves, protecting much of the shore. Fans of the TV series *Magnum PI* may recognise the beach here, as it's where Magnum was often seen taking a swim after a hard day of sleuthing.

Waimanalo has three beach parks, all with camping facilities; see Camping in the Facts for the Visitor chapter for details. The setting is scenic, although the area isn't highly regarded for safety.

## Waimanalo Beach Park

Waimanalo Beach Park has an attractive beach of soft white sand, and the water is excellent for swimming. This is an in-town county park, with a grassy picnic area, rest rooms, showers, ball fields, basketball and volleyball courts and a playground. Camping is allowed is an open area near the road.

The park has ironwood trees, but overall it's more open than the other two Waimanalo parks to the north. The scalloped hills of the lower Koolau Range rise up behind the park, and Manana Island and Makapuu Point are visible to the south. Bus No 57 stops at the park entrance.

## Waimanalo Bay Beach Park

This county park about a mile north of Waimanalo Beach Park has Waimanalo

Bay's biggest waves, thus its popularity with board surfers and bodysurfers.

Locals call the park 'Sherwood Forest,' because hoods and car thieves used to hang out here in days past – it hasn't totally shaken its reputation, so keep an eye on your belongings. The park itself is quite appealing, with beachside camp sites shaded by ironwood trees. There are barbecue grills, drinking water, showers, rest rooms and a lifeguard station.

Bus No 57 stops on the main road in front of the park, and from there it's a third of a mile walk to the beach and camping ground.

## Bellows Field Beach Park

The beach fronting Bellows Air Force Station is open to civilian beachgoers and campers on weekends only, from noon Friday until 8am Monday. This long beach has fine sand and a natural setting, backed by ironwood trees. The small shore-break waves here are good for beginning bodysurfers and board surfers.

There are showers, rest rooms, drinking water, a lifeguard and a caretaker, and the 50 campsites are set among the trees. Although it's military property, camping permits are issued through the county **Department of**

**Parks & Recreation** *(☎ 523-4525; 650 S King St)* in downtown Honolulu.

The marked entrance to this beach park is a quarter of a mile north of Waimanalo Bay Beach Park. Bus No 57 stops in front of the entrance road and from there it's 1½ miles to the beach.

## Places to Stay & Eat

Waimanalo is a tiny town, mostly suburban, but there are a number of family-run accommodation options.

Try **On the Beach Suite** *(☎ 259-6729; 41-929 Laumilo St; W www.beachhousehawaii .com/onthebeachsuite.html; 1-bedroom apartments $150)*, where you'll have back-door access to the fabulous white-sand beach, free boogie boards and gracious, knowledgeable hosts. Phone ahead.

Just north of Waimanalo Beach Park, on Hwy 72 near the post office, you'll find the local eatery **Keneke's** *(plate lunches $5)* and **Leoni's**, a bakery that also serves pizzas and subs. There are food marts and fast-food eateries just south of Waimanalo Bay Beach Park and in a cluster of shops about a mile north of Bellows Field Beach Park.

Nearby Kailua (see the Windward Coast chapter) has more to offer hungry travellers.

# Windward Coast

Windward Oahu, the island's eastern side, follows the Koolau Range along its entire length. The mountains looming inland are lovely, with scalloped folds and deep valleys. In places they come so near to the shore that they almost seem to crowd the highway into the ocean.

The two main towns are Kaneohe and Kailua, both largely nondescript bedroom communities for workers who commute to Honolulu, about 10 miles away. North of Kaneohe, the Windward Coast is rural Hawaii, where many Hawaiians toil close to the earth, making a living with small papaya, banana and vegetable farms. The windward side of the island is generally wetter than other parts of the island, and as a result, the vegetation here is lush and green.

Because the Windward Coast is exposed to the northeast trade winds, it's a popular area for anything that requires a sail – from windsurfing to yachting.

There are some attractive swimming beaches on the Windward Coast – notably at Kailua Bay, Kualoa Regional Park and Malaekahana State Recreation Area – although many other sections of the coast are too silted for swimming. Swimmers should keep an eye out for the stinging Portuguese man-of-wars that often wash in close to shore during stormy weather.

Most of the offshore islets that you will see along this coast have been set aside as bird sanctuaries, providing vital habitat for ground-nesting seabirds.

## Orientation

The Windward Coast runs from Makapuu Point in the south to Kahuku Point in the north. (For the Waimanalo to Makapuu area, see the Southeast Oahu chapter.)

There are two highways cutting through the Koolau Range from central Honolulu to the Windward Coast. The Pali Hwy (Hwy 61) goes straight into Kailua, while the Likelike Hwy (Hwy 63) runs directly into Kaneohe. Although the Likelike (pronounced lee-kay-lee-kay) Hwy doesn't have the scenic stops the Pali Hwy has, in some ways it is more dramatic. Driving away from Kaneohe it feels as if you're heading straight into towering fairy-tale

### Highlights

- Enjoying the panoramic view of the Windward Coast from Nuuanu Pali Lookout
- Windsurfing or kayak at lovely Kailua Beach Park
- Ringing the brass bell for luck at the picturesque Byodo-In temple in Kaneohe
- Stopping for a picnic and a swim at scenic Kualoa Regional Park

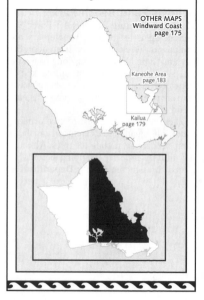

mountains – then you suddenly shoot through a tunnel and emerge on the Honolulu side, the drama gone.

If you're heading both to and from Windward Oahu through the Koolau Range, take the Pali Hwy up from Honolulu and the Likelike Hwy back for the best views afforded by both.

### THE PALI HIGHWAY

The Pali Hwy (Hwy 61), which runs north from Honolulu toward Kailua, is a scenic little highway with a ridge lookout that offers a sweeping vista of the Windward Coast. If it's been raining heavily, every

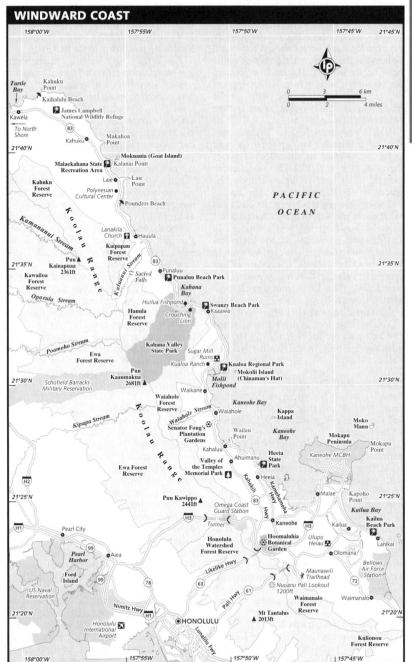

# WINDWARD COAST

158°00'W · 157°55'W · 157°50'W · 157°45'W · 21°45'N

*Turtle Bay*
Kahuku Point
Kaihalulu Beach
Kawela
James Campbell National Wildlife Refuge
*To North Shore*
(83)
Kahuku
Makahoa Point

21°40'N · 21°40'N

Mokuauia (Goat Island)
Malaekahana State Recreation Area
Kalanai Point
Kahuku Forest Reserve
Laie
Laie Point
Polynesian Cultural Center
Pounders Beach

*PACIFIC OCEAN*

Lanakila Church
Hauula
Kaipapau Forest Reserve

21°35'N · 21°35'N

Puu Kainapuaa 2361ft
Kawailoa Forest Reserve
*Kamananui Stream*
*Koolau Range*
*Kaluanui Stream*
*Opaeula Stream*
Sacred Falls
Punaluu
Punaluu Beach Park
*Kahana Bay*
Huilua Fishpond
Hauula Forest Reserve
Crouching Lion
Swanzy Beach Park
Kaaawa

*Poamoho Stream*
Ewa Forest Reserve
Kahana Valley State Park
Sugar Mill Ruins
Kualoa Ranch
Kualoa Regional Park

21°30'N · 21°30'N

Puu Kaaumakua 2681ft
Schofield Barracks Military Reservation
Waikane
Mokolii Island (Chinaman's Hat)
*Molii Fishpond*
Waiahole Forest Reserve
*Waiahole Stream*
Waiahole
*Kaneohe Bay*
Kappa Island
Moko Manu

*Kipapa Stream*
*Koolau Range*
Senator Fong's Plantation Gardens
Wailau Point
*Kaneohe Bay*
Mokapu Peninsula
Mokapu Point

Kahaluu
Ahuimanu
Heeia State Park
Kaneohe MCBH

Ewa Forest Reserve
Valley of the Temples Memorial Park
Heeia
Malae
Kapoho Point

21°25'N · 21°25'N

(H2)
Puu Kawippo 2441ft
Omega Coast Guard Station
(83)
*Kailua Bay*
Kailua Beach Park
(H1)
Pearl City
(99)
Aiea
(99)
*Pearl Harbor*
Ford Island
*US Naval Reservation*
(78)
Tunnel
(H3)
Honolulu Watershed Forest Reserve
Kaneohe
(H3)
Kailua
Lanikai
Hoomaluhia Botanical Garden
Ulupo Heiau
Olomana
*Bellows Air Force Station*

21°20'N · 21°20'N

Nimitz Hwy
(H1)
Likelike Hwy
(63)
Pali Hwy
(61)
Maunawili Trailhead
Nuuanu Pali Lookout 1200ft
Waimanalo Forest Reserve
Waimanalo
(72)
Honolulu International Airport
HONOLULU
*Lunalilo Fwy*
Mt Tantalus 2013ft
Kulionou Forest Reserve

158°00'W · 157°55'W · 157°50'W · 157°45'W

0 — 3 — 6 km
0 — 2 — 4 miles

fold and crevice in the Koolau Range will have a lacy waterfall streaming down it.

Many Kailua residents commute to work over the Pali, so Honolulu-bound traffic can be heavy in the morning and outbound traffic heavy in the evening. It's less of a problem for visitors, however, as most day-trippers will be traveling against the traffic. Public buses travel the Pali Hwy, but none stop at the Nuuanu Pali Lookout.

Heading north up the Pali Hwy, just past the four-mile marker look up and to the right to see two notches cut about 15ft deep into the crest of the *pali* (cliff). These notches are thought to have been dug as cannon emplacements by Kamehameha the Great.

The original route between Honolulu and Windward Oahu was an ancient footpath that wound its way perilously over these cliffs. In 1845 the path was widened into a horse trail and later into a cobblestone carriage road. In 1898 the Old Pali Hwy (as it's now called) was built in place of the carriage road. It was abandoned in the 1950s after tunnels were blasted through the Koolau Range and the present multilane Pali Hwy opened.

You are able to still drive a loop of the Old Pali Hwy (called Nuuanu Pali Dr) and hike another mile of it from the Nuuanu Pali Lookout.

### Nuuanu Pali Drive
For a scenic side trip through a shady green forest, turn off the Pali Hwy onto Nuuanu Pali Dr, a half mile past the two-mile marker on the highway.

The two-mile-long Nuuanu Pali Dr runs parallel to the Pali Hwy and then comes back out to it before the Nuuanu Pali Lookout, so you don't miss out on any scenery by taking this side loop – in fact, quite the opposite.

The drive is through mature trees that form a canopy overhead, all draped with hanging vines and wound with philodendrons. The lush vegetation includes banyan trees with hanging aerial roots, tropical almond trees, bamboo groves, flowering impatiens, angel trumpets and golden cup – a tall climbing vine with large golden flowers.

### Nuuanu Pali Lookout
Whatever you do, don't miss the Nuuanu Pali Lookout with its broad view of the Windward Coast from a height of 1200ft.

From the lookout you can see Kaneohe straight ahead, Kailua to the right and Mokolii Island and the coastal fishpond at Kualoa Regional Park to the far left.

This is *windward* Oahu – and the winds that funnel through the *pali* are so strong that you can sometimes lean against them. It gets cool enough to appreciate having a jacket.

In 1795, Kamehameha the Great routed Oahu's warriors up the Nuuanu Trail during his invasion of the island. On these steep cliffs, Oahu's warriors made their last stand. Hundreds were thrown to their death over the *pali* as they were overcome by Kamehameha's troops. A hundred years later, during the construction of the Old Pali Hwy, more than 500 skulls were found at the base of the cliffs.

The abandoned Old Pali Hwy winds from the right of the lookout, ending at a barrier near the current highway about a mile away. Few people realize the road is here, let alone venture down it. It makes a nice walk, taking about 20 minutes one way. There are good views looking back up at the jagged Koolau Range and out across the valley.

When you return to the highway, it's easy to miss the sign leading you out of the parking lot, and instinct could send you in the wrong direction. Go to the left if you're heading toward Kailua, to the right if heading toward Honolulu.

### Maunawili Trail
The 10-mile-long Maunawili Trail connects Nuuanu Pali with Waimanalo on the coast. Popular with both hikers and mountain bikers, this scenic trail winds along the back side of Maunawili Valley, following the base of the lofty Koolau Range. Along the way, there are panoramic views of the valley, mountains and Windward Coast.

This trail consists of many climbs up and down gulches, across streams and along ridges. Going in an easterly direction is the less strenuous way, as you will be following the trail from the mountain crest down to the coast. Because Maunawili Trail is subject to erosion, mountain bikers are asked to stay off the trail when it's raining or if the trail is wet. If you come across muddy sections, always dismount and walk your bike.

For visitors on foot, it's generally most practical to take the trail for a couple of miles and then turn around and return the

'Hawaiian George & Etta' strumming ukuleles at a local craft fair

Hula dancer with the trio 'The Islanders', Halekulani Hotel, Waikiki

Young sisters making leis with their teacher

Eating shave ice, Kailua

Chinatown produce market, Honolulu

Auction at the fish market, Honolulu

same way. Even hiking the trail for just an hour will reward you with some fine views of both the coast and Maunawili Valley's lush, forested interior.

Maunawili Trail can be accessed by driving about a mile past the Nuuanu Pali Lookout in the Kailua direction. Pull off to the right into the scenic turnout that's at the hairpin turn just before the 7-mile marker. There's parking here. Walk through the break in the guardrail where a footbridge takes you over a drainage ditch to begin the hike.

The trail can also be picked up from the Nuuanu Pali Lookout by walking the mile-long stretch of the abandoned Old Pali Hwy that starts to the right of the lookout and ends near the Maunawili Trailhead.

## KAILUA
### pop 36,500

In ancient times Kailua (meaning 'two seas') was a place of legends. It was home to a giant that turned into a mountain ridge, the island's first *menehunes* and numerous Oahuan chiefs. Rich in stream-fed agricultural land, fertile fishing grounds and protected canoe landings, Kailua once served as a political and economic center for the region. The area supported at least three heiaus, one of which, Ulupo Heiau, you can still visit today.

Kailua is Windward Oahu's largest town. Although the inland section may appear to be little more than an average suburban community, Kailua's shoreline is graced with miles of lovely beach – a generous portion of which is public park, and the rest lined with oceanfront homes.

Kailua has long been known as a windsurfing mecca and today it draws increasing numbers of kayakers too. Considering its size, the town has an excellent variety of restaurants and shops. It also has an agreeable mix of locals and visitors, making it a refreshing alternative to overtouristed Waikiki.

## Information

Kailua has several banks, including a **Bank of Hawaii** (☎ 266-4600; 636 Kailua Rd; open 8:30am-4pm Mon-Thur, 8:30am-6pm Fri).

The Kailua **post office** (☎ 266-3996; 335 Hahani St; open 8am-4:30pm Mon-Fri, 8am-2pm Sat) is in the town center.

**Bookends** (☎ 261-1996; 590 Kailua Rd) sells books and newspapers. **Kailua Public Library** (☎ 266-9911; 239 Kuulei Rd; open

10am-5pm Mon, Wed, Fri & Sat, 1pm-8pm Tues & Thur) has periodicals to browse.

## Ulupo Heiau

Ulupo Heiau is a large open-platform temple made of stones stacked some 30ft high and 180ft long. Its construction is attributed to the *menehunes*, the little people who, according to legend, created much of Hawaii's stonework, magically finishing each project in just one night (see the boxed text 'Little People, Big Tasks' in the Facts about Oahu chapter). Fittingly, Ulupo means 'night inspiration.'

In front of the heiau, which is thought to have been a *luakini* type (a place of human sacrifice), is an artist's rendition of how the site probably looked in the 18th century, before Westerners arrived.

If you walk the path across the top of the heiau, you get a view of **Kawainui Swamp**. Legends say the fishpond that stood here in precontact times had edible mud at the bottom and was home to a *moo*, or lizard spirit. In the 1880s, the fishpond was converted into rice fields by Chinese farmers. However, in the early 20th century, the fields were abandoned by the farmers and reverted back to marshland. Today, Kawainui Swamp is one of Hawaii's largest habitats for endangered waterbirds.

Ulupo Heiau is 1 mile south of Kailua center. To get there, turn west off Hwy 61 onto Uluoa St (just north of the Hwy 72 junction); then turn right on Manu Aloha St and right again onto Manuoo St. The heiau is behind the YMCA.

## Kailua Beach Park

Kailua Beach Park is a stunningly beautiful stretch of glistening white sand at the southeastern end of Kailua Bay. The beach is long and broad with lovely turquoise waters, and the park is popular for long walks, family outings and a full range of water activities. It draws a particularly large crowd on sunny weekends, when it can be a challenge to even find a parking space.

Kailua Bay is the top windsurfing spot on Oahu. Onshore trade winds are predominant and windsurfers can sail at Kailua year round. In different spots around the bay there are different water conditions, some good for jumps and wave surfing, others for flatwater sails. Two windsurfing companies,

Naish Hawaii and Kailua Sailboards, give lessons and rent boards at the beach park on weekdays and Saturday mornings.

Kailua Beach has a gently sloping sandy bottom with waters that are generally calm. Swimming conditions are good all year, but sunbathers beware – the breezes favored by windsurfers also give rise to blowing sand. The park has rest rooms, showers, lifeguards, a volleyball court and large grassy expanses partly shaded by ironwood trees.

Kaelepulu Canal divides the park into two sections, although a sand bar usually prevents the canal waters from emptying into the bay. Because of pollution from runoff, the canal itself should be avoided. Windsurfing activities are centered to the west of the canal; there's a small boat ramp on the eastern side.

The island offshore, **Popoia Island** (Flat Island), which is a bird sanctuary where landings are allowed, is a popular destination for kayakers.

For further information on windsurfing and kayaking, see those sections in the Activities chapter.

### Kalama Beach Park

Kalama, a small beach park north of Kailua Beach Park, usually has one of the largest shore breaks in the bay. When the waves are up, both board surfers and bodysurfers can find decent conditions here. Board surfers also sometimes head to the northern end of Kailua Bay to Kapoho Point (see the Kaneohe Area map), which has a decent break during swells.

### Lanikai

If you follow the coastal road as it continues southeast from Kailua Beach Park, you will shortly come to Lanikai, an exclusive residential neighborhood. It's fronted by **Lanikai Beach**, which is an attractive stretch of powdery white sand – at least what's left of it. Much of the sand has washed away as a result of the retaining walls built to protect the homes constructed right on the shore. The sandy bottom slopes gently and the waters are calm, offering safe swimming conditions similar to those at Kailua.

From Kailua Beach Park, the road turns into the one-way Aalapapa Dr, which comes back around as Mokulua Dr to make a 2½-mile loop. There are 11 narrow beach access walkways off Mokulua Dr. For the best stretches of beach, try the one opposite Kualima Dr or any of the next three.

The twin **Mokulua Islands**, Moku Nui and Moku Iki, sit directly offshore. Both islands are set aside as seabird sanctuaries. It's possible to kayak from Kailua Beach Park to Moku Nui, which has a lovely beach; for kayaking information, see the Activities chapter. Landings are prohibited on Moku Iki, the smaller of the two islands.

### Places to Stay

Kailua has no hotels, but there are furnished beachfront cottages, studios and B&B-style rooms in private homes. Although the majority are handled by the vacation rental services listed at the end of this section, the following places can be booked directly with the owners.

**Paradise Palms Bed & Breakfast** (☎ 254-4234, fax 254-4971; e ppbb@pixi.com; 804 Mokapu Rd; rooms $70 & 75) consists of two meticulously decorated studios at the side of Marilyn and Jim Warman's home, at the northwestern end of Kailua. The more expensive room has a king bed, while the cheaper one has a queen bed. Each has a private entrance, bathroom and a kitchenette with refrigerator, microwave and coffeemaker. The units also have cable TV, ceiling fans, air-con and phone. Fruit, coffee and fresh-baked bread are provided upon arrival. Smoking is not allowed. The minimum stay is three days. There's a grocery store and fast-food restaurants just across the street.

**Manu Mele Bed & Breakfast** (☎ 262-0016; e manumele@pixi.com; 153 Kailuana Place, Kailua, HI 96734; small/large room $70/80) consists of two attractive guest rooms in the contemporary home of English-born host Carol Isaacs. The largest, the Hibiscus Room, has a king bed, and the smaller but perfectly suitable Pikake Room has a queen bed. Each has a private entrance, bathroom, refrigerator, microwave, coffeemaker, air-con, ceiling fan and cable TV. A basket of fruit and baked goods is provided on the first morning. The minimum stay is two days. The house has a pool, and a short footpath leads to the beach. Smoking is not allowed in the units.

**Sheffield House** (☎ 262-0721; e rachel@sheffieldhouse.com; 131 Kuulei Rd, Kailua, HI 96734; rooms $75 & $95), a couple of minutes walk from Kailua Beach, consists of two cozy rental units in the home of Paul and

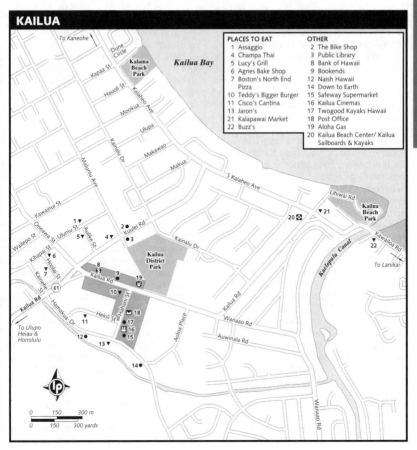

**KAILUA**

To Kaneohe

Kalama Beach Park

*Kailua Bay*

Kailua Beach Park

To Lanikai

To Ulupo Heiau & Honolulu

| PLACES TO EAT | OTHER |
|---|---|
| 1 Assaggio | 2 The Bike Shop |
| 4 Champa Thai | 3 Public Library |
| 5 Lucy's Grill | 8 Bank of Hawaii |
| 6 Agnes Bake Shop | 9 Bookends |
| 7 Boston's North End Pizza | 12 Naish Hawaii |
| | 14 Down to Earth |
| 10 Teddy's Bigger Burger | 15 Safeway Supermarket |
| 11 Cisco's Cantina | 16 Kailua Cinemas |
| 13 Jaron's | 17 Twogood Kayaks Hawaii |
| 21 Kalapawai Market | 18 Post Office |
| 22 Buzz's | 19 Aloha Gas |
| | 20 Kailua Beach Center/ Kailua Sailboards & Kayaks |

0  150  300 m
0  150  300 yards

Rachel Sheffield. There's a guest room with a wheelchair-accessible bathroom for $75 and a more expensive one-bedroom suite that has a queen bed and a separate sitting area with a queen futon. Each unit has a private entrance, bathroom, TV, microwave, toaster oven, coffeemaker, small refrigerator and ceiling fan. The Sheffields, who have three young children of their own, welcome kids. There's a three-day minimum stay; a basket of pastries, coffee and tea are provided on the first day.

**Papaya Paradise Bed & Breakfast** *(☎/fax 261-0316; e kailua@compuserve.com; 395 Auwinala Rd, Kailua, HI 96734; singles or doubles $85, plus $15 each additional person)* is a 15-minute walk from Kailua Beach. Bob and Jeanette Martz, retired from the

army and home most of the time, rent two rooms adjacent to their home. One room has a queen bed and a trundle bed, the other two twin beds; each has a private entrance, bathroom, phone, air-con, ceiling fan and TV. Rates include a continental breakfast, and guests have access to a refrigerator, microwave and swimming pool. Boogie boards and snorkel gear can be borrowed for free. There's usually a three-day minimum stay.

**Kailua Tradewinds** *(☎ 262-1008; e kailua@compuserve.com; 391 Auwinala Rd, Kailua, HI 96734; singles or doubles $80, plus $10 each additional person)*, a vacation rental next door to Papaya Paradise, consists of two studio units at the home of Jona Williams, the Martz' daughter. Breakfast is not provided, but each unit has a refrigerator, microwave and coffeemaker as well as a private entrance, a king or two twin beds, TV and phone. One of the units also has a double futon. There's a swimming pool, and beach gear is available for guests to use. The minimum stay is three days.

**Akamai Bed & Breakfast** (*☎/fax 261-2227, 800-642-5366; *e* akamai@aloha.net; 172 Kuumele Place, Kailua, HI 96734; rooms $85)* has two pleasant studio units in a private home about a 10-minute walk from Kailua Beach. Each is modern and comfortable, with a refrigerator, microwave, coffeemaker, small bathroom, cable TV and private entrance. Both units have a king bed as well as a sofa bed. The rate includes a fruit basket and breakfast items. There's a laundry room ($1 per load) and a quiet courtyard with a pool. The minimum stay is three days. Smoking is limited to the outdoors.

**Hawaii's Hidden Hideaway** (*☎ 262-6560, 877-443-3299, fax 262-6561; *e* hhhide away@yahoo.com; 1369 Mokolea Dr, Kailua, HI 96734; studio $95, suite $135)* consists of three inviting units in an upscale neighborhood just a block from Lanikai Beach. Each unit has a private entrance, a bathroom, a lanai and a kitchenette that includes a refrigerator, microwave, coffeemaker and hot plates. Special touches include a collection of Hawaiiana books perfect for perusing in the evening and beach gear that guests are free to borrow. The suite, which has a queen size canopy bed and a private Jacuzzi, would be a fun choice for honeymooners or those just looking for a romantic getaway. All of the units come stocked with juice, cereal, pastries, fruit and coffee. There's a three-day minimum stay. Smoking is not allowed.

**Vacation Rental Agencies** There are several agencies that will book accommodation for you in the Kailua area. These are not drop-in agencies; call ahead to make reservations.

**Affordable Paradise Bed & Breakfast** (*☎ 261-1693, fax 261-7315; *w* www.afford able-paradise.com; 332 Kuukama St, Kailua, HI 96734; rooms/cottages/condos from $45/60/80)* books studios, cottages, condos and rooms in private homes in the Kailua area.

**All Islands Bed & Breakfast** (*☎ 263-2342, 800-542-0344, fax 263-0308; *w* www.all-islands.com; 463 Iliwahi Loop, Kailua, HI 96734;

rooms $65-75, studios $75-85, cottages $85-95)* also books Kailua-area rooms, studio apartments and cottages.

**Pat's Kailua Beach Properties** (*☎ 261-1653; fax 261-0893; *w* www.10kvacation rentals.com/pats; 204 S Kalaheo Ave, Kailua, HI 96734; studios per day/month $70/1700, large homes $500/12,000)* handles a few dozen properties on or near the beach, which range from small studios that can sleep two people to large beachfront houses with five bedrooms and four bathrooms that sleep a dozen people.

## Places to Eat
**Near the Beach** *The* place to stop for coffee, **Kalapawai Market** (*☎ 262-4359; 305 S Kalaheo Ave; open 6am-9pm daily)* is on the way to the beach. You have a choice of fresh brews, with a cup costing just $1. It also has takeout items including good bagels and some fantastic sandwiches, as well as a fine selection of wine and beer.

**Kailua Beach Restaurant** (*☎ 263-2620; 130 Kailua Rd; combination meals $5-7; open 7am-9pm daily)*, in the Kailua Beach Center, is a simple place with good food, cheap prices and outdoor tables. Surfers start the morning here with the omelette breakfasts ($3.75), available until 10:30am. At other times of the day, the place specializes in Chinese food with lots of selections.

**Island Snow** (*☎ 263-6339; 130 Kailua Rd; open 10am-6pm daily)*, also in the Kailua Beach Center, is popular for its shave ice in tropical flavors, such as da-kine lemon and banzai banana.

**Buzz's** (*☎ 261-4661; 413 Kawailoa Rd; lunch mains $7-10, dinner mains $14-24; open 11am-2:30pm & 5pm-10pm daily)*, opposite Kailua Beach Park, has lunches such as fresh fish sandwiches, burgers, and salads. However, it's most popular as an evening steak house, with various cuts of beef to choose from. It also has a range of fresh fish, and meals come with the small but fresh salad bar. Ask for an open-air table under the banyan tree. Credit cards are not accepted.

**Town Center** All of the following eateries are in Kailua's town center, within a mile of each other.

**Agnes Bake Shop** (*☎ 262-5367; 46 Hoolai St; open 6am-6pm Tues-Sun)* is a fantastic little bakery that makes whole-grain breads, inexpensive pastries and Portuguese *malasadas* (sweet fried dough ball). The *malasadas*, which are served hot, take about 10 minutes to fry up and cost 60¢ each. The shop also sells coffee, tea and Portuguese bean soup, and has a half a dozen café tables where you can sit and eat. You can also log onto the Internet here.

**Boston's North End Pizza** (*☎ 263-7757; 29 Hoolai St; pizza $12-18; open 11am-8pm Mon-Fri, 11am-9pm Sat & Sun)* has excellent pizza. In addition to whole pizzas it sells huge slices, each equal to a quarter of a large pizza, for $3 to $4.65 depending on the toppings. The spinach and fresh garlic version is awesome.

**Teddy's Bigger Burgers** (*☎ 262-0820; 539 Kailua Rd; burgers $4; open 10:30am-9pm daily)* has fabulous burgers prepared in myriad ways. Skip the dry garlic fries and go for the crispy onion rings.

**Cisco's Cantina** (*☎ 262-7337; 131 Hekili St; 2-item combination plates $10; open 11am-10pm Sun-Thur, 11am-11pm Fri & Sat)* is an unpretentious Mexican restaurant that serves generous portions at reasonable prices. In addition to combination plates, you can get a single taco ($6) or enchilada ($8), served with rice and beans.

**Jaron's** (*☎ 261-4600; 201 Hamakua Dr; lunch $7-12, dinner $10-20; open lunch 11am-4pm Mon-Sat, dinner 4pm-9pm Sun-Thur, 4pm-10pm Fri & Sat)* is a reliable favorite with a jazzy decor and a varied menu. Lunch choices include a nice blackened ahi salad, and a variety of sandwiches served with soup. The dinner menu features pasta, fresh fish and steak dishes, with a green salad included in the price.

**Champa Thai** (*☎ 263-8281; 306 Kuulei Rd; dishes $7-10; open 11am-2pm Mon-Fri, 5pm-9pm daily)* has the best Thai food on the Windward Coast. The Penang curry, with coconut milk and shrimp, is a knockout, and it also makes good noodle dishes and Thai salads.

**Assaggio** (*☎ 261-2772; 354 Uluniu St; lunch mains $7-10, dinner mains $10-20; open 11:30am-2:30pm & 5pm-9:30pm Tues-Sat)* serves good, moderately priced Italian food in a somewhat upmarket setting. Its menu is extensive, with more than 50 pasta, seafood and meat dishes, including the house special chicken Assaggio, a tasty dish brimming with garlic.

**Lucy's Grill** (*☎ 230-8188; 33 Aulike St; appetizers $7-12, mains $16-26; open 5pm-10pm Tues-Sat)* has an agreeable ocean theme with surfboards hanging from the walls and a menu featuring seafood. Specialties include fresh fish tacos with papaya salsa, oysters on the half shell and Szechuan-spiced prawns. There are a handful of creative chicken and beef dishes as well – good food, fun place, with nice tables outside.

**Down To Earth** (*☎ 262-3838; 201 Hamakua Dr; open 8am-9pm daily)* is a large natural food store with just about everything you could imagine from bulk granola and organic produce to vitamins and herbal supplements. For a conventional supermarket, a 24-hour **Safeway** (*200 Hamakua Dr)* is one of several supermarkets nearby.

## Entertainment
**Jaron's** (*☎ 261-4600; 201 Hamakua Dr)* usually has reggae, slack key or contemporary Hawaiian bands Wednesday to Saturday nights, and there's a dance floor.

The multiscreen **Kailua Cinemas** (*☎ 263-4171; 345 Hahani St)* shows first-run movies.

## Getting There & Away
If traffic is light, by car it's a 20-minute drive along the Pali Hwy (Hwy 61) from Honolulu to Kailua. To get to Kailua Beach Park, simply stay on Kailua Rd, which begins at the end of the Pali Hwy and continues as the main road through town before reaching the coast.

Both bus Nos 56 and 57 run between the Ala Moana Center and downtown Kailua roughly once every 15 minutes from about 6am to 10pm; the trip takes about 40 minutes. To get to Kailua Beach Park or Lanikai, get off in downtown Kailua at the corner of Kailua Rd and Oneawa St and transfer to bus No 70 Lanikai-Maunawili. However, bus No 70 only operates about once every 90 minutes, so check the schedule in advance.

## KANEOHE & AROUND
**pop 35,000**
Kaneohe is Windward Oahu's second largest town. Kaneohe Bay, which stretches from Mokapu Peninsula all the way to Kualoa Point, 7 miles north of Kaneohe, is the state's largest bay and reef-sheltered lagoon. Although inshore it's largely silted and not good for swimming, the near-constant trade

winds that sweep across the bay are ideal for sailing. Much of the town stretches along the highways and consists of charmless strip malls. Kailua is a much better stop.

Two highways run north to south through Kaneohe. Kamehameha Hwy (Hwy 836) is both closer to the coast and more scenic and goes by Heeia State Park. The Kahekili Hwy (Hwy 83), which is more inland, intersects the Likelike Hwy (Hwy 63) and continues on north past the Byodo-In temple.

Kaneohe Marine Corps Base Hawaii (MCBH) occupies the whole of Mokapu Peninsula. The H3 Fwy terminates at its gate.

## Valley of the Temples & Byodo-In

The Valley of the Temples is an interdenominational cemetery in a beautiful setting just off the Kahekili Hwy, 1½ miles north of Haiku Rd. For visitors the main attraction is **Byodo-In** (☎ 239-8811; adult/child $2/1; open 8am-5pm daily), the 'Temple of Equality,' a replica of the 900-year-old temple of the same name in Uji, Japan. This one was dedicated in 1968 to commemorate the 100th anniversary of Japanese immigration to Hawaii.

Byodo-In sits against the Koolau Range. The rich red of the temple against the verdant fluted cliffs is strikingly picturesque, especially when mist settles in on the *pali*. The temple is meant to symbolize the mythical phoenix. Inside the main hall is a 9ft-tall gold-lacquered Buddha sitting on a lotus.

Wild peacocks roam the grounds and hang their tail feathers over the temple's upper railings. A carp pond with cruising bullfrogs and cooing doves fronts the temple. The 3-ton brass bell beside the pond is said to bring tranquillity and good fortune to those who ring it.

It's all very Japanese, right down to the gift shop selling sake cups, *daruma* dolls and happy Buddhas. This scene is as close as you'll get to Japan without having to land at Narita.

On the way out, you might want to head up to the hilltop mausoleum with the cross on top and check out the view.

No buses go to Byodo-In, but bus No 55 can drop passengers off near the cemetery entrance on Kahekili Hwy. From there, it's two-thirds of a mile to the temple.

## Hoomaluhia Botanical Garden

Hoomaluhia (☎ 233-7323; 45-680 Luluku Rd; admission free; open 9am-4pm daily), a 400-acre park in the uplands of Kaneohe, is the island's largest botanical garden. The park is planted with groups of trees and shrubs from tropical regions around the world. It's a peaceful, lush green setting, with a stunning *pali* backdrop. Fittingly enough, the name Hoomaluhia means 'peace and tranquillity.'

Hoomaluhia is not a formal landscaped flower garden, but more of a natural preserve. A network of trails wind through the park and up to a 32-acre reservoir (no swimming allowed).

The visitor center, although small, has displays on flora and fauna, Hawaiian ethnobotany and the history of the park, which was originally built by the US Army Corps of Engineers as flood protection for the valley below. Guided two-hour nature hikes are held at 10am Saturday and 1pm Sunday; call ahead to register.

The park entrance is at the end of Luluku Rd, which is off the Kamehameha Hwy, about 2¼ miles north of its intersection with the Pali Hwy. Bus Nos 55 and 56 stop at the Windward City Shopping Center, opposite the start of Luluku Rd, but there's no bus service to the park. It's 1½ miles up Luluku Rd from the highway to the visitor center and another 1½ miles from the visitor center to the far end of the park – so if you're getting around by bus, expect to do some walking.

For information on camping at Hoomaluhia Botanical Garden, see the Places to Stay section that follows.

## Places to Stay

**Hoomaluhia Botanical Garden** (☎ 233-7323; 45-680 Luluku Rd; no fee), at the base of the Koolau Range, has five grassy camping areas, each with rest rooms and drinking water. The park can accommodate up to 650 people, but often only a couple of the areas need to be opened. If you don't mind being inland rather than on a beach, this botanical park makes an interesting camping option, and with a resident caretaker and gates that close to noncampers at 4pm it's among the safest parks on Oahu. On the minus side, it's out of the way for those who don't have their own transportation. Camping is allowed Thursday to Monday nights and there's no fee, but a permit from the county is required.

# KANEOHE AREA

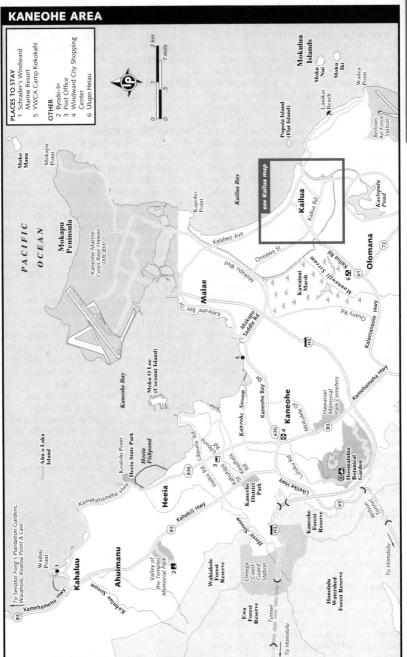

PLACES TO STAY
1 Schrader's Windward Marine Resort
5 YWCA Camp Kokokahi

OTHER
2 Byodo-In
3 Post Office
4 Windward City Shopping Center
6 Ulupo Heiau

Mokulua Islands
Moku Nui
Moku Iki
Wailea Point

Lanikai Beach

Popoia Island (Flat Island)

Moko Manu

Mokapu Point

PACIFIC OCEAN

Mokapu Peninsula

Kaneohe Marine Corps Base Hawaii (MCBH)

Kailua Bay

Kapoho Point

see Kailua map

Kailua
Kailua Rd

Kaelepulu Pond

Bellows Air Force Station

Kalaheo Ave

Oneawa St

Olomana
72

Kawainui Marsh

Maunawili Stream

Kailua Rd
61

Quarry Rd

Malae

Mokapu Blvd

Kaneohe Bay Dr

Mokapu Saddle Rd

Kalanianaole Hwy

H3

Ahu o Laka Island

Kaneohe Bay

Moku O Loe (Coconut Island)

Kamehameha Hwy

5

Kaneohe Stream

Kaneohe Bay Dr

Kaneohe
Mokulele
630 4
83

Hawaiian Memorial Park Cemetery

Kealohi Point
Heeia State Park
Heeia Fishpond

Lilipuna Rd

Haiku Rd
836

Kahuhipa St
Keaahala Rd

3

Kaneohe District Park

Luluku Rd

63

Likelike Hwy

Hoomaluhia Botanical Garden

Heeia

Kahekili Hwy

Kamehahameha Hwy

83

Heeia Stream

Kaneohe Forest Reserve

Wilson Tunnel

H3

To Honolulu

To Senator Fong's Plantation Gardens, Waiahole, Kualoa Point & Laie

Wailau Point
1

Kahaluu
Kahaluu Stream

Ahuimanu

Valley of the Temples Memorial Park
2

Wahiahole Forest Reserve

Omega Coast Guard Station

Kaneohe Forest Reserve

Honolulu Watershed Forest Reserve

Ewa Forest Reserve

Tunnel

To Honolulu

83

2 km
1 mile
1
.5
0
0

PACIFIC

For more information, see Camping in the Facts for the Visitor chapter.

**YWCA Camp Kokokahi** (☎ *247-2124; fax 247-2125; e kokokahi@gte.net; 45-035 Kaneohe Bay Dr; tent sites $8, single cabins $25, double cabins per person $16)* is a budget option 1½ miles northeast of Kaneohe center. Although the camp gives priority to groups, it also accepts individual travelers. Accommodations are simple – opt for a tiny cabin all to yourself, get a double cabin with two single beds, or pitch your own tent on the grounds. You can rent linen for $5 per stay if you don't have your own, and guests have access to kitchen, lounge and laundry facilities. Though the camp overlooks Kaneohe Bay, the water is too silted for swimming, but there's a heated pool on the grounds. Two things to keep in mind: the place sometimes fills up completely, so call ahead to make reservations before heading all the way out, and plan on checking in before the office closes at 5pm. Bus No 56 (1¼ hours from Ala Moana Center) stops out front.

**Alii Bluffs Windward Bed & Breakfast** *(☎ 235-1124, 800-235-1151; e donm@lava .net; 46-251 Ikiiki St, Kaneohe, HI 96744; rooms $60 & $75)* has two bedrooms in a cozy home filled with Old World furnishings, oil paintings, antique toys and collectibles. The Victorian Room has one double bed, while the cheaper Circus Room has two twin beds. Each room has a private bathroom. Originally from the Scottish Highlands, where his mother ran a B&B, host Don Munro and his partner De, a retired New York fashion designer, give guests the run of the house. Beach towels and coolers are provided; breakfast and afternoon tea are included in the rates. There's a small pool and a view of Kaneohe Bay.

### Getting There & Away
By car, the main route from Honolulu is the Likelike Hwy (Hwy 63), which leads into Kaneohe's main commercial strip.

Kaneohe is connected to Honolulu by bus No 55, with the first bus leaving the Ala Moana Center at 6:15am. The bus operates about once every 30 minutes during the day, less frequently in the evening. Bus No 65 also covers the same route but only operates about once an hour. Travel time between Honolulu and Kaneohe on either bus is about 35 minutes.

Bus No 56 connects Kailua with Kaneohe an average of twice an hour and takes 20 minutes. You can also take this bus from the Ala Moana Center to Kaneohe, but it takes much longer as it goes via Kailua.

## KAHALUU
This small enclave marks the start of the best bit of the Windward Coast drive.

### Heeia State Park
Heeia State Park is on Kealohi Point, just off Kamehameha Hwy. It has a good view of Heeia Fishpond on the right and Heeia-Kea Harbor on the left.

Before contact with the West, stone-walled fishponds used for raising fish for royalty were common along the coasts of Hawaii. The **Heeia Fishpond** is an impressive survivor that remains largely intact despite the invasive mangrove that grows along its walls and takes root between the rocks. Several key scenes for *Karate Kid II* were filmed here.

**Coconut Island (Moku O Loe)**, just offshore and to the southeast of the fishpond, was a royal playground in times past. It was named for the coconut trees planted there by Princess Bernice Pauahi Bishop. In the 1930s it was the estate of Christian Holmes, heir to the Fleischmann Yeast fortune, who by dredging doubled the island's size to 25 acres. During WWII the estate served as an R&R facility for military personnel. Airbrushed shots of Coconut Island were used in opening scenes for the *Gilligan's Island* TV series. Today, the Hawaii Institute of Marine Biology of the University of Hawaii occupies a portion of the island, while the rest is privately owned.

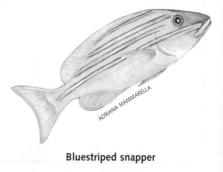

**Bluestriped snapper**

## Senator Fong's Plantation & Gardens

Set on 725 acres, these gardens (☎ 239-6775; 47-285 Pulama Rd; admission $10; open 10am-4pm daily) are a labor of love of one of Hawaii's most famous politicians. Hiram Fong served in the US Senate until he retired in 1977. Since then he has been the tireless sponsor of these lovely gardens dedicated to preserving Hawaii's flora for future generations. Macadamias, bananas, sandalwood, myriad tropical flowers and more are grown. A 45-minute tram ride gives visitors an overview of the plants. On weekends, the Senator – now well into his 90s – can be found hard at work. There's a small snack stand serving items grown on the grounds, which are about 1 mile off of Hwy 83, the Kahekili Hwy.

## Places to Stay & Eat

**Schrader's Windward Marine Resort** (☎ 239-5711, 800-735-5711, fax 239-6658; 47-039 Lihikai Dr, Kaneohe, HI 96744; 1-/2-bedroom units from $100/160) has 57 units in low-rise wooden buildings in a residential neighborhood. Despite the name, the ambience is more like a motel than a resort. So many of the guests are military families that Schrader's provides free transport to the Kaneohe MCBH. All units have refrigerators, microwaves, TVs, air-con and phones. It overlooks Heeia State Park.

Just north of the Kahaluu Regional Park and the fishponds is **Kahaluu Bar-B-Q**, a roadside stand with tables, which does great fish, pork and prawns. It's across from the entrance to Wailehua Rd.

Back by the fishponds, the **Hygenic Store** is an old-time grocery that's good for picnics and supplies.

## WAIAHOLE & WAIKANE

The area north of Kahaluu has a sleepy, local feel to it, with some lovely beaches, interesting hiking opportunities and fine scenery. The Kamehameha Hwy, really just a modest two-lane road, runs the length of the entire coast, doubling as Main St for each of the small towns along the way. There are loads of fruit stands, orchid shops and nurseries, giving the drive a real feel of old Hawaii.

Waiahole and Waikane mark the beginning of rural Oahu. This area is home to a number of family-run orchid nurseries and small farms growing coconuts, bananas, papayas and taro.

Large tracts of Waikane Valley were taken over by the military during WWII for training and target practice, a use that continued until the 1960s. The government now claims the land has so much live ordnance it can't be returned to the families it was leased from, a source of ongoing contention with local residents who are upset that much of the inner valley remains off-limits.

## KUALOA

Kualoa was once one of the most sacred places on Oahu. In fact, the name Kualoa means 'long ancestral background.' When a chief stood on the point, passing canoes lowered their sails in respect. The children of chiefs were brought here to be raised, and it may also have been a place of refuge where *kapu* (taboo) breakers and fallen warriors could seek reprieve from the law. Reflecting its historic importance, the double-hulled canoe *Hokulea* landed at Kualoa in 1987, following a two-year voyage through Polynesia that retraced the ancient migration routes. Because of its rich significance to Hawaiians, Kualoa Regional Park is listed in the National Register of Historic Places.

## Kualoa Regional Park

The Kualoa Regional Park, a 153-acre county beach park on Kualoa Point, is bounded on the southwest by **Molii Fishpond**. From the road southwest of the park, the fishpond is visible through the trees as a distinct green line in the bay.

Kualoa is a nice beach park in a scenic setting. The mountains looming precipitously across the road are called, appropriately

### North of Kaneohe by Bus

Bus No 55 services the Kamehameha Hwy from Kaneohe to the Turtle Bay Resort in Kawela. From Kaneohe, the bus runs approximately every 30 minutes from dawn to 6pm and then less frequently until 10:45pm. By bus from Kaneohe, it takes about 30 minutes to reach Kualoa Regional Park, an hour to the Polynesian Cultural Center in Laie and 1½ hours to the Turtle Bay Resort.

enough, Pali-ku, meaning 'vertical cliff.' When the mist settles, it looks like a scene from a Chinese watercolor.

The main offshore island is **Mokolii**. In Hawaiian legend, Mokolii is said to be the tail of a nasty lizard or a dog – depending on who's telling the story – that was slain by a god and thrown into the ocean. Following the immigration of Chinese laborers to Hawaii, this cone-shaped island also came to be called Papale Pake, Hawaiian for 'Chinese hat.'

**Apua Pond**, a 3-acre brackish salt marsh on Kualoa Point, is a nesting area for the endangered *aeo* (Hawaiian stilt). If you walk down the beach beyond the park, you'll see a bit of Molii Fishpond, but it's hard to get a good perspective on it from there because its rock walls are covered with mangrove, milo and pickleweed.

The park is largely open lawn with a few palm trees. It has a long, thin strip of white-sand beach with shallow waters and safe swimming. There are picnic tables, rest rooms, showers and sometimes a lifeguard.

Camping is allowed from Friday to Tuesday night, with a permit from the county; see Camping in the Facts for the Visitor chapter for more details.

### Kualoa Ranch

The horses grazing on the green slopes across the road from Kualoa Regional Park belong to Kualoa Ranch (☎ 237-8515). Parts of the scenic 4000-acre ranch has been used as settings for several movies, including *Jurassic Park* and *Godzilla*. The ranch offers all sorts of activities, including horseback riding, target shooting and a 'movie set bus tour,' with much of it packaged for Japanese tourists who are shuttled in from Waikiki.

Back in 1850, Kamehameha III leased 625 acres of this land for $1300 to Dr Judd, a missionary doctor who became one of the king's advisers. Judd planted the land with sugarcane, built flumes to transport it and imported Chinese laborers to work the fields. His sugar mill trudged along for a few decades but went under just before a reciprocity agreement with the USA opened up mainland sugar markets.

You can still see the **ruins** of the sugar mill's stone stack and a bit of its crumbling walls half a mile north of the beach park, right alongside the road.

## KAAAWA
### pop 1325

In the Kaaawa area, the road tightly hugs the coast and the *pali* moves right on in, with barely enough space to squeeze a few houses between the base of the cliffs and the road.

**Swanzy Beach Park**, a narrow neighborhood beach used mainly by fishers, is fronted by a shore wall. Camping is allowed on weekends (see Camping in the Facts for the Visitor chapter for permit details), but because there's little privacy and it's smack in the middle of town, it's a bit like invading somebody's backyard.

Across the road from the park is a convenience store and plate-lunch place, a gas station and a postage-stamp-sized post office – pretty much the commercial center of town, such as it is.

### Crouching Lion

Just north of Kaaawa center is a rock formation known as the crouching lion. In Hawaiian legend, the rock is said to be a demigod from Tahiti who was cemented to the mountain during a jealous struggle between Pele, the volcano goddess, and her sister Hiiaka. When he tried to free himself by pulling into a crouching position, the demigod was turned to stone.

To find him, pull into the Crouching Lion Inn parking lot, just north of the 27-mile marker. Stand at the Crouching Lion Inn sign with your back to the ocean and look straight up to the left of the coconut tree. You will see the figure, which bears some resemblance to a lion, on a cliff in the background.

### Places to Eat

**Crouching Lion Inn** (☎ 237-8511; 51-666 Kamehameha Hwy; lunch mains $8-10, dinner mains $11-25; open lunch 11am-3pm, dinner 5pm-9pm daily), the area's main sit-down restaurant, attracts a fair number of day-trippers, many of whom have no choice as it seems every tour bus pulls in here. Lunch is mainly sandwiches and salads, though there are a few hot chicken and beef dishes. Dinner features the usual steaks, chicken and seafood. Torches are lit at dinnertime and there's a sea view, which makes the restaurant's veranda a pleasant place to dine at sunset.

## KAHANA VALLEY

In old Hawaii the islands were divided into *ahupuaa* – pie-shaped land divisions reaching from the mountains to the sea. They provided everything the Hawaiians needed for subsistence. Kahana Valley, 4 miles long and 2 miles wide, is the only publicly owned *ahupuaa* in Hawaii.

Kahana is a wet valley. Annual rainfall ranges from about 75 inches along the coast to 300 inches in the mountains. Before Westerners arrived, Kahana Valley was planted with wetland taro. Archaeologists have identified the overgrown remnants of more than 130 agricultural terraces and irrigation canals, as well as the remains of a heiau, fishing shrines and numerous house sites.

In the early 20th century, the area was planted with sugarcane, which was hauled north to the Kahuku Mill via a small railroad. During WWII, the upper part of Kahana Valley was taken over by the military and used for training soldiers in jungle warfare. In 1965 the state bought Kahana Valley from the Robinson family of Kauai (owners of the island of Niihau) in order to preserve it from development.

About 30 Hawaiian families live in the lower valley. The upper valley remains undeveloped and is mostly used by local hunters who come here on weekends to hunt feral pigs.

While many of Kahana's archeological sites are deep in the valley and inaccessible, the park's most impressive site, **Huilua Fishpond** on Kahana Bay, is visible from the main road and can be visited simply by going down to the beach.

### Kahana Valley State Park

The signposted entrance to Kahana Valley State Park is 1 mile north of the Crouching Lion Inn.

When the state purchased Kahana, it also acquired tenants, many of whom had lived in the valley for a long time. Rather than evict a struggling rural population, the state created a plan allowing the 140 residents to stay on the land. The concept is to eventually incorporate the families into a 'living park,' with the residents acting as interpretive guides. The development of the park is a slow process, but after a couple of decades of planning and negotiating, the 'living park' concept is inching forward. There's now a simple orientation center near the park entrance and tours are being provided to school children and local organizations.

Although there are no tours for individual travelers, you can walk through the valley on your own. The **orientation center** (☎ 237-7766; open 7:30am-4pm Mon-Fri) provides a map and has the latest information on trail conditions. Keep in mind that the trails can be slippery when wet, and this is the wettest side of Oahu.

The most accessible of the park trails is the 1¼-mile **Kapaeleele Koa and Keaniani Lookout Trail**, which begins at the orientation center. It goes along the old railroad route, passes a fishing shrine called Kapaeleele Koa and leads to Keaniani Kilo, a lookout that was used in ancient times for spotting schools of fish in the bay. The trail then goes down to the bay and follows the highway back to the park entrance.

If you want to get into the rain forest, there's the **Nakoa Trail**, which makes a 2½-mile loop through tropical vegetation. This trail makes a couple of stream crossings and passes a swimming hole en route. However, the start of the Nakoa Trail is 1¼ miles inland from the orientation center on a rough dirt road, so the total walking distance equals 5 miles.

The park also encompasses **Kahana Bay** with its tree-lined beach and fishpond. The bay is set deep and narrow, and the protected beach provides safe swimming, with a gently sloping sandy bottom.

There are 10 beachside **camp sites**, but they're primarily used by island families, so there may be some turf issues for tourists. Camping is allowed with a permit from the state, however; see Camping in the Facts for the Visitor chapter for details.

## PUNALUU

### pop 880

Punaluu is a scattered little seaside community that doesn't draw many tourists, although the many small art galleries would like to change that. At **Punaluu Beach Park**, a long, narrow beach offers fair swimming, as the offshore reef protects the shallow inshore waters in all but stormy weather. Be cautious near the mouth of the Waiono Stream and in the channel leading out from it, as currents are strong when the stream is flowing quickly or when the surf is high.

## Places to Stay & Eat

**Punaluu Guesthouse** (☎ 946-0591; 53-504 Kamehameha Hwy; $22 per person), a home in the Punaluu's center, belongs to the owners of Hostelling International Honolulu. Because there are only two rooms and it's a cozy situation, the hostel prescreens potential guests – so if you want to stay here, you need to go to the Honolulu hostel first to meet with the staff there and get a referral. Punaluu Guesthouse has a couple of guest rooms, one with twin beds, another with a double bed; there's a shared bathroom and a shared kitchen. House parents live on site.

**Pat's at Punaluu** (☎ 293-2624; 53-567 Kamehameha Hwy) is a 136-room puce-colored fortresslike condominium complex midway between the 23- and 24-mile markers. The unattractive place is largely residential, older and a bit neglected, but on the plus side, it's on the water, the units face the ocean and there's a swimming pool. There's no front desk. The units are handled by individuals and realtors, some of whom post their listings at the condo bulletin board. Call the number listed above to speak to the resident manager, who might be able to make a recommendation.

**Paul Comeau Condo Rentals** (☎ 467-6215, fax 293-0618; PO Box 589, Kaaawa, HI 96730; studios $80, 1-bedroom unit $100, 3-bedroom unit $180) handles a number of units at Pat's at Punaluu; all have a three-day minimum stay.

**Ahi's** (☎ 293-5650; 53-146 Kamehameha Hwy; meals $8-15; open 11am-9pm Mon-Sat), a third of a mile north of the 25-mile marker, is Punaluu's only restaurant. And in fact it has something of a split personality as it is also called the Punaluu Restaurant. You can get fried chicken, fish or steaks, but the specialty is fresh shrimp in a variety of preparations, including shrimp scampi, shrimp tempura and shrimp cocktail.

Near milepost 24, there's a small stand with hot dogs and all the usual plate lunches.

## HAUULA

### pop 3650

Hauula is a small coastal town set against a scenic backdrop of hills and majestic Norfolk pines. There are scenic hiking trails in the forest reserve above town.

As with most other windward towns, the shoreline area in the village is largely set aside for the community to use as a park. Although the beach is not particularly appealing for swimming, it does occasionally get waves that are big enough for local kids to ride.

The main landmark in town is the stone ruins of **Lanakila Church** (c.1853), which sit perched on a hill opposite Hauula Beach, next to the newer Hauula Congregational Church.

If you're in need of a quick bite to eat, Hauula has a couple of small eateries and a convenience store.

## Trails

The **Division of Forestry & Wildlife** (☎ 587-0166) maintains two trails in the Kaipapau Forest Reserve above Hauula. Both trails share the same access point and both head into beautiful hills in the lower Koolau Range.

The **Hauula Loop Trail** is a scenic 2½-mile hike that makes a couple of gulch crossings and climbs along a ridge with broad views of the forested interior, the ocean and the town of Hauula. This trail, which forks off to the right shortly after you enter the forest reserve, passes native vegetation such as ohia trees as well as thickly planted groves of shaggy ironwood trees and towering Norfork pines. The hike takes about two hours.

The **Maakua Ridge Trail**, which begins on the left about half a mile after entering the forest reserve, makes a 2½-mile loop that climbs in and out of a couple of gullies and follows the narrow Maakua Ridge. Much of the trail is open and dry but there are sections that close in, including some thickets of acacia trees that create tunnel effects. There are ridgetop views of the coast and Hauula along the way. The hike takes about 2½ hours.

The signposted trailhead to both hikes is at a bend in Hauula Homestead Rd, about a quarter of a mile up from Kamehameha Hwy. Hauula Homestead Rd is located right in town, at the northern end of Hauula Beach Park.

Backcountry camping is permitted along the Maakua Ridge Trail, but a permit from the Division of Forestry & Wildlife is required. For details on obtaining a permit, see Backcountry Camping in the Facts for the Visitor chapter.

## LAIE

**pop 4585**

Laie is thought to have been the site of an ancient *puuhonua* – a place where *kapu* breakers and fallen warriors could seek refuge. Today, Laie is the center of the Mormon community in Hawaii.

The first Mormon missionaries to Hawaii arrived in 1850. After an attempt to establish a Hawaiian 'City of Joseph' on the island of Lanai failed amid a land scandal, the Mormons moved to Laie. In 1865 they purchased 6000 acres of land in the area and slowly expanded their influence.

In 1919 the Mormons constructed a **temple**, a smaller version of the one in Salt Lake City, at the foot of the Koolau Range. This stately temple, at the end of a wide promenade, is like nothing else on the Windward Coast. Although there's a visitor center where enthusiastic guides will tell you about Mormonism, tourists are not allowed to enter the temple itself.

Nearby is the Hawaii branch of **Brigham Young University**, with scholarship programs that recruit students from islands throughout the Pacific.

### Information

The **Laie Shopping Center** *(55-510 Kamehameha Hwy)*, about half a mile north of the Polynesian Cultural Center, has a **Bank of Hawaii** (☎ *293-9238; open 8:30am-4pm Mon-Thur, 8:30am-6pm Fri)* and a **post office** (☎ *293-0337; open 9am-3:30pm Mon-Fri, 9:30am-11:30am Sat)*. The center also has a coin laundry, the **Laie Washerette** (☎ *293-2821; 55-510 Kamehameha Hwy; open 6am-8pm Mon-Sat)*.

### Polynesian Cultural Center

The Polynesian Cultural Center (☎ *293-3333, 800-367-7060;* **w** *www.polynesia.com; adult/child 5-11 yrs $39/24; open 12:30pm-9pm Mon-Sat)*, called PCC by locals, is a 'nonprofit' organization belonging to the Mormon Church. The center covers 42 acres and draws about 900,000 tourists a year, more than any other attraction on Oahu, with the exception of the USS *Arizona* Memorial.

The park has seven theme villages representing Samoa, New Zealand, Fiji, Tahiti, Tonga, the Marquesas and Hawaii. The 'villages' contain authentic-looking huts and

ceremonial houses, many elaborately built with twisted sennit ropes and hand-carved posts. In the huts there are examples of weavings, tapa cloth, feather work and other handicrafts. People of Polynesian descent dressed in native garb demonstrate *poi* pounding, coconut frond weaving, dances, games and the like.

There's also a replica of an old mission house and a missionary chapel representative of those found throughout Polynesia in the mid-19th century.

Many of the people working here are Pacific Island students from the nearby Brigham Young University (BYU), who pay their college expenses with jobs at PCC. The interpreters are amiable and you could easily spend a few hours wandering around chatting or trying to become familiar with a craft or two.

The admission price also includes boat rides along the winding waterway through the park; the Pageant of the Long Canoes, a sort of trumped-up floating talent show at 2:30pm; 45-minute van tours of the Mormon temple grounds and BYU campus; movies at the center's IMAX theater; and the evening Polynesian song and dance show. The Polynesian show, which runs from 7:30pm to 9pm, can be fun – partly authentic, partly Hollywood-style and much like an enthusiastic college production, with elaborate sets and costumes.

There is a wide range of admission prices. You can skip the show for $29/19 per adult/child or throw in a buffet dinner for $54/37. At the top end, the Super Ambassador Package yields the services of a fresh-faced personal guide for $165/115.

Although PCC has many interesting features, it's also very touristy and hard to recommend at the variety of admission prices. You might be better off enjoying the nearby parks and beaches with a picnic. You can always stage your own show.

### Beaches

The 1½ miles of beach fronting the town of Laie between Malaekahana State Recreation Area and Laie Point are used by surfers, bodysurfers and windsurfers.

**Pounders Beach**, a half mile south of the main entrance to PCC, is an excellent bodysurfing beach, but the shore break, as the name of the beach implies, can be brutal.

There's a strong winter current. The area around the old landing is usually the calmest. Summer swimming is generally good at this nice and simple stretch of sand.

From **Laie Point** lookout, there's a good view of the mountains to the south and of tiny offshore islands. The island to the left, with the hole in it, is **Kukuihoolua**, otherwise known as Puka Rock. To get to Laie Point, head toward the ocean on Anemoku St, opposite the Laie Shopping Center, turn right on Naupaka St and go straight to the end.

## Places to Stay & Eat

**Laie Inn** (☎ 293-9282, 800-526-4562, fax 293-8115; ℮ laieinn@hawaii.rr.com; 55-109 Laniloa St; rooms $89), right outside the Polynesian Cultural Center, is a two-story motel with 49 rooms surrounding a courtyard swimming pool. Although not special, it's comfortable enough, and each room has a lanai, cable TV, air-con and mini-refrigerator. Rates include a continental breakfast.

The Laie Shopping Center has a grocery store and a couple of fast-food chain eateries selling the usual Chinese, burgers, sandwiches and pizza.

## MALAEKAHANA STATE RECREATION AREA

Malaekahana Beach is a beautiful strand that stretches between Makahoa Point to the north and Kalanai Point to the south. The long, narrow, sandy beach is backed by ironwood trees. Swimming is generally good year-round, although there are occasionally strong currents in winter. This popular family beach is also good for many other water activities, including bodysurfing, board surfing and windsurfing.

**Kalanai Point**, the main section of the state park, is less than a mile north of Laie and has picnic tables, barbecue grills, camping, rest rooms and showers.

**Mokuauia (Goat Island)**, a state bird sanctuary just offshore, has a nice, sandy cove with good swimming and snorkeling. It's possible to wade over to the island – best when the tide is low and the water's calm – but be sure to ask the lifeguard first about water conditions and the advisability of crossing. Be careful of the shallow coral and sea urchins.

You can also snorkel across to Goat Island and off its beaches. Beware of a rip current

that's sometimes present off the windward end of the island where the water is deeper.

Malaekahana State Recreation Area has the best **camping grounds** at this end of the Windward Coast. You are allowed to pitch a tent in the park's main Kalanai Point section if you have a state park permit; for details, see Camping in the Facts for the Visitor chapter.

You can also rent a rustic cabin or camp for a fee in the Makahoa Point section of the park, which has a separate entrance off Kamehameha Hwy, three-quarters of a mile north of the main park entrance. **Friends of Malaekahana** (☎ 293-1736; tent sites per person $5, 4-/8- person cabins Mon-Thur $55/66, Fri-Sun $66/80), a local nonprofit group dedicated to cultural preservation, maintains this end of the park. It's a relatively secure place to stay, with gates locked to vehicles between 7pm and 7am.

## KAHUKU
**pop 2100**

Kahuku is a former sugar town with little wooden cane houses lining the road. The mill in the center of town belonged to the Kahuku Plantation, which produced sugar from 1890 until it closed in 1971. The operation was a relatively small concern, unable to keep up with the increasingly mechanized competition of Hawaii's bigger mills. When the mill shut down, Kahuku's economy skidded into a slump that still lingers today.

A small shopping center now occupies Kahuku's old sugar mill, with small shops set among the old machinery. The mill's enormous gears, flywheels and pipes are painted in bright colors to help visitors visualize how a sugar mill works. The steam systems are painted red, the cane-juice systems are light green, hydraulic systems are dark blue and so forth. It looks like something out of *Modern Times* – you can almost imagine Charlie Chaplin caught up in the giant gears.

The center has not been wildly successful, but there's a famous plate-lunch eatery, food mart, gas station, post office, bank and a few other shops.

About one mile north of Kahuku, **The Only Show in Town** (☎ 293-1295; 56-901 Kamehameha Hwy), is a fun antique and collectible store in an old grocery.

## James Campbell National Wildlife Refuge

This wildlife refuge *(reservations ☎ 637-6330; free tours 4pm-5:30pm Thur & 3:30pm-5pm Sat)* is a rare freshwater wetland that provides a habitat for Hawaii's four endangered waterbirds – the Hawaiian coot, the Hawaiian stilt, the Hawaiian duck and the cootlike Hawaiian gallinule.

During stilt nesting season, normally mid-February through July, the refuge is off-limits to all visitors. The rest of the year, it can be visited only through guided tours, which are provided by refuge staff. Tours are free, but reservations are required. Near the refuge you'll see acres of shrimp farms. You can buy the buggers fresh by the pound or already cooked at Giovanni's Shrimp in Kahuku.

The refuge, which is signposted, is 2 miles north of Kahuku's town center.

## Places to Stay & Eat

The only hotel in the Kahuku area is the **Turtle Bay Resort**. For more information on the resort and the neighboring **Turtle Bay Condos**, see Kahuku Point in the North Shore chapter. Turtle Bay Resort also has a couple of restaurants.

**Giovanni's Shrimp** *(open 10:30am-6:30pm daily)*, a white truck that parks along the highway just south of the Kahuku Sugar Mill, is the place to go if you like shrimp. Popular with both locals and sightseers from Honolulu, Giovanni's offers a choice of tasty shrimp scampi (the best choice), lemon-butter grilled shrimp or hot and spicy shrimp. A plate with half a pound of jumbo shrimp and two scoops of rice will cost you $11. There is also a covered picnic area where you can sit, peel and eat to your heart's content.

# North Shore

Oahu's North Shore is synonymous with surfing and wicked winter waves. Sunset Beach, the Banzai Pipeline and Waimea Bay are among the world's most famous surf spots and attract top surfers from around the globe. Other North Shore surf breaks may be less well known, but with names such as Himalayas and Avalanche, it's obvious they are not exactly for neophytes.

Early Polynesian settlers were drawn to the North Shore by the region's rich fishing grounds, cooling trade winds and moderate rain. The areas around Mokuleia, Haleiwa and Waimea all once had sizable Hawaiian settlements and abandoned taro patches still remain in their upland valleys.

By the early 20th century the Oahu Railway & Land Company had extended the railroad from Honolulu to the North Shore, and the first beachgoers began to arrive. Hotels and private beach houses sprang up to accommodate the tourists, but when the railroad stopped running in the 1940s the hotels shut down for good. Sections of abandoned track are still found along many of the beaches.

Waikiki surfers started taking on North Shore waves in the late 1950s and big-time surf competitions followed a few years later. In 1963, the Beach Boys' hit song *Surfin' USA* rolled through a list of the best surf breaks in the country, and the names Sunset Beach and Waimea Bay suddenly became part of the country's vernacular.

These days the grandest surfing event of them all is the Triple Crown, consisting of three major surf competitions that take place in early winter, with prize purses reaching six figures.

Surf mania prevails even in the restaurants, which serve up omelettes with names such as 'Pumping Surf' and 'Wipe Out.' When the surf's up, half the North Shore population can be found on the beach. On winter weekends, convoys of cars make the trip up from Honolulu to watch surfers ride the waves. If you want to avoid the traffic, simply head to the North Shore on a weekday.

The order of the chapter follows on from the Windward Coast chapter and starts at the north. Alternatively you can go clockwise around the island starting in the pineapple fields of central Oahu. Besides

NORTH SHORE

## Highlights

- Watching the world's top surfers tackle towering winter waves at Banzai Pipeline

- Treating yourself to shave ice, a favorite Hawaiian treat, in Haleiwa

- Taking a free surfing lesson at Haleiwa Alii Beach Park

- Donning a mask to snorkel amid the colorful fish at Pupukea Beach Park

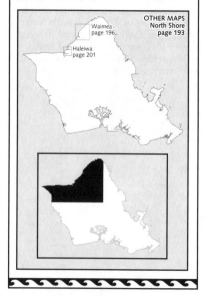

the crashing waves along the coast road, you will see one stand after another selling succulent local fruit.

## Getting There & Away

If you're coming from the Windward Coast on the Kamehameha Hwy, the first town you'll encounter is Kawela, and more notably, the Turtle Bay Resort. The Kamehameha Hwy (Hwy 83), a two-lane coastal road along the North Shore, connects the North Shore's main sightseeing locales and beaches with Haleiwa in the south. This chapter follows the Kamehameha Hwy from the north along the coastline until the highway veers inland after Haleiwa and becomes Hwy 99.

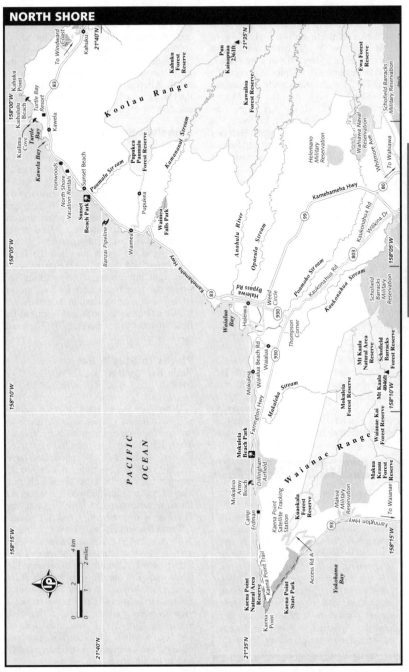

The quickest route to the North Shore from Honolulu is to take the H1 Fwy west and then exit north onto the H2 Fwy to Wahiawa, where you can continue north via the Kamehameha Hwy. (If that's your route, you'll be reading this chapter in reverse.)

Bus No 52 is the main route serving the North Shore. It runs from the Ala Moana Center in Honolulu all the way to the Turtle Bay Resort, near Kawela. En route, the bus stops in Wahiawa (1¼ hours), Haleiwa (1½ hours), Waimea (1¾ hours) and Sunset Beach (two hours) before terminating at Turtle Bay (2¼ hours). The bus leaves the Ala Moana Center twice an hour from 6:30am to 6:15pm and then once again at 7:15pm and 8:15pm.

Bus 52 bypasses Waialua, but the local bus No 76 connects Haleiwa and Waialua once every 40 minutes throughout the day; travel time between the two towns is 15 minutes.

## KAHUKU POINT

North of the township of Kahuku, this point marks the division between the North Shore and the Windward Coast.

### Kuilima Cove

The shallow Kuilima Cove, also known as Bay View Beach, is fronted by the Turtle Bay Resort, the only hotel in the Kahuku area. This pleasant white-sand beach, protected by a reef, is one of the area's best swimming spots. It also has a few coral patches that are good for snorkeling. While it's mostly used by resort guests, it's open to everyone.

### Seasonal Changes

With the exception of Haleiwa Beach Park, North Shore beaches are notorious for treacherous winter swimming conditions. There are powerful and dangerous currents along the entire shore. If the water doesn't look as calm as a lake, it's probably not safe for swimming or snorkeling.

During the summer, surf conditions along the whole North Shore can mellow right out. Shark's Cove in Waimea then becomes a prime snorkeling and diving spot, and Waimea Bay, internationally famous for its winter surf, turns into a popular swimming and snorkeling beach.

The beach concession stand rents snorkel sets and boogie boards for $12 a day, floats and tubes for $10, lounge chairs for $4.

You can park at one of the free spaces for beachgoers, on the right just before the guard booth, and walk 10 minutes to the beach. Alternatively, there's parking inside the hotel lot for $1.50 for the first half-hour and 50¢ for each additional half-hour.

### Kaihalulu Beach

Kaihalulu is a beautiful, curved, white-sand beach backed by ironwoods. Although a shoreline lava shelf and rocky bottom make the beach poor for swimming, it's good for beachcombing – you can walk east about a mile to Kahuku Point. Local fishers cast thrownets from the shore and pole fish from the point. The dirt road just inland of the beach is also used as a horse trail.

To get to the beach, turn into the Turtle Bay Resort and just before the guard booth turn right into an unmarked parking lot, where there are free spaces for beachgoers. It's a five-minute walk out to the beach; just walk east on the footpath that begins at the field adjacent to the parking lot. There are no facilities here.

### Places to Stay & Eat

**Turtle Bay Condos** (☎ 293-2800, fax 293-2169; e trtlbayest@aol.com; Box 248, Kahuku, HI 96731; studios $95, with loft $105, 1-/2-bedroom apartments $115/160) handles units at Kuilima Estates, a modern condominium complex on the grounds fronting the Turtle Bay Resort. Each unit has a complete kitchen, washer/dryer, TV, phone and lanai. Weekly rates are six times the daily rate; monthly rates are 2½ times the weekly rate. There's a one-time $50 to $75 cleaning fee for all rentals, no matter how long you stay. There are two tennis courts and five pools.

**Turtle Bay Resort** (☎ 293-8811, 800-203-3650, fax 293-9147; e res@turtlebayresort .com; 57-091 Kamehameha Hwy; rooms $139-295), perched on Kuilima Point between Turtle Bay and Kuilima Cove, is the only resort hotel on the Windward Coast and the North Shore. Each of the 485 rooms has an ocean view as well as all the expected first-class amenities. Turtle Bay is a self-contained resort with a couple of restaurants, two golf courses, two swimming pools, horse stables and 10 tennis courts.

## A Ton of Turtles

Turtle Bay, the wide bay at the western side of the Turtle Bay Resort, takes its name from the green sea turtles that swim into the bay to feed on algae.

Green sea turtles, which can weigh upwards of 200lb, are the most abundant of the three native species of sea turtles *(honu)* found in Hawaiian waters. The turtles are not permanent residents of the main Hawaiian Islands. About once every four years they return to their ancestral nesting grounds in the remote French Frigate Shoals, 500 miles east of Oahu, where they mate and nest.

Hawaii's other two native turtles are the hawksbill, which is about the same size as the green sea turtle but far rarer, and the leatherback, a huge turtle that weighs up to a ton and is found in deep offshore waters.

There are a couple of restaurants at the Turtle Bay Resort that offer moderately priced all-you-can-eat meals and boast fine ocean views. The lobby-side **Bayview Lounge** (☎ 293-8811, ext 6512; buffet adult/ child under 12 $12/8) serves a simple evening buffet, some nights it's a pizza and pasta spread, while other nights it's a taco bar or barbecue; the buffet is offered 5:30pm to 8:30pm every night. The hotel's **Sea Tide Room** (☎ 293-8811, ext 6504; buffet adult/ child under 12 $22/12.50) has an extensive brunch buffet from 10am to 2pm Sunday, which includes fresh shrimp, sushi, fish, various meat dishes, an omelette station, and salad and dessert bars.

### SUNSET BEACH PARK

Sunset Beach Park is a pretty white-sand beach that invites sunbathing, but the main action is in the water. This beach is Oahu's classic winter surf spot, with incredible waves and challenging breaks.

Because of the tremendous surf activity in winter, the slope of the beach becomes increasingly steeper as the season goes on. In the summer, as the sand washes back in, the shoreline begins to smooth out.

Winter swells create powerful rips. Even when the waves have quieted down in the summer, there's still an along-shore current for swimmers to deal with.

Despite Sunset Beach's legendary reputation, unless there's a surf meet going on, the site is surprisingly low-key. The beach has rest rooms, showers and a lifeguard tower.

**Backyards**, the surf break off Sunset Point at the northern end of the beach, draws a lot of top windsurfers. There's a shallow reef and strong currents to contend with, but Backyards has the island's biggest waves for sailing.

### EHUKAI BEACH PARK

Most people come to Ehukai Beach Park to watch the pros surf the world-famous **Banzai Pipeline**, which is off the southern side of the park. It breaks over a shallow coral reef and can be a death-defying wave to ride. The Pipeline takes its name from the near-perfect tubes that are formed when huge westerly swells hit the shallow reef, exploding into a forward curl as they break.

At Ehukai Beach, many board riders and bodysurfers brave a hazardous current to ride the waves. Water conditions mellow out in summer, when it's good for swimming, but even then there can occasionally be strong currents.

Even in old Hawaii, Ehukai was known for its powerful breaking surf – the name means 'sea spray.'

Some of the Triple Crown surfing events that take place in late November and early December each year are held at Ehukai Beach (others are held at nearby Sunset Beach).

The entrance to Ehukai Beach Park is opposite Sunset Beach Elementary School. The beach has a lifeguard, rest rooms and showers. Because the beach is small, parking is limited; don't park on the highway or you'll risk getting towed.

## WAIMEA

Waimea Valley was once heavily settled. The lowlands were terraced in taro, the valley walls were dotted with house sites and the ridges were topped with heiaus (stone temples). Just about every crop grown in Hawaii thrived in this valley, including a rare pink taro favored by the *alii* (royalty).

Waimea River, now blocked at the beach by a sandbar, originally emptied into the bay. The river served as a passage for canoes traveling to villages upstream. Surfing was immensely popular here centuries ago, with the early Hawaiians riding Waimea's huge waves on their long boards.

In 1779, when Captain Cook's ships sailed into Waimea to collect water (shortly after Cook's death), an entry in the ship's log noted that the valley was uncommonly beautiful and picturesque.

However, contact with the West did nothing to preserve that beauty. Logging and the clearing of land to build plantations caused deforestation above the valley.

One of the consequences of the massive deforestation was a devastating flood in Waimea in 1894. In addition to water damage, an enormous volume of mud washed through the valley, so much so that it permanently altered the shape of Waimea's shore. After the flood, residents abandoned the valley and resettled elsewhere.

The **St Peter & Paul Church** stands beneath the tall, unassuming tower on the northern side of Waimea Bay. The structure was originally a rock-crushing plant that was built to

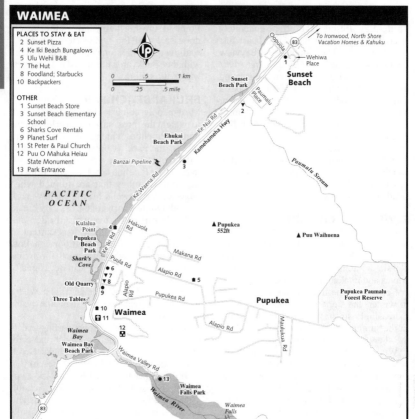

**WAIMEA**

PLACES TO STAY & EAT
2 Sunset Pizza
4 Ke Iki Beach Bungalows
5 Ulu Wehi B&B
7 The Hut
8 Foodland; Starbucks
10 Backpackers

OTHER
1 Sunset Beach Store
3 Sunset Beach Elementary School
6 Sharks Cove Rentals
9 Planet Surf
11 St Peter & Paul Church
12 Puu O Mahuka Heiau State Monument
13 Park Entrance

supply gravel for the construction of the highway in the 1930s. After it was abandoned, the Catholic Church converted it into Oahu's most unlikely chapel.

## Puu O Mahuka Heiau State Monument

Puu O Mahuka is a long, low-walled platform temple perched on a bluff above Waimea, at an elevation of 300ft. The largest heiau on Oahu, its stacked stone construction is attributed to the legendary *menehunes*, elflike people who are said to have completed their work in just one night.

Puu O Mahuka means 'hill of escape,' a bit ironic given that it was a *luakini* heiau where human sacrifices took place.

The terraced stone walls are a couple of feet high, although most of the heiau is now overgrown. Collectively, the three adjoining enclosures that form the main body of the heiau are more than 550ft in length. This was a dramatic site for a temple, and it's well worth the drive for the view, especially at sunset. The site, which is under the jurisdiction of the state park system, is a national historic landmark.

For a view of Waimea Valley and Waimea Bay, walk from the parking lot along the left side of the heiau. To the west, you can see the coast all the way to Kaena Point.

To get to the heiau, turn up Pupukea Rd at the Foodland supermarket. The marked turnoff to the heiau is about a half mile up the road, and from there it's three-quarters of a mile in to the site.

## Waimea Falls Park

This park (☎ 638-8511; 59-864 Kamehameha Hwy; adult/child 4-12 yrs $24/12, child under 4 yrs free; after 3pm adult/child 4-12 yrs $14/7; open 10am-5:30pm daily), across from Waimea Bay Beach Park, is a combination botanical garden and cultural theme park.

The main path inside the park, which leads up the Waimea Valley to a waterfall, is flanked by extensive naturalized gardens that are arranged by theme. There are sections of ginger, hibiscus, heliconia, native food plants and medicinal species. In all, they feature some 6000 plant species, including many that are rare and endangered.

The park contains several ancient stone platforms and terraces dating back hundreds of years, as well as replicas of thatched buildings similar to those used by the early Hawaiians. Traditional hula dances, Hawaiian games and other demonstrations are held during the day. In addition, several times a day, a cliff diver plunges 60ft into the waterfall pool, thrilling spectators.

Although the valley's natural beauty and ethnobotanical heritage is nicely preserved, the cost of admission is a little on the steep side. One way to cut the cost is to enter after 3pm. You will still have time to catch the last dive show and wander through the gardens, though it will be a bit late for most other activities.

Bus No 52 stops on the highway in front of the park, from where it's a half-mile walk to the park entrance.

## Pupukea Beach Park

Pupukea Beach Park is a long beach along the highway that includes Three Tables to the south and Shark's Cove to the north. In the middle is **Old Quarry**, where a fascinating array of jagged rock formations and tide pools are exposed at low tide. This is a very scenic beach, with deep-blue waters, a varied coastline and a mix of lava and white sand. The waters off Pupukea Beach are protected as a marine-life conservation district. The rocks and tide pools are tempting to explore, but be careful – they're razor sharp, and if you slip, it's easy to get a deep cut. Pupukea, incidentally, means 'white shell.'

There are showers and rest rooms in front of Old Quarry. The entrance to the beach is opposite an old gas station; bus No 52 stops out front.

Snorkel sets and other water-sports equipment can be rented from **Planet Surf**, across from the Foodland supermarket. It sells cheap bikinis, and should love bloom while you are hanging 10, it also arranges weddings.

**Three Tables**, at the southern end of the beach, gets its name from the ledges rising above the water. In summer when the waters are calm, Three Tables is a good place for snorkeling and diving. It is possible to see some action by snorkeling around the tables, but the best coral and fish, as well as some small caves, lava tubes and arches, are in deeper water farther out. However, this is a summer-only spot. In the winter, dangerous rip currents flow between the beach and the tables. Beware of sharp rocks and coral.

**Shark's Cove** is beautiful, both above and below the water's surface. The naming of the cove was done in jest – sharks aren't a particular problem. In the summer, when the seas are calm, Shark's Cove has good snorkeling and swimming conditions, as well as Oahu's most popular cavern dive. A fair number of beginning divers take lessons here, while the underwater caves will thrill advanced divers.

To get to the caves, swim out of the cove and around to the right. Some of the caves are very deep and labyrinthine, so exercise caution when exploring them. There have been a number of drownings in these caves.

The large boulders out on the end of the point, at the far right of the cove, are said to be followers of Pele, the Hawaiian volcano

### King of the Waves

If there's one name that every surfer hitting the waves here knows, it's unquestionably the Duke's. Born on Oahu in 1890, Duke Paoa Kahanamoku so revived the ancient Hawaiian art of surfing that he earned the title 'father of modern surfing.'

A full-blooded Hawaiian, he was as much at home in the water as he was on land. Between 1912 and 1932, Duke won six Olympic medals, including three gold medals for swimming.

But it was surfing, not swimming, that was his greatest passion. Duke was an ardent traveler who spread the sport of surfing far and wide, traveling with his board along the west and east coasts of the Americas, to Europe and Australia.

In 1925, while surfing off Corona del Mar, California, he became a national hero when he used his surfboard to rescue the passengers of a yacht that had capsized in heavy seas. Battling stormy conditions, Duke managed to paddle between the yacht and the shore several times, saving the lives of eight people.

From 1932 to 1960, Duke was elected sheriff of Honolulu for 13 consecutive terms. He loved meeting people and often mingled with visiting tourists, offering impromptu surf lessons and spreading good cheer. He so greatly symbolized Hawaii that to millions of people he was also known as the 'Hawaii Ambassador,' an honorary title he held his entire adult life. He died in 1968 at the age of 77.

goddess. To acknowledge their loyalty, Pele gave her followers immortality by turning them to stone.

## Waimea Bay Beach Park

Waimea Bay is a beautiful, deeply inset bay with turquoise waters and a wide white-sand beach almost 1500ft long. Ancient Hawaiians believed its waters were sacred.

Waimea Bay's mood changes with the seasons: It can be tranquil and as flat as a lake in summer, then savage with incredible surf and the island's meanest rip currents in winter.

Waimea boasts Hawaii's biggest surf and holds the record for the highest waves ever ridden in international competition. The huge north swells bring out throngs of spectators who crowd to watch surfers perform near-suicidal feats on waves of up to 35ft.

On winter's calmer days, the boogie boarders are out in force, but even then sets come in hard and people get pounded. Winter water activities at this beach are not for novices. Usually, the only time the water is calm enough for swimming and snorkeling is from June to September.

Waimea Bay Beach Park is the most popular North Shore beach. There are showers, rest rooms and picnic tables, and a lifeguard is on duty daily. Parking is often tight. Don't be tempted to park along the highway, even if you see others doing so; police have some notoriety for calling in tow trucks and hauling away dozens of cars at once, particularly when surf competitions are taking place.

### Places to Stay

In addition to the places listed here, the bulletin board at Pupukea's Foodland has roommates-wanted notices and the occasional vacation rental listing.

**Backpackers** (☎ 638-7838, fax 638-7515; w www.backpackers-hawaii.com; 59-788 Kamehameha Hwy; dorm beds $15-20, rooms $45-65, studios $80-114, cabins $110-200), opposite Three Tables, is pretty much a surfers' hangout. A durable place that's been in business for years, it has a few different setups, most of them beach-house casual. The main house has the $15 bunks, while a three-story house behind it has the cheapest rooms. Both houses have shared bathrooms and kitchens. Expect spartan decor and aging furniture, but if you're just looking for a place to crash between waves, it's an option that won't take a deep bite out of your wallet. It also has info on local vacation house rentals. Rates vary and you supply the kegs.

A small beachfront building across the road has eight studios with TVs, kitchens and great views. Units on the bottom floor have $20 dorm beds, while those on the top floor are rented as private studios. Backpackers' third property, a few hundred yards away on the inland side of the road, consists of fully equipped cabins that can sleep four to eight people.

**Sharks Cove Rentals** (☎ 779-8535, fax 638-7980; e info@sharkcoverentals.com; 59-672 Kamehameha Hwy; dorm beds $25, private rooms $50-60) consists of two adjacent three-bedroom houses across from Pupukea Beach Park. One of the houses has a setup with bunk beds, and as there is only two people to a room it's relatively quiet. The other house has three comfortable bedrooms; the more expensive rooms have their own TV and refrigerator. All guests have access to a fully equipped kitchen, a living room with cable TV and a washer and dryer. The place is within easy walking distance of a grocery store.

**Ironwoods** (☎ 293-2554, fax 293-2603; 57-531 Kamehameha Hwy; studio per day/week $70/450), 2 miles north of Sunset Beach, is a studio within the beachside home of Ann McMann. The studio has a private entrance, a loft bedroom with one king (or two twin beds) that's reached via a steep ladder staircase, and a downstairs sitting area with cable TV, bathroom, kitchenette and a single sofa bed. The nightly rate includes a simple breakfast, the weekly rate is with no breakfast; there's a three-night minimum stay. The unit is recommended for two people. The road is nearby, so expect to hear traffic noise, though it's usually drowned out by the sound of crashing waves. The beach is literally in the backyard. Ann speaks a little German.

**Ulu Wehi B&B** (☎/fax 638-8161; e tj4 dogs@aol.com; 59-416 Alapio Rd; studio singles or doubles $85, plus $15 additional person) is 1½ miles up the hill from Pupukea Beach Park. Tina Jensen and her French husband, Bernie Moriaz, an artist, operate a small nursery at their home and rent out a simple studio unit. The unit has both a double bed and a single bed, a TV (no cable, but there's a VCR and an extensive movie collection),

microwave, refrigerator, toaster and coffeepot. The toilet and shower are in a rustic bathhouse in the rear garden. There's a $10 nightly discount on weekly stays. A breakfast that includes a variety of fresh tropical fruit from their gardens and homemade baked goods is included. The house has a lovely 75ft lap pool in the backyard and a poolside barbecue that guests are free to use. Smoking is not allowed.

**Ke Iki Beach Bungalows** (☎ 638-8229; e info@keikibeach.com; 59-579 Ke Iki Rd; streetside 1-bedroom units low/high season $60/80, beachside 1-bedroom units from $130/150, beachside 2-bedroom units from $165/195) consist of 10 renovated apartments fronting a beautiful white-sand beach just north of Pupukea Beach Park. The units are comfortably furnished with a tropical decor of floral prints, rattan chairs and the like. Each unit has a full kitchen, TV and phone, and guests have access to a barbecue, picnic tables and hammocks lazily strung between coconut trees. The location is an absolute gem – the beachside units are right on the sand, the others just a minute's walk from the water.

**North Shore Vacation Homes** (☎ 638-7289, 800-678-5263, fax 638-8736; e luckyc@rr .com; 59-229C Ke Nui Rd; 2-bedroom unit low/high season $145/165, 3-bedroom unit low season $195-220, high season $225-245) consists of four pleasant beachside houses sharing a one-acre lot between Sunset Beach and Turtle Bay. The cheapest unit has two bedrooms, one bathroom and a living room with a sofa bed, and can accommodate up to four people. The other three units have three bedrooms and two baths and can hold up to six people. Each house has a full kitchen, washer and dryer, cable TV, VCR, phone and a spacious deck looking out over the ocean. There's typically a seven-night minimum stay, but shorter stays can sometimes be arranged.

## Places to Eat

**Foodland** (☎ 638-8081; 59-720 Kamehameha Hwy; open 6am-10pm daily), a supermarket opposite Pupukea Beach Park, has the best grocery prices and selection on the North Shore. It has a deli selling good, fried chicken, perfect for a beachside picnic.

**Starbucks** (☎ 638-0341; 59-720 Kamehameha Hwy; open 5:30am-8pm daily), inside

Foodland, sells coffee, brownies, scones and muffins. If you don't want to eat on the premises, you can find cheaper bakery items at Foodland itself.

**The Hut** (☎ 638-8442; dishes $5-7; open 11am-7pm daily), a little white trailer that parks along the highway about 100 yards north of Foodland, has good burgers, fish sandwiches and chicken teriyaki plates. There are a few tables where you can sit and eat, with a view of the beach across the road.

**Sunset Pizza** (☎ 638-7660; 59-176 Kamehameha Hwy; pizzas $9-18; open 7am-9pm daily), opposite Sunset Beach Park, has $5 meatball subs, $3 pizza slices and whole pizzas made to order. It has palm-shaded outdoor tables.

## HALEIWA
### pop 2250
Haleiwa is the southern gateway to the North Shore and the main town catering to the multitude of day-trippers who make the circle-island ride. It's a great place to wander around and have lunch, especially as options are slim elsewhere along the coast.

The townspeople are a multiethnic mix of families who have lived in Haleiwa for generations as well as more recently arrived surfers, artists and New Age folks.

Most of Haleiwa's shops are strung out along Kamehameha Hwy, the main drag through town, and the town has a picturesque boat harbor that is bordered on both sides by beach parks. There are lots of old storefronts and some sympathetically designed newer shopping areas. The southern side is known for its winter surfing, and the northern side is known for the North Shore's safest year-round swimming conditions. For information on renting surfboards and other water-sports gear, see the Activities chapter in the front of the book.

The Anahulu River, which flows out along the boat harbor, is spanned by the Rainbow Bridge, so nicknamed for its distinctively curved arches. From the bridge, take a glimpse up the river. It's still a lush green scene, and it's easy to imagine how this area must have looked in ancient Hawaii, when the riverbanks were lined with taro patches.

## Information
There's a **First Hawaiian Bank** (☎ 637-5034; 66-135 Kamehameha Hwy; open 8:30am-4pm

Mon-Thur, 8:30am-6pm Fri) at the northern side of Haleiwa Shopping Plaza.

The Haleiwa **post office** (☎ 637-1711; 66-437 Kamehameha Hwy; open 8am-4pm Mon-Fri, 9am-noon Sat) is at the southern end of town.

## Things to See & Do
For a sense of just how integral surfing is to the area's character, visit the **North Shore Surf & Cultural Museum** (☎ 637-8888; 66-250 Kamehameha Hwy; admission by donation; generally open 11am-6pm daily) in the North Shore Marketplace. The museum collection includes about 50 vintage surfboards, period photos and surfing videos. There's a neat display of lost items and artefacts found on the beaches and in the water by surfers. Run by volunteers, it is open most afternoons, but call to confirm.

**Liliuokalani Protestant Church** (☎ 637-9364; 66-090 Kamehameha Hwy) takes its name from Queen Liliuokalani, who spent summers on the shores of the Anahulu River and attended services here. Although the church dates from 1832, the current building was built in 1961. As late as the 1940s, services were held entirely in Hawaiian. Of most interest is the church's unique seven-dial clock that was donated by Queen Liliuokalani in 1892. It shows the hour, day, month and year, as well as the phases of the moon, with the queen's 12-letter name replacing the numerals on the clock face. The church is open whenever the caretaker is in, which is typically in the morning.

And of course there's surfing and other water activities. At the southern end of town, **Deep Ecology** (☎ 637-7946; 66-456 Kamehameha Hwy) has a full range of gear ($1 beach mats etc) and clothes. But it's most notable as the headquarters for the Center for Turtle Rescue, which does just that. Staff can provide a lot of information and have tales to tell about turtles and the local ecology. They are also able to organize whale – watching tours and scuba and surfing classes.

If you arrive without gear, **Surf-N-Sea** (☎ 637-9887; 62-595 Kamehameha Hwy), north of the Rainbow Bridge, rents boogie boards, surfboards, windsurfing equipment, kayaks, clothes, diving gear and snorkel sets. It also sells new and used surfboards and sailboards. It has a mileage marker out front that notes that Australia and New York are 5075 and 4958 miles away respectively.

## Kaiaka Bay Beach Park
The 53-acre Kaiaka Bay Beach Park is on Kaiaka Bay, about a mile west of town. With its shady ironwood trees, the park is a nice place for a picnic, but the in-town beaches are better choices for swimming. Two streams empty into Kaiaka Bay, leaving the beach muddy after heavy rainstorms. Kaiaka has rest rooms, picnic tables, showers, drinking water and camp sites.

## Haleiwa Alii Beach Park
Surfing is king at Haleiwa Alii Beach Park. This attractive park with its generous white-sand beach is the site of several surfing

tournaments in the winter, when north swells can bring waves as high as 20ft.

When waves are less than 5ft, lots of young kids bring out their boards. Any time the waves are 6ft or better there are strong currents and conditions are more suited to experienced surfers. In winter, the county's **Haleiwa Surf Center** (☎ 637-5051; *Haleiwa Alii Beach Park, Haleiwa*) gives free surfing lessons here on weekend mornings; see the Activities chapter for more details.

The 20-acre beach park has rest rooms, showers, picnic tables and lifeguards. The shallow areas on the southern side of the beach are generally the calmest places to swim.

The park's knotty-pine beachfront community building may look familiar. It served

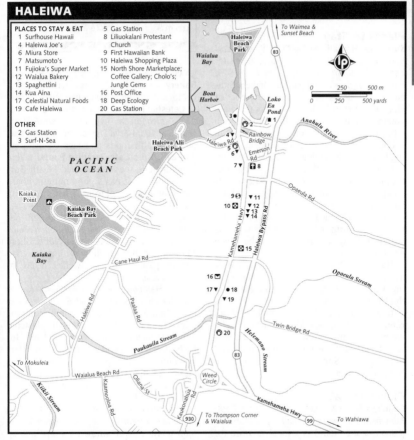

as the lifeguard headquarters in the TV show *Baywatch Hawaii*, which used this beach park as its main setting when the show was filmed in Hawaii from 1999 to its demise in 2001.

## Haleiwa Beach Park

Haleiwa Beach Park is on the northern side of Waialua Bay. The beach is protected by a shallow shoal and a breakwater, so the water is usually very calm, making it a good choice for swimming. There's little wave action, except for the occasional north swells that ripple into the bay.

Although the beach isn't Haleiwa's most appealing, this 13-acre county park has a complete range of beach facilities, as well as basketball and volleyball courts, an exercise area and a softball field. It also offers a good view of Kaena Point.

## Places to Stay

**Surfhouse Hawaii** (☎ 637-7146; ⓦ www.surf house.com; 62-203 Lokoea Place; tent sites per single/double $9/15, dorm beds $15, bungalow $45) is a backpacker's haven. Situated on 2 acres at the northern end of Haleiwa, Surfhouse Hawaii offers three accommodation options: eight tent sites in a citrus grove; a simple dorm-style cabin with six beds; and a private bungalow overlooking its own little garden. All guests have access to kitchen facilities. Sofie, who runs the place, speaks French. Some water-sports equipment is available for rent; if you don't have a tent, that can be arranged for a small fee as well. The location, on a side road immediately north of Rainbow Bridge, is within walking distance of both the beach and town center.

Haleiwa's other camping option is at Kaiaka Bay Beach Park. For details on obtaining a permit, see Camping in the Facts for the Visitor chapter.

In addition, people occasionally rent out rooms in their homes. You can often find a couple of room-for-rent notices on the bulletin boards at Celestial Natural Foods and the Haleiwa Super Market in Haleiwa Shopping Plaza.

## Places to Eat

**Fujioka's Super Market** (☎ 637-4520; 66-190 Kamehameha Hwy; open 8am-8pm Mon-Sat, 8:30am-5:30pm Sun) is a local favorite for

### Sweet Treat

For many people, the circle-island drive isn't complete without lining up for shave ice at **Matsumoto's** (66-087 Kamehameha Hwy) tin-roofed general store.

Hawaiian shave ice is totally drenched with industrial-strength sweet syrup like the snow cones found on the US mainland, but it's much better, because the ice is shaved finer. It costs about $1.20 for a small, plain shave ice and $2 for a fancy large one with ice cream and sweetened adzuki beans. The entire concoction begins dripping into a sticky mess the second you get yours, so don't dawdle.

Although most tourists flock to Matsumoto's, many locals actually prefer the lesser-known **Miura Store**, (66-057 Kamehameha Hwy) another unassuming spot just up the road. Shave ice topped with coconut cream is a favorite choice at Miura's.

groceries. Across the parking lot, **Waialua Bakery** (☎ 637-9079) has fresh breads, cookies, sandwiches and smoothies.

**Celestial Natural Foods** (☎ 637-6729; 66-443 Kamehameha Hwy; open 9am-6:30pm Mon-Sat, 10am-6pm Sun) carries a good variety of health foods and has a vegetarian deli called the **Cafe Paradise Found** where items include the aptly named Bomb Burrito for $7.95. It has a good bulletin board out front if you want to see what's going on locally.

**Coffee Gallery** (☎ 637-5571; 66-250 Kamehameha Hwy; snacks $2-6; open 8am-8:30pm daily), located in the North Shore Marketplace, has a mellow setting and good coffees, pastries and sandwiches. It has Internet access as well.

**Cafe Haleiwa** (☎ 637-5516; 66-460 Kamehameha Hwy; breakfast $3-6, lunch $5-8; open 7am-2pm daily) is an unpretentious joint with formica tables and walls plastered with surf memorabilia. A popular haunt for both local surfers and day-trippers, it offers good food at cheap prices. A great breakfast choice is the hearty blueberry pancakes ($3.50). Lunch is predominantly sandwiches and Mexican fare.

**Kua Aina** (☎ 637-6067; 66-214 Kamehameha Hwy; sandwiches $4-7; open 11am-8pm daily) is well known for grilling up the North Shore's best burgers and fish sandwiches.

**Spaghettini** *(☎ 637-0104, 66-200 Kamehameha Hwy; medium pizzas $10; open 11am-8pm daily)* is popular for its long list of pizzas. Many locals grab a slice and eat it on the little porch outside.

**Cholo's** *(☎ 637-3059; 66-250 Kamehameha Hwy; combination plates $8-11; open 8am-9pm daily)*, also in the North Shore Marketplace, serves good Mexican food. A great choice is the fresh ahi taco, which costs $4 or $7 with rice and beans. All the usual Mexican standards are available as well.

**Haleiwa Joe's** *(☎ 637-8005; 66-001 Kamehameha Hwy; appetizers $5-10, lunch $8-15, dinner $14-20; open 11:30am-9:30pm daily)* has superb food and a pleasant seaside setting. You can't go wrong ordering the fish, which literally comes right off the boats in the adjacent harbor. Favorites include sashimi, blackened ahi and crunchy coconut shrimp. It also serves chicken and steak dishes. Hands down, it's the best upmarket restaurant on the North Shore.

## Shopping
Haleiwa boasts myriad little shops run by local crafts people and artists. One example is **Jungle Gems** *(☎ 637-6609, 66-250 Kamehameha Hwy)* in the North Shore Marketplace, which has jewelry made onsite from gemstones and crystals.

## WAIALUA
### pop 3750
Waialua, a small former plantation town a mile southwest of Haleiwa, is centered around the dusty Waialua Sugar Mill. The mill shut down in 1996, bringing an end to the last commercial sugar operation on Oahu.

Although the Waialua area remains economically depressed, with many of the surrounding fields overgrown with feral sugarcane, other sections are newly planted with coffee trees – a labor-intensive crop that holds out promise for new jobs. You can see the coffee trees, planted in neat rows, as you come down the slopes into Waialua.

The old **Waialua Sugar Mill**, which now serves as the coffee operation's headquarters, is chock full of racks where the coffee beans are sorted and dried. You can poke around the place a bit, but there's not much to see, as the visitors center has closed.

As for other sights, this sleepy town has a handful of period buildings, the most interesting being the local watering hole, the **Sugar Bar**, which occupies the old Bank of Hawaii building down by the mill.

## MOKULEIA
### pop 1850
The Farrington Hwy (Hwy 930) runs west from Thompson Corner to Dillingham Airfield and Mokuleia Beach. (Both this road and the road along the Leeward Coast are called Farrington Hwy, but they don't connect, as each side reaches a dead end about 2½ miles short of Kaena Point.)

Mokuleia Beach is a 6-mile stretch of white sand running from Kaiaka Bay toward Kaena Point. Although some GIs and locals come this way, the beaches don't draw much of a crowd and the area has feels a bit like the boondocks. This is certainly not a prime tourist area – there's little traffic and no bus service, and the only beach facilities are at Mokuleia Beach Park.

**Dillingham Airfield** is a take-off site for glider rides and skydiving. For details, see the Activities chapter.

---

### Surfspeak

Hit the waves in Hawaii, and you're likely to hear some of these terms:

**brah** – friend, surfing buddy
**da kine** – a great wave, top quality
**goofy-footing** – surfing with the right foot forward
**kaha** – traditional Hawaiian term for board surfing
**kaha nalu** – body surfing
**keiki waves** – small, gentle waves suitable for kids
**macker** – huge wave, one big enough to drive a Mack truck through
**malihini** – newcomer, tenderfoot
**pau** – quitting time
**Pipe** – also Pipeline, referring to the Banzai Pipeline
**snake** – steal; as in 'that dude's snaking my wave'
**stick** – local slang for a surfboard
**wahine** – female surfer
**wipeout** – get knocked down by a big wave

---

## Mokuleia Beach Park

Mokuleia Beach Park, opposite Dillingham Airfield, has a large, open grassy area with picnic tables, rest rooms and showers. Camping is allowed with a county permit (see Camping in the Facts for the Visitor chapter).

Mokuleia is sandy, but it has a lava shelf along much of its shoreline. It has fairly consistent winds, making it a popular spot with windsurfers, particularly in spring and fall. In the winter there are dangerous currents.

## Mokuleia Army Beach

Mokuleia Army Beach, opposite the western end of Dillingham Airfield, is the widest stretch of sand on the Mokuleia shore. Once reserved exclusively for military personnel, the beach is now open to the public, but the army no longer maintains it, and there are no beach facilities.

The beach is unprotected, and there are very strong rip currents, especially during winter high surf. Locals sometimes surf here in the winter, but water conditions can be dangerous, and this beach has had a number of fatalities over the years.

## Army Beach to Kaena Point

From Army Beach, you can drive another 1½ miles down the road, passing still more white-sand beaches with aquamarine water. The paved road goes past **Camp Erdman**, a facility run by the YMCA, and then ends at a locked gate.

The terrain is scrubland reaching up to the base of the Waianae Range, and the shoreline is wild and windswept. The area is not only desolate, but can also be a bit trashed, and this is certainly not a must-do drive.

From the road's end, it is possible to walk 2½ miles to Kaena Point, but it is a more attractive walk from the other side of the point (for details, see Kaena Point State Park in the Leeward Coast chapter).

# Central Oahu

Central Oahu forms a saddle between the Waianae Range on the west and the Koolau Range on the east.

Three routes lead north from Honolulu to Wahiawa, the town smack in the middle of Oahu. The freeway, H2, is the fastest route. Hwy 750, the farthest west, is the most scenic. The least interesting option is Hwy 99 (Kamehameha Hwy), which catches local traffic as it runs through Mililani, a nondescript residential community.

Most people just zoom up through central Oahu on their way to the North Shore. If your time is limited, this isn't a bad idea. There are a few sights along the way, but Wahiawa, the region's commercial center, doesn't really warrant much more than a quick visit anyway.

From Wahiawa two routes, Hwy 803 (Kaukonahua Rd) and Hwy 99, lead through pineapple country to the North Shore. Hwy 803 is a slightly shorter route to Mokuleia, and both routes are about the same distance to Haleiwa. The two roads are equally picturesque, and if you're not circling the island, you might as well go up one and down the other.

## VIA HIGHWAY 750

Highway 750 (Kunia Rd) adds a few miles to the drive through Central Oahu, but if you have the time it's worth it. Follow H1 to the Kunia/Hwy 750 exit, 3 miles west of where H1 and H2 divide.

As you drive up Hwy 750, the first mile takes you through creeping suburbia, but then you enter plantation lands. The road runs along the foothills of the Waianae Range and the countryside is solidly agricultural all the way to Schofield Barracks Military Reservation.

Two miles into the drive, you'll come to a strip of cornfields planted by the Garst Seed Company. Three generations of corn are grown here each year, making it possible to develop hybrids of corn seed at triple the rate it takes on the mainland. Incidentally, the little bags covering each ear of corn are there to prevent cross-pollination.

One of the prettiest pineapple fields in Hawaii is a bit farther north. It's a landscape without buildings or development – just red

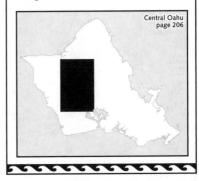

Central Oahu
page 206

earth carpeted with long, green strips of pineapples stretching to the edge of the mountains.

From the Hawaii Country Club, just up the highway on the right, there's a distant view of Honolulu all the way to Diamond Head.

### Kunia

Kunia, a little town in the midst of the pineapple fields, is home to the field-workers employed by Del Monte. If you want a look at a current-day plantation village, turn west off Hwy 750 onto Kunia Dr, which makes a 1¼-mile loop through town.

Rows of gray-green wooden houses with corrugated tin roofs stand on low stilts. Residents take pride in their little yards, with bougainvillea and other colorful flowers adding a splash of brightness despite the wash of red dust that blows in from the surrounding pineapple fields.

Kunia Dr intersects Hwy 750 at around 5½ miles north of the intersection of Hwy 750 and H1 (there's a store and post office near the turnoff) and again at the 6-mile marker.

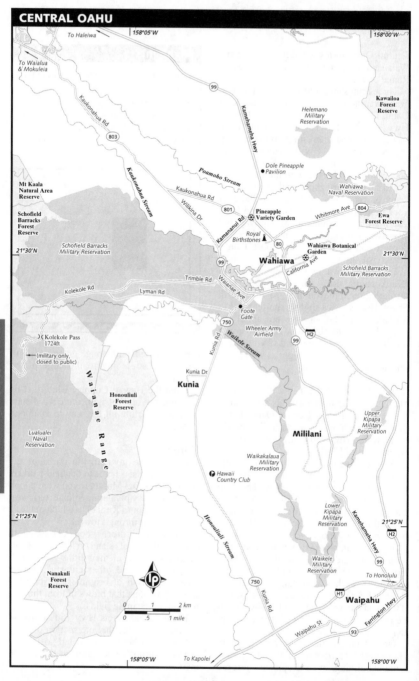

# CENTRAL OAHU

158°05'W · 158°00'W

To Haleiwa

To Waialua & Mokuleia

Kaukonahua Rd

99

Kamehameha Hwy

803

Kaukonahua Stream

Helemano Military Reservation

Kawailoa Forest Reserve

Poamoho Stream

Dole Pineapple Pavilion

Mt Kaala Natural Area Reserve

Kaukonahua Rd

Wilikina Dr

801

Wahiawa Naval Reservation

Schofield Barracks Forest Reserve

Kamananui Rd

Pineapple Variety Garden

Whitmore Ave

804

Ewa Forest Reserve

21°30'N

Schofield Barracks Military Reservation

Royal Birthstones

80

Wahiawa Botanical Garden

99

Wahiawa

California Ave

Schofield Barracks Military Reservation

21°30'N

Trimble Rd

Waianae Ave

Kolekole Rd

Lyman Rd

750

Foote Gate

Wheeler Army Airfield

H2

Kolekole Pass 1724ft

(military only, closed to public)

Kunia Rd

Waikele Stream

99

Kunia Dr

Kunia

Honouliuli Forest Reserve

Mililani

Upper Kipapa Military Reservation

W a i a n a e   R a n g e

Lualualei Naval Reservation

Waikakalaua Military Reservation

Hawaii Country Club

21°25'N

Honouliuli Stream

Lower Kipapa Military Reservation

Kamehameha Hwy

21°25'N

H2

Nanakuli Forest Reserve

Waikele Military Reservation

99

To Honolulu

LP

0   1   2 km
0   .5   1 mile

750

Kunia Rd

H1

Waipahu

Farrington Hwy

Waipahu St

93

158°05'W

To Kapolei

158°00'W

## WAHIAWA

pop 16,150

Wahiawa, whose name means 'place of noise' in Hawaiian, is a GI town, sitting on the edge of Schofield Barracks, Hawaii's largest army base. Just about every fast-food chain you can think of is found in Wahaiwa's center. Tattoo parlors and pawnshops are the town's main refinements, and if you're looking for a little excitement, there are some rough-and-tumble bars.

Despite its current drab commercial center, Wahiawa once played a significant role in Oahu's history. Just north of town is the site where women of royalty went to give birth in precontact times. Back then, vast stretches of this upland region, including the site of the present botanical garden, were thick with sandalwood trees. Unfortunately, foreign traders had a penchant for the fragrant wood, and soon after the arrival of the first merchant ships, the native sandalwood forests were depleted. Today, most of the former forested plains are planted with endless rows of pineapple, although subdivisions are making inroads into the bright orange dirt.

To go through town and visit the botanical garden, healing stones and royal birthstones, take Kamehameha Hwy (which is Hwy 80 as it goes through town, although it's Hwy 99 before and after Wahiawa). To make the bypass around Wahiawa, stick with Hwy 99.

### Kolekole Pass

Kolekole is the gap in the Waianae Range that Japanese fighter planes flew through on their way to bomb Pearl Harbor. Film buffs may recognize the landscape, as the historic flight was re-created here 30 years later for the classic war film *Tora! Tora! Tora!*

Kolekole Pass, at an elevation of 1724ft, sits on military property above Schofield Barracks. It can be visited as long as the base isn't on some sort of military alert.

Access the pass through Foote Gate, on Hwy 750, a third of a mile south of the highway's intersection with Hwy 99. After passing through the gate, take the first left onto Road A, then the first right onto Lyman Rd. The pass is 5¼ miles up past the barracks, golf course and bayonet assault course. The parking lot is opposite the hilltop with the big white cross that's visible from miles away.

A five-minute walk to the top of the pass ends at a clearing with a view straight down to the Waianae Coast. The large, ribbed stone sitting atop the ridge here is said to have been a woman named Kolekole. According to Hawaiian legend, she took the form of this stone in order to become the perpetual guardian of the pass.

Note the series of ridges on the stone's side. One drains down from the bowl-like depression on the top. Shaped perfectly for a guillotine, the depression has given rise to a more recent 'legend' that Kolekole served as a sacrificial stone for the beheading of defeated warriors. The fact that military bases flank the pass has no doubt had a little influence on forming this tale.

Just west of the pass the road continues through the Lualualei Naval Reservation down to the Waianae Coast, but you can't take it. The reservation is a storage site for nuclear weapons, and there's no public access through that side.

### Wahiawa Botanical Garden

This botanical garden (☎ 621-7321; 1396 California Ave; admission free; open 9am-4pm daily) is a mile east of Kamehameha Hwy (Hwy 80). What started out in the 1920s as a site for forestry experiments by the Hawaii Sugar Planters' Association is now a 27-acre city park with shady paths, grand old trees and a wooded ravine.

### Juicy Tidbits

- In 1901 James Dole planted Oahu's first pineapple patch in Wahiawa.
- Dole's original 12-acre Wahiawa plot has since grown to 8000 acres.
- Each acre of a pineapple field supports about 6500 plants.
- It takes nearly two years for a pineapple plant to reach maturity.
- Each plant produces just two pineapples, one in its second year and one in its third year.
- Pineapples are harvested year-round, but the long, sunny days of summer produce the sweetest fruit.
- The average pineapple weighs 5lbs.
- Pineapples are unique among fruits in that they don't continue to ripen after they're picked.

CENTRAL OAHU

If you're venturing out of the concrete of Waikiki for the first time, this is a great place to stop and immerse yourself in a tropical forest.

Interesting 80-year-old exotics such as cinnamon, chicle and allspice are grouped in one area. Loulu palms (fan palms), ginger and other Hawaiian natives are in other sections. The trees are identified by markers, and the air is thick with birdsong.

Note the tree ferns at the left side of the visitor center. These are *hapuu*, a huge fern that reaches heights of 20ft and forms the understory of Hawaii's wetter forest areas. The silky 'wool' at the base of the fronds was used in ancient Hawaii as a surgical dressing, and until the late 19th century it was harvested commercially as a filling for mattresses.

For a description of other plants found here, pick up the free garden brochure at the visitor center.

## Healing Stones

Among the odder sights to be labeled with a visitors bureau marker are the 'Healing Stones' that are caged inside a small marble 'temple' next to the Methodist church on California Ave, half a mile west of its intersection with Kamehameha Hwy.

The main stone is thought to be the gravestone of a powerful Hawaiian chief. Although the chief's original burial place is in a field a mile away, the stone was moved long ago to a graveyard at this site. In the 1920s people thought the stone had healing powers, and thousands made pilgrimages to it before interest waned. The housing development and church came later, taking over the graveyard and leaving the stones sitting on the sidewalk.

A local group with roots in India, which sees a spiritual connection between Hawaiian and Indian beliefs, now visits the temple, so you may see flowers or little elephant statues placed around the stones. The story of the healing stones is actually more interesting than the sight, however.

## Royal Birthstones

Kukaniloko, just north of Wahiawa, is a collection of royal birthstones where Hawaii's queens gave birth. The stones are thought to date back to the 12th century. Legend held that if a woman lay properly against the stones while giving birth, her child would be blessed by the gods, and indeed, many of Oahu's great chiefs were born at this site.

These stones are at one of only two documented birthstone sites in Hawaii (the other is on Kauai). Many of the petroglyphs on the stones are of recent origin, but the eroded circular patterns are original.

To get to the site from town, go three-quarters of a mile north on Kamehameha Hwy (Hwy 80) from its intersection with California Ave. Turn left onto the red dirt road directly opposite Whitmore Ave. The stones, marked with a state monument sign, are a quarter of a mile down the road, through a pineapple field, among a stand of eucalyptus and coconut trees. If it's been raining, be aware that the red clay can cake onto car tires, and once back on the paved road, the car may slide as if you're driving on ice.

## Pineapple Variety Garden

Del Monte maintains a historic pineapple demonstration garden in a triangle at the junction of Hwys 99, 80 and 801. A broad range of plants bearing the spiky fruit is gathered here from around the world.

Smooth cayenne, the commercial variety of pineapple grown in Hawaii, is shown in various growth stages. Other commercial varieties of pineapple grown in Australia, the Philippines and South America are on display, as are some varieties of purely decorative bromeliads (pineapples are in the *Bromeliaceae* family). The range of sizes, shapes and colors is fun; note the stiff-leaved *'Erectifolius Amazon'*, which comes from Brazil. Also look for the nifty mutant varieties that feature multiple heads.

You can pull off to the side of the road and walk through the garden on your own at any time.

## Dole Pineapple Pavilion

This popular pineapple pavilion (☎ 621-8408; 64-1550 Kamehameha Hwy (Hwy 99); admission free; open 9am-5:30pm daily) is on Hwy 99, less than a mile north of its intersection with Hwy 80. This touristy complex in the heart of Oahu's pineapple country consists of a bustling gift shop, ornate gardens, a tram and an expansive hibiscus hedge maze. Dole's processing plant sits across the street, and miles of pineapple fields surround the area.

Monument to Kamehameha the Great, Aliiolani Hale, Honolulu

Kuan Yin Temple offerings, Honolulu

Image of Ku, Bishop Museum, Honolulu

USS *Arizona* Memorial, Pearl Harbor

Diamond Head lookout

Sea kayaking off Lanikai, Windward Coast

Antler coral tree, white spot damsels and diver

Hikers, Manoa Falls Trail

The gift shop sells pineapple in many forms – juice, freezes, pastries and pineapples boxed to take home. But the real fun occurs outdoors in the gardens and the maze.

If you feel like getting lost, you can wander through the **'world's largest maze'** *(adult/child $5/3)*, a claim confirmed by the *Guinness Book of Records* (and sorry, there's no helpful Lonely Planet map for this one, so you're on your own). The maze covers nearly 2 acres and contains 1.7 miles of pathways. The goal is to find six different stations and things get quite challenging as there's no cheese (or pineapple) waiting at the end of the correct path to lure you. Most people take 15 to 30 minutes to get through.

## Places to Eat

You'll find a thick run of generic fast-food chains on Kamehameha Hwy, the main drag in downtown Wahiawa, and some better island-style choices – Sushiman and Wok & Grill Express – on California Avenue at the Wahiawa Shopping Center.

## Getting There & Away

To go through town and visit the botanical garden, healing stones and royal birthstones, take Kamehameha Hwy (which is Hwy 80 as it goes through town, although it's Hwy 99 before and after Wahiawa). To make the bypass around Wahiawa, stick with Hwy 99.

Although exploring many of Central Oahu's sights is only practical for those with their own transportation, you can get from Honolulu to Wahiawa (and onward to Haleiwa) via bus No 52. It runs from the Ala Moana Center in Honolulu twice an hour from 6:30am to 6:15pm and then once again at 7:15pm and 8:15pm, stopping at Wahiawa (1¼ hours) en route. Wahiawa can also be reached via bus No 62, which leaves the Ala Moana Center about once every 30 minutes, which takes approximately 1½ hours and stops by the botanical garden.

# Leeward Oahu

Leeward Oahu, the western side of the island, encompasses some curious extremes: the Ewa area, the most rapidly growing district on Oahu, and the Waianae Coast, a sleepy area that is resistant to change and wary of outsiders.

## Ewa Area

The Ewa area, at the southwestern tip of Oahu, is a district in transition. Not only does it contain boomtown Kapolei, the state's fastest growing community, but it's home to the former Barbers Point Naval Air Station, which was demilitarized in 1999 and is now being converted for civilian use.

In Waipahu, the Hawaii's Plantation Village complex preserves important remnants of the sugar plantation era. Ewa, the village southwest of Waipahu, also has its roots in sugar, and its main attraction – the restored Hawaiian Railway – takes visitors back in time with antique trains.

The area's other attractions are designed around water – the splashy thrills of the Hawaiian Waters Adventure Park and the quiet beaches at Ko Olina Resort.

Other beaches in this area are mostly used by local residents and military personnel. The best of the lot is Ewa Beach, a decent span of white sand, of which 5 acres is a county beach park and the rest set aside for the military. Oneula Beach and Nimitz Beach are predominantly rocky, with marginal swimming conditions, while Barbers Point Beach, just south of the industrial park, is outright unappealing.

### HAWAII'S PLANTATION VILLAGE

This plantation village (☎ 677-0110; 94-695 *Waipahu St, Waipahu; adult/senior or child 7-12 yrs $7/4; guided tours on the hour 9am-3pm Mon-Fri, 10am-3pm Sat)* will reward visitors with insights into Hawaii's multiethnic heritage.

The site has 30 homes and buildings set up to re-create a typical plantation village of the early 20th century. The houses are furnished with period pieces illustrating the lifestyles of the eight different ethnic groups – Hawaiian, Japanese, Okinawan, Chinese, Korean,

## Highlights

• Hitting the beach at Makaha, where surfing is awesome in the winter and diving is great in the summer

• Visiting Kaneaki Heiau, the most authentically restored Hawaiian temple on Oahu

• Hiking the coastal Kaena Point Trail, around the westernmost tip of Oahu

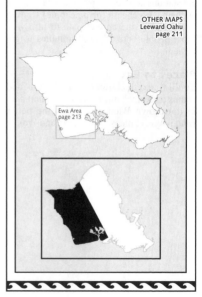

OTHER MAPS
Leeward Oahu
page 211

Ewa Area
page 213

Portuguese, Puerto Rican and Filipino – that worked the sugar plantations. The Chinese cookhouse (circa 1909) was originally on this site, and the Japanese shrine (1914) was moved here; the other structures are replicas authentic to the time period.

The setting is particularly evocative, as Waipahu was one of Oahu's last plantation towns, and its rusty sugar mill, which operated until 1995, still looms on a knoll directly above this site. While you're waiting for the tour to begin, you can stroll through the small museum off the lobby. All in all, it's a quality, community-based production.

To get there by car, take the H1 to exit 7, turn left onto Paiwa St, then right onto Waipahu St, continue past the sugar mill

LEEWARD OAHU

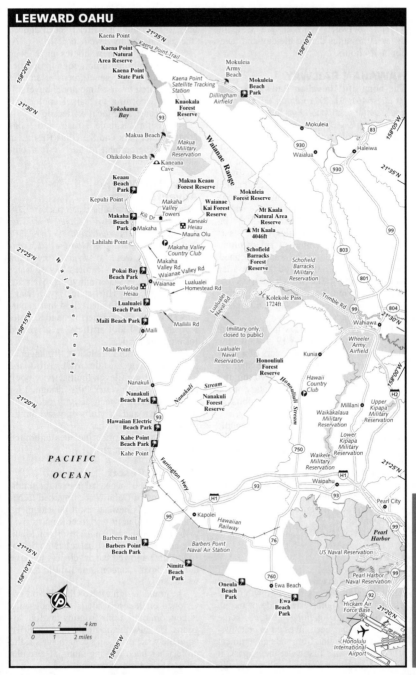

# LEEWARD OAHU

21°35'N
Kaena Point
Kaena Point Natural Area Reserve
Kaena Point Trail
Kaena Point State Park
Kaena Point Satellite Tracking Station
Mokuleia Army Beach
Mokuleia Beach Park
Dillingham Airfield
Kuaokala Forest Reserve
158°01'W
21°30'N
*Yokohama Bay*
(93)
Makua Beach
*Makua Military Reservation*
Ohikilolo Beach
Kaneana Cave
Keaau Beach Park
Makua Keaau Forest Reserve
Kepuhi Point
*Makaha Valley Towers*
*Waianae Range*
Waianae Kai Forest Reserve
Mokuleia Forest Reserve
Mt Kaala Natural Area Reserve
Makaha Beach Park
*Kili Dr*
Makaha
Kaneaki Heiau
Mauna Olu
▲ Mt Kaala 4046ft
Lahilahi Point
Makaha Valley Country Club
Schofield Barracks Forest Reserve
*Schofield Barracks Military Reservation*
Pokai Bay Beach Park
Makaha Valley Rd
Waianae Valley Rd
*Kuilioloa Heiau*
Waianae
Lualualei Homestead Rd
Lualualei Beach Park
Maili Beach Park
Mailiilii Rd
*Maili*
Lualualei Naval Rd
Kolekole Pass 1724ft
Trimble Rd
(military only, closed to public)
Maili Point
*Lualualei Naval Reservation*
Honouliuli Forest Reserve
*Honouliuli Stream*
Nanakuli
*Nanakuli Stream*
Nanakuli Forest Reserve
Nanakuli Beach Park
(93)
Hawaiian Electric Beach Park
Kahe Point Beach Park
Kahe Point
Hawaii Country Club
Kunia
Mililani
Upper Kipapa Military Reservation
*Waikakalaua Military Reservation*
Lower Kipapa Military Reservation
Waikele Military Reservation
(750)
PACIFIC OCEAN
Farrington Hwy
(93)
Waipahu
(H1)
(93)
Pearl City
Barbers Point
Barbers Point Beach Park
*Barbers Point Naval Air Station*
Nimitz Beach Park
Oneula Beach Park
Ewa Beach
Ewa Beach Park
(760)
(95)
Kapolei
Hawaiian Railway
(76)
(H1)
*US Naval Reservation*
*Pearl Harbor*
*Pearl Harbor Naval Reservation*
Hickam Air Force Base
(92)
Honolulu International Airport
(99)

*Waianae Coast*

Mokuleia
(930)
Waialua
Haleiwa
(83)
(930)
21°35'N
99
803
801
804
Wahiawa
21°30'N
158°00'W
H2
Wheeler Army Airfield
21°25'N
21°20'N

158°15'W
158°10'W
158°05'W
21°25'N
21°20'N

0   2   4 km
0   1   2 miles

and turn left into the complex. By bus, No 42 runs between Waikiki and Waipahu every 30 minutes during the day and takes about 1¾ hours.

## HAWAIIAN RAILWAY

The nonprofit **Hawaiian Railway Society** (☎ 681-5461; 91-1001 Renton Rd, Ewa; fare adult/senior or child 2-12 yrs $8/5; train rides at 12:30pm & 2:30pm Sun only) offers train rides along 6½ miles of restored railroad track that once belonged to the Oahu Railway & Land Company (OR&L). If you're a railroad buff, you won't want to miss it.

From 1890 until 1947, the OR&L carried sugarcane and passengers along its narrow-gauge tracks, from Honolulu all the way to Kahuku on the North Shore. With the increasing use of automobiles in the years after WWII, the number of riders plummeted and the rail service was abandoned. But thanks to the efforts of the Hawaiian Railway Society, the stretch of track between Ewa and Nanakuli has been preserved and is now on the National Register of Historic Places.

The society offers rides to the general public on Sundays only. A 1944 Whitcomb diesel locomotive pulls four cars of a similar vintage, one of which is wheelchair accessible. Each ride takes about 90 minutes roundtrip and includes a commentary on the railway's history, spiced with tidbits of local interest.

In addition to the ride, there are a couple of stationary locomotives on display in the yard, including the coal engine that pulled the first OR&L train in 1889.

To get there, take exit 5A off the H1, drive south 2½ miles on Fort Weaver Rd and then turn right at the 7-Eleven store onto Renton Rd. By bus, you can get there from Waikiki via No 42, which operates about twice an hour.

## KAPOLEI

**pop 75,000**

Kapolei is a planned community that was created to shift Oahu's future growth to the less-developed southwestern side of the island. Since first 'opening' in 1992, some $600 million has been invested in construction projects, ranging from state government offices to Hawaii's first water theme park. It is envisioned that Kapolei will eventually grow into an urban center that will be second only to Honolulu; it's already been dubbed 'the second city' by developers.

So far, 25,000 new homes have been built, ranging from million-dollar properties overlooking golf course greens to smaller houses geared to first-time home buyers. If all goes according to plan, Kapolei will double in size over the next decade.

For visitors, Kapolei's main attractions are the water park and Ko Olina Resort, an upscale development at the western outskirts of the city.

## Hawaiian Waters Adventure Park

This multimillion-dollar water park (☎ 674-9283; 400 Farrington Hwy, Kapolei; ⓦ www.hawaiianwaters.com; adult/child 4-11 yrs $30/20; open 10:30am-4pm Mon-Fri, 10:30am-5pm Sat & Sun, closed Wed winter), covering more than 25 acres, features lots of water slides and other water activities. Main attractions include Hurricane Bay, a wave pool the size of a football field that generates 3ft waves for bodysurfing; and Kapolei Kooler, an 800-foot artificial river geared for inner-tube rides.

Other attractions include Cliffhanger, a seven-story speed slide; Waterworld, the 20,000-sq-ft multilevel, multiactivity pool; Keiki Kove, with water slides designed for young children; a teen activity pool with rope ladders; and an adults-only swimming pool with a swim-up bar.

The admission price includes unlimited access to all attractions.

## Ko Olina Resort

In the late 1980s, a coastal tract at the southwestern end of Oahu was earmarked to become Hawaii's newest resort development. Named Ko Olina, it was to be Oahu's rival to the Kaanapali and Wailea resorts on Maui. The only problem was, that it had no beach, so the state allowed the developers to carve out four lovely lagoons and haul in tons of white sand.

The grand design for Ko Olina Resort envisioned eight resort hotels and thousands of condominium units fronting the four lagoons. Because the original financing dried up in the wake of Japan's banking crisis, the project has been moving along at a snail's pace. At the time of writing, one hotel and about 200 condominiums were completed, along with a golf course and a 270-slip yacht marina. The development plan is now focused on building upmarket housing.

The four artificial lagoons at Ko Olina Resort have white-sand beaches that are open to the public. The largest lagoon, more than 200m across, borders the JW Marriott Ihilani Resort & Spa; the other three are about half that size. The lagoons are constructed with small islets at their mouths, a design that creates channels for water circulation. Swimmers should be aware of the seaward currents going out through the middle channels; signs posted at each lagoon detail water safety issues.

If you are up for a walk, there is a shoreline path that connects the four lagoons. Each lagoon has rest rooms and parking spaces for about 20 cars.

## Places to Stay & Eat

**JW Marriott Ihilani Resort & Spa** *(☎ 679-0079, 800-626-4446, fax 679-0080; ☎ www .marriotthotels.com; 92-1001 Olani St; rooms $339, with ocean view $415)* is a luxury resort hotel with extensive spa facilities. The 387 rooms are equipped with lanais, deep soaking tubs, large-screen TVs, minibars and pampering touches such as Japanese-style *yukata* robes and slippers. The grounds include six tennis courts, a championship golf course and a spa that specializes in Thalasso therapy, which utilizes warmed seawater. Packages that include spa treatments and golf are available.

The more affordable of the resort's eateries are the **Poolside Grill** *(☎ 679-0079; snacks from $10; open 7am-10pm daily)*, which serves salads, burgers and sandwiches, and **Niblick** *(☎ 676-6703; open 8:30am-7pm daily)*, which overlooks the golf course and offers similar fare at similar prices.

Outside the resort, the **Kapolei Shopping Center** *(Farrington Hwy)*, has a bevy of fast-food establishments and a supermarket.

## Getting There & Away

Kapolei is near the western terminus of the H1. To get to the Kapolei Shopping Center by car, take exit 2 off H1; to get to Hawaiian Waters Adventure Park, take exit 1. The road to Ko Olina Resort is off the southern side of

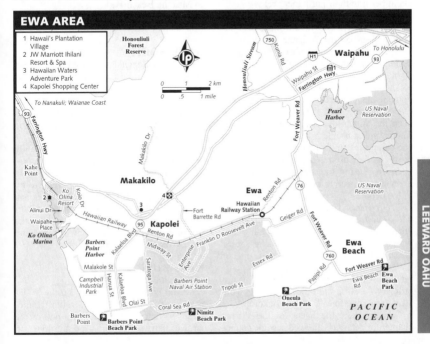

EWA AREA

1 Hawaii's Plantation Village
2 JW Marriott Ihilani Resort & Spa
3 Hawaiian Waters Adventure Park
4 Kapolei Shopping Center

LEEWARD OAHU

the Farrington Hwy (Hwy 93). Bus Nos 40 and 40A, which connect Honolulu with Leeward Oahu, make stops in Kapolei at both Hawaiian Waters Adventure Park and the shopping center. The bus ride to Kapolei takes about 1¼ hours from Ala Moana Center in Honolulu. Buses run an average of every 30 minutes from 5:30am to 7pm, and then about once an hour until midnight.

There's no bus into the Ko Olina Resort – the bus stops along the Farrington Hwy, and from there it's a mile walk to the nearest beach.

# Waianae Coast

In 1793, English captain George Vancouver was the first Westerner to drop anchor on the Waianae Coast. He found a barren wasteland with only a few scattered fishing huts. Just two years later, Kamehameha the Great invaded the island, and the population density along the remote Waianae Coast swelled with Oahuans who were forced to flee from their homes elsewhere on the island. This arid, isolated western extreme of Oahu became their permanent refuge.

Today, it still stands separate from the rest of the island. There are no gift shops or sight-seeing buses on the Waianae Coast. When you get right down to it, other than watching surfers at Makaha, there aren't a whole lot of sights to see.

The area has a history of resisting development and a reputation for not being receptive to outsiders. In the past, visitors have been the targets of assaults and muggings. There's still a problem with thefts from cars and camp sites, and although things aren't as hostile as they used to be, some locals aren't keen on sharing their space with tourists. Overall, you need to be attuned to the mood of the people.

The Waianae Coast has long stretches of white-sand beaches, some quite attractive, others a bit trashed. In winter, swimming conditions are treacherous at most beaches, but at the same time, these conditions offer some of the island's more challenging surfing opportunities. Although the towns themselves are ordinary, the cliffs and valleys cutting into the Waianae Range form a lovely backdrop.

Camping (see the Facts for the Visitor chapter for details) is allowed at some county beach parks along the Waianae Coast, but because of safety concerns none of them are recommended for tourists.

## Getting There & Away

This is basically a one-road region. All through traffic, both by car and bus, is along the Farrington Hwy, the coastal road connecting the Waianae Coast's towns and beaches.

Bus Nos 40 and 40A connect Honolulu with the Waianae Coast, stopping in every town as far north as Makaha. If you're going to Makaha Beach Park, bus No 40 is the more direct option, because it stays along the coast. Bus No 40A goes up Makaha Valley Rd to the golf course and the Makaha Valley Towers condominiums and then comes down Kili Dr to the beach.

The two buses, which alternate throughout the day, run the same route before reaching Makaha. From the Ala Moana Center in Honolulu, buses run about every 30 minutes from 5:30am to 7pm, and then about hourly until midnight. Travel time from Honolulu is about 1¾ hours to Nanakuli, two hours to Maili and 2½ hours to Makaha Beach Park.

There is no public bus service beyond Makaha.

## KAHE POINT

**Kahe Point Beach Park**, despite its name, does not have a beach, just the rocky cliffs of Kahe Point. The park has running water, picnic tables and rest rooms, but little else to recommend it. The backdrop is punctuated by the smokestacks of the electric power plant across the way.

**Hawaiian Electric Beach Park**, a sandy beach north of Kahe Point, is more commonly known as Tracks, the name given to it by beachgoers who used to go there by train before WWII. In the summer this is a fairly calm place to swim, and in the winter it's frequented by surfers. To get there, take the first turnoff after the power plant and drive over the abandoned railroad tracks.

## NANAKULI
### pop 10,800

Nanakuli is the biggest town on the Waianae Coast. The site of a Hawaiian Homesteads settlement, Nanakuli has one of the largest native Hawaiian populations on

Oahu. The town has supermarkets, a court-house, a bank and a few fast-food places.

Nanakuli is lined by a broad, sandy beach park. There's swimming, snorkeling and diving during the calmer summer season. In winter, high surf can create rip currents and dangerous shore breaks.

To get to the beach park, turn left at the traffic lights on Nanakuli Ave. This is a community park, with a playground, sports fields, beach facilities and camp sites.

Nanakuli's eateries are along the Farrington Hwy. In the Pacific Shopping Mall, at the southern side of town, you will find several eateries, including **Nanakuli Korean Bar-B-Q**, which does tasty plate lunches.

## MAILI
**pop 5950**
Maili is fronted by **Maili Beach Park**, a long, grassy roadside park with an endless stretch of white-sand beach. Like other places on the Waianae Coast, the water conditions are often treacherous in winter but usually calm enough for swimming in summer. The park has a lifeguard station, a playground, beach facilities and a few castrated coconut palms that provide limited, but safe, shade.

To the north of Maili Beach Park is **Lualualei Beach Park**. Its shoreline is less desirable than Maili Beach and not suitable for swimming; this park is mainly used by local fishers and campers.

## WAIANAE
**pop 10,500**
Waianae is the second largest town on the Waianae Coast. It has a beach park, a protected boat harbor and a satellite city hall.

Protected by both Kaneilio Point and a long breakwater, **Pokai Bay Beach Park** has calm year-round swimming conditions. Waves seldom break inside the bay, and the sandy beach slopes gently, making it a popular spot for families with children.

Snorkeling is fair by the breakwater, where fish gather around the rocks. The bay is also used by local canoe clubs, and you can watch them rowing if you happen by in the late afternoon. There are showers, rest rooms and picnic tables, and a lifeguard is on duty daily.

Kaneilio Point, which runs along the south side of the bay, is the site of **Kuilioloa**

**Heiau**. Partially demolished by the army during WWII, this stone temple has been reconstructed by local conservationists.

To get to the beach park and heiau, turn seaward onto Lualualei Homestead Rd at the traffic light immediately north of the Waianae post office.

For a quick eat, there are numerous fast-food options along the Farrington Hwy. If you prefer cheap – but not chain – you'll find a couple of inexpensive Chinese restaurants in the Waianae Mall Shopping Center, behind Burger King.

## MAKAHA
**pop 7750**
Makaha means 'ferocious,' and in days past the valley was notorious for the bandits who waited along the cliffs to ambush passing travelers. Today, Makaha is best known for its world-class surfing. It has a fine beach, a golf course, a few condominiums and Oahu's best-restored heiau.

### Makaha Beach Park
Makaha Beach is broad, sandy and crescent-shaped, with some of the most daunting winter surf in the islands. Experienced surfers and bodysurfers both take to the waves here.

Over the years Makaha Beach has hosted a number of major surf events. In the early 1950s it was the site of Hawaii's first international surfing competition. Although the biggest surfing events have since shifted to Oahu's North Shore, Makaha Beach is still favored by longboarders. Each March, the beach is the site of the **Buffalo Surf Meet**, with competitors using old-style surfboards called tankers that can reach 15ft in length.

When the surf's not up, Makaha is a popular beach for swimming. When the surf is up, rip currents and a strong shore break make swimming hazardous.

In the summer the slope of the beach is relatively flat, but in winter it has a steeper drop due to the turbulent wave action. The beach sand is slightly coarse and of calcareous origin, with lots of mollusk shell fragments. As much as half of the sand temporarily washes away during winter erosion, but even then Makaha is still an impressive beach.

Snorkeling is good offshore during the calmer summer months. Makaha Caves, out where the waves break farthest offshore, feature underwater caverns, arches and tunnels at depths of 30ft to 50ft. It's a popular leeward diving spot.

The beach has showers and rest rooms, and lifeguards are on duty daily.

## Makaha Valley

For a little loop drive, turn inland from the Farrington Hwy onto Kili Dr, opposite Makaha Beach Park. The road skirts up along scalloped green cliffs into Makaha Valley. If you're in the area around noon, stop to visit Kaneaki Heiau – one of Hawaii's most authentically restored temples.

To get to the heiau, take Kili Dr to the Makaha Valley Towers condominium complex and turn right onto Huipu Dr. A half mile down, make a left onto Mauna Olu St, which leads a mile into Mauna Olu Estates and up to Kaneaki Heiau.

**Kaneaki Heiau** This heiau (☎ 695-8174; *admission free; open 10am-2pm Tues-Sun)* sits in the center of Makaha Valley, midway between the valley's wet, forested uplands and its dry, coastal lowlands.

Its construction dates to around 1545, and the heiau was originally a temple dedicated to Lono, the god of agriculture. As with many Hawaiian temples, over time it went through transformations in both its physical structure and its use. In its final phase it was rededicated as a *luakini* (dedicated to Ku, the god of war) temple, and it's thought that Kamehameha the Great used Kaneaki Heiau as a place of worship after he conquered Oahu. The heiau remained in use until his death in 1819.

The social and religious upheaval introduced by Kamehameha's successors resulted in the abandonment of Kaneaki Heiau – and all other Hawaiian temples as well. Although many of Hawaii's more accessible coastal heiaus were dismantled and their stones used to build cattle fences and other structures, Kaneaki Heiau, protected by its remoteness, survived largely intact.

Constructed of stacked basalt rocks, Kaneaki Heiau has two terraced platforms and six enclosed courtyards. Its restoration, undertaken by the Bishop Museum, was completed in 1970. The heiau was authentically reconstructed using ohia logs handhewn with adzes and thatch made from native *pili* grass gathered on the Big Island. The project added two prayer towers, a taboo house, a drum house, an altar and god images – items representative of those that would have been here.

For those interested in precontact Hawaiian culture, it's a special place; the immediate setting surrounding the heiau remains undisturbed, even though the site is in the midst of a residential estate.

An estimated 3000 wild peacocks live in Makaha Valley. They can be spotted, or at least heard, throughout the upper valley, and if you visit the heiau, it's not unusual to see some of them performing their courting rituals in the field adjacent to the parking lot.

The guard at the Mauna Olu Estates gatehouse usually lets visitors enter to see the heiau during the listed hours. However, you might want to call the gatehouse in advance to inquire, as they can be a bit inconsistent in providing access. Also, you'll need to show your rental vehicle contract and driver's license, and there's typically no access if it's raining.

## Places to Stay

Makaha doesn't have many accommodations for short-term visitors. There are a handful of condos geared primarily to permanent residents, but none are terribly appealing and they generally require a stay of at least a week.

**Makaha Surfside** (☎ 696-6991 or 524-3455; **e** *riess@lava.net; 85-175 Farrington Hwy; studios/1-bedroom apartments per week $325/425)* is a four-story cinder-block apartment complex a mile south of Makaha Beach. Although it's predominantly residential, some of the 450 units are rented out on a weekly basis. Studios and units both have full kitchens. There's nothing special about this place, but it does have a pool.

**Makaha Shores** (☎ 696-8415, fax 696-4499; Hawaii Hatfield Realty, 85-833 Farrington Hwy, suite 201, Waianae, HI 96792; studios per week/2 weeks/month $500/800/ 1000)* has a prize location right on the northern end of Makaha Beach, with lanais overlooking the surf. In addition to the studios, there are one-bedroom units that cost about 20% more. Many retired people winter at this condo so it can be tough to book accommodations in the high season. Hawaii Hatfield Realty also handles similarly priced

## Nanaue the Shark Man

Hawaiian legend tells of a child named Nanaue who was born with an open space between his shoulders. Unbeknownst to Nanaue's mother, the father of the child was the king of sharks, who had taken on the guise of a man in order to woo her. Nanaue was born half human, half shark. He was human on land, but when he entered the ocean, the open space on his back became a shark's mouth.

After a nasty spell in which several villagers were ripped to shreds by a mysterious shark, Nanaue's secret was discovered, and he was forced to swim from island to island as he was hunted down. For a while he lived near Makua and took his victims into Kaneana Cave via an underwater tunnel.

units in **Makaha Valley Towers**, the high-rise complex that's tucked into the valley.

## Places to Eat

**Makaha Valley Country Club** (☎ 695-7111; 84-627 Makaha Valley Rd; dishes $4-8; open 7am-2pm Mon-Fri, 6am-3pm Sat & Sun), overlooking the golf course, is a popular lunch spot with a varied menu that includes sandwiches, fried *mahimahi* and teriyaki beef. Until 10:30am, you can get pancakes, omelettes and similar breakfast fare.

**Makaha Drive-In** (☎ 696-4811; 84-1150 Farrington Hwy; dishes $2-5; open 6am-8pm Mon-Sat), at the corner of Makaha Valley Rd, serves $5 plate lunches and burgers and sandwiches for around $2.

There are no places to eat north of Makaha.

## NORTH OF MAKAHA

**Keaau Beach Park** is a long, open, grassy strip that borders a rocky shore. It has rest rooms, showers, drinking water, picnic tables and camp sites. A sandy beach begins at the very northern end of the park, although a rough reef, sharp drop and high seasonal surf make swimming uninviting.

Driving north along the coast you'll see lava cliffs, white-sand beaches and patches of *kiawe*, a relative of the mesquite tree. On the inland side you'll get a glimpse into a run of little valleys.

**Kaneana Cave**, a massive cave on the inland side of the road, about 2 miles north of Keaau Beach Park, was once underwater (see the boxed text 'Nanaue the Shark Man'). Its impressive size is the result of wave action that wore away loose rock around an earthquake crack. Over the millennia, the cavern expanded as the ocean slowly receded. It's a somewhat uncanny place – often strong gusts of wind blow near the cave, while just down the road it's windless.

Hawaiian kahunas (priests) once performed rituals inside the cave's inner chamber. Older Hawaiians consider it a sacred place and won't enter the cave for fear that it's haunted by the spirits of deceased chiefs. From the collection of broken beer bottles and graffiti inside, it's obvious not everyone shares their sentiments.

From **Ohikilolo Beach**, which is below the cave, you can see Kaena Point to the north. Ohikilolo Beach is sometimes called Barking Sands, because the sand is said to make a woofing sound when it's very dry and someone walks on it.

Scenic **Makua Valley** opens up wide and grassy, backed by a fan of sharply fluted mountains. It serves as the ammunition field of the Makua Military Reservation. The seaside road opposite the southern end of the reservation leads to a little graveyard that's shaded by yellow-flowered be-still trees. This solitary site is all that remains of the Makua Valley community that was forced to evacuate during WWII when the US military took over the entire valley for bombing practice. War games still take place in the valley, which is fenced off with barbed wire and signs that warn of stray explosives.

**Makua Beach**, the white-sand beach opposite the Makua Military Reservation, was a canoe landing in days past. A movie set was built on the beach for the 1966 movie *Hawaii*, based on James Michener's classic novel and starring Julie Andrews and Max von Sydow, but no trace of the set remains.

Immediately before the gate to Kaena Point State Park, a road leads up to **Kaena Point Satellite Tracking Station**, operated by the US Air Force. The tracking station's antennae and domes sit atop the mountains above the point, where they resemble giant white golf balls.

There are **hiking trails** above the tracking station, including a scenic 2½-mile ridge trail that leads to Mokuleia Forest Reserve. To get past the air force's guard station, you will need to obtain a hiking permit in advance from the **Division of Forestry & Wildlife** (☎ 587-0166) in Honolulu.

## KAENA POINT STATE PARK

Kaena Point State Park is an undeveloped 853-acre coastal strip that runs along both sides of Kaena Point – the westernmost point of Oahu.

Until the mid-1940s, the Oahu Railway ran up here from Honolulu and continued around the point, carrying passengers on to Haleiwa on the North Shore.

The attractive, mile-long sandy beach on the southern side of the point is Yokohama Bay, named for the large numbers of Japanese fishers who came here during the railroad days.

Winter commonly brings huge, pounding waves, making Yokohama a popular seasonal surfing and bodysurfing spot. It is, however, best left to the experts, because of the submerged rocks, strong rip currents and dangerous shore break. Swimming is pretty much limited to the summer, and then only during calm conditions. When the water's flat, it's possible to snorkel; the best spot with the easiest access is at the southern side of the park. Rest rooms, showers and a lifeguard station are also at the southern end of the park.

In addition to being a state park, Kaena Point is designated as a natural area reserve

### Slipping Away

Early Hawaiians believed that when people went into a deep sleep or lost consciousness, their souls would wander. Souls that wandered too far were drawn west to Kaena Point. If they were lucky, they were met there by their *aumakua* (ancestral spirit helper), who led their soul back to their body. If unattended, their soul would be forced to leap from Kaena Point into the endless night, never to return.

On clear days, the island of Kauai is visible from Kaena Point. According to legend, it was from this point that the demigod Maui attempted to cast a huge hook into Kauai in order to pull it closer to Oahu and join the two islands. But the line broke and Kauai slipped away, with just a small piece of it remaining near Oahu. Today, this splintered rock, off the end of Kaena Point, is known as Pohaku O Kauai.

because of its unique ecosystem. The extensive dry, windswept coastal dunes that rise above the point are the habitat of many rare native plants. The endangered *kaena akoko* growing on the talus slopes is found nowhere else in the world. In the winter you can identify it by its pale green leaves, but it drops all of its leaves in the summer.

Other plants growing here include beach *naupaka*, a native shrub with white flowers that look like they have been torn in half;

ANNE JEFFREE

**The humpback whale is one of the most acrobatic of all whales**

*pau-o-hiiaka*, a vine with blue flowers; and beach morning glory, sometimes found entwined with *kaunaoa*, a parasitic vine that looks like orange fishing line.

Seabirds seen at Kaena Point include shearwaters, boobies and the common noddy – a dark-brown bird with a grayish crown. You can often see schools of spinner dolphins off the beach, and in winter humpback whale sightings are not unusual.

Dirt bikes and 4WD vehicles once created a great deal of disturbance in the dunes, but after Kaena Point became a natural area reserve in 1983, vehicles were restricted and the situation improved. The reserve is once again a nesting site for the rare Laysan albatross, and Hawaii's endangered monk seals occasionally bask in the sun here.

## Kaena Point Trail

A 2½-mile (one way) coastal hike runs from the end of the paved road at Yokohama Bay to Kaena Point, utilizing the old railroad bed. This easy-to-follow hike offers fine views the entire way, with the ocean on one side and the lofty cliffs of the Waianae Range on the other. Along the trail there are tide pools, sea arches and a couple of lazy blowholes that occasionally come to life on high-surf days.

The hike typically takes three to four hours roundtrip. The trail is exposed and lacks shade (Kaena means 'the heat'), so take sunscreen and plenty of water. Be cautious near the shoreline, as there are strong currents, and the waves sometimes reach extreme heights. In fact, winter waves at Kaena Point are the highest in Hawaii, sometimes towering in excess of 50ft.

Don't leave anything valuable in your car. Telltale mounds of shattered windshield glass litter the road's-end parking area used by most hikers. Parking closer to the rest rooms or leaving your doors unlocked can decrease the odds of having your car windows smashed.

# Language

The unifying language of Hawaii is English, but it's liberally peppered with Hawaiian phrases, loan words from the various immigrant languages and pidgin slang.

It's not uncommon to hear islanders speaking in other languages, however, as the main language spoken in one out of every four homes in Hawaii is a mother tongue other than English. The Hawaiian language itself is still spoken among family members by about 9000 people, and Hawaiian is, along with English, an official state language.

Closely related to other Polynesian languages, Hawaiian is melodic, phonetically simple and loaded with vowels and repeated syllables.

Some 85% of all place-names in Hawaii are in Hawaiian, and as often as not they have interesting translations and stories behind them.

The Hawaiians had no written language until the 1820s, when Christian missionaries arrived and rendered the spoken language into the Roman alphabet.

## Pronunciation

The written Hawaiian language has just 12 letters. Pronunciation is easy and there are few consonant clusters.

There are five vowel sounds, which sound similar to their English equivalents. Each vowel has both a short and a long pronunciation:

| | |
|---|---|
| a | as in 'father' |
| e | as in 'egg' |
| i | as in 'ski' |
| o | as in 'home' |
| u | as the 'ue' in 'blue' |

Hawaiian has diphthongs, a combination of two vowels where the two sounds glide into one another. The stress is on the first vowel, although in general if you pronounce each vowel separately, you'll have no trouble being understood.

The consonant **w** is usually pronounced like a soft English 'v' when it follows the letters **i** and **e** (the town Haleiwa is pronounced Haleiva) and like the English 'w'

when it follows **u** or **o**. When **w** follows **a**, it can be pronounced either 'v' or 'w' – thus you will hear both *Hawaii* and *Havaii*.

The other consonants – **h**, **k**, **l**, **m**, **n**, **p** – are pronounced much the same as they are in English.

### Glottal Stops & Macrons

Written Hawaiian uses both glottal stops and macrons, although in modern print both are often omitted.

The glottal stop (') indicates a break between two vowels, which produces an effect similar to saying 'oh-oh' in English. A macron – a short straight line over a vowel – indicates that the vowel sound is lengthened.

Glottal stops and macrons not only affect pronunciation, but can give a word a completely different meaning. For example, *ai* can mean 'sexual intercourse' or 'to eat,' depending on the pronunciation.

All this takes on greater significance when you learn to speak Hawaiian in depth. When using Hawaiian words in an English-language context, eg, 'this *poi* (mashed kalo) is *ono* (good),' there shouldn't be much of a problem.

## Compounds

Hawaiian may seem more difficult than it is because many proper names are long and look similar. Many begin with *ka*, meaning 'the,' which over time simply became attached to the beginning of the word.

When you break each word down into its composite parts, some of which are repeated, it all becomes much easier. For example, *Kamehameha* consists of the three compounds Ka-meha-meha. *Humuhumunukunukuapuaa*, which is Hawaii's state fish, is broken down into humu-humu-nuku-nuku-a-pu-a-a.

Some words are doubled to emphasize their meaning. For example: *wiki* means 'quick,' while *wikiwiki* means 'very quick.'

There are some easily recognizable compounds repeatedly found in place-names, and it can be fun to learn a few. For instance, *wai* means 'freshwater,' Waikiki means 'spouting water' (so named for the freshwater springs that were once there);

## Sharing the *Shaka*

Islanders greet each other with a *shaka* sign, which is made by folding down the three middle fingers to the palm and extending the thumb and little finger. The hand is then usually held out and shaken in greeting. It's as common as waving.

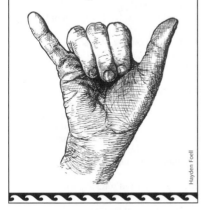

Hayden Foell

*kai* means 'seawater,' Kailua means 'two seas,' *lani* means 'heavenly,' Lanikai means 'heavenly sea,' *hana* means 'bay' and Hanalei means 'crescent bay.'

### Common Hawaiian Words

Learn these words first: *aloha* (love, welcome, goodbye) and *mahalo* (thank you), which are everyday pleasantries; *makai* (toward the sea) and *mauka* (toward the mountains), commonly used in giving directions; and *kane* (man) and *wahine* (woman), often on bathroom doors.

For more Hawaiian words see the Glossary at the back of the book.

### Pidgin

Hawaii's early immigrants communicated with each other in pidgin, a simplified, broken form of English. It was a language born of necessity, stripped of all but the most needed words.

Modern pidgin is better defined as local slang. It is an extensive language, lively and ever changing. Whole conversations can take place in pidgin, or often just a word or two is dropped into a more conventional English sentence.

Even Shakespeare's *Twelfth Night* has been translated (by local comedian James Grant Benton) to *Twelf Nite O Wateva*. Malvolio's line 'My masters, are you mad?' becomes 'You buggahs crazy, o wat?'

Short-term visitors will rarely win friends by trying to speak pidgin. It's more like an insider's code that you're allowed to use only after you've lived in Hawaii long enough to understand the nuances.

Some characteristics of pidgin include a fast staccato rhythm, two-word sentences, dropping the soft 'h' sound from words that start with 'th,' the use of loan words from many languages (often Hawaiian), and double meanings that can easily trip up the uninitiated.

Some of the more common words and expressions include the following:

*blalah* – big Hawaiian fellow
*brah* – brother, friend; it's also used for 'hey you'
*broke da mouth* – delicious
*buggah* – guy
*chicken skin* – goose bumps
*coconut wireless* – word of mouth
*cockaroach* – steal
*da kine* – that kind of thing, whatchamacallit etc; used whenever you can't think of the word you want but you know the listener knows what you mean
*gee vem* – go for it, beat them
*grinds* – food, eat; *ono grinds* is good food
*haolefied* – become like a *haole* (Caucasian)
*howzit?* – hi, how's it going?
*how you stay?* – how are you?
*humbug* – a real hassle
*like beef?* – wanna fight?
*mo' bettah* – much better, the best
*slippahs* – flip-flops, thongs
*stick* – surfboard
*stink eye* – dirty look, evil eye
*talk story* – any kind of conversation, tales, gossip
*tanks* – thanks; more commonly, *tanks brah*
*tree* – three

# Glossary

ahi – yellowfin tuna

ahu – stone cairns used to mark a trail; or an altar or shrine

ahupuaa – traditional land division, usually in a wedge shape that extends from the mountains to the sea

aikane – friend

aina – land

akamai – clever

aku – skipjack tuna

akua – god, spirit, idol

akule – bigeye mackerel

alii – chief, royalty

aloha – the traditional greeting meaning love, welcome, good-bye

aloha aina – love of the land

amaama – mullet

amakihi – small, yellow-green bird; one of the more common native birds

ao – Newell's shearwater (a seabird)

apapane – red native Hawaiian honey-creeper

au – marlin

aumakua – ancestral spirit helper

awa – kava, made into an intoxicating brew; milkfish

awapuhi – wild ginger

bento – the Japanese word for a box lunch

cilantro – coriander leaves (also known as Chinese parsley)

crack seed – snack food, usually dried fruits or seeds; can be sour, salty or sweet

elepaio – a brownish native bird with a white rump, common to Oahu forests

gyoza – a grilled dumpling made of minced pork and garlic

hala – pandanus plant; the leaves are used in weaving mats and baskets

hale – house

hana – work; a bay, when used as a compound in place names

haole – Caucasian; literally 'without breath'

hapa – half; person of mixed blood

hau – indigenous lowland hibiscus tree whose wood is often used for outrigger canoes

haupia – coconut pudding

heiau – ancient stone temple, a place of worship in Hawaii before contact with the West

Hina – Polynesian goddess (wife of Ku, one of the four main gods)

holoholo – to walk, drive or ramble around for pleasure

holoku – a long dress similar to the muumuu, but more fitted

honu – turtle

hoolaulea – celebration, party

hui – group, organization

hukilau – fishing with a seine (a large net), involving a group of people; the word can also refer to the feast that follows

hula – traditional Hawaiian dance

hula halau – hula school or troupe

humuhumunukunukuapuaa – triggerfish

iiwi – a bright-red forest bird with a curved, salmon-colored beak

iliahi – Hawaiian sandalwood

iliili – stones

ilima – native plant, a ground cover with delicate yellow-orange flowers

imu – underground earthen oven used in traditional luau cooking

kahili – a feathered standard, used as a symbol of royalty

kahuna – wise person in any field, commonly a priest, healer or sorcerer

kahuna nui – high priest

kaiseki ryori – a formal Japanese meal consisting of a series of small dishes

kalua – traditional method of baking in an underground oven (imu)

kamaaina – native-born Hawaiian or a longtime resident; the literal meaning is 'child of the land'

Kanaloa – god of the underworld

kane – man; also the name of one of four main Hawaiian gods

kapu – taboo, part of strict ancient Hawaiian social system

kaunaoa – a thin, parasitic vine

kava – a mildly narcotic drink made from the Piper methysticum, a pepper shrub

keiki – child, children

kiawe – a relative of the mesquite tree introduced to Hawaii in the 1820s, now very common; its branches are covered with sharp thorns

**kii** – image, statue

**ko** – sugarcane

**koa** – native hardwood tree often used in woodworking of native crafts

**kona** – leeward, or a leeward wind

**koolau** – windward side

**Ku** – Polynesian god of many manifestations, including god of war, farming and fishing (husband of Hina)

**kukui** – candlenut tree; the official state tree, its oily nuts were once burned in lamps

**kuleana** – an individually held plot of land

**kupuna** – grandparent

**kuula** – fishing shrine

**Laka** – goddess of the hula

**lanai** – veranda

**lapaau** – to heal with medicine

**lauhala** – leaves of the hala plant used in weaving

**laulau** – bundles of pork or beef with salted fish, which are wrapped in leaves and steam cooked

**lei** – garland, usually of flowers, but also of leaves or shells

**lilikoi** – passionfruit

**limu** – seaweed

**lolo** – stupid, crazy

**lomi** – raw, diced salmon marinated with tomatoes and onions

**lomilomi** – massage

**Lono** – Polynesian god of harvest, agriculture, fertility and peace

**loulu** – native fan palms

**luakini** – a type of heiau (temple) dedicated to the war god Ku and used for human sacrifices

**luau** – traditional Hawaiian feast

**mahalo** – thank you

**mahimahi** – also called 'dolphin,' but actually a type of fish unrelated to the marine mammal

**maile** – native plant with twining habit and fragrant leaves; often used for leis

**makaainana** – commoners; literally 'people who tend the land'

**makaha** – a sluice gate, used to regulate the level of water in a fishpond

**makahiki** – ancient four-month-long winter-harvest festival dedicated to Lono, during which sports and celebrations replaced all warfare

**makai** – toward the sea

**makaku** – creative, artistic mana

**malasada** – a fried dough served warm, similar to a doughnut

**malihini** – newcomer, visitor

**malo** – loincloth

**mana** – spiritual power

**manini** – convict tang (a reef fish); also used to refer to something small or insignificant

**mano** – shark

**mauka** – toward the mountains; inland

**mele** – song, chant

**menehune** – 'little people' who, according to legend, built many of Hawaii's fishponds, heiaus and other stonework

**milo** – a native shade tree with beautiful hardwood

**moo** – water spirit, water lizard or dragon

**mu** – a 'body catcher' who secured sacrificial victims for the heiau altar

**muumuu** – a long, loose-fitting dress introduced by the missionaries

**naupaka** – a native shrub with delicate white flowers

**Neighbor Islands** – the term used to refer to the main Hawaiian Islands outside of Oahu

**nene** – a native goose; Hawaii's state bird

**nisei** – people of Japanese descent

**noni** – Indian mulberry; a small tree with yellow, warty, smelly fruit, used medicinally

**nuku puu** – a native honeycreeper with a bright-yellow underside

**ohana** – family, extended family

**ohia lehua** – native Hawaiian tree with tufted, feathery, pom-pom like flowers

**olo** – surfboards used by Hawaiian royalty

**onaga** – red snapper

**ono** – delicious; also the name of the wahoo fish

**opae** – shrimp

**opakapaka** – pink snapper

**opihi** – edible limpet

**pakalolo** – marijuana; literally means 'crazy smoke'

**pali** – cliff

**palila** – native honeycreeper

**pau** – finished, no more

**Pele** – goddess of fire and volcanoes

**pho** – a Vietnamese soup of beef broth, noodles and fresh herbs

**piko** – navel, umbilical cord
**pili** – a bunchgrass, commonly used for thatching houses
**pilikia** – trouble
**pipikaula** – salted, dried beef that is broiled
**poha** – gooseberry
**poi** – a gooey paste made from taro roots; a staple of the Hawaiian diet
**poke** – chopped raw fish marinated in soy sauce, oil and chilli pepper
**Poliahu** – goddess of snow
**pua aloalo** – a hibiscus flower
**puka** – any kind of hole or opening
**pupu** – snack food, hors d'oeuvres; shells
**puu** – hill, cinder cone
**puuhonua** – place of refuge

**saimin** – a Hawaiian noodle soup
**sashimi** – thin slices of raw fish

**tabi** – Japanese reef-walking shoes
**talk story** – to strike up a conversation, make small talk
**tapa** – cloth made by pounding the bark of the paper mulberry tree, used for early Hawaiian clothing ('kapa' in Hawaiian)
**taro** – a plant with green heart-shaped leaves; cultivated in Hawaii for its edible rootstock, which is mashed to make *poi* ('kalo' in Hawaiian)
**teishoku** – Japanese word for fixed-plate meal
**teppanyaki** – Japanese style of cooking using an iron grill
**ti** – common native plant; its long shiny leaves are used for a variety of things, including wrapping food and making hula skirts ('ki' in Hawaiian)

**ukulele** – a stringed musical instrument derived from the 'braginha,' which was introduced to Hawaii in the 1800s by Portuguese immigrants
**ulu** – breadfruit

**wahine** – woman
**wana** – sea urchin
**wikiwiki** – hurry, quick

# LONELY PLANET

You already know that Lonely Planet produces more than this one guidebook, but you might not be aware of the other products we have on this region. Here is a selection of titles that you may want to check out as well:

**Diving & Snorkeling Hawaii**
ISBN 1 86450 090 5
US$17.95 • UK10.99

**Hawaii: The Big Island**
ISBN 1 74059 345 6
US$16.99 • UK£9.99

**Maui**
ISBN 1 74059 271 9
US$14.99 • UK£8.99

**Hawaii**
ISBN 1 74059 142 9
US$21.99 • UK£14.99

**Available wherever books are sold**

# Index

## Text

### A

AAA 52-3
accommodations 61-5
  B&Bs 63
  camping 61-2
  hostels 62-3
  hotels 63-4
  rental 64-5
  reservations 61
  travel club discounts 64
  YMCAs/YWCAs 63
activities 71-82, see also
  individual listings
Aiea Loop Trail 164
Aihualama Trail 115-18
Aina Moana State Recreation
  Park 111
air travel
  buying tickets 84-5
  departure tax 85
  to/from Oahu 83-8, 89-90
  within Hawaii 87-8
airlines 83
airport 83, 89-90
Ala Moana 111-15, 127-9, **112**
Ala Moana Beach Park 111
Ala Moana Center 111, 128
Ala Wai Canal 143
alcoholic drinks 66-7
alii 19
Aliiolani Hale 104-6
Aloha Stadium 68
Aloha Stadium Swap Meet 165
Aloha Tower 107
Aloha Tower Marketplace 107,
  125
American Automobile
  Association 52-3
annexation 19, 21
arboretum 118
aquarium 142
area code 40
*Arizona* Memorial 160-2, 163
arts 31-3, see also individual
  listings
ATMs 38

### B

B&Bs 63
Banzai Pipeline 195
bargaining 39

beaches 73, 138-40, **72**, see
  *also* ocean safety
  Ala Moana Beach Park 111
  Bellows Field Beach Park 173
  Central Waikiki Beach 139
  Diamond Head Beach 168
  Ehukai Beach Park 195
  Fort DeRussy Beach 138-9
  Gray's Beach 139
  Haleiwa Alii Beach Park
    201-2
  Haleiwa Beach Park 202
  Halona Cove 170
  Hanauma Bay Nature
    Preserve 169-70
  Hawaiian Electric Beach Park
    214
  Kahanamoku Beach 138
  Kahe Point Beach Park 214
  Kaiaka Bay Beach Park 201
  Kaihalulu Beach 194
  Kailua Beach Park 177-8
  Kalama Beach Park 178
  Kapiolani Beach Park 140
  Keaau Beach Park 217
  Kualoa Regional Park 185-6
  Kuhio Beach Park 139-40
  Kuilima Cove 194
  Lanikai Beach 180
  Lualualei Beach Park 215
  Maili Beach Park 215
  Malaekahana Beach 190
  Makaha Beach Park 215-16
  Makapuu Beach Park 172
  Makua Beach 217
  Mokuleia Army Beach 204
  Mokuleia Beach Park 204
  Ohikilolo Beach 217
  Pokai Bay Beach Park 215
  Pounders Beach 189-90
  Punaluu Beach 187
  Pupukea Beach Park 197-8
  Sand Island State Recreation
    Area 122
  Sandy Beach Park 170-1
  Sans Souci Beach Park 140
  Swanzy Beach Park 186
  Sunset Beach Park 195
  Waimanalo Bay Beach Park
    172-3
  Waimanalo Beach Park 172
  Waimea Bay Beach
    Park 198
Bellows Field Beach Park 173
bicycling 80-1, 94

birds 27-8, 219
bird sanctuaries 172, 178, 179,
  180, 190, 191
Bingham, Hiram 16
Bishop Museum (Honolulu)
  120-1
Bishop Museum (Kalia) 141
bodysurfing 72
boogie boarding 72-4
books 32-3, 42-4
botanical gardens
  Foster Botanical Garden 110
  Hoomaluhia Botanical
    Garden 182
  Wahiawa Botanical Garden
    207-8
  Waimea Falls Park 197
*Bowfin* Submarine Museum &
  Park 162
bowls, wooden 32, 68-9
British 17-18
bus travel 90-1
  tours 94-5
business hours 57
business travelers 53
Byodo-In 182

### C

camping 61-2
car travel 91-3
  AAA 52-3
  driver's license 37
  driving times 91
  insurance 93
  parking 93
  rental 92-3
  road rules 92
central Honolulu 111-15,
  127-9, **112**
central Oahu 205-9, **206**
Central Waikiki Beach 139
children
  activities for 111-14, 212
  travel with 51-2, 85
Chinatown 108-11, 126-7
Chinatown Cultural Plaza 109
Chinese 14-15, 17
Chinese medicine 109
ciguatera poisoning 49
cinemas 131, 157, see also
  films
Circle-Island route 91
Circle Pacific tickets 84-5
climate 25-6
clothing 69

**Bold** indicates maps.